FIFTY YEARS IN SCIENCE AND RELIGION

Ian Barbour's distinguished and distinctive contribution to the increasingly creative dialogue between science and religion is, in this volume, celebrated by an appropriately matching collection of distinguished and distinctive essays on the variegated themes of his work. It provides valuable surveys of the past and insightful pointers to the future of this dialogue which is so essential for the vitality, fruitfulness and beneficence of both science and religion.
Arthur Peacocke, Former Director of the Ian Ramsey Centre, University of Oxford.

Ian Barbour is an unparalleled leader in the contemporary dialogue between science and religion. This volume is a wonderful witness from key scholars in the field to the breadth, depth and integrity of his contribution. It also offers fresh and exciting insights on the diverse range of key issues we face as we move into a new moment in this dialogue.
Denis Edwards, School of Theology, Flinders University, South Australia.

Ian G. Barbour is the internationally acknowledged pioneer in the field of 'science and religion'. Although public opinion is often swayed by strident voices which attempt to place science and religion in conflict or keep them totally isolated, Barbour's voluminous contributions over the past fifty years have carved out a trusted pathway to constructive dialogue and creative mutual interaction between science and religion.

Fifty Years in Science and Religion brings together nineteen leading scholars in the field to offer an appreciative yet critical assessment of the impact of Barbour's work on science and religion and to point ahead towards future critical areas, goals and tasks that await new research and visionary exploration. This book includes a unique autobiography by Barbour in which for the first time he shares and reflects on his life and work, as well as a detailed bibliography of Barbour's works. Together, the authors demonstrate how Barbour's writings and the hundreds of scholars who have now become part of the field have changed the course of intellectual history in the West by making possible and necessary a truly constructive engagement between science and religion in the context of inter-religious dialogue and the global human and environmental challenges of our time.

Ashgate Science and Religion Series

Series Editors:

Roger Trigg, *Department of Philosophy, University of Warwick, UK*
J. Wentzel van Huyssteen, *James I. McCord Professor of Theology and Science, Princeton Theological Seminary, USA*

Science and religion have often been thought to be at loggerheads but much contemporary work in this flourishing interdisciplinary field suggests this is far from the case. The *Ashgate Science and Religion Series* presents exciting new work to advance interdisciplinary study, research and debate across key themes in science and religion, exploring the philosophical relations between the physical and social sciences on the one hand and religious belief on the other. Contemporary issues in philosophy and theology are debated, as are prevailing cultural assumptions arising from the 'post-modernist' distaste for many forms of reasoning. The series enables leading international authors from a range of different disciplinary perspectives to apply the insights of the various sciences, theology and philosophy and look at the relations between the different disciplines and the rational connections that can be made between them. These accessible, stimulating new contributions to key topics across science and religion will appeal particularly to individual academics and researchers, graduates, postgraduates and upper-undergraduate students.

Other titles published in this series:

Theology and Psychology
Fraser Watts
0 7546 1672 X (HBK)
0 7546 1673 8 (PBK)

Islam and Science
Muzaffar Iqbal
0 7546 0799 2 (HBK)
0 7546 0800 X (PBK)

Science, Theology, and Ethics
Ted Peters
0 7546 0824 7 (HBK)
0 7546 0825 5 (PBK)

Fifty Years in Science and Religion

Ian G. Barbour and his Legacy

Edited by
ROBERT JOHN RUSSELL
Graduate Theological Union, Berkeley, California, USA

ASHGATE

Published by
Ashgate Publishing Limited
Gower House
Croft Road
Aldershot
Hants GU11 3HR
England

Ashgate Publishing Company
Suite 420
101 Cherry Street
Burlington, VT 05401-4405
USA

Ashgate website: http://www.ashgate.com

British Library Cataloguing in Publication Data
Fifty years in science and religion : Ian G. Barbour and his legacy. – (Ashgate science and religion series) 1.Barbour, Ian G. (Ian Graeme) 2.Religion and science I.Russell, Robert J. II.Barbour, Ian G. (Ian Graeme)
215

Library of Congress Cataloging-in-Publication Data
Fifty years in science and religion : Ian G. Barbour and his legacy / edited by Robert John Russell.
       p. cm. – (Ashgate science and religion series)
    Includes bibliographical references and index.
    ISBN 0-7546-4117-1 (als. paper) – ISBN 0-7546-4118-X (pbk. : alk. paper)
    1. Barbour, Ian G. 2. Religion and science. I. Russell, Robert J. II. Series

BL241.F57 2003
201'.65–dc22

2003063727

ISBN 0 7546 4117 1 (Hbk)
ISBN 0 7546 4118 X (Pbk)

Typeset by Bournemouth Colour Press, Parkstone, Poole, Dorset.
Printed in Great Britain by MPG Books Ltd, Bodmin.

This *Festschrift* is dedicated to Ian Graeme Barbour, whose pioneering work in the 1950s–1960s helped create the interdisciplinary field of science and religion and whose ongoing work over the past fifty years has explored every aspect of it in depth.

Contents

C. Buddhist Theology

List of Contributors

Jensine Andresen, Visiting Scholar, Columbia University Center for Buddhist Studies, New York; Director, International Faith and Science Exchange (InterFASE), Lunenburg, Massachusetts, USA.

Ian G. Barbour, Emeritus Professor of Physics and Religion, Emeritus Bean Professor of Science, Technology and Society, Carleton College, Northfield, Minnesota, USA.

Christian Berg, Wissenschaftlicher Mitarbeiter, the Technical University of Clausthal, Germany.

Philip Clayton, Ingraham Chair, Claremont School of Theology and Professor of Philosophy at the Claremont Graduate University, Claremont, California, USA.

Anne M. Clifford, Associate Professor of Theology, Duquesne University, Pittsburgh, Pennsylvania, USA.

John B. Cobb, Jr, Founding Co-Director, Center for Process Studies, and Emeritus Professor, Claremont School of Theology and Claremont Graduate School, Claremont, California, USA.

Niels Henrik Gregersen, Research Professor in Theology and Science, University of Aarhus, Denmark.

John F. Haught, Landegger Distinguished Professor of Theology, Georgetown University, Washington, DC, USA.

Martinez J. Hewlett, Professor Emeritus, Department of Molecular and Cell Biology Emeritus, University of Arizona, Tucson, USA.

Paul O. Ingram, Professor of Religion, Pacific Lutheran University, Tacoma, Washington, USA.

Nancey Murphy, Professor of Christian Philosophy, Fuller Theological Seminary, Pasadena, California, USA.

Ted Peters, Professor of Systematic Theology, Pacific Lutheran Theological Seminary and the Graduate Theological Union, Berkeley, California, USA.

W. Mark Richardson, Professor of Systematic Theology, General Theological Seminary, New York City, New York, USA.

Robert John Russell, Founder and Director, The Center for Theology and the Natural Sciences, and Professor of Theology and Science in Residence, the Graduate Theological Union, Berkeley, California, USA.

Judith N. Scoville, Assistant Professor of Religion and Philosophy, Hulings Distinguished Chair in the Humanities, Northland College, Ashland, Wisconsin, USA.

Roger L. Shinn, Reinhold Niebuhr Professor Emeritus of Social Ethics, Union Theological Seminary, New York, USA.

Ernest Simmons, Professor of Religion and Director, the Dovre Center for Faith and Learning, Concordia College, Moorehead, Minnesota, USA.

Christopher Southgate, Honorary University Fellow in Theology, University of Exeter, Exeter, United Kingdom.

William R. Stoeger, SJ, Staff Astrophysicist and Adjunct Associate Professor of Astronomy, Vatican Observatory, Vatican Observatory Research Group, Steward Observatory, University of Arizona, Tucson, USA.

Carl M. York, former Professor of Physics and Assistant Chancellor for Research, University of California in Los Angeles, California, and Chair, Board of Directors, The Center for Theology and the Natural Sciences, Berkeley, California, USA.

Preface

Robert John Russell

'Science and religion' stands for a rapidly growing international, intercultural, interreligious and interdisciplinary movement of scholars held together by their commitment to responsible dialogue and creative mutual interaction between scientists and religious leaders. This commitment is crucial if we are to appropriate the wealth of discoveries of contemporary science in reshaping our religious understanding of life and its ultimate meaning, if we are to critically engage the philosophical and theological elements in contemporary science and the ethical challenges of technology and the environment as new directions in research arise in both areas and if we are to envision a future which is genuinely wholesome for all life on earth. It has broadened beyond the academy to include the general public from all walks of life whose imaginations are kindled by science and who recognize the deeper spiritual questions which science raises but cannot answer – and which religion has often overlooked. Still the major thrust comes from scholars who are willing to look beyond the narrow expertise of their fields and raise questions and insights that are foundational to life.

What is both crucial and unique is that these scholars are committed to the pursuit of such dialogue based on *mutual respect* and a willingness to hold their beliefs self-critically and hypothetically in hopes that such dialogue will lead to deeper understanding and even mutual transformation. They are motivated in part by the stunning discoveries of the natural sciences in the last hundred years, discoveries which raise profound questions about the universe, its origins and future, and the role and meaning of life in it. Such questions push beyond the traditional boundaries of science. They inspire and challenge us to seek answers which, along with science, draw on all aspects of human knowledge, including philosophy, ethics, aesthetics, religion and spirituality. These scholars are concerned, too, by the diversity of contemporary technologies which challenge us to shape a future that supports all life on earth. World religions are an essential reservoir of wisdom and truth which, when brought together with the discoveries of science and the challenges of technology, can serve the betterment of human life and the environment and the envisioning of the role and destiny of life in the universe.

The purpose of this book is to assess the current state of these discussions and to point forward to future challenges and dreams as we enter fully into the twenty-first century in view of science and religion. This book is also a celebration of the scholar who most clearly made this interdisciplinary field possible and who has continued for fifty years to inspire its many participants. This scholar is Ian Graeme Barbour – universally acclaimed as *the* pioneer of science and religion in the twentieth century. It is in his honor that we gladly dedicate this *Festschrift*.

Clearly there were numerous scientists, theologians, philosophers in the nineteenth and early twentieth centuries who anticipated to one degree or another today's questions and insights – Karl Heim, Michael Polanyi, and Pierre Teilhard de Chardin come immediately to mind, along with many others. Still, as history shows, their contributions did not result in the kind of international movement among both scholars and the general public such as we see today. Instead, the overwhelming climate of positivism, empiricism, reductionism, materialism, fideism, and atheism made conflict or independence the inevitable options for most of culture.

Even today, we do not yet have a full analysis of Barbour's role in initiating the new paradigm of science and religion in the 1950s–1960s or a detailed analysis of the intellectual, historical, sociological, cultural and religious factors which made it possible. Still, I believe we can already identify a convergence of three relatively autonomous factors in this period which played a crucial role in making science and religion possible and which provide a context for understanding Barbour's unique role. Each factor involves a watershed change in a prevailing paradigm.

The first factor is the enormous changes in Christian theology by the 1960s. In Protestant circles neo-Orthodox and existential theologians had long advocated a 'two-language' model of science and religion, but by the 1960s the dominance of such luminaries as Karl Barth, Paul Tillich, Reinhold Niebuhr, H. Richard Niebuhr, Rudolf Bultmann and Langdon Gilkey, was beginning to subside. In its place a diversity of new approaches were on the rise, many of which were radically engaged with secular thought. Similarly Vatican II opened Roman Catholic theology to the results of biblical and historical criticism, encouraged ecumenical dialogue and advanced the engagement between church scholars and secular intellectual culture.[1] The Graduate Theological Union was formed in 1962 out of this new ecumenism, and the GTU, in turn, provided an ideal context for me to create CTNS as a GTU Affiliate in 1981.

The second factor stems from the philosophy of science. The empiricism that dominated the first half of the century was being challenged by scholars such as Gerald Holton, Norwood Hanson, Stephen Toulmin, Thomas Kuhn, and Imre Lakatos. In its place, a new philosophy of science arose in which historical, cultural, philosophical, and even religious, aesthetic and gender elements were included as cognitively relevant within the project of the natural sciences. Similarly, philosophers of religion such as Ian Ramsey, William Austin, and Frederick Ferré, were pointing to the cognitive element of religious language against previous claims for its purely expressivist function.

The third factor is the combined effect of groundbreaking scientific discoveries and the development of new technologies. In evolutionary and molecular biology this period saw the discovery of the molecular structure of DNA and with it a deepening understanding of the evolution of life on earth. In cosmology the Big Bang model triumphed over its competitor, the steady state model, and with it the paradigm of an expanding universe and its possible origins at 't = 0'. In physics, the profound epistemological and ontological challenges raised by quantum mechanics in the first third of the century were rekindled and deepened by the discovery of Bell's theorem and its eventual implications for such concepts as non-locality and non-separability. During the same period, the search for a unified theory in fundamental physics began again in earnest. Meanwhile the 1950s–1960s saw the development of technologies that would change the course, and challenge the future, of global civilization and the environment, from nuclear energy to modern medicine and agriculture, from global communications to the exploration of space.

Together these three independent factors provided a unique intellectual context for the creation of 'science and religion'. It was here that Barbour constructed 'critical realism': the methodological 'bridge' which spanned the gulf previously separating scientific and religious communities and made possible the development of genuine, two-way commerce and, eventually, the global dialogue we enjoy today.

Although Barbour published a number of important works in the 1950s, his first major textbook, *Issues in Science and Religion* (1966), marks the birth of this new period of interaction. Here Barbour showed us how to move beyond the two-language model by constructing a 'bridge' between the methodologies, languages, and assumptions of science and religion. Using this bridge, a wealth of ideas, values and insights have begun to flow with ever-increasing momentum to the benefit of both communities. Over the ensuing decades, Barbour's voluminous writings have provided a dependable foundation and a compelling vision for the interaction, and many extraordinary scholars from all cultures and religions of the globe have joined the conversations and contributed their own unique gifts and insights to the dialogue. In the process, Barbour's own personal style of scholarship, with its chiseled fairness to and tireless inclusiveness of every deserving voice on each issue, his gentle but persuasive critique of their preferred options, and then the sure development of his own quietly held views, by its very nature has invited everyone 'to the table' and made them feel as honored guests. This unique approach that honors the other, begun in *Issues*, has marked every publication by him since then, a fine example being his magisterial Gifford Lectures in 1990 and 1991. He has inspired others in the field to emulate his example of radical fairness, generous expansiveness, and intentional inclusiveness. I believe that Barbour's gifts – an approach to dialogue that requires mutual respect and self-critical engagement around issues as potentially explosive as are those in science and religion and in ethics and technology, the creation of a bridge between disparate fields which makes the exchanges between them possible for any scholar who is willing to undertake the arduous journey, and his own substantive contributions to our understanding of God and nature based on that interaction – constitute the extraordinary legacy he has given us all.

The chapters in this *Festschrift* attest to Barbour's enormous influence and compelling vision. The contributors here write with two foci in mind: a critical assessment of the importance of Barbour's work for their own area of specialization in science and religion, and a vision of the field's wider dimensions and frontier challenges. The book begins with an autobiography by Barbour. It is then divided into four parts: the first surveys his scientific research and contributions to teaching science; the second looks at his contributions to methodology and the underlying philosophical issues raised in relating science and religion; the third surveys Barbour's contributions to theological issues regarding physics, cosmology, evolution, anthropology and neuroscience, and ethical issues surrounding technology and the environment; and the final part includes prerspectives on Barbour's work from process theology, Roman Catholicism, and Buddhist theology. What unites the contributors to *Fifty Years* is both their admiration of Barbour and their commitment, each in their own way, to what I see as the fundamental purpose driving the field: the pursuit and celebration of the creative mutual interaction between science and religion. These scholars are exploring ways in which constructive theology engages the methods and discoveries of the natural sciences as well as ways in which philosophical, cultural, and theological elements play a creative role in ongoing theoretical research in the natural sciences.

Fifty Years should help the reader, whether new to the discussion or a scholarly partner, gain a clear sense of the diversity and the depth of the field as well as its overall unity and vision. Its varied chapters mark the unique community of authors gathered here as indicative of the international, intercultural, interreligious and interdisciplinary dimensions of science and religion today. Moreover, the impact of Barbour's lifetime of research, lectures, teaching, and public presentations can be seen in how it has influenced successive generations of scholars as represented in this volume, all of whom trace portions of their intellectual history to Barbour. It is indeed a rare legacy for an individual scholar to have achieved such an impact on intellectual history and on the lives of some of its leading figures – one worthy of honoring in a *Festschrift*. It is particularly appropriate therefore that it be dedicated to the one scholar who is the pioneer of the field.

It is my hope that *Fifty Years* will provide a lasting assessment of science and religion circa 2000: what has been accomplished in fifty years of an exponentially growing dialogue and what lies ahead as we look into the coming decades of the new millennium – and how all of this is, in such large measure, due to the life and writings of one person, Ian Graeme Barbour.

Note

1. It was in large measure due to Vatican II that the possibility arose for three Roman Catholic seminaries to join the existing Protestant seminaries in Berkeley to form the ecumenical consortium called the Graduate Theological Union in 1962. I like to describe the GTU as a 'lived experiment in institutional ecumenism' and I am very proud of such an experiment. It is for this and related reasons that I chose to locate CTNS in Berkeley in 1981 as an Affiliate of the GTU.

Acknowledgements

Special thanks go to Ted Peters for his help with the initial design and planning of this project and his crucial suggestions along the way, and to Wentzel van Huyssteen for recommending the publication of this manuscript. I am grateful to Jamie and Heidi Haag for revising the bibliography and producing the indices, to Kevin Lucid for copy-editing the notes in the manuscript, and to Sylvia Chan López for securing permission to reprint copyright material.

Introduction

Robert John Russell

Fifty Years in Science and Religion: Ian G. Barbour and his Legacy explores the current frontier in science and religion both to assess ongoing research at that frontier and to point forward to future challenges and vistas. The approach here, though, is unique: amidst the growing literature of both scholarly and non-technical publications in science and religion, it is the first *Festschrift* in the field and its focus is on *the* scholar, Ian G. Barbour, whose pioneering work in the 1950s–1960s helped create the field and whose ongoing work over the past fifty years has explored every aspect of it in depth. The contributors to *Fifty Years*, each of whom is a leading figure in the field, write then with two foci in mind: a critical assessment of the importance of Barbour's work for their own area of specialization in science and religion, and an envisioning of the field's wider dimensions and frontier challenges. Moreover, they are committed to the fundamental vision driving the field: the creative mutual interaction between science and religion in an age all too often held captive by trenchant voices urging heated conflict or by passionless voices counseling fruitless isolation.

Fifty Years begins with Ian Barbour's autobiographical sketch, 'A Personal Odyssey.' Barbour was raised in Beijing where his mother taught religious education, his father geology – and Teilhard de Chardin was a close friend of the family! In 1943 he graduated from Swarthmore College and spent three years in Civilian Public Service, during which he met and married Deane Kern. Following doctoral research in cosmic ray physics at the University of Chicago, Barbour taught physics at Kalamazoo College. In 1953, a Ford fellowship took him to study theology and ethics at Yale Divinity School. He then joined the faculty of Carleton College, teaching physics half-time while developing a department of religion. During the 1960s, Barbour participated in a study group of scientists and theologians, read Whitehead avidly, and developed the groundbreaking undergraduate textbook, *Issues in Science and Religion.* He writes that 'what had started as an attempt to fit together two halves of my own life had become a wider intellectual inquiry in which I found that many other people were interested.' Following *Myths, Models, and Paradigms* in 1973, Barbour turned on ethical issues in technology and the environment. Through a series of grants he then developed an interdepartmental minor at Carleton, 'Science, Technology and Public Policy,' and in 1980 published *Technology, Environment and Human Values.* A decade later, Barbour gave two sets of Gifford Lectures in Scotland which were published as *Religion in an Age of Science* and *Ethics in an Age of Technology.*

Next Barbour reflects on people, programs, and themes which have been particularly meaningful to him, including the Center for Theology and the Natural Sciences (CTNS), the Vatican Observatory/CTNS conferences on divine action, the

Science and the Spiritual Quest program, and the financial gift he made to CTNS after receiving the Templeton Prize for Progress in Religion in 1999. Barbour emphasizes the importance of methodological issues in science and religion and the crucial role of inter-religious conversations about science. He acknowledges scholars who have strongly influenced him, including Nancey Murphy, Sallie McFague, John Cobb, Charles Hartshorne, David Griffin, and Arthur Peacocke. Poignantly, Barbour closes his autobiography by sharing with the reader his return trip to Beijing with Deane in 2002: 'My odyssey had returned to the point where it had started.'

Part I: Barbour's Scientific Contributions

The first Part attends to Barbour's scientific research and teaching before his move to science and religion. Carl M. York is uniquely qualified to write on 'Ian G. Barbour's Contributions as a Scientist.' As a physicist in the same generation as Barbour and working in the same specialization – cosmic rays – York is able to fluently assess Barbour's scientific research as well as tell us about his early teaching career before moving into science and religion. We enter the scene shortly after World War II where experimentalists had not only to master the theoretical dimensions of their field of study but to face the double challenge of the laboratory: deploying available tools and developing innovative new techniques. After completing a Master's degree at Duke University, where he built an ingenious device that analyzed electroencephalograms into their component waves, Barbour entered the doctoral program of the University of Chicago. Here emulsion plates were used to detect high energy particles. Barbour designed and built a special tracking microscope and a klystron magnet ideal for high altitude work. His research contributed to the eventual discovery of the mass and charge of the pion and the muon. He continued to extend his research on high energy particles and thermal neutrons at Carleton College.

Through teaching physics, Barbour helped undergraduates experience some of the exciting aspects of genuine research as well as to discover for themselves the limitations inherent in scientific methods. In an early publication, Barbour called for 'integration' between diverse academic fields, themes that would come to fruition in Barbour's future pioneering work in science and religion, including the relation of science and public policy, the relation of the physical and the social sciences, and the impact of science on worldviews.

Part II: Barbour's Contributions to Methodology

The second Part focuses on a cornerstone issue in science and religion: how can and should these two seemingly disparate fields relate constructively? Four articles contribute to our understanding of the methodology Barbour developed as a pioneering response to this cornerstone issue, a methodology he terms 'critical realism.'

Robert John Russell's chapter surveys critical realism as the most prevelant methodology in the past fifty years of science and religion, focusing on Barbour's constructive arguments and the contributions of other scholars to it. Critical realism includes three topics: the role of metaphor in religious and scientific language, a correspondence theory of truth, and a methodological analogy between the ways scientific and religious communities construct, deploy and test theories against evidence. Barbour's central claim is that there is an analogy between scientific and theological rationality, although there are also significant differences. The analogy forms the linguistic, epistemic and methodological 'bridge' between the fields that has made 'science and religion' possible. He traces the ways Barbour drew on the philosophy of science of the 1960s, with its understanding of scientific revolutions, paradigms, models, and the philosophy of religion, with its growing appreciation for the referential status of religious language and verification as intersubjectivity. Russell describes how the work of other scholars, including Arthur Peacocke, John Polkinghorne, Nancey Murphy, Philip Clayton, Wolfhart Pannenberg, Wentzyl van Huyssteen, Niels Gregersen, and Ted Peters, have developed and criticized this approach. He also points to a wider horizon of discussion, including Continental postmodernism, feminist critiques of science, and historians of science and religion, in which broader concerns and challenges have been voiced to the way critical realism has shaped the field, and he suggests new ways in which the conversation can be genuinely interactive.

Christian Berg's chapter, 'Barbour's Way(s) of Relating Science and Theology,' is an outgrowth of his recent dissertation in Germany. Berg gives us a fascinating historical account of the way Barbour developed his now famous fourfold typology of ways to relate science and religion: Conflict, Independence, Dialogue, and Integration. He begins with Barbour's early thought during the 1950s and 1960s. Here Barbour argued against positivism by drawing on the writings of Karl Heim, stressing the existentialist dimensions of practicing scientists and the difference between I–It and I–Thou relations in science and religion. He even suggested that science and religion could provide complementary descriptions of reality as wave-particle modes do in physics. In his middle period Barbour moved from complementarity between science and religion to critical realism and its focus on the unity of the world. Here, as Berg demonstrates, we see a growing interest in metaphysics and the importance for Barbour of both Teilhard de Chardin and Alfred North Whitehead. Finally, in his late period following retirement in 1986, Barbour deployed his typology in a variety of publications from the prestigious Gifford Lectures to his recent popular book, *When Science Meets Religion*.

Next Berg offers a fascinating analysis of the development of Barbour's views over the past four decades, according to which Barbour's typology mirrors cornerstones and phases of his development. Berg then questions how well the typology really works. For example, is 'conflict' the best way to categorize the opposition between biblical literalists and scientific materialists? Is 'systematic synthesis' too ambitious and costly for theology? In response, Berg proposes a dimensional metaphor for the relations of science and theology, and closes by placing Barbour's position within this three-dimensional analysis.

Niels Gregersen explores subtle and important nuances in the origin and development of critical realism in the science-religion dialogue before turning to current criticisms. According to Ernan McMullin, only some sciences can be said to 'approximate reality,' while Willem B. Drees and Kees van Kooten Niekerk are skeptical about the use of realism in theology. Nancey Murphy urges us to move beyond the modernist view of referentiality to postmodern epistemology. Wentzel van Huyssteen focuses our attention on the epistemic values of participants in religious and scientific communities. Wesley Robbins commends a turn to pragmatism. Gregersen's own position is that realist cognitive claims are built into both science and theology. The hard task, particularly for theology, is justifying them, and this can be done through a coherentist form of realism in which the role of theology is to 're-describe a world already described and partially explained by science.'

Gregersen's approach supports metaphysical realism, that is, the claim that the world has a mind-independent structure, and semantic realism, that is, the idea that scientific theories are truth-conditioned descriptions of their intended domains, both observable and unobservable. Gregersen, however, is skeptical about theoretical-explanatory realism, that is, the view that the entities posited by mature scientific theories actually inhabit the world. He sides with Christian Berg that a more apt comparison might be between science and theology than science and religion, and with Arthur Peacocke's stress on the religious community as providing first-order experience and an identity of reference for theological language. In short, a coherence theory of truth is a healthy approach to theological rationality.

In 'Religion, Theology, and the Philosophy of Science: An Appreciation of the Work of Ian Barbour,' Nancey Murphy considers several aspects of Barbour's position on the relation between religion and science. His scholarship, both encyclopedic and irenic, often leads to a *via media* that takes into account the strengths and the weaknesses of opposing sides. For example, critical realism for Barbour is a middle position on the truth and language of both science and religion, one lying between naive realism and relativism. More than offering a mere compromise, though, Barbour is constructing a real alternative in which religion as a whole, and not just theology, is that which is to be related to science.

In his recent work, Barbour views the Christian tradition as containing various internal Kuhnian-like paradigms. Murphy, however, prefers Alasdair MacIntyre's definition of tradition as 'an historically extended, socially embodied argument about how best to interpret and apply a set of formative texts' over Kuhn's notion of paradigm. On a large scale, traditions can contain, and be contained in, other traditions. On a finer scale we find schools with enough agreement on fundamentals to be designated *research programs* as defined by Imre Lakatos. A further advantage of using Lakatos and MacIntyre over Kuhn is their stress on rational criteria in choosing between competing traditions. Finally, MacIntyre is helpful specifically for the science and religion dialogue because both theists and atheists stand within traditions in need of rational analysis.

Returning to the issue of critical realism, Murphy expresses concern that here at least Barbour's irenic spirit leads him to seek a midpoint between positions that are not, in fact, on a spectrum. Critical realism, for example, is intended as a compromise between rationalistic and sociological accounts of science, one which allows 'external' sociological factors to play a corrective to the 'internalist' views of realism without thoroughly relativizing them. However, rationalism and sociology of science are answers to two different sets of questions rather than extremes on a spectrum of answers to the same question. Thus, Murphy concludes contrary to Barbour that there is no middle position between them, and no compromise need be found.

Part III: Barbour's Contributions to Theological and Ethical Issues

We now begin the first of the two longest Parts in the volume, this one dealing with both theological and ethical issues. It is divided into four sections.

Section A addresses the relations between God and nature. In 'Barbour's Panentheistic Metaphysic,' Philip Clayton focuses on three aspects of Barbour's advocacy of process philosophy. First, Barbour uses process philosophy as a mediation between science and religion. Second, instead of pulling in random analogies and metaphors as might be helpful for each new topic, Barbour has sought to use mediating principles that form a consistent, systematic whole. Third, this methodology has (rightly) caused Barbour at different points to alter both science and theology. This third feature is the source of two fundamental principles which represent one of Barbour's greatest legacies. (1) The primary discussion partner for religion is science as interpreted metaphysically. (2) Since the dialogue entails genuine *interaction*, theology will be probed as well. The theology that is capable of stepping outside of the blinders of its faith commitments and engaging in this sort of dialogue – and Clayton sees this as Barbour's great insight – is philosophical theology. Clayton identifies this theology as 'Christian metaphysical theism.'

Clayton then focuses on Barbour's advocacy of panentheism. His core thesis is that while Barbour's panentheism remains true to the Whitehead–Hartshorne trajectory, it has been adapted, modified and extended because of his specialization in the religion–science dialogue. He then draws attention to problematic areas in Barbour's project: (1) The tension between emergence, which Barbour endorses, and process metaphysics is never resolved. (2) Dual-aspect monism, which Barbour advocates, is inconsistent with both traditional process thought and emergence. (3) These problematic areas should cause us to modify Barbour's panentheism in two directions. The first strengthens the dimension of emergence while the second adds a deeper element to the divine mystery and strengthens the dimension of faith. According to Clayton, were this to occur, Barbour would have to leave open a larger place for doctrinal considerations in his thought about God.

Section B focuses on physics and cosmology. William R. Stoeger writes on 'What is "the Universe" which Cosmology Studies?' He initially defines cosmology as the physical and astronomical investigation of the universe taken as a 'single object of study' or 'the universe as a whole.' This definition, however, leads to complex scientific and philosophical issues. Since our knowledge is limited to the observable universe, 'the universe as a whole' must refer to that reality which makes the observable universe intelligible. But can we establish the existence of this reality and determine whether it is infinite? And what are the theological implications of its existence?

In responding, Stoeger follows Barbour's lead in adopting a critical realist interpretation of science. In specific, Stoeger employs retroduction, an inferential argument developed by C.S. Peirce and Ernan McMullin by which hypotheses are constructed to explain observable phenomena in terms of hidden realities, causes, and relationships. In light of Big Bang, inflationary and quantum cosmology, Stoeger then argues that everything we can observe shares the same origin, evolutionary history, and laws of nature, and that the observable universe is unbounded. But does this suggest that the universe as a whole is infinite in space and time? In Stoeger's carefully argued view we cannot rule out the universe being spatially infinite. An infinitely old universe poses additional complications, since time, unlike space, is given sequentially, not 'all at once,' and in some cosmologies our universe emerged from a primordial universe with no temporal characteristics. Stoeger concludes with the provocative suggestion that the universe as a whole 'is not to be identified with the totality of all that exists, only with the largest physical system of which our observable universe is a part.' Thus we can speak of 'all that is' as greater than 'the universe as a whole,' opening the door for theological reflection on cosmology.

In 'Barbour's Assessment of the Philosophical and Theological Implications of Physics and Cosmology,' Robert John Russell offers an illuminating overview of Barbour's methodology, the key role he sees for process metaphysics, and crucial insights into his theological commitments. After discussing Barbour's views on complementarity and holism in quantum mechanics and the challenge to realism, Russell compares the way he and Barbour relate quantum mechanics and divine action. Both interpret quantum mechanics as pointing to ontological indeterminacy in nature. Both agree that quantum mechanics offers a non-interventionist approach to objective special providence. Both point out that such divine action would be scientifically undetectable even while occasionally leading to significant macroscopic effects. But Barbour believes process metaphysics is needed to avoid theological determinism and to address the problems of free will and theodicy while Russell argues it is not. Meanwhile they both must face the challenge posed by quantum non-separability to critical realism.

Russell praises Barbour's analysis of special relativity, including his sharp criticism of idealist and relativizing interpretations and his wisdom in stressing the limitations of science, the partiality of scientific theory, and the difficulties fraught by a move from science to metaphysics. Russell then focuses on Barbour's critique of the 'block universe' interpretation of relativity in favor of a 'flowing time' interpretation. Barbour argues that relativity depicts events in nature as radically isolated and yet, unlike other scholars, he also sees them as interconnected. In Russell's opinion, it is actually Barbour's presupposition of a process metaphysics, and not relativity *per se*, that allows him to include interconnectedness. Russell then asks whether process metaphysics suggest insights for research in physics, and whether other metaphysical systems in current theology offer promising options for a relational ontology. Finally, Russell analyzes Barbour's discussion of the relation of God's temporal knowledge of and influence on the universe from a process perspective.

The third topic is the beginning of time, 't = 0' as depicted by (standard) Big Bang cosmology, in relation to a theology of creation. Russell traces the evolution of Barbour's position and its dependence on Langdon Gilkey's separation of the meaning of 'origin' into ontological versus historical categories. Russell then moves beyond the Gilkey/Barbour position by adopting a Lakatosian methodology in which *creatio ex nihilo* includes both an ontological and a historical, empirical claim about t = 0. As Barbour was the first scholar to discuss Lakatos in the context of theological methodology, Russell sees this as a fitting way to explore yet another dimension of Barbour's pioneering contributions.

Section C is devoted to evolutionary biology, anthropology, and the neurosciences. It begins with W. Mark Richardson's chapter, 'Case Studies in Barbour's Integrative Model: Liberal Anglo-Catholicism in the 1920s.' Richardson starts with Barbour's essay in *Neuroscience and the Person*, where Barbour describes various Christian views of the human person in relation to relevant data from the neurosciences, computational sciences and informational systems. Barbour closes with an exposition of the integrating power of process philosophy to bridge the conceptual distance between theology and the neurosciences. Richardson builds on Barbour's 'integrative' model by taking up the nature of the human being in theological anthropology and opening it to revision in light of contemporary science.

Through a 'case study' method, Richardson explores Barbour's thesis that the relation of scientific data and theory to theology is mediated philosophically. His study focuses on early twentieth-century liberal Anglo-Catholic theologians including N.P. Williams, William Temple, and Charles Gore. Here crucial differences arise in the way these theologians revised their view of human origins and sin in light of evolution by moving from an Augustinian 'fall' theology toward a 'soul-making' theology. Still, these differences are only due in part to the influence of evolution; other factors such as philosophical idealism played a role too. Richardson concludes that Gore and Temple are closer in their views than either of them is to Williams. Unlike Williams, they do not see nature's laws as evidence of a fallen world or, behind that, a heavenly rebellion. Temple, in turn, tends to view evil as necessary, whereas Gore holds to a more classical form of ethical monotheism.

Next comes Martinez Hewlett's incisive chapter, 'DNA, Darwin, and Doxology: A Contemporary Conversation Between Biology and Faith.' Hewlett begins by drawing out the subtle philosophical relations between biology and theology as twentieth-century biology came to be dominated by the burgeoning field of Genomics and its reductive approach. But, as Hewlett warns, we should not lose sight of the higher order complexities that cannot be reduced to the chemistry of the nucleic acids. Here too Barbour's influence has been felt in the philosophical basis of this interchange, as well as in the ethical and theological implications of the ensuing dialogue. His fourfold typology for the relations between science and religion have been an immensely helpful 'roadmap' for these conversations. More importantly, Barbour's use of process philosophy provides a metaphysics that is consistent with the methodology of biology while avoiding the ever-present snares of reductionism and determinism. His views on critical realism are closely aligned with how most practicing scientists view their work.

But in Hewlett's opinion, it is Barbour's integrationist approach to biology and theology that opens the most promising door to future directions of interaction. For example, the Human Genome Project promises to offer crucial knowledge for dealing with gene-based diseases, but it could also be used by those wishing to justify abhorrent social agendas. Once again, Barbour's challenge to reductionistic and materialistic views of the human person and its support, instead, of viewing human nature as a multi-leveled unity is crucial. In closing, Hewlett recalls the basically religious experience of the biologist encountering 'yet another seeming miracle of life.' Modern science has no method to describe this kind of experience, but Barbour's integration model might allow one to move beyond the limits of science *per se* and create a new hymn of praise to the Creator that uses 'the music of the gene' as its thematic content.

Ted Peters begins his chapter, 'Selfish Genes and Loving Persons,' by focusing on Barbour's emphasis on hope and the possibilities for change in the world brought about by a future open to newness and the power of *agape* love. Barbour assumes that humanity, inspired by God's transformatory power, can be guided to change towards what is genuinely good, while his belief in the openness of nature lies in Darwinian evolution supported by an evolutionary metaphysics which underscores temporality and change. But Peters asks, how much change lies within the reach of human resolve if from our evolutionary past we human beings have inherited a propensity to selfishness? And are we able to love without self-regard, without reciprocity, without dependence on the drive for reproductive fitness?

Peters responds by starting with sociobiological research on altruism in nonhuman species and comparing it with the theological mandate to love our neighbor. Sociobiological theories such as kin preference and reciprocal altruism seem to imply that biological constraints make *agape* love impossible since *agape*, as compared with altruism, is dedicated to the welfare of those from a different gene pool. To address this challenge, Peters moves to the issue of biological determinism at the level of organism, then to adaptation in evolutionary psychology, and finally to culturally created values that appear to transcend their biological prehistory. In the process, he uses Francisco Ayala's arguments against reductionism to make his case that genetic determinism or even adaptive functionalism cannot fully account for, or undermine the possibility of, the human experience of *agape* as an apparently nonadaptive phenomenon. Instead it requires a distinctively theological epistemology, since self-sacrificial love is invisible to science. Indeed, *agape* love has never been considered theologically as a mere phenomenon of human culture – let alone of our biology – but rather as a goal towards which an individual strives, and a goal that requires the gift of divine grace.

He then sketches several ways theologians have reflected on *agape* in light of sociobiology: some scholars rely on intervention by the Holy Spirit; others redefine *agape* love to make it compatible with genetic selfishness and kin preference; still others turn to kenotic theology. Instead, Peters moves to an eschatology which sharply contrasts the divine call toward selfless loving with precedents set by natural selection and genetic selfishness. He closes by suggesting that God calls us towards an eschatological future that transcends the precedents of our biological past.

Section D moves our attention from theology to ethics in relation to technology and the environment. In 'Technology Requires Ethical Decisions,' Roger L. Shinn begins by reminding us that from Biblical times to the present, the assessment of the importance of technology in shaping human culture has varied widely. Hellenic philosophers largely neglected it, while Christian theologians and monastics often recognized its role in the service of God. Recent historians and philosophers have stressed the contribution of Christianity to the rise of modern science, while ecological critics have sought to blame Christianity for environmental disasters. Shinn then turns to Barbour's writings in general, citing how they display his broad expertise in the sciences, philosophy and theology, his discernment of their cultural impacts, a fairness in evaluating controversial issues and decisiveness in taking his own position. From this he raises five themes for discussion.

First, in exploring the relation between science and technology, Barbour sees both differences (understanding versus activity; verifiability versus effectiveness) and similarities (relativity leads to energy and weapons). Secondly, Barbour claims that technology is not value-neutral since it leads to power and, with it, moral ambivalence. Like Barbour, Shinn rejects both the messianic hopes of a 'technological fix' and the demonization of technology as typified in the debate between Jacques Ellul and Margaret Mead. Thirdly, new technologies require an 'exploratory ethics' for arriving at decisions which cannot simply be read off of sacred texts or philosophical sources. At the same time, science and technology cannot deliver ethically sound decisions; we need to proceed on a case-by-case basis. Fourthly, are the electorate and their governmental representatives competent to make these decisions, given the powerful influence of Congressional committees, political lobbies, the National Academy of Sciences, and the Office of Technology Assessment? Finally, Gandhi's distinction between 'need and greed' is convoluted and ambiguous today, calling as Shinn puts it for 'an immense task of social reconstruction.' What then can we project about the goals and tasks ahead? Shinn argues that the world wants modernization without decadence, sexual excess, drug addiction, and rampant individualism. Globalization is ambiguous: is it allegiance to the global community against nationalism, or is it westernization in disguise? Clearly, technological advance does not equate with the advance of freedom and peace. Shinn shares with Barbour a hope for an expansion of liberal democracy, repentant of ecological extravagance and heavily committed to a just and sustainable world society, though Shinn has deeper forebodings about its realization and the costs to get there. Still, neither of them is a utopian or 'futilitarian;' both are committed to redirecting technology for 'faith without works is dead.'

In 'Ethics, Technology, and Environment,' Judith N. Scoville begins by praising Barbour for his unique contribution to science and religion: his writings connect both Christian theology and its engagement with the natural sciences, on the one hand, and Christian ethics and its concerns over technology and the environment on the other. In comparison, most scholars in 'religion and science' have given relatively little attention to environmental ethics, while many ecotheologians have given inadequate attention to the important work being done in 'religion and science'. Moreover, in his writings on ethics and technology, Barbour's inclusion of the environment distinguishes his writings from most scholars who focus entirely on such human-centered concerns as medical and reproductive technologies. Finally, Scoville commends Barbour for attending to social ethics and to values such as justice and participation.

She notes, however, that the division of the Gifford lectures into two volumes has obscured the connections Barbour identifies between 'science and religion' and 'ethics and technology,' and her objective is to more fully develop them. She begins with Barbour's unique approach to environmental ethics: he focuses on the ethics of technology since it is through technology and its social embedding that we enact our relationship to the environment. He views technology as a value-laden social construct, shaped by culture and purpose. He then outlines three approaches to Christian ethics: the ethics of the good, of duty, and of response, and deploys them to develop a series of human and environmental values. Here his focus on intrinsic as well as environmental values reflects Barbour's commitment to process philosophy and its attention to the universality of experience.

Scoville is critical, however, of the primacy Barbour gives to human-centered environmental ethics, and she seeks to extend it to a broader range of non human-centered values by turning to the science of ecology and its focus on communities over individuals. She also argues that including ecology explicitly in the discussions of 'science and religion' would yield rich implications for both an environmental theology and ethics. She then utilizes Barbour's four-part typology for relating religion and science to illuminate the different ways in which such an environmental ethics could be developed. How, then, does process thought fit into this typology? Her conclusion is that, while process theology exemplifies Barbour's 'integration' model in science and religion, it seems to fall more into the independence model when it comes to ethics and the environment.

In her final section, Scoville evaluates Barbour's discussion of agriculture. Though he seeks to stress both 'the holism of ecosystem ethics and the individualism of animal rights,' Scoville argues that ecological interrelatedness does not play a significant role in Barbour's ethical analysis. She concludes by underscoring the complexity of these issues and by thanking Barbour for his honesty, accuracy, and willingness to live with tension and to empower others to enter into the conversations.

Christopher Southgate writes on 'Environmental Ethics and the Science–Religion Debate', giving a British perspective on Barbour's work. Here too we find a probing analysis of the relation between both streams of Barbour's writings: science and religion, and technology and values. Southgate first takes us back to Barbour's early work in the 1970s – the era of Lynn White, Jr's (in)famous indictment of Christianity for its role in fostering the growing ecological crisis – and moves carefully through Barbour's many writings, emerging at the Gifford Lectures in 1991. He notes Barbour's early insight in linking ecological wisdom with social justice and his criticism of social institutions that lead to environmental devastation. Barbour's process ethic allows him to avoid two extremes: deep-ecology that values all species as equal, and systemic values that undercut the status of the individual.

Southgate compares Barbour's development of the image of 'spaceship earth' in the 1970s with more recent language about 'Gaia' and touches on Barbour's defense of stewardship in the 1980s. He then offers a helpful comparison of the constructive optimism of the science–religion dialogue and the skepticism prevalent in the 'green' theology movement. Turning to the science–religion dialogue, Southgate compares the way Barbour developed critical realism with particular attention to models and metaphors. He cites the striking influence of Barbour's philosophical work on Arthur Peacocke and John Polkinghorne, 'the major British contribution' to the dialogue. And though process theology has not been particularly influential in British circles, Southgate stresses that one can learn much from Barbour's use of it without adopting it. Southgate closes with deep appreciation for Barbour's philosophical skills, which mapped the territory and grounded and opened the science–religion conversation to a wider audience, and for his keeping in our attention both the debates over the environment and the concern for a scholarly theological appropriation of science.

Part IV: Theological Perspectives on Barbour's Work

The second longest Part focuses on three distinct types of theological perspectives on Barbour's work. *Section A* centers on process theology. In 'God and Physics in the Thought of Ian Barbour,' John Cobb, Jr assesses Barbour's accomplishments in terms of 'the larger project of process theology.' This project challenges the contemporary view of knowledge as fragmented into differing subjects and methods and views substance thinking as a chief cause of such fragmentation. Instead Cobb assumes that events, processes and experiences provide an alternative model of reality which can overcome fragmentation by assuming that relations are intrinsic and constitutive. Changes in twentieth-century science, such as quantum theory and relativity, are particularly promising in support of this model. Though most process theologians are ill-equipped for the task of engaging physics and theology, Barbour is a rare and brilliant exception. Cobb was initially attracted to Whitehead because his thought about God and humanity was coherent with science. Decades later, Barbour's extensive work has strengthened that judgment. Cobb's critique, however, is that Barbour does not show how a process perspective leads to new directions within, and even a thorough revision of, the various sciences.

After discussing examples drawn from economics and from biology, Cobb then turns to the main area of Barbour's work, physics and cosmology. While Barbour shows that the philosophical implications of quantum theory, such as temporality and historicity, chance and law, and wholeness and emergence, are 'congenial' with process philosophy, he does not advocate changing quantum theory in light of process metaphysics. Cobb, however, urges that a process-based approach to interrelated events can generate better theories in physics than existing ones based on substance metaphysics. Turning next to relativity, Cobb notes that, although Whitehead accepted Einstein's special theory of relativity, he was critical of Einstein's substantialist treatment of space-time in general relativity. In 1922, Whitehead developed an alternative theory based on multiple time systems and represented this in four different sets of equations. Cobb reports in detail on how these equations were received, rejected, and recently reassessed within the scientific community. Finally Cobb turns to the implications of cosmology for process theology. Big Bang cosmology, with its discovery of a cosmic beginning, seemed to challenge Whiteheadian commitment to a universe of many epochs. Cobb lauds Barbour for showing that Big Bang cosmology does not challenge the more fundamental commitment of process philosophers against substantialism, but he continues to call for a deeper interaction between theology and science.

Ernest Simmons's chapter, 'Barbour in Process: Contributions to Process Theology,' offers a second careful assessment of Barbour's appropriation and critique of process theology. Though highly sympathetic, Barbour has consistently sought to enlarge process theology by relying more fully on Christian religious experience and historical revelation through the theology of continuing creation. From his earliest work, Barbour drew on both Whitehead and Hartshorne while deploying a theology of nature reminiscent of the work of Joseph Sittler. His themes included the worshipping community as the context of theology, nature as a dynamic process with multiple levels of activity, and the sovereignty of God as love, not coercive power. In his Gifford Lectures, Simmons sees Barbour as developing an 'ecological metaphysics' through his understanding of God as 'creative participant' in light of the biblical understanding of Spirit and the Christian community. Thus Barbour 'is not trying to reconcile theology and science with process thought but using process thought to reconcile theology and science.' Barbour's process response to God and evil is to stress divine power as suffering love and to extend this beyond the human community to the evolution of life on earth – in what Simmons calls the greatest contribution that process theology in general has to offer us.

Barbour's most recent writings are the ones 'many of us have been waiting for' since they carry Barbour's strongest endorsement of process theology. Still he calls for a more integrated sense of self than Whitehead offers, pointing to the emergence of higher capacities and underplaying the atomistic character of process thought. He defends his preference for metaphysical limits on God's power rather than divine self-limitation but he still argues that a God of empowerment is indeed worthy of worship. Simmons concludes by briefly assessing the relation between Polkinghorne and Barbour on several counts. Simmons is critical of Polkinghorne for failing to recognize that Barbour calls for more continuity in natural processes than does Whitehead. He also believes that Barbour sees himself not so much as a theologian than as a philosopher of science and religion. But Simmons finds Barbour's greatest contribution to be the synthesizing of the vast literature in the field and the raising of ethical implications of technology. These truly make Barbour 'the father of the field of science and religion in the United States.'

Barbour's relation to Roman Catholic theology is the theme of *Section B*. In 'Catholicism and Ian Barbour on Theology and Science', Anne M. Clifford argues that the term 'catholic' has two distinct, yet related, meanings – universal and confessional – that apply to Barbour's life project. She then addresses Barbour's position in three areas in science and theology: the Galileo affair; science as a necessary partner for theology; and evolution, especially of *homo sapiens*. Barbour speaks of the Galileo affair as an example of conflict between science and religion, although he is more nuanced in this than many other commentators. Clifford, though, feels the situation is difficult to categorize without a careful analysis of its complex historical development and surrounding factors: an 'ecclesiastical biblicism' which drove Cardinal Bellarmine to interpret Scripture literally and thus to require Galileo to treat heliocentrism as a mere hypothesis, and the fact that the heliocentric system tended to undermine such central Church teachings as the incarnation and humanity's being created as *imago Dei*. She recounts how Galileo's views later underwent a 'gradual rehabilitation' culminating in the work of the special commission created by John Paul II. In his 1992 address, John Paul II, like Barbour, is careful to identify the real conflict as between science reframed as scientism and religion turned into religionism and used against science as a pseudoscience. Instead of conflict or independence, John Paul II has called for genuine conversation and dialogue.

When it comes to evolution, the situation is once again complex. On the one hand, John Paul II affirms the reasonableness of evolution and its wide acceptance in the scientific community while challenging reductionist and materialist philosophical interpretations of evolution. On the other hand, he adopts Pope Pius XII's position that, while the human body evolved, the soul is created immediately by God – what Clifford calls 'the Roman Catholic form of "creationism".' Barbour turns instead to biblical anthropology, contemporary science, and process philosophy to develop the view of the person as a psychosomatic unity. Clifford leaves us to choose between these two positions and their relative merits, concluding that in an era in which Catholic theologians continue to neglect the natural sciences, much of value can be learned from the 'catholicity' of Ian Barbour.

In '"Seeing" the Universe: Ian Barbour and Teilhard de Chardin,' John F. Haught carefully places the visions of these two pioneers in dialogue and articulates his understanding of their strengths and differences. He begins by asking why Teilhard's thought has been so neglected in recent discussions of theology and science. Perhaps Teilhard's argument that evolution does not require a materialist metaphysics drives his critics to see him as a vitalist, or perhaps his vision of cosmic directionality is mistaken for a teleology being forced into science. Haught admits that Teilhard may have opened the door to being misinterpreted in these ways, his real concern was to counter the materialist agenda of dismissing consciousness as a mere epiphenomenon of matter by arguing that science should include the datum of conscious experience – the 'withinness' of things. Haught sees strong links here between Teilhard's approach and the philosophies of William James and Alfred North Whitehead.

How does Barbour relate to these views? According to Haught, Barbour too sees consciousness as an objective feature of nature that deserves empirical study, but urges that such study can be handled more appropriately through an experientially grounded metaphysics, such as Whitehead provides, than by expanding our idea of natural science to include consciousness, as Teilhard urged. Since Thomistic metaphysics could not provide Teilhard with what process metaphysics does for Barbour, he had no choice but to urge the expansion of science itself. Still, whether one follows Teilhard or Barbour here, the advantage to the relation of science and religion of placing mind on a continuum with nature is profound. A prime example is the new approach to divine action in nature. Conversely, seeing matter and mind as tendencies and not distinct substances overcomes the challenge to religion posed by eliminative materialism. Thus one of Barbour's most important contributions is his insistence on the objectivity of mind in evolutionary nature, a vision which Haught believes Teilhard would have gladly endorsed.

Section C focuses on the impact of Barbour's work on one element of the growing interreligious/inter-faith conversations about science and religion: the dialogue between Buddhism and science. This focus is motivated in part because Barbour was born in China and its impact on his life and thought has been enduring. But more importantly, many attempts at relating science and religion against the backdrop of Western reductionism and atheism have been used by popularizers who have sought to draw quick parallels between 'Eastern mysticism,' particularly Buddhism, and modern science. Barbour has been critical of these attempts while devoting considerable time to his own suggestions for relating Buddhism and science. In this section, two chapters assess his work in this regard.

In 'A Reflection on Buddhist–Christian Dialogue with the Natural Sciences', Paul O. Ingram explores several ways in which Christians and Buddhists are currently engaging the natural sciences. He first draws on Barbour to argue that several features of science constitute a challenge to all religious traditions: the success of scientific methods, the difference between scientific and traditional cosmologies, and scientific understandings of human nature. He then lays out his working assumptions: science gives us real knowledge about the universe best understood through critical realism, a philosophy that is also valid in Christian theology. Moreover, both scientific and theological insights carry ethical implications for human action, and scientific cosmology offers a 'metadiscourse' for discussing ethics, politics and various religious traditions. Still, as Ingram notes, science has strongly challenged Christian faith, while it has had little if any impact on Buddhism. The exploration of this dissimilarity forms the body of his paper.

Ingram first discusses Big Bang cosmology, including the origin of the universe and the anthropic principle, and reviews the debates over their implications in the writings of several Buddhist and Christian scientists. While Christians claim that God created the universe, the Buddhist response is nontheistic: it harmonizes well with Big Bang cosmology in which there is no time before the universe, and in any case, Buddhists tend to dismiss such questions as meaningless. Ingram then turns to discussions of evolution and its stress upon interdependence as well as the problem of suffering in nature. B. Alan Wallace disagrees with critical realism, affirming the 'two-truth' epistemology of Nāgārjuna and arguing that scientific theories have no ontological status. Victor Mansfield sees Buddhism and science, especially psychology, as highly compatible. Shoyo Taniguchi claims that Buddhism in its empirical and experimental methods is scientific in ways that other religions are not, and is thus superior to Western monotheism.

In closing Ingram returns to his initial issue: is it in fact true that the encounter with science poses no important conceptual challenges to Buddhism? Perhaps the Buddhist attempt to relieve suffering by nonviolent means is actually an illusion, given the essential role of suffering in evolution. Do we really cause our own suffering by clinging to impermanence, and free ourselves of suffering by not clinging, if the universe demands suffering and death as the price for life? Finally, can Awakening really mean anything beyond a mere awareness of universal pointlessness as suggested by science? Of course, Ingram recognizes that the most genuine response must come from Buddhists themselves, but the process of coming to such a response in the context of Buddhist–Christian dialogue may lead to a new form of creative transformation in both traditions.

Jensine Andresen writes on 'Barbour, Buddhism, Bohm, and Beyond.' She praises Barbour for discussing Asian thought within various topics in his major works, particularly metaphysical holism seen from the contrasting viewpoints of physics and mysticism. As a result, the religion and science dialogue has been extended into a pluralistic context. Still, Barbour's reliance on secondary sources on Asian thought causes him to reify Asian perspectives and to present them in too general a way.

To address these issues, Andresen first takes Buddhist views on consciousness as illustrative of how a deeper grounding in a particular Asian tradition would enhance Barbour's discussion. Barbour is rightly critical of such thinkers as Fritjof Capra who find easy parallels between concepts of wholeness in physics and in eastern mysticism. But when he attempts to show the difference between the relation of time and timelessness in physics and mysticism, Andresen claims that Barbour overgeneralizes what he characterizes as timelessness in Buddhism, conflating subtle distinctions in the process.

To remedy this problem, Andresen selects a specific tradition for analysis: Madhyamaka Buddhist philosophy as expressed in the second-century scholar Nāgārjuna and his discussion of 'timelessness.' Here, the 'two truths' interpretation (worldly or conventional and ultimate truths) allows Buddhists to recognize that both time and timelessness can co-exist. According to Andresen, the experience of enlightenment includes the ability to perceive this co-existence, although physics seems to be restricted to time's worldly reality. She points out that David Bohm seems to make a similar claim about the relationship between both conventional and ultimate reality, as well as between local connectedness and global wholeness. This leads Andresen into a careful exploration of the differing views of consciousness in physics and in Buddhist Tantra. Here, unlike scholars who claim that science does not challenge Buddhism, the neurosciences do in fact challenge Buddhist notions of enlightenment by underscoring the grounding of experience in brain activities. Andresen then discusses Barbour's writings on Eastern traditions as a resource for environmental ethics, his use of complementary models in physics, in mystical experience and in theological doctrines of God, and paradigm analysis in comparing differing religions such as Hinduism and Christianity. She concludes that her critique of Barbour as a generalist in the context of Asian thought is really only a caveat to the fact that Barbour's writings genuinely further the interreligious dimension of the religion and science dialogue.

In sum, *Fifty Years* will help the reader, whether new to the discussion or a scholarly partner, gain a clear sense of the diversity and the depth of the field as well as its overall unity and vision. These chapters should provide a lasting assessment of science and religion at the turn of the century: what has been accomplished in fifty years of an exponentially growing dialogue and what lies ahead as we look into the coming decades of the new millenium – and how all of this is, in such large measure, due to the life and writings of one person, Ian G. Barbour.

A Personal Odyssey

Ian G. Barbour

My dictionary defines an odyssey as 'an extended adventurous wandering.' My intellectual and spiritual journey over the past 80 years has been an adventure and it has certainly wandered.

I was born in Peking (Beijing) in 1923. My mother was an Episcopalian, the daughter of Dr Robert L. Dickinson of Brooklyn, who was one of the earliest medical advocates of family planning. My father was Presbyterian, son of a physician with similar medical interests in Edinburgh, Scotland, where the two families had met. Soon after they were married my parents went to China to teach at Yenching University – he in the geology department and she in religious education. Dad was a close friend and colleague of the Jesuit paleontologist, Pierre Teilhard de Chardin. They were part of the team that discovered the hominid skull which was dubbed *Sinanthropus* or Peking Man. Some of their conversations and correspondence over four decades are recorded in George B. Barbour's *In the Field with Teilhard de Chardin.*[1]

My family left China in 1931 on the advice of physicians concerned about the health of my older brother Hugh (who retired a few years ago from teaching at Earlham College and writing numerous volumes on the history of Quakerism). My younger brother, Freeland, died in 1953 of brain cysts while a medical student at Harvard; the doctors thought that a long history of undiagnosed high fevers might have been caused by something acquired in China. During the Depression years, Dad had leave-replacement jobs in Pasadena, Cincinnati, New York, and London before returning to Cincinnati as Dean. I attended five schools in five years, which did not facilitate long-term friendships. In England I was in an excellent Quaker boarding school for three years, long enough to be a prefect in the final year. I have a report card signed by W.H. Auden who had us writing poetry – though we had no inkling he would soon be recognized as a major poet. In three years at Deerfield Academy in Massachusetts I had my first serious exposure to science and to literature – but not much on the side of religion, except for required church services, the thoughtful radio sermons of Harry Emerson Fosdick, and a congenial roommate who later became an Episcopal priest.

I entered Swarthmore College in 1940, starting as an engineer but switching to physics because its theories and experiments intrigued me. The experience of being a lab assistant to an exciting young physics teacher confirmed the choice. One of my few humanities courses was Philosophy of Religion, a rather uninspiring analysis of the classical arguments for theism. But a summer in a Quaker work camp was an important experience of close community and shared meditation and discussion. Graduating on an accelerated schedule in 1943, I tried to join an overseas ambulance unit, the American Field Service, but was turned down when changes in the law excluded me as a British subject. Influenced by my contact with Quakers, I registered as a conscientious objector.

My three years in Civilian Public Service were divided between building forest access roads and fighting forest fires in Oregon and working with mental patients in North Carolina. Those years saw hard work, intense discussions, and strong friendships. Two unexpected results were the opportunity to take some graduate physics courses at Duke and the companionship and joy of knowing Deane Kern, a Duke undergraduate from Washington, DC, whom I married soon after her graduation. I have been profoundly thankful for our life together in all the years since then, and for her sharing in my unpredictable odyssey.

At the University of Chicago I was a teaching assistant under Enrico Fermi, who had presided over the first sustained atomic reaction a few years earlier. Many graduate students had delayed their studies to work on war-related projects, and competition for the PhD exams was intense. One of the students who took the exams with me did not pass, but he persisted, took them a second time, and subsequently won a Nobel Prize. My thesis was on the use of photographic emulsions to study cosmic ray mesons deflected by the field of a 70-pound magnet, carried to high altitudes by a huge helium-filled balloon. Physics absorbed most of my time in Chicago, but we were members of a group of four couples who met alternate weeks for readings, reflection and a simple meal together. We lived on the top floor of Frank Lloyd Wright's prairie-style Robie House, then owned by Chicago Theological Seminary in which Deane was enrolled in graduate courses.

We were invited to be counselors in a Congregational work camp in Germany during the summer of 1948. Students from Holland, the USA and Germany cleared rubble from a bombed-out university to prepare the site for rebuilding. The presence of the Dutch students was impressive, since many of them had had close relatives imprisoned or killed during the Nazi occupation, and the German students included former soldiers and even a former SS officer. I will never forget conversations at work, at meals, and in our tents, in which the linguistic skills of the Dutch students helped us to communicate.

I had taken Quantum Mechanics from Edward Teller, who was soon recruiting students to go with him to Los Alamos to work on the H-bomb. But I knew I wanted to teach in a liberal arts college, and in 1949 accepted a position at Kalamazoo College in Michigan, where I greatly enjoyed teaching physics. I received a grant to continue some cosmic ray experiments and was appointed department chair after the death of the former chair. Deane and I were active in an interdenominational, intercampus student fellowship whose minister, John Duley, helped us all to seek the meaning of Christian community in an academic context. Our first two children, John and Blair, were born in Kalamazoo and we had time to enjoy them in our home on Faculty Row.

The Ford Foundation was offering fellowships for faculty to study for a year in a discipline other than their primary field. In 1953 I applied to study theology and ethics at Yale Divinity School, and was fortunate to have courses with H. Richard Niebuhr, Roland Bainton, and Robert Calhoun, among others. I was so fascinated by these courses that I asked for my leave to be extended for a second year, and then faced a difficult decision. I believed that a vocational choice should reflect a person's abilities, interests and (in a religious context) response to God and human needs. I enjoyed physics and was familiar enough with it that I could teach and still have time for other activities. Moreover I knew that scientists are respected in the academic world, and their voices carry some weight on educational, ethical and religious issues. In addition, I shared the Reformation's conviction that any useful vocation can serve God and human need. But I increasingly felt that it would be more interesting and more significant to spend at least part of my time learning and teaching in religious studies. I completed a divinity degree at Yale, with the help of two summer sessions at Union in New York.

Carleton College in Minnesota offered me a job teaching half-time in physics and half-time in religion in the philosophy department (there was then no religion department). Between teaching a great variety of new courses, advising student religious groups, and continuing some cosmic ray experiments, I was under too much pressure during my first five years here, and I greatly regret that I did not spend more time with our children while they were young, especially the third and fourth, David and Heather. All four of our children have continued to enrich my life immeasurably. By 1960 the establishment of a religion department had been approved, and I dropped the physics teaching to be chair and teach full-time in the new religion department which included first an exceptional colleague, Bardwell Smith, and then other faculty (totaling five within a few years). Starting in 1961 I was fortunate to be in a group of scientists and theologians, convened by Harold Schilling (physicist and Dean at Penn State) which for a decade met twice a year for a weekend. It included William Pollard, Frederick Ferré, Huston Smith, Roger Shinn, and Dan Williams (who first introduced me to process theology), along with two philosophers and five other scientists. I later edited some of the papers written for this group under the title *Earth Might Be Fair: Reflections on Ethics, Religion and Ecology.*[2]

I received a fellowship to do research at Harvard in 1963. After attending a seminar on Whitehead led by Gordon Kaufman, I read extensively in the process theology of Charles Hartshorne, John Cobb, and David Griffin, to whom I have been deeply indebted ever since. Back at Carleton I wrote some chapters which I tried out in classes before revising them as *Issues in Science and Religion* (1966). What had started as an attempt to fit together two halves of my own life had become a wider intellectual inquiry in which I found that many other people were interested. The book was widely used as a college text at a time when there were few attempts to relate the two fields by authors familiar with both. The journal *Zygon*, founded in 1965 by Ralph Burhoe and subsequently edited by Philip Hefner, was an important catalyst for the continuing dialogue.

A few years later I was awarded Guggenheim and Fulbright Fellowships to explore epistemological questions in Cambridge, England. Deane and I greatly enjoyed our time there with our three younger children enrolled in local schools, and we formed lasting friendships with several British families. I attended some seminars and wrote *Myths, Models, and Paradigms* (1973). Positivistic philosophers had contrasted the objectivity of science with the subjectivity of religion. But new themes in the philosophy of science (such as Mary Hesse's writing on models and Thomas Kuhn's on paradigms), and new views of religious language in British analytic philosophy, suggested similarities as well as differences between the fields. The critical realism I defended was later endorsed by Arthur Peacocke and John Polkinghorne and has been of interest to philosophers and theologians. But I have found that methodological issues are less likely to engage the interest of scientists.

Ever since the nuclear weapons discussions in Chicago I had been deeply concerned about ethical issues in the applications of science, and by the early 1970s I had done some writing on environmental and technological ethics. Working with a Carleton colleague in political science I obtained grants from the National Science Foundation and the National Endowment for the Humanities to develop a program on Science, Technology and Public Policy. Students and faculty were drawn from the natural sciences, economics, political science, history, philosophy, and other fields, in courses and seminars that students could take separately or grouped together as an interdisciplinary 'minor.' My courses teaching half-time in this program took up ethical issues in policies for energy, agriculture and the environment, and later genetic engineering and computer applications. I drew from these courses in writing *Technology, Environment, and Human Values*, published in 1980. I was appointed the first Winifred and Atherton Bean Professor of Science, Technology and Society, a chair endowed by several friends of the college to honor an outstanding trustee (and former Rhodes Scholar) and his wife. I lectured on many of these topics during a year at Purdue as the first Eli Lilly Visiting Professor of Science, Theology and Human Values, and enjoyed a year at the National Humanities Center in North Carolina writing *Energy and American Values* with three co-authors.[3]

The invitation to give the Gifford Lectures in Scotland in 1989 and 1990 offered an opportunity to try to bring together my theological and ethical interests – and, of course, to see my Scottish relatives and a beautiful country. The first series, *Religion in an Age of Science* (1990), has been widely used as a text, especially in the expanded edition which included three historical chapters.[4] The second Gifford series, *Ethics in an Age of Technology* (1993), has not had such wide circulation though it has been used as a text in a few courses in engineering schools, seminaries, and liberal arts colleges. In order to make it more useful in secular institutions, I had analyzed policy choices in terms of such values as social justice and environmental preservation, for which I tried to provide justification on both theological and philosophical grounds. I thought this broader approach would be helpful to students looking at policy choices in the public arena, but as a consequence the theological ideas are not very extensively developed. I wanted the second volume to stand on its own, but perhaps I should have done more to integrate the two volumes.

On several occasions we stayed at Iona Abbey on an island off the coast of Scotland for memorable weeks of work, discussion, and worship. The Iona community has combined the journey inward with the journey outward in response to social injustice and human suffering; it has also written some powerful contemporary hymns set to Celtic melodies. In Northfield we have found in the United Church of Christ (Congregational) a community of acceptance, commitment, and concern for social justice, centering in the person of Christ and the work of the Spirit but remaining open to differences in theological interpretation.

The theme of sin and forgiveness has of course been central in the Christian tradition, but I have learned from Paul Tillich and others to appreciate some relational terms that go beyond moral judgment: alienation and reconciliation, brokenness and healing, bondage and liberation. The invitation to the communion table given by our minister for many years, Gordon Forbes, presents what I take to be the heart of the Gospel:

> If you know the brokenness of life, its fractures within and its division without, then you have participated in the broken body of Christ, and you are invited to share in the breaking of bread.
> If you desire to know the love of God that overcomes indifference and despair, if you desire the reconciliation that overcomes estrangement and alienation, then you are invited to share the cup of the new covenant.

During the 1990s I took up new questions concerning human nature in the light of evolutionary history, genetics, neuroscience, and the artificial intelligence of computers and robots.[5] There were opportunities to speak at conferences on evolution, cosmology, process theology, artificial intelligence, environmental ethics, the church in an age of science, and a variety of other topics. Living next to the Carleton campus, Deane and I have been able to hear lectures and concerts and to participate in smaller groups, and we are grateful for friendships in the church and the community. We have treasured the time with our adult children, their spouses or friends, and our three grandchildren, gathered at Christmas or for a few days in a rented house at a conference center on a Wisconsin lake.

I have been enduringly grateful to Robert Russell personally and for his innovative leadership in founding and directing the Center for Theology and the Natural Sciences (CTNS) in Berkeley, California. He had taught physics for three years at Carleton, where we had offered a science and religion course together a couple of times before he moved to Berkeley in 1980. The series of working groups on 'Divine Action' sponsored by CTNS and the Vatican Observatory, and the workshops of the CTNS science/religion course program funded by the Templeton Foundation, were for me invaluable opportunities for intellectual exchange and personal friendship. The program on 'Science and the Spiritual Quest,' led by Phillip Clayton and Mark Richardson, brought together prominent scientists from diverse religious traditions. The participants were more open to each other's religious views because they respected each other as scientists, and they brought to their discussion some of the spirit of inquiry they had known in science, even as they acknowledged the differences between the fields. When I received the Templeton Prize for Progress in Religion in 1999, I was glad that I could give most ($1 million) of it to CTNS to support what I see as the most significant program of courses, conferences and publications on science and religion anywhere in the world. The broadening of the science–religion dialogue to include all the world's major religious traditions is an exciting challenge. I have regretted that my knowledge of Hinduism and Buddhism was limited to two courses at Yale and my own subsequent reading, and I was until recently even less familiar with the rich legacy of Islam. The future dialogue must be interreligious as well as interdisciplinary.

Looking back over the years, I can see that my writing has elicited rather diverse responses. To keep these comments brief, I will say nothing about technology and ethics, or substantive issues in science and religion, and will focus on methodological questions only – and even there I can mention only a few of the people with whom I have had significant exchanges in the past. The contributions to the present volume had not been submitted when this article was due, so I am not responding to them specifically.

Paradigms and Research Programs

In earlier writing I criticized Karl Popper's empiricism which claims that individual theories can be definitively falsified because the data are objective and independent of theory. I accepted Thomas Kuhn's thesis that both data and theory are dependent on paradigms that are strongly influenced by wider cultural assumptions and beliefs.[6] Nancey Murphy recommends that instead of using the concept of *paradigm* we should use two concepts on differing scales: (1) a large-scale *tradition* as portrayed by Alisdair MacIntyre, 'a historically extended socially embodied argument about how best to interpret and apply a set of formative texts;' and (2) within a tradition, a smaller-scale *research program*, as described by Imre Lakatos, which is not embodied in a distinct community. Lakatos held that the 'positive heuristic' of a program can be explored while its 'hard core' is protected by modifying its 'auxiliary hypotheses.'[7]

In a 1999 symposium on her own work, Murphy makes a proposal as summarized in her abstract:

> The writing of Ian Barbour and Arthur Peacocke can be construed as initial contributions to a Lakatosian research program on the relation between theology and science, the core theory of which is the thesis that theology belongs at the top of an irreducible hierarchy of sciences. The positive heuristic of this program involves showing that theology and the sciences have enough in common epistemologically to be so related and arguing for nonreducibility. The author of this essay 'rationally reconstructs' some of her philosophical work as a contribution to these tasks.[8]

It is nice to be nominated as the founder of a research program, especially when accompanied by Arthur Peacocke with whom I probably have more in common on both methodological and substantive issues that any other author today. Peacocke, Murphy, and I do indeed agree that there is an irreducible hierarchy of levels of organization in the world corresponding to which there is an irreducible hierarchy of sciences. But I am not sure that I agree that theology and the sciences are so epistemologically similar that they can be placed in a hierarchy with theology at the top.[9]

Murphy states that theological reasoning can be enough like that in science 'to count theology as a science.' Moreover, 'the relation of theology to a particular science should be analogous to the relation of any science in the hierarchy to its neighbor below.'[10] In my own writing I have pointed to differences as well as similarities between theological and scientific reasoning. Though no data are free of interpretation, and all theories are underdetermined by the data, scientific theories are far more strongly constrained by data than are theological doctrines.

Murphy goes on to suggest that Peacocke's program has two auxiliary hypotheses: an emergentist-monist account of the human person (which she equates with her own non-reductive physicalism), and the thesis that divine action in the world is analogous to top-down causation among the levels of an organism (though she herself defends divine action at the quantum level which would have a bottom-up causal effect on higher levels). Perhaps in discussing divine action my use of process philosophy (which she does not mention) could be considered an alternative auxiliary hypothesis differing from both Peacocke's and her own. In process thought, God is present in the unfolding of all integrated events at all levels as one of the sources of both order and novelty, but God does not act unilaterally as the sole cause of any event (see pp. 25–7 below). In short, I am glad to be considered a charter member of a research program, as long as membership allows recognition of the differences between science and theology and the possibility of diverse auxiliary hypotheses.

Critical Realism and Feminist Critiques

Since my early writings I have presented critical realism as a middle ground between classical realism and instrumentalism. In the *classical realism* of the age of Newton, theories were taken to be descriptions of nature as it is in itself, apart from the observer. In contemporary *instrumentalism* theories are taken to be useful human constructions, calculating devices for making predictions and controlling nature. Between these extremes, *critical realism* sees theories as limited accounts of aspects of the world as it interacts with us. Here the criteria for evaluating theories are agreement with data, coherence with other accepted theories, scope, and fertility for ongoing research.[11]

These three views are exemplified in three influential interpretations of quantum physics. Albert Einstein was a classical realist in holding that the indeterminacy of quantum theory reflects our current ignorance of the underlying deterministic mechanisms which will eventually be understood through a more adequate theory. Niels Bohr has usually been seen as an instrumentalist for whom indeterminacy is a product of the conceptual and experimental limitations which make it impossible to say what is going on in the atomic world apart from our interactions with it (the 'Copenhagen Interpretation'). We have to use differing and inadequate complementary models (such as wave and particle) to visualize what cannot be directly observed. I have suggested, however, that in his later writings, Bohr was closer to critical realism than to instrumentalism. Werner Heisenberg was a critical realist in ascribing indeterminacy to the atomic world but recognizing the limitation of human knowledge.[12]

Critical realism has come under attack by postmodern and feminist authors. Sallie McFague is appreciative of my writing on metaphors and models but suggests that I have perpetuated the Enlightenment (modernist) understanding of objectivity and have given insufficient attention to the social location of the knower and the gender biases pervading science. In place of the criteria advocated by critical realists she defends the pragmatic criterion of what is good for people and the planet. She points to the third-world critique of male Euro-American hegemony in science today.[13] I would reply that I have tried to reformulate the notion of objectivity rather than to perpetuate modernist or empiricist views of it. The third-world critique is mainly directed at applied science and technology, which are indeed dominated by first-world industrial and military interests. Theoretical science is never as 'pure' as its defenders think, but the roles of gender and cultural biases vary greatly in various aspects and fields of scientific inquiry.

Clearly gender biases are very strong in the job opportunities and professional life of scientists. Cultural assumptions can also influence the choice of problems to study and can affect the interpretation of data and the evaluation of theories. Such influences are stronger in the social and behavioral sciences, and in the historical sciences such as evolution, than in biochemistry or mathematical physics. The periodic table of the elements is the same for all cultures around the world. I also believe that the distorting influence of ideologies and interests can be reduced by the participation of scientists with a wider range of worldviews and by continual testing against intersubjectively reproducible data. The data are always paradigm-dependent, but they place greater constraints on theories than postmodernists acknowledge. In this more limited sense I see objectivity as a valid though never attainable goal.

While I disagree with some of the claims of feminist epistemology, I am deeply indebted to feminist thinkers (and Sallie McFague in particular) on many substantive issues. I share their rejection of the mind/body dualism in Western thought and its correlation with male/female stereotypes, and I welcome their view of the integral embodied self. I welcome their objections to reductionism and their elaboration of a more holistic understanding of interdependent systems and communities at all levels. I have learned much from their writings on contextuality and relatedness. Feminists reject patriarchal models of both human relationships and divine power. In both cases they urge us to envision power not as power over other beings but as the empowerment of other beings. On all these questions I see common ground between feminist and process thought, and I am grateful for it.

The Fourfold Typology

In *Issues*, I suggested a threefold typology for discussing constructive relationships between science and religion. In *Religion in an Age of Science* I presented a broader fourfold typology that included the category of Conflict in addition to Independence, Dialogue, and Integration. This fourfold scheme is used in *When Science Meets Religion* as the format for each chapter, and it has been widely cited by other authors. It is given prominence in *God, Humanity and the Cosmos*, an excellent and comprehensive text of which Christopher Southgate is coordinating editor.[14] But a recent article by Geoffrey Cantor and Chris Kenny is devoted to an extended critique of the typology. These authors claim that all typologies are too simple and too static to illuminate the complex and changing historical interactions of science and religion. They assert that I present ahistorical ('essentialist') types of relationships, and they urge us to rely instead on biographies of individual scientists in their particular historical and cultural contexts.[15]

In replying to Cantor and Kenny, I indicated that in my historical chapters I had given considerable attention to the differences among historical periods and national cultures. I said that in introductory courses it is helpful to survey a broad range of options – which does not exclude a more biographical approach to a few individuals. I also maintained that in modern science in the West there are common patterns (or 'family resemblances,' as the philosopher Ludwig Wittgenstein calls them) among diverse sciences and periods, as well as distinctive features of each. I cited the sociologist Max Weber's concept of an 'ideal type' as a useful intellectual construct in research in the social sciences, even though individual cases may diverge from it. Weber was aware of the danger that a typology may be overextended to suggest timeless and universal social structures, but he held the danger could be avoided by continual return to empirical data.[16]

In my reply I also discussed some problems I had encountered in classifying particular authors and I described alternative typologies proposed by other writers, including John Haught's fourfold typology, Ted Peters's use of eight categories, Willem Drees's ninefold classification, and Bob Russell's scheme which allows for several ways in which theology has influenced science. I asked whether my typology developed to classify diverse responses to modern science in the Christian tradition had any relevance to members of Islamic or Asian traditions, and I referred to comments, both appreciative and critical, I had received on this topic from people in non-Western cultures. I will be interested in hearing further reactions now that *When Science Meets Religion* is being published in nine languages.

Process Thought

My use of the process philosophy of Alfred North Whitehead and authors influenced by him has been the most controversial aspect of my writing. Some critics, especially those sympathetic with analytic philosophy or postmodernism, hold that all attempts to formulate an inclusive metaphysical system are suspect if we take seriously the diverse functions of human language and the role of culture in the formation of all interpretive concepts. Evangelical authors have said that in reformulating traditional doctrines I have departed too far from the gospel.

John Cobb, on the other hand, agrees with most of my conclusions but takes issue with the way I present them. He thinks I should start by describing process metaphysics, since it influences my selection and interpretation of scientific theories.[17] In the strategy I have usually followed, I first discuss alternative ways of relating science and religion and then explore forms of integration for which there is support from science and from philosophical and theological positions apart from process theology. Many of the insights of process thinking can be conveyed without the formal terminology of process philosophy, which is unfamiliar to most readers. Only at the end of a chapter (or as a separate chapter in the first Gifford volume) do

I indicate how process thought brings together in a distinctive way what I see as valid in other schools of thought.

Take the themes of *holism* and *interdependence*, for example. I have suggested that many scientific fields support the claim that the whole is more than the sum of its parts, and that we must look at the properties of systems. Quantum physics points to the participation of the observer in what is observed, and relativity shows the inseparability of space and time. The wave function for two electrons in an atom cannot be represented as the sum of wave functions of two separate electrons. In experiments on 'quantum entanglement' or 'nonlocality' a correlation is found in the behavior of two particles from a single source when they reach detectors too distant from each other for communication at the speed of light. Complexity theory deals with the self-organization of subsystems into integrated wholes whose behavior does not violate lower-level laws but sets boundary conditions for them. Successively higher levels of organization are found in molecules, cells, organisms, populations, and ecosystems. Process thinkers (notably Charles Hartshorne) have portrayed reality as a hierarchy of levels, but they are not unique in doing so.

There is a striking parallel between holism in science (especially quantum physics) and the holism of Eastern religions expressed as the unity of all things and the loss of selfhood experienced in meditation. The physicist David Bohm is a follower of Krishnamurti and develops a strong version of holism in the quantum formalism of the 'implicate order' which encompasses past, present, and future. He ends with a deterministic view of all events. I have suggested that process philosophy can combine holism with indeterminism and human freedom because each momentary entity arises in a network of interdependent relationships but expresses its individuality in a synthesis which is not totally determined by its past.[18]

I have defended *emergence* against *reductionism* (the claim that events at higher levels can in principle be explained by the laws governing events at lower levels and are determined by lower-level events). Research at the molecular level is of course enormously powerful. In the height of enthusiasm for a new scientific theory it is easy to think it will explain everything. In the eighteenth century many scientists thought Newtonian mechanics would be able to explain all events. Some molecular biologists today think we will find molecular explanations for all biological phenomena. But I would insist that explanations of activities at higher levels require concepts that are not chemical and physical. I have been impressed by the suggestion of Bruce Weber and Terrence Deacon that the most complex form of emergence occurs when levels and scales of causality are linked across wide spans of time and space. If the state of a system can be represented as a historical memory, the information can be repeatedly re-entered at lower levels, as occurs in biological evolution and in the development of an embryo.[19] Such top-down causality has been strongly defended by Arthur Peacocke and is consistent with process thought.[20]

Consider an example from theology. John Polkinghorne recently convened a working group whose papers he edited as *The Work of Love: Creation as Kenosis*.[21] In my chapter I outlined five reasons shared by most of the participants for questioning divine omnipotence: the integrity of nature, the problem of evil and suffering, the reality of human freedom, the Christian understanding of the cross, and feminist critiques of patriarchal models of God. I then indicated how process theology brings these ideas together by arguing that God's power is not sovereign control over other beings but more like the power of persuasion or empowerment from within. I suggested that in process thought unilateral power is ruled out by metaphysical necessity rather than by God's voluntary self-limitation, but this is a reflection of God's nature and not an external restriction imposed on God, as in gnosticism. I also criticized process writers for overemphasizing divine immanence in reaction to the traditional emphasis on transcendence. In short I tried to develop (and criticize) process themes in dialogue with other theological positions.

But there is one feature of process philosophy for which it is more difficult to find allies from other schools of thought, namely the attribution of *experience* or *inwardness* to lower-level entities, and it is of course a crucial feature. Following David Griffin I call this panexperientialism rather than panpsychism because at least rudimentary forms of experience are postulated in unified entities at all levels (but not in rocks and other aggregates without any unified activity).[22] Consciousness is postulated only at very high levels in organisms with a central nervous system. I have tried to defend this claim on grounds of metaphysical generality, evolutionary and ontological continuity, and immediate access to human experience. I would argue that radically new kinds of behavior emerge at higher levels, but the distinction between inner and outer applies at all levels. In dealing with the mind-body problem there is among philosophers, theologians, and some scientists considerable dissatisfaction with materialism and with the classical dualism of mind and body (or soul and body). My hope is that this will lead to greater appreciation of the *dipolar monism* and *organizational pluralism* of process philosophy: the claim that all unified entities have both internal and external aspects but that there are great differences in the way entities are organized, and therefore great differences in their behavior. Perhaps this view will have a wider appeal as the limitations of alternative views are more evident.

In summary I can say that my life has indeed been an odyssey, 'an extended adventurous wandering.' The years in my twenties were devoted mainly to physics, in my thirties mainly to studying and teaching religion, my forties to relating science and religion, and my fifties (starting in 1973) to technology and ethics. In my sixties I had time to work further on both the science/religion and the technology/ethics interfaces. Since turning seventy I have taken up new questions concerning evolution, human nature, environmental ethics, and religious pluralism. I am profoundly grateful for interaction with colleagues who have labored in the same vineyards – especially for those who amid busy schedules have found time to contribute to the present volume for my eightieth birthday.

In 2002 I was invited to return to Beijing. Deane and I saw my childhood home, still used as faculty housing, next to Peking University, which took over the Yenching campus in 1952. The campus water tower, disguised as a graceful pagoda by the lake, still stands at the spot where my father had told the college to drill for an artesian water supply; as a geologist he had helped select some 500 well sites in northern China. My lecture was sponsored by the Department of Religious Studies, newly established after two generations of Communist hostility to religion. A few months earlier, *When Science Meets Religion* had been translated into the classical Chinese of Taiwan, but for both political and linguistic reasons the Taiwanese edition was not available in mainland China. While I was in Beijing I found that the book would be published there in modern (simplified) Chinese. My odyssey had returned to the point where it had started.

Notes

1. George B. Barbour, *In the Field with Teilhard de Chardin* (New York: Herder & Herder, 1965).
2. Ian G. Barbour (ed.), *Earth Might Be Fair: Reflections on Ethics, Religion and Ecology* (Englewood Cliffs, NJ: Prentice Hall, 1972).
3. I.G. Barbour, Harvey Brooks, Sanford Lakoff, and John Opie, *Energy and American Values* (New York: Praeger, 1982).
4. I.G. Barbour, *Religion and Science: Historical and Contemporary Issues* (San Francisco: HarperSanFrancisco, 1997).
5. I.G. Barbour, *Nature, Human Nature, and God* (Minneapolis: Fortress Press, 2002).
6. I.G. Barbour, *Myths, Models, and Paradigms* (London: SCM Press, 1974).
7. Nancey Murphy, *Theology in the Age of Scientific Reasoning* (Ithaca, NY: Cornell University Press, 1990), and *Anglo-American Postmodernity: Philosophical Perspectives on Science, Religion, and Ethics* (Boulder, CO: Westview Press, 1997).
8. Eadem, 'Theology and Science within a Lakatosian Program,' *Zygon*, 34 (1999), 629.
9. Nancey Murphy and George F.R. Ellis, *On the Moral Nature of the Universe: Theology, Cosmology, and Ethics* (Minneapolis: Fortress Press, 1996), 204. These authors propose a hierarchy starting at the bottom with physics, chemistry and biology, followed by two branches (one running through astrophysics and cosmology, the other through the social sciences and ethics), both culminating in metaphysics and theology.
10. Murphy, 'Theology and Science within a Lakotosian Program,' 631.
11. Barbour, *Religion and Science*, 109, 113.
12. Ibid., 167–73.
13. Sallie McFague, 'Ian Barbour: Theologian's Friend, Scientist's Interpreter,' *Zygon*, 31 (1996), 21–8.
14. Christopher Southgate (ed.) et al., *God, Humanity and the Cosmos: A Textbook in Science and Religion* (Harrisburg, PA: Trinity Press International, 1999).
15. Geoffrey Cantor and Chris Kenny, 'Barbour's Fourfold Way: Problems with his Taxonomy of Science–Religion Relationships,' *Zygon*, 36 (2001), 765–81.
16. I.G. Barbour, 'On Typologies for Relating Science and Religion,' *Zygon*, 37 (2002), 345–59.
17. John B. Cobb, Jr, 'A Personal Appreciation,' *Zygon*, 31 (1996), 43–9.
18. I.G. Barbour, 'Bohm and Process Philosophy: A Response to Griffin and Cobb,' in *Physics and the Ultimate Significance of Time*, ed. by David Ray Griffin (Albany: State University of New York Press, 1986).
19. Bruce H. Weber and Terrence Deacon, 'Thermodynamic Cycles, Developmental Systems, and Emergence,' *Cybernetics and Human Knowing*, 7:1 (2000), 21–43. See Barbour, *Nature, Human Nature, and God*, 22–3.
20. Arthur Peacocke, *Theology for a Scientific Age*, enlarged edition (Minneapolis: Fortress Press, 1993), 157–60.
21. John Polkinghorne (ed.), *The Work of Love: Creation as Kenosis* (Grand Rapids, MI: Wm. B. Eerdmans Publishing Co., 2001).
22. David Ray Griffin, *Unsnarling the World-Knot: Consciousness, Freedom, and the Mind–Body Problem* (Berkeley and Los Angeles: University of California Press, 1998).

I

BARBOUR'S SCIENTIFIC CONTRIBUTIONS

Chapter 1

Ian Barbour's Contributions as a Scientist

Carl M. York

Introduction

In this chapter I will review the contributions that Ian Barbour made to the fields of cosmic ray physics, nuclear physics, and undergraduate teaching in a small liberal arts college. His experimental work was carried out in the rapidly changing field of particle physics just after World War II. Before high energy accelerators were built the only source of energetic nuclear particles was found in the cosmic radiation which was composed mainly of high energy protons bombarding the earth's atmosphere from outer space. He first participated in experiments that showed that the variation in the numbers and types of particles with altitude in the atmosphere could not be explained on the basis of current understandings of nuclear processes and their constituent particles. As new discoveries about these processes and particles were made, he turned to the study of the properties of the particles produced in cosmic ray generated nuclear interactions. In an ingenious set of observations and measurements using special photographic emulsions in a magnetic field, he was able to measure both the mass and electric charge of the newly discovered 'pions' and their decay products, the 'muons.' Not only did these measurements yield corroborating evidence of the properties of these particles, but they verified that pions are produced by the cosmic rays in equal numbers of positive and negative charges in the atmosphere. He next turned to the measurement of nuclear interactions at high energies in various elements. Again using photographic emulsions flown to high altitudes in balloons, he showed that the total interaction cross sections of these high energy cosmic rays varied with atomic number of the target nuclei as predicted by theory. Many years later this result was corroborated by experiments using accelerators.

After completing his PhD Barbour began teaching and attacking the problems that would occupy him for the rest of his career. He used physics as a vehicle to teach the students critical thinking and to guide them in integrating their newly acquired class room information into their daily lives. He introduced them to the value and pitfalls of comparing disciplines by asking them to write essays identifying the similarities and differences of such diverse fields as physics and English literature, or any other subject of interest to them. The design of these courses gives considerable insight into Barbour's early attempts to build a coherent methodology for dealing with the issues and problems of the interaction between science and religion.

A word of explanation is in order to tell why I am an appropriate person to comment on the scientific accomplishments of Barbour. He is several years older than I, and he was finishing his Bachelor's degree at Swarthmore College, while I was finishing high school. When he had finished his Master's degree at Duke University and published a paper on an electronic device to analyze low frequency electric waves, I was finishing my Bachelor's degree at University College Berkeley and learning how to build and operate Wilson cloud chambers. He moved to the University of Chicago to do doctoral work in cosmic ray physics, while I stayed at Berkeley and joined the Cosmic Ray group there to begin my own doctoral program. After graduation Barbour went to Kalamazoo College as an Assistant Professor and after several years of post doctoral work, I joined the Cosmic Ray group at the University of Chicago as an Assistant Professor. So although we never worked together, we were involved in the same research field and shared many similar experiences in our scientific lives. Later, as Barbour's interests shifted toward a degree in theology from Yale while he continued to teach physics and courses in religion, I moved into the fields of high energy physics and university administration. In spite of this seemingly close paralleling of our early professional careers, we never met until about thirteen years ago. Since then we both have had the privilege of serving together on the Board of Directors of the Center for Theology and the Natural Sciences in Berkeley. It is with great pleasure that I shall tell you a little bit about the world of experimental physics and cosmic ray studies where we both started our careers.

The field of physics is divided into those who do experimental work and those who do theoretical studies. Although experimentalists are expected to know and understand the conclusions of the theoretician's calculations, they are also expected to devise apparatus to measure the predicted physical consequences of those calculations. Both Barbour and I were involved in the doubly challenging world of experimental work. No one pretended to know all about either world, but when a known technology could be applied to a problem, then it was used, even if the experimentalist often had to go to the library and take a crash self-study course to learn how to use it. The interplay between the available tools and their innovative application to new experimental problems is a theme that underlies all experimental science and will be referred to below in the commentary on Barbour's series of published works in physics. Another theme is the availability of equipment either developed especially for scientific use, or built originally for some other purpose, but then adapted for use in an experiment. Barbour made use of both of these approaches in his work. He not only designed and built new equipment, but also innovatively modified existing equipment to use in his measurements.

Before World War II the field of cosmic ray studies had emerged as a separate branch of physics. The fact that high energy radiation of some kind was striking the earth's atmosphere from somewhere in outer space was established in the 1920s. The early studies were directed toward learning the nature of this radiation and identifying its origin. Early on it was found that the intensity of the radiation increased as you went higher in the atmosphere, so studies were made at mountain observatories or used high-altitude balloons to carry equipment to even greater heights. The University of Chicago, which is very nearly at sea level, developed a balloon program that originally launched the balloons from the campus football field, Stagg Field. It was under the west grandstand of this field that the world's first nuclear reactor was secretly housed during World War II. After the war, balloons were launched by the military from air bases and were made available to civilian scientists.

As the nature of this radiation of 'cosmic' origin became better understood, the field of study split into two different aspects. The first continued to study the phenomenology, or nature, of the radiation. The second was based on the observation that the particles that made up the cosmic radiation could be used as a way to observe high energy collisions of particles with nuclei. The findings of this branch regarding the nature of elementary particles stimulated the construction of high energy accelerators that are at the heart of the field of high energy physics today. As we shall see below, Barbour published in both the phenomenology and the high energy particle branches of the field, and the majority of his work was focused on the latter.

A Review of Barbour's Scientific Publications

An Instrumentation Project

Having prepared the reader for a discussion of Barbour's contributions to cosmic ray research, I must first report on a very elegant piece of work he did while completing his Master's degree at Duke University.[1] While there he collaborated with a brain researcher named Dr H. Lowenbach in the analysis of human brain waves, or electroencephalograms (EEGs). These waves are detected by placing electrodes on the patient's scalp and measuring the variations of voltage between them that are generated by brain activity inside the skull. The voltage variations can be amplified and displayed on a moving chart with a pen recorder. The wavy lines that this generated formed patterns for normal people that were quite different from those for patients with brain disorders such as brain tumors and epilepsy. The analysis of these patterns was qualitative at best, but they could be grouped roughly into several types. What was needed was a simple way to analyze these wave patterns. The French mathematician J.B.J. Fourier had shown at the end of the eighteenth century that any wave form can be synthesized by superimposing a series of sine waves of varying frequency and amplitude. In Barbour's task it was necessary to take a wave form and analyze it into its component sine waves. There were instruments available to do this in the audio range of frequencies and at higher radio frequencies. However, the brain waves observed in an EEG are in the very low frequency range of 2 to 25 cycles per second. Barbour designed and built an ingenious electronic device to perform a sweep of this frequency range and plot a curve of the amplitude of each of the constituent sine waves against its frequency. The equipment repeated the analysis, every 4 seconds and automatically displayed the result on a pen recorder mounted just above the EEG record that was being observed. This enabled the clinician to simultaneously observe a brain wave pattern and the amplitudes of the various frequencies in that pattern. Normal individuals have patterns that show most of their brain waves clustering near a narrow band of frequencies around 11 cycles per second, but patients with encephalitis show a different, broader range of frequencies. Other patients with still different brain disorders show distinct patterns that are easily classified and recognized by the clinician using this equipment.

In designing this analyzer Barbour had to develop a stable, low frequency oscillator to use as a standard against which the measured frequencies could be compared. No such device was available. After a careful study of the literature in electronic engineering, he worked out a design, built several versions of it and selected the one that best suited the requirements of this instrument. He then systematically tested the stability of the device, an essential requirement. Finally he assembled the electronic circuits to complete the apparatus for trials in the clinic. As in his later work, this whole process is written up in such a way that anyone else can get out the reference books, design the instrument and build it for herself. Or one could use the circuit diagrams and other details given in this paper to make a similar instrument.

A Phenomenological Cosmic Ray Experiment

When Barbour started doctoral work at the University of Chicago, he joined the Cosmic Ray group headed by Professor Marcel Schein. By this time it was known that 'primary' cosmic rays strike the top of the atmosphere from outer space and interact with the atoms in the stratosphere to cause showers of particles cascading down toward the earth's surface. These 'secondary' particles were absorbed by the atmosphere as they descended and this explained the original observation that the intensity increased with altitude. But since those first studies, the nature of the particles in these cascades had been determined to include electrons, positrons and gamma rays as well as 'mesotrons,' protons and neutrons. 'Mesotrons' were particles of mass about two hundred times greater than that of an electron, but about one-fifth that of a proton. So the research questions centered on determining the intensity and energy distribution of the various particles that were cascading down through the atmosphere.

The Chicago group had developed equipment that could distinguish between electron–positron showers and charged 'penetrating' particles, which were a mixture of 'mesotrons,' and a few protons. Neutrons could also be detected when they interacted with a paraffin block inserted between Geiger counters in the apparatus. By changing the lead absorber in the Geiger counter telescope, they could measure different energy ranges of the charged penetrating particles. In 1943 the group had used a similar device to measure the energy distribution of penetrating particles at an elevation of 14,250 feet (4343.5 m) on Mount Evans in Colorado. In this experiment[2] the equipment was flown by a US Army Air Force plane to Denali Pass at 18,100 feet (5.5 km) in Alaska and dropped by parachute to the researchers who had climbed to the pass. The experiment was operated in a small cabin in the pass to record the energy distribution at this higher altitude. The two distributions were compared, after carefully correcting for the fact that mesotrons were known to decay in flight and that they would lose energy in traversing the atmosphere as they descended. The group found to their surprise that there were many more low energy mesotrons at the lower altitude than they would have expected. They correctly deduced that these additional particles had been produced in the intervening layer of the atmosphere. As a more detailed picture of the complex array of particles and their interactions became better known, this unexpected result would be more fully explained. The significance of the experiment is that it pointed to the fact that new particles and processes were needed to explain their surprising result.

A Series of Studies of Elementary Particles

The rapidly changing understanding of the nature of the particles observed in the cosmic rays is reflected in the titles of this series of papers.[3] The 'mesotrons' of the previous paper have now become 'mesons.' In 1947 a 'mesotron' was observed to decay into another lighter 'mesotron.' The particle community decided to drop 'mesotron' and adopt the name 'meson:' the heavier 'pi meson' decayed into the 'mu meson' which was still much heavier than an electron and later was found to decay into an electron. These names were later contracted into 'pion' and 'muon,' and either terminology is now in general use. So in this set of papers Barbour was developing special equipment to measure the properties of mesons in cosmic rays.

By the end of World War II both British and American film companies were producing special photographic emulsions for the detection of nuclear particles and making them available to the scientific community for the first time. These emulsions had been developed as radiation monitors for the wartime effort in nuclear energy and enabled one to detect the passage of a charged particle by viewing its track of developed grains in the emulsion. The grains were very small (of the order of one or two microns in diameter), but with a standard optical microscope they could easily be seen. The Chicago group began using these emulsions in their studies as soon as they became available. They were relatively small, rather light, and ideally suited to flying in a balloon to high altitudes.

There had been a suggestion by the British group at Bristol University to mount two emulsions with an air gap between them in a magnetic field. The idea was that a charged particle would start in one of the plates, cross the air gap where it was deflected by the magnetic field, and then come to rest in the second plate. By measuring the deflection of the track in the magnetic field and the distance it took to come to rest, one could determine the mass of the particle and the sign of its electrical charge. This idea was worked on by several groups. As a graduate student in Berkeley, I was assigned to help one of our more senior doctoral students who was trying to make this scheme work. Neither we, nor the people at Bristol, were very successful and eventually abandoned the project. But Barbour made it work. The main difficulty was to find a track that stopped in one plate and then follow it back across the air gap and unambiguously connect it with a track in the other plate. In characteristic fashion, Barbour devised a clever way to do this. He modified the stage of a microscope so that it could be tilted to view a longer section of a track in each field of view. The angle of tilting was measured by ingeniously attaching a protractor to the microscope's stage. A pantograph arrangement enabled the scanner to plot the position of a track on one plate, move to the other plate and locate the track's position in that plate by comparing the angle of tilt and its projected range of positions which depended on its deflection in the magnetic field between the plates.

During the war very strong permanent magnets had been developed for use on radar klystron tubes. Later, these magnets proved an excellent source for the deflecting magnetic field in this experiment. Barbour first used such a klystron magnet to demonstrate that he could make the overall system work. But he then designed and built a larger magnet,which was ideal for balloon work because it was rugged, required no power supply, and could be flown to high altitudes.

Having solved the measurement problem, a series of balloon flights were made at altitudes around 90,000 feet (27.4 km). The emulsions were scanned to find pi meson decays in one plate, and after following the pi meson's track back to its entry point in the emulsion, its track in the other emulsion was sought. Barbour was able to find a number of pi meson decays. They were all positively charged and gave good measurements of their mass. But when negative pi mesons came to rest, they were absorbed in nuclei of the emulsion and blew the nucleus apart showing a characteristic 'star' of nuclear fragments radiating from the stopping point. The incoming particle could be traced backward along its track to its entry point in the emulsion and then found in the other emulsion. All of these events had negative charge and gave the same mass as the positive pi mesons. The mu mesons were recognized by a different set of criteria. Stopping mu mesons do not interact with nuclei but decay into high energy electrons. Unfortunately these electrons did not produce observable tracks in the emulsion. Stopping particles had their mass determined from their range in the emulsion and their deflection in the magnetic field. These events were classified as mu mesons, because their mass values were less than that of the pi mesons and corresponded to the muon masses from the decaying pions. They had both positive and negative deflections in the magnetic field.

The events observed on the entire series of balloon flights were combined and the data yielded values of the masses of the pion and muon that agreed well with others' results. The data provided an independent verification of the masses and charges of these new particles. The fact that there were roughly equal numbers of both positive and negatively charged pions and muons near the top of the atmosphere (90,000 feet/27.4 km) had never been observed before.

Studies of Nuclear Interactions Produced by Cosmic Rays

As Barbour was winding up the work on pi and mu mesons described above, vast changes were taking place in the study of those particles. In Berkeley the 184-inch (72.5 cm) cyclotron had begun to operate at a proton beam energy that was sufficient to make beams of the pi mesons that had been discovered earlier in cosmic rays. Even higher energy cyclotrons were beginning to operate at Chicago and Columbia Universities and other institutions around the world. This meant that the mass, charge, lifetime, and other characteristics of the new particles could be studied with great statistical accuracy and effectively made further cosmic ray studies in this field obsolete.

Barbour had by now obtained his PhD from the University of Chicago and accepted a position as an Assistant Professor at Kalamazoo College in Michigan. He had mastered the art of measuring particle tracks that traverse one emulsion plate, cross a gap and continue into another plate, where others had failed. So he chose to apply this skill to new cosmic ray measurements which were begun in Chicago. In a series of papers[4] he described how a 'sandwich' consisting of an emulsion mounted on a glass slide was placed with the emulsion side facing a metal foil, and then another emulsion was placed on the other surface of the metal foil to form a closely packed sandwich. A set of these sandwiches, each with a different kind of metal foil between the two emulsions, was flown in a balloon at 93,000 feet (28 km) for six hours. Each pair of plates was then scanned to find 'stars' or nuclei that had been struck by an incident cosmic ray and had exploded into nuclear fragments that diverge from points that lay in the metal foil. Because the incoming cosmic ray particles have different energies, the stars were classified by the number of fragments that emerged from the collision. The idea was that the more energy in, the more nuclear fragments, or 'prongs,' that would come out. For each of the foils the number of observed events was plotted against the measured star size. It was of course necessary to make detailed corrections to the observed data and these were meticulously presented and analyzed, again in the best tradition of making it possible for others to verify what had been done. By a careful comparison of the number of stars formed in each of the different foils, it was possible to determine the relative probability of nuclear interactions, the 'nuclear cross section,' as a function of the nuclear size. The shape of a nucleus is essentially spherical and depends on the number of neutrons and protons in it (the element's 'atomic number,' A). So one would expect that for the high energy cosmic ray particles bombarding these foils the cross sections would increase as the cross sectional area of the nuclear sphere increased. This was indeed the case. A final summary of the results compared to the results of others was presented, so that the reader could assess for herself how consistent the new data were with what was already known.

The significance of these results was that at a time when very little data on the interaction of high energy particles with complex nuclei was available, and when all of the data came from cosmic ray studies, this work presented more data on a larger number of different elements than had ever been available before. It would be many years before the new accelerators would turn to the study of nuclear interactions of proton and pi meson beams with complex elements, because they were all preoccupied with the 'fundamental' interactions of those beams with hydrogen and other light elements.

A Final Phenomenological Study

After moving to Carleton College, Barbour took part in 'the International Geophysical Year, 1958.'[5] This was the first truly international cooperative scientific effort after World War II and its aim was to carry out observations of geophysical quantities all over the face of the earth for at least one year. In addition to oceanographic and meteorological data, cosmic ray observations were made to study the intensities of the various cosmic ray particles on the earth's surface and at high altitudes by balloon flights. The surface measurements included Geiger counter telescopes similar to those described above to measure the mu meson, or 'penetrating' component of the cosmic radiation, but a different method was used to detect neutrons. Barbour chose to measure the neutrons produced by cosmic rays in the atmosphere as his contribution to this international endeavor.

The purpose of the program was to monitor variations in the intensity of the low energy portion of the primary cosmic ray energy spectrum. These primary particles strike the upper atmosphere and produce most of the secondary component which is composed mostly of protons and neutrons that are observed deep in the atmosphere at the earth's surface. The secondary particles are in the energy range of a few hundred Mev[6] to 1000 Mev and interact with the atoms of the atmosphere to produce 'stars' like the ones seen in the emulsions of Barbour's earlier experiments. These stars emit nuclear fragments such as the charged protons, deuterons and alpha particles seen as prongs in the emulsion, as well as uncharged neutrons, all in the energy range of 1 to 20 Mev. Near sea level the star production is in equilibrium with the flux of neutrons each star emits. The rate of star production is most conveniently and reliably monitored by detecting the disintegration neutrons rather than the charged fragments observed in the emulsions.

It is not easy to detect neutrons in the 1 to 20 Mev range, but it is easy to detect those at much lower 'thermal' energies of a fraction of an electron volt. The detector used is a variation of a Geiger counter, which is called a proportional counter and is filled with a special gas, boron trifluoride, BF^3. Thermal neutrons are absorbed by the boron atom's nucleus which then disintegrates to give a large characteristic pulse in the counter that is easy to distinguish from all other pulses that are present. To slow the cosmic ray neutrons from millions of volts of energy to a fraction of a volt, the counter is placed inside a cube of either graphite or paraffin, just as is done in a nuclear reactor. This layer is called a 'moderator' and does the job of slowing the neutrons down. Just as before in the nuclear emulsion experiments, a layer of dense material outside of the moderator was used to produce stars which emitted neutrons. A standard geometry of local star producer, moderator and BF^3 counter was prescribed for all of the neutron intensity monitoring stations to use and was called 'the neutron monitor pile.'

Data was recorded bi-hourly of the number of neutron counts and of the atmospheric pressure. It had been shown that pressure variations were the only atmospheric effect on the neutron count rate, so all count rates were corrected to correspond to a single 'standard' pressure in order that the variations in the intensity of the incoming radiation could be observed. The data were submitted each month to the central repository. Barbour submitted this data from the 'Northfield Station' for all twelve months of the calendar 1958 year, the year of the International Geophysical Year, and then the station was closed.

This work was not written up as a scientific report in the usual way because it was part of the overall collaboration, and it contributed to a massive international effort.

An Innovative First Year Laboratory Experiment

While at Kalamazoo College, Barbour, in collaboration with R.O. Kerman, designed and introduced a new type of experiment for first-year physics students studying heat. As reported in the subsequent paper,[7] Barbour was trying to give beginning students a sense of the 'research spirit' that excites and drives those working in the field. In this experiment he broke with the tradition of having the students come to the laboratory to a lab bench which contained all of the equipment needed for the experiment, open their lab manuals and follow a recipe of steps to perform the required measurements. To break this 'cookbook' tradition, he restated this particular experiment to more closely model the experience of the researcher. Here one starts with a physical problem and then must select which equipment to use, and figure out how to operate it, to measure the desired physical quantities.

In this case the problem was to measure the temperature of a mixture of 'dry ice' (frozen carbon dioxide) and alcohol. He immediately demonstrated to the class that any standard method, such as a mercury thermometer, would freeze solid and even sometimes shatter in this liquid. The class was divided into pairs, and a laboratory assistant was on hand to help them find any equipment they might need and even do some glass blowing or make other equipment as needed. The first lab period was devoted to choosing a method and selecting and assembling their equipment. During the second period the students made their measurements and calculated their results complete with estimates of the errors in their answers. At the end of the second period the students came together, presented their results, and discussed which method gave the most accurate values for the temperature of the solution.

Over several semesters the students came up with eleven different ways to measure the temperature of the dry ice/alcohol mixture. With each method they were able to explore and compare the problems of assembling and calibrating equipment, the reliability of standards used in the calibration, the accuracy of the measured values, and the limits of extrapolating calibrations to heretofore unknown regions of the temperature scale. The students had a very positive response to this 'real life' approach to laboratory problems. Most were strongly motivated by the challenge of selecting a method and pursuing it. They all benefited from the class discussions that clarified the basic principles of 'heat.' During the class discussions, great stress was placed on reviewing the fundamental assumptions underlying the analysis of their method and finding ways to test those assumptions, on the limits of extrapolating data, and on error analysis.

It is clear that Barbour wanted to share with the students in the laboratory the set of principles that he had used throughout his own experimental career. Those who have read his later work, will recognize at least one as part of his emphasis on the limits of the scientific method that are introduced in this work.

An Attempt to 'Integrate' Science into the Overall Curriculum

The first publication in which Barbour attacked the problems of compartmentalization and isolation of subject matter at the college level is in a paper called 'Integration as an Objective in Physical Science.'[8] The educational objective of *integration* is 'the insight into relationships of one's own field to other areas of life.' In this paper he outlines a two-week unit which deals with the *impact of science on man's life and thought* (Barbour's italics). After discussing the way facts are fragmented and science is isolated from real life, he assures the reader that this goal of integration is not in conflict with any other goals of a college curriculum. Furthermore, there are at least four ways to integrate science with other fields. The first might be called the 'practical approach' in which you take a familiar object of everyday life such as an automobile and identify the various scientific principles that come into its design and operation. Then there is the more abstract way of engaging in a discussion of the 'realm of ideas' and exploring how ideas in one field interweave with those in another. A 'case history approach' is yet another means of demonstrating the interrelationship of ideas in different fields by discussing the development of a single idea and its dependence on knowledge gleaned from other areas of study. This method can be extended to include the whole 'history of science approach.'

In laying out the contents of this course, three topics were covered which in fact are themes that Barbour has pursued throughout the rest of his career. The first is 'Science and Society' in which he explored the responsibilities of science to society to inform and help shape the public policies of society. It is not surprising that only six years after the bombing of Hiroshima and Nagasaki the prime example for discussion was the use of atomic energy and nuclear power.

The second topic was 'the Relation of Physical Sciences to the Social Sciences.' Here he especially emphasized the limits in applying the methods of the physical sciences to other fields. His comparison of methods used in the two areas stressed both the similarities and differences in their approaches to problems. This clearly foreshadows Barbour's later work. He found that this approach led to a better understanding of both areas by the students.

Finally, the third topic was 'the Impact of Science on Man's Thinking.' Here he cites the impact of Newton's thinking on the world's history and how the limits of the scientific method as it was evolving led to distortions and unjustified conclusions that persist to this day. He noted that in classroom discussions 'religious issues are unnecessary to avoid just because they are controversial.' He also emphasized questions such as: 'Does science describe the whole of reality? or does it deliberately limit itself?' The general approach he used was to engage the students in a way that encouraged the individuals to express their own ideas and thoughts.

The students were asked to write two papers. One was to explore the application of scientific principles to some everyday device such as a radio or a jet plane. The other was to deal with the relation of science to a field of major interest to the student, for example, English Literature or perhaps a comparison of research methods in the physical and life sciences. Clearly he was forcing the students to think about their personal lives and to reflect on them in relation to the science they had learned.

The importance for me of Barbour's paper on integration was not only to be again impressed with the care and concern that Barbour gave to helping his individual students learn the art of critical thinking. I also found in it a summary statement of the research program that would guide Barbour throughout the rest of his professional career: 'It is desirable in a general education science course to stress the scientific facts and principles, but also give both implicit and explicit consideration to the contributions of science to intellectual, spiritual, and material aspects of life.'

Conclusion

In this review of Barbour's scientific publications I hope it is clear that in my opinion, his work exhibited adherence to the highest ideals of experimental science. His choice of problems to attack was always carefully thought out and explained in its proper context. His choice of parameters to measure and the apparatus to be used was equally well described. When he presented the experimental results, the data were displayed in graphic or tabular form in such a way that the reader could easily follow the discussion in the text and understand the conclusions that were drawn. One of the greatest strengths of these papers was the discussion of uncertainties in the results and the limits on the conclusions that could be drawn. A meticulous comparison with other similar data obtained by other observers and the care given to credit others' ideas in their relation to his own work are another hallmark of these papers. To those who have read Barbour's later works it should be clear that at least some of his basic methods and style were developed during his early years as a physicist.

While Barbour's experimemntal work in cosmic ray physics did not produce any outstanding discoveries, it did contribute important supportive evidence on the masses and charges of the newly discovered mesons; it helped to explain the anomalies in the observed fluxes in the cosmic rays in the atmosphere; and it gave the most comprehensive treatment of high energy nuclear cross sections that was available at the time. These were all significant contributions to the fields of cosmic rays and nuclear physics.

Notes

1. I.G. Barbour, 'An Automatic Low Frequency Analyzer', *Review of Scientific Instruments*, 18:7 (July 1947), 516–22.
2. Thomas D. Carr, Marcel Schein, and Ian Barbour, 'Cosmic Ray Investigations on Mt. McKinley', *Physical Review*, 73 (1948), 1419.
3. Ian G. Barbour, 'On the Use of Nuclear Plates in a Magnetic Field', *Physical Review*, 74 (1948), 507; 'A Pantograph and Tilting Stage for Use with Nuclear Plates', *Review of Scientific Instruments*, 20 (1949), 530; 'Magnetic Deflection of Cosmic-Ray Mesons Using Nuclear Plates', *Physical Review*, 76 (1949), 320; 'Magnetic Deflection of Cosmic-Ray Mesons Using Nuclear Plates', *Physical Review*, 78 (1950), 518.
4. Ian Barbour and L. Greene, 'Emulsion Studies of Cosmic-Ray Stars Produced in Metal Foils', *Physical Review*, 79 (1950), 406; Ian Barbour, 'Emulsion Studies of Cosmic-Ray Stars Produced in Metal Foils', *Physical Review*, 82 (1951), 280; 'Emulsion Studies of Cosmic-Ray Stars Produced in Metal Foils', *Physical Review*, 93 (1954), 535.
5. I.G. Barbour, 'Cosmic-Ray Neutron Monitor Data for Northfield, Minnesota', *Annals of the International Geophysical Year*, 36 (1964), 11.

6. Mev stands for Million electron volts, the unit of measure used for the energy of nuclear particles.
7. I.G. Barbour and R.O. Kerman, 'An "Original" Experiment in Heat for the First-Year Laboratory', *American Journal of Physics*, 20 (1952), 493.
8. I.G. Barbour, 'Integration as an Objective in the Physical Sciences', *American Journal of Physics*, 20 (1952), 565.

II

BARBOUR'S CONTRIBUTIONS TO METHODOLOGY

Ian Barbour's Methodological Breakthrough: Creating the 'Bridge' between Science and Theology[1]

Robert John Russell

Introduction

The question of methodology lies at the heart of the theology and science community: how are we to relate these two disparate fields? I will take the question as broadly including issues in epistemology and the nature of scientific and religious language, as well as issues more clearly arising in methodology per se. The past decades have seen a variety of important such methodological proposals; here we'll briefly review some of the most promising. I believe we will see that, though they differ significantly on key questions, they still form a somewhat continuous developmental path, leading from early insights to cutting edge research questions. More importantly for the purposes of this book, however, we will find that the original contributions by Ian Barbour to methodology in the 1960s form the initial 'bridge' across which so much traffic now flows – in both directions! – and that his contributions to methodology have continued from the 1960s through the present discussion. Barbour called this methodology 'critical realism,' a phrase taken up by almost all of the scholars who have adopted, adapted, extended, and critiqued Barbour's methodological bridge.

Critical Realism: Barbour's Original 'Bridge' between Science and Religion

In his groundbreaking 1966 publication, *Issues in Science and Religion*, Ian G. Barbour laid out a series of well-crafted arguments involving issues in epistemology (the kinds of knowledge we have), language (how it is expressesd), and methodology (how it is obtained and justified).[2] Together these arguments provide what I call the 'bridge'[3] between science and religion; more than any other scholar's work, these arguments, in my opinion, have made possible the developments of the past five decades. Barbour has explored these arguments in detail since then, principally through his 1990 Gifford Lectures, together with their revisions in 1997[4] and 2000.[5] From the outset, Barbour used the term 'critical realism'[6] to stand for the specific set of arguments he first developed in 1966. Most scholars in the field have adopted and developed the term, although some, while sharing one or more of its arguments, have moved away from the term (as we shall see below).

Barbour viewed critical realism as an alternative to three competing interpretations of scientific theories: (1) classical or 'naive' realism: scientific theories provide a 'photographic' representation of the world; (2) instrumentalism: scientific theories are mere calculative devices, and (3) idealism: scientific theories depict reality as mental. Instead, from a critical realist perspective, scientific theories yield partial, revisable, abstract, but referential knowledge of the world. Linguistically, scientific theories are expressed through metaphors and models which ' ... selectively represent particular aspects of the world for specific purposes ... [They] are to be taken seriously but not literally.'[7] Scientific models are thus systematically developed metaphors. Turning to religion, he defined 'metaphor' similarly as an open-ended analogy. Although more than a useful fiction, the meaning of a religious metaphor cannot be reduced to a set of literal statements.[8]

Barbour then turned to the current discussion of scientific methodology, with major breakthroughs by such philosophers of science as Norwood R. Hanson, Gerald Holton, Thomas Kuhn, Michael Polanyi, and Stephen Toulmin, and with special emphasis on the writings of Imre Lakatos.[9] He began with the empiricism of Carl Hempel, whose 'hypothetico-deductive' method brought together inductivist and deductivist approaches to the construction and testing of theories *vis*. Popperian falsificationism. In the 1960s, this method was fundamentally recast. It was now seen to operate within both the historicist and contextualist elements which characterize the scientific community. These elements include the 'theory-ladenness of data', the presence of intersubjectivity rather than strict objectivity in scientific rationality, the structure of science through paradigms and their revolutions in the history of science, the presence of metaphysical assumptions about nature in scientific paradigms, and the role of aesthetics and values in theory choice. Scientific theories are a human construction and their conclusions are inherently tentative and subject to revision. Nevertheless, according to Barbour, they are to be assessed by four criteria which are reasonably transparadigmatic: agreement with data, coherence, scope, and fertility.

Barbour used these criteria to articulate what he called a 'critical realist' theory of truth.[10] Like classical realism, the meaning of truth in critical realism is correspondence with reality (that is, reference) and the key criterion of truth is agreement of theory with data. But we often have only indirect evidence for our theories; moreover, networks of theories are tested together. Thus internal coherence and scope also serve as criteria of truth, as stressed by rationalists and philosophical idealists. Even this is insufficient when competing theories are equally coherent and comprehensive; hence fruitfulness serves as a fourth criterion of truth – as pragmatists, instrumentalists, and linguistic analysts stress. Thus intelligibility and explanatory power, and not just observableness or predictive success, is a guide to the real.[11]

Turning to philosophy of religion, Barbour constructed a similar defense of critical realism. Here his sources in religious epistemology, methodology and language include the writings of John Wisdom, John Hick, Ian Ramsey, and Frederick Ferré.[12] With these arguments in place, Barbour was prepared to make his crucial, methodological claim that 'bridges' science and religion: 'the basic structure of religion is similar to that of science in some respects, though it differs at several crucial points.'[13] *Similarities*: Both science and religion make cognitive claims about the world using a hypothetico-deductive method and a contextualist and historicist framework. Both communities organize observation and experience through models seen as analogical, extensible, coherent, and symbolic, and these models are expressed through metaphors.[14] *Differences*: But there are important differences in the 'data' of religion compared to that of science.[15] Religious models serve noncognitive functions which are missing in science, such as eliciting attitudes, personal involvement and transformation. Moreover, compared to science, where theories tend to dominate models, in religion models are more influential than theories.[16] Religion lacks lower-level laws such as those found in science, and the emergence of consensus seems 'an unrealizable goal.' Religion also includes elements not found in science such as story, ritual, and revelation through historical events.[17] Barbour's argument culminates in his use of paradigm analysis to place science and religion on a continuous spectrum in which both display 'subjective' as well as 'objective' features, though the former are more prominent in religion and the latter in science.[18] The subjective features include 'the influence of theory on data, the resistance of comprehensive theories to falsification, and the absence of rules for choice among paradigms.'[19] Objective features include 'the presence of common data on which disputants can agree, the cumulative effect of evidence for or against a theory, and the existence of criteria which are not paradigm-dependent.' It is the dynamic tension between similarities and differences, and between subjective and objective features in both science and religion, that together make Barbour's analysis so original and fruitful.

Further Developments of Critical Realism in Theology and Science

Barbour's arguments have been developed in significant and diverse ways by a variety of scholars. In his 1979 Bampton Lectures[20] and in his 1983 Mendenhall Lectures,[21] Arthur Peacocke endorsed critical realism in both science and religion.[22] In science, where challenges to realism from sociologists of knowledge were mounting, Peacocke draw on arguments for realism by Ernan McMullin, Hilary Putnam, and Ian Hacking.[23] In his 1993 Gifford Lectures,[24] Peacocke acknowledged the diversity of positions held by scientific realists but argued for a 'common core' of claims: that scientific change is progressive and that the aim of science is to depict reality. Peacocke made a similar case for critical realism in theology, where the social conditioning of beliefs is generally assumed. As in science, theological concepts and models are partial, inadequate, and revisable, and, unlike those in science, they include a strong, affective function. Still Peacocke views them as the 'necessary and, indeed, the only ways of referring to "God" and to God's relation with humanity,' though he stresses that referring to God (for example, the *via positiva*) does not mean describing God (the *via negativa*). Its grounding in a continuous community and interpretive tradition make it 'reasonable' to accept theology's explication of religious experience, though metaphorical and revisable, as an inference to the best explanation.[25]

Other scholars in theology and science have taken similar approaches. According to John Polkinghorne, critical realism is the best explanation of the success of science, the only philosophy adequate to scientific experience, and the view most congenial to scientists themselves. In his 1994 Gifford Lectures, Polkinghorne drew on Thomas Torrance and Polanyi to highlight the doubly circular character of knowledge: belief and understanding are mutually entailing, and what is known and the knowledge of it are mutually conforming.[26] Scientific theories are shaped by the way things are, offering an ever increasing degree of verisimilitude as suggested by his motto, 'epistemology models ontology.'[27] Polkinghorne offers similar arguments for theology, too: '[F]rom a theological perspective, all forms of realism are divinely underwritten, for God will not mislead us ...' Wentzel van Huyssteen, in his earlier writings, also viewed theology from a realist perspective, claiming that 'theology ... is scientifically committed to a realist point of view' and describing the referential power of theological language about God as 'reality depiction.' For van Huyssteen, the hypothetical status of scientific statements become the eschatological dimension of theological statements.[28] Thomas F. Torrance, too, argues for the scientific character of theology because, like the natural sciences, it adopts a method which is determined by its object. For theology, the object is God, known to us by God's revelation in the incarnation and resurrection of the Word. Thus the theoretical structures of theology disclose knowledge of God just as the theoretical structures in science, such as Einstein's general relativity, provide objective knowledge of this world.[29] According to Torrance, natural theology can find a place within positive theology, though not as a prolegomenon to it – a view which he reports he persuaded Karl Barth eventually to accept.[30]

Widening Use of Metaphors, Models, and Paradigms

The central role Barbour gave to metaphors, models, and paradigms in both science and theology has stimulated wide discussion, too. In 1982, Sallie McFague drew directly from Barbour's work in pointing to basic similarities between models in theology and in science, but she also stressed four important differences: they provide order in theology while stimulating new discoveries in science; they more clearly carry meaning in theology than in science; and unlike in science, in theology they are ubiquitous and hierarchical; and they elicit feelings and action. McFague combined this with Paul Ricoeur's notion of metaphor as 'is and is not' in developing what she then termed 'metaphorical theology.' Using this approach she has developed new metaphors for God as Mother, Lover, and Friend, and the world as the body of God, which challenge theology's patriarchical and androcentric distortions and fund her work in ecological theology.[31]

In 1984, Mary Gerhart and Allan Russell[32] contrasted two meanings of analogy: (1) as an extension of our conceptual network from a known to an unknown, and (2) as a new and dynamic relation between two separate networks which distorts both and induces tension. They call the latter 'metaphor,' concluding that the relation between science and religion is itself a metaphor.[33] In 1985 Janet Soskice[34] published a thorough study of metaphor in religious and scientific language, emphasizing the distinction between metaphor and model which she found conflated in Max Black, Barbour, Ferré and David Tracy. Although she vigorously defended theological realism, Soskice also stressed the social and contextual nature of scientific realism, in which theoretical terms 'are seen as representing reality without claiming to be representationally privileged.' Theological realism, in turn, distinguishes between referring to God and defining 'God,' and employs a causal theory of reference.[35]

In 1988, Hans Küng applied paradigm analysis to the history of theology and compared the results to the history of science.[36] In contrast to the way paradigms are successively replaced in science, giving it an irreversible history, in theology contrasting paradigms, such as Thomism, Reformation theology, modernity, may well coexist in history. In science the next revolution comes at the limits of the existing paradigm. In theology the 'primal testimony' of scripture and the events of the history of Israel and Jesus Christ are the sources of each new revolution.

Consonance as a Growing Theme in Theology and Science

An important development has been the theme of 'consonance' introduced in 1981 by Ernan McMullin. His concern was the search for a 'coherence of world-view' to which all forms of human knowing can contribute. The consonance that characterizes such a worldview does not require or even expect direct support. Instead it would involve mutual contributions in a relation that is tentative and open to 'constant slight shift.' Beginning in 1989, I picked up and developed McMullin's term, consonance, in several ways. I combined McMullin's idea with McFague's epistemic claim about the 'is and is not' structure of metaphor to include and thus to learn from both consonance and what I called 'dissonance' between scientific and theological theories. Rather than undercutting a coherent worldview, dissonance points to the dynamic character of our worldview, specifying where problems arise, shifts are required, and potentially greater coherence can be sought. Moreover, by recognizing that theories in both science and theology evolve and are eventually replaced, we can build change directly into the relation between science and theology rather than being threatened by it.[37]

Ted Peters has also developed this approach in terms of what he calls 'hypothetical consonance.'[38] If consonance in the 'strong sense' means complete harmony or accord, we might 'hope to find [it], but we have not found it yet.' What we do have are shared domains of inquiry or consonance in a 'weak sense', but this is enough to encourage further exploration. He bases this on his critical realist assumption that theologians and scientists are seeking to understand the same reality.[39] The qualifier 'hypothetical' reminds theologians to treat their assertions as fallible and subject to possible disconfirmation as well as confirmation.

Willem B. Drees, though exploring the concept of consonance, has pointed out the problematic assumptions underlying realism and a correspondence theory of truth. Instead he proposes 'constructing a consonance world' which includes God's otherness and the prophetic challenge of lived values.[40] Our religious traditions invite us to wander through, and our sciences to wonder about, the reality which transcends and sustains our lives and to engage ethically with the challenge of the future.[41]

The Importance of Lakatos in Theology and Science

Although Barbour was apparently the first scholar in the field to discuss the potential importance to theology of the writings of Imre Lakatos in the philosophy of science, Lakatos's ideas have been extensively discussed by Nancey Murphy and Philip Clayton. Murphy's arguments arose in 1990 through her criticism of Wolfhart Pannenberg's methodology.[42] Pannenberg uses Stephen Toulmin's claim that theories in history, science, and hermeneutics serve as explanations by placing facts in a broader context. For theology, the explanatory context becomes the whole of reality, including the future. Pannenberg then developed a criterion for acceptability of both theological and scientific theories: the most adequate theory is the one that can incorporate its competitors. However, according to Murphy, Pannenberg cannot answer the Humean challenge to theological rationality[43] because Hume's point of view is incommensurable with Pannenberg's, and thus it cannot be incorporated into Pannenberg's system, as Pannenberg's methodology requires.

In place of Toulmin, Murphy urges us to adopt the work of Lakatos, with its view of scientific theories as structured by a central core and a surrounding belt of auxiliary hypotheses. Following Lakatos, we should judge the relative progress or degeneration of such research programs on the basis of their ability to predict and corroborate novel facts.[44] Murphy then offers a crucial modification of Lakatos's conception of 'novel facts': 'A fact is novel if it is one not used in the construction of the theory T that it is taken to confirm … [that is] one whose existence, relevance to T, or interpretability in light of T is first documented after T is proposed.'[45] This modification allows Murphy to apply Lakatos's methodology to theology, to decide rationally which theological research programs are empirically progressive, and thus to complete the argument for the scientific status of theology. It also would allow Pannenberg's theological research program, when properly modified, to be progressive against the challenge of Hume.

Philip Clayton has also advocated the theological appropriation of Lakatosian methodology.[46] Clayton views 'explanation' as the key concept embracing both the natural and social sciences and, ultimately, theology – one with sufficient diversity to span vastly differing disciplines while retaining an underlying unity. Here the revisionist, contextualist, and historicist arguments in recent philosophy of science become crucial. In the natural sciences, where one interprets physical data, the truth of an explanation is pivotal. In the social sciences, however, where one interprets both physical data and the experience of actor-subjects (that is, the 'double hermeneutic'), explanation means 'understanding' (*Verstehen*). Theological explanations, then, are subject to validation not by verificationist/foundationalist standards, but by intersubjective testability and universalizability, as performed by the disciplinary community. Clayton supports his case by relying on the discovery/justification distinction: religious claims can be truthful even if their sources are in social, and not just physical, data. The key, though, is Lakatos's requirement that a previously specified set of criteria is held by the community by which competing explanatory hypotheses can be assessed, including the stipulation of 'novel facts.'

Over the past decade, Murphy and Clayton have offered important critiques of their corresponding positions which have further revealed the layers of complexity that underlie theological rationality.[47] Meanwhile, Murphy's approach has been implemented in discussions of theological anthropology by Philip Hefner,[48] pragmatic evaluation of religion by Karl Peters,[49] and the theological implications of cosmology in my own work.[50] I believe that further pursuit of the suggestions by both Murphy and Clayton is an extremely important task at the frontiers of theology and science today.[51]

Key Critiques by Social Constructivists and Feminists

Even while Barbour was developing this position, scientific realism was being challenged in a number of ways.[52] Though Kuhn had focused primarily on factors *internal* to the scientific community, sociologists from the 1970s onwards explored the social construction of science. These *externalist* accounts of science emphasized the social history of science and the variety of political and economic influences on science. According to the 'strong program,' the theory-ladenness of data and the underdetermination of theories by evidence almost entirely influence the formation and content of scientific theories and the ways they are assessed.[53] Marxists argued that science is a source of power over nature and thus over people, power rationalized by appeals to the myth of objectivity. Meanwhile the diversity of philosophical views on realism in science was growing, along with an increasing number of anti-realist positions.[54] Against their critics, realists tended to argue that social and personal influences are gradually filtered out by the methods of testing used in the sciences, and that the increasing success in predictive power and technological application implies that scientific knowledge is referential.[55]

Feminist critiques of science have also stressed the crucial role of gender analysis in uncovering distortions in scientific research. According to Evelyn Fox Keller and Helen E. Longino,[56] the roots of the feminist critique lie in externalist arguments of Kuhn but the focus is on the novel concept of 'gender' as the social constitution of 'masculine' and 'feminine' applied independently of the biological categories of male and female. Early feminists sought a 'gender-free' science by urging greater access for women in science education and research, and by retrieving the stories of women whose outstanding scientific accomplishments had been forgotten or repressed. More recent writings have used the concept of gender to analyze the content and practice of science, to detect the distortions introduced by gender bias, to uncover the sexual metaphors used for nature that legitimate dominance over nature.[57] Still some seek an alternative philosophy of knowledge that includes a commitment to objectivity.[58]

Barbour's assessment of these diverse externalist accounts is that they provide a 'valuable corrective' to the internalist view, particularly regarding the context of discovery. However, the appeal to interests is hard to document, the shift towards relativism '… underestimates the constraints on theories by the data' and testing of theories reduces distortions due to ideologies and interests. He agrees with feminists in their challenge of dualist thought and the pervasive role of values and interests in scientific inquiry, but he calls for a rejection of dualism and not their inversion. While data and theory criteria are objective features of science, he agrees that scientific inquiry involves participation and he affirms holistic thinking in science. At bottom, 'absolutizing the feminine seems as dubious as absolutizing the masculine,' and he lays the charge of cultural relativism against the externalist claim as well.[59]

I would add to Barbour's discussion a concern for what can be called a 'feminist critique of science and religion.' While feminist theology emerged in roughly the same period as the secular feminist views of science,[60] a feminist critique of science and religion is only just emerging but its importance is worth underscoring. On one level the issue is numbers. Even today very few women are active in 'theology and science,' and the number of feminist women (or men) is even fewer.[61] However, the more pressing issue lies in the claim that gender effects the content of the field. Lisa Stenmark urges scholars in science and religion to listen to the 'voices from the margins' and to turn to postmodernist views of knowledge, to honor the importance of diversity in community, and to adhere to participatory values.[62] Recent historical studies have led to a clearer understanding of gender bias in 'science and religion.' Margaret Wertheim[63] has argued for a parallel between the marginalization of women in religion and in physics. Historically women were excluded from European universities, and thus from participating in the rise of science. Today, 'the struggle women have faced to gain entry into science parallels the struggle they have faced to gain entry into the clergy.' Wertheim advocates instead 'a culture of physics that would encourage both men and women to pursue different kinds of goals and ideals ... more concerned with human beings and our needs.'[64]

I believe that a sustained focus on issues of gender as a clue to how scientific and theological voices have influenced – and distorted – each other and the inclusion of womanist, mujerista, and other womens' voices will mark an important new development in 'science and religion.' Finally, the growing ecofeminist interaction between feminist and ecological concerns promises to add a much-needed fresh perspective on the long-standing relation between 'theology and science' and 'ethics and technology.'[65]

An Interaction Model of Theology and Science

A major challenge continues to be whether science and theology are genuinely *inter*active in a *creative and constructive* sense, each offering something of intellectual value to the other although in different ways, or is the theological role one of mere hermeneutics? Philosophy and theology have been influential in the rise of modern science with both creative and distortive consequences, as historians of science now stress,[66] and such influences continue to play a role in theory formation and theory choice in contemporary science,[67] as we have just seen. But can such influences be constructive and beneficial? In recent writings,[68] I have explored the possibility that theology can, at least in some cases, lead to creative suggestions for scientific research which science would find beneficial as judged by its own, independent criteria.

My proposal combines the depiction of the sciences and humanities (including theology) as ordered in an epistemic hierarchy, as proposed by Peacocke and by Murphy, with Barbour's proposal of an analogy between theological and scientific methodologies. The result is striking: we can identify a number of distinct 'paths' between theology and science. Five paths move upwards as influences by science on theology, while three paths move downwards conveying suggestive ideas for research programs in science from theology. I believe that each path represents what has actually happened historically and what happens, though often unacknowledged, in current research. By reflecting on all eight paths together we can discern something about the interaction of theology and science as a whole, something which we have not appreciated by taking each path separately. The overall perspective might also tell us something about the direction for 'theology and science' in the future.

Summary of the Status of Critical Realism and Open Issues

Over the past five decades, the predominant school of thought among scholars in theology and science, particularly of those coming from a liberal theological perspective, has been critical realism. The term stood for a 'packaged deal' whose elements were brought together from a variety of various philosophical contexts.[69] They include:

1   the ubiquitous role and complex epistemic structure of metaphor in all language (against literalism and expressivism);
2   a Hempelian hypothetico-deductive methodology embedded in a contextualist/explanatory and historicist/competitive framework (against positivism, empiricism and instrumentalism);
3   a hierarchy of disciplines with both constraints and autonomy (against epistemic reductionism);
4   a commitment to referentiality, whether of individual terms or of entire theories (against some aspects of the sociology of knowledge), and with it a theory of truth combining correspondence, coherence, and pragmatism; and yet
5   a genuine division over metaphysical issues, whose most representative alternatives are emergent monism versus panexperientialism.

Each of these elements, of course, raised complex issues that were highly debated. Still there was sufficient agreement for these elements to form what can be called the 'consensus view' in theology and science since the 1960s. For these scholars, critical realism was seen as providing the crucial 'bridge' between theology and science, making possible real dialogue and growing interaction.

During this period, however, each of these elements has come under criticism. Some scholars working in theology and science have stressed the difficulties facing a realist interpretation of specific scientific theories, such as quantum mechanics,[70] as well as key theological terms, such as the concept of God.[71] Some have acknowledged the diversity of realist positions taken by philosophers[72] as well as the continuing challenge to realism by the sociology of knowledge.[73] Some have given increased attention to the diversity of models of rationality and their relative appropriateness for 'science and religion'[74] and the importance of differences, as well as similarities, between theology and science from the standpoint of pragmatism.[75] Some have moved to a non-foundationalist (and in this specific sense a postmodernist) epistemology, either keeping correspondence and referentiality[76] or shifting to a pragmatic theory of truth.[77] Some working with an all-embracing philosophical system, such as Whiteadian metaphysics, have developed a broad set of theological positions in light of science[78] while others who make more limited use of metaphysics have developed equally broad theological arguments.[79] Other positions have emerged at increasing distances from the 'consensus view.' For some, a postmodernist view offers an attractive approach, drawing on Continental and/or Anglo-American sources, and, for growing numbers, feminist critiques of science are crucial. Some have abandoned realism as a whole while continuing to find some of its elements helpful in relating science and religion.[80]

On balance, though, critical realism, as originally constructed by Barbour five decades ago, has continued to be defended, deployed and diversified widely in theology and science, and it continues to be presupposed by most working scientists, by many theologians, and in much of the public discourse about both science and religion. On balance I believe it to be of enduring importance, both for its crucial role in the historical developments of the past decades and as a point of departure for future research. Surely Barbour's proposal constitutes the key methodological contribution that the 'first generation' gave to make discourse regarding theology and science possible today.

Notes

1. This material is drawn from portions of Robert John Russell, 'Theology and Science: Current Issues and Future Directions' (2000), from Center for Theology and the Natural Sciences website: <http://www.ctns.org/Publications/publications.html>
2. Ian G. Barbour, *Issues in Science and Religion* (New York: Harper & Row, 1971; originally published in 1966 by Prentice Hall). See especially Part Two: 'Religion and the Methods of Science.'
3. I discuss this metaphor in Robert John Russell, 'Bridging Theology and Science: The CTNS Logo', *Theology and Science*, 1:1 (April 2003), 1–3. For a critique, see W. Mark Richardson and Wesley J. Wildman (eds), *Religion and Science: History, Method, Dialogue* (New York: Routledge, 1996), xi–xiii.
4. I.G. Barbour, *Religion and Science: Historical and Contemporary Issues* (San Francisco: HarperSanFrancisco, 1997).
5. Idem, *When Science Meets Religion* (San Francisco: HarperSanFrancisco, 2000).
6. Barbour, *Issues in Science and Religion*, ch. 6/III and IV; *Myths, Models, and Paradigms: A Comparative Study in Science and Religion* (New York: Harper & Row, 1974), ch. 3/2; *Religion in an Age of Science: The Gifford Lectures; 1989–1990 Volume 1* (San Francisco: Harper & Row, 1990), 43. Note that many of the writers in theology and science described here draw on philosophers of science who defend what is more commonly called 'scientific realism' though

typically using Barbour's term, 'critical realism'. For an overview of realist positions, see Jarrett Leplin (ed.), *Scientific Realism* (Berkeley: University of California Press, 1984).

7. Barbour, *Religion in an Age of Science*, ch. 2/II, esp. p. 43; *Issues in Science and Religion*, ch. 6/II/3; *Myths, Models, and Paradigms*, 3/2–3.

8. Idem, *Myths, Models, and Paradigms*, ch. 2.

9. Barbour, *Religion in an Age of Science*, ch. 2, esp. I/1, II/1, III/1; Ibid., ch. 6/I/1,2, II/1; *Myths, Models, and Paradigms*, ch. 6.

10. Idem, *Religion in an Age of Science*, 34–5.

11. Idem, *Issues in Science and Religion*, 170, 173.

12. Idem, *Religion in an Age of Science*, chs. 2, 3; Issues in Science and Religion, chs. 8, 9; *Myths, Models, and Paradigms*, chs. 4, 5, 7, 8, 9.

13. Idem, *Religion in an Age of Science*, 36.

14. Ibid., ch. 2/II; Barbour, *Issues in Science and Religion*, ch. 8/I/4; *Myths, Models, and Paradigms*, chs. 4, 5.

15. Barbour, *Religion in an Age of Science*, ch. 2, esp. I/1–3 and Figs. 1 and 2.

16. Ibid., 46–7, 65; *Issues in Science and Religion*, chs. 8/II, 9/I/3; *Myths, Models, and Paradigms*, ch. 4/5.

17. Barbour, *Religion in an Age of Science*, ch. 2/I/3; *Issues in Science and Religion*, ch. 8/III; *Myths, Models, and Paradigms*, ch. 7/4.

18. Barbour, *Myths, Models, and Paradigms*, ch. 7, esp. pp. 118, 144–5; *Religion in an Age of Science*, ch. 2 Section III, IV, esp. p. 65.

19. For a response to Anthony Flew and others on falsifiability in religion, see Barbour, *Myths, Models, and Paradigms*, ch. 7/2.

20. Arthur R. Peacocke, *Creation and the World of Science: The Bampton Lectures, 1979* (Oxford: Clarendon Press, 1979).

21. Idem, *Intimations of Reality: Critical Realism in Science and Religion: The Mendenhall Lectures, 1983* (Notre Dame, IN: University of Notre Dame Press, 1984).

22. Idem, *Creation and the World of Science*, 21–2. His exact phrase at that time was a 'skeptical and qualified realism' and he attributes the term 'critical realism' to Barbour, *Myths, Models and Paradigms*. Peacocke's note #38 includes helpful references to the complex discussion in philosophy of science at the time. In earlier writings Peacocke adopts a 'realist' perspective, though without a detailed discussion. See A.R. Peacocke, *Science and the Christian Experiment* (London: Oxford University Press, 1971).

23. Idem, *The Sciences and Theology in the Twentieth Century* (Notre Dame: University of Notre Dame Press, 1981); *Intimations of Reality*, 18–29, esp. 19–22. Note that Peacocke's comparison of models in theology and in science (pp. 40–46) draws directly from Barbour, *Myths, Models, and Paradigms* (as does A.R. Peacocke, 'Intimations of Reality: Critical Realism in Science and Religion,' *Religion and Intellectual Life*, II:4 [Summer 1985]).

24. A.R. Peacocke, *Theology for a Scientific Age: Being and Becoming – Natural, Divine and Human*, enlarged edn (Minneapolis: Fortress Press, 1993).

25. Idem, *Theology for a Scientific Age*, 11–19.

26. John C. Polkinghorne, *The Faith of a Physicist: Reflections of a Bottom-up Thinker* (Princeton, NJ: Princeton University Press, 1994), 32.

27. Idem, *One World: The Interaction of Science and Theology* (Princeton: Princeton University Press, 1986), 22–4; Idem., *The Faith of a Physicist*, 25, 156, and see the following quotation.

28. J. Wentzel van Huyssteen, *Theology and the Justification of Faith: Constructing Theories in Systematic Theology* (Grand Rapids, MI: Eerdmans, 1989), 162; see also Wentzel van Huyssteen, 'Seriously, But Not Literally: Pragmatism and Realism in Religion and Science,' *Zygon*, 23:3 (September 1988).

29. Thomas F. Torrance, *Theological Science* (London: Oxford University Press, 1969), viii–x, ch. 6.

30. Idem, *Space, Time and Resurrection* (Grand Rapids: Eerdmans, 1976), ix–xiii.

31. Sallie McFague, *Metaphorical Theology: Models of God in Religious Language* (Philadelphia:

Fortress Press, 1982), ch. 3, esp. 101–8; see also 'Ian Barbour: Theologian's Friend, Scientist's Interpreter', *Zygon*, 31:1 (March 1996), 21–8.

32. Mary Gerhart and Allan Melvin Russell, *Metaphoric Process: The Creation of Scientific and Religious Understanding* (Fort Worth: Texas Christian University Press, 1984).

33. See also Mary Gerhart and Allan Melvin Russell, 'Bidisciplinary Fusion: New Understandings in Theology and Natural Science', *CTNS Bulletin*, 13:2 (Spring 1993), 1–6; Mary Gerhart and Allan Melvin Russell, 'Metaphoric Process as the Tectonic Reformation of Worlds of Meaning in Theology and Natural Science', *CTNS Bulletin*, 13:2 (Spring 1993), 7–13.

34. Janet Martin Soskice, *Metaphor and Religious Language* (Oxford: Oxford University Press, 1985). See also 'Knowledge and Experience in Science and Religion: Can We Be Realists?', in *Physics, Philosophy, and Theology: A Common Quest for Understanding*, ed. by Robert J. Russell, William R. Stoeger, SJ, and George V. Coyne, SJ (Vatican City State: Vatican Observatory Publications, 1988), 173–84.

35. Soskice, *Metaphor and Religious Language*, esp. 101–7, 131–2, 137, 140, 148.

36. Hans Küng, *Theology for the Third Millennium: An Ecumenical View*, trans by Peter Heinegg (New York: Doubleday, 1988), B/II, 156.

37. Robert John Russell, 'Cosmology, Creation, and Contingency', in *Cosmos as Creation: Theology and Science in Consonance*, ed. by Ted Peters (Nashville: Abingdon Press, 1989), esp. pp. 188, 194, 204; 'Contemplation: A Scientific Context,' *Continuum*, 2 (Fall 1990). See also 'Theological Lessons from Cosmology', *Cross Currents: Religion and Intellectual Life*, 41:3 (Fall 1991), esp. pp. 313–14; 'Finite Creation Without a Beginning: The Spiritual and Theological Significance of Stephen Hawking's Quantum Cosmology', *The Way: Review of Contemporary Christian Spirituality*, 32:4 (October 1992); 'Cosmology from Alpha to Omega', *Zygon*, 29:4 (December 1994); 'Cosmology: Evidence for God or Partner for Theology?' in *Evidence of Purpose*, ed. John Marks Templeton (New York: Continuum, 1994); 'T=0: Is It Theologically Significant?', in *Religion and Science: History, Method, Dialogue*, ed. by W. Mark Richardson and Wesley J. Wildman (New York: Routledge, 1996), esp. p. 213.

38. Ted Peters, 'On Creating the Cosmos', in *Physics, Philosophy, and Theology: A Common Quest for Understanding*, ed. by Robert J. Russell, William R. Stoeger, SJ, and George V. Coyne, SJ (Vatican City State: Vatican Observatory Publications, 1988), esp. 274–6; 'Cosmos as Creation', in *Cosmos as Creation: Theology and Science in Consonance*, ed. by Ted Peters (Nashville: Abingdon Press, 1989), 45–114; Ted Peters (ed.), *Science and Theology: The New Consonance* (Boulder, CO: Westview Press, 1998), esp. 18–19.

39. See the Introduction to Wolfhart Pannenberg, *Toward a Theology of Nature: Essays on Science and Faith*, ed. by Ted Peters (Louisville, KY: Westminster/John Knox Press, 1993), 5. (Note: Peters edited this collection and wrote the Introduction being cited.)

40. Willem B. Drees, *Beyond the Big Bang: Quantum Cosmologies and God* (La Salle, IL: Open Court, 1990), esp. 1.2.5 and 5.5; 'A Case Against Temporal Critical Realism? Consequences of Quantum Cosmology for Theology', in *Quantum Cosmology and the Laws of Nature: Scientific Perspectives on Divine Action*, ed. by Robert J. Russell, Nancey C. Murphy, and Chris J. Isham, Scientific Perspectives on Divine Action Series (Vatican City State; Berkeley, CA: Vatican Observatory Publications; Center for Theology and the Natural Sciences, 1993), esp. 2.1.

41. Drees, *Religion, Science and Naturalism* (Cambridge: Cambridge University Press, 1996), esp. ch. 5.

42. Wolfhart Pannenberg, *Theology and the Philosophy of Science*, trans. Francis McDonagh (Philadelphia: Westminster Press, 1976).

43. Nancey Murphy, *Theology in the Age of Scientific Reasoning* (Ithaca: Cornell University Press, 1990), esp. chs. 2, 3. Murphy noted that Ian Barbour had anticipated the importance of Lakatos in Barbour, *Myths, Models, and Paradigms*, pp. 99–102, 107–8, 112–18, 133–7.

44. See Murphy, *Theology in the Age of Scientific Reasoning*, ch. 3, esp. pp. 58–61.

45. Eadem, *Theology in the Age of Scientific Reasoning*, 68. Note that without careful attention to

Murphy's modification, the notion of 'prediction' might seem to undercut the applicability of Lakatos to theology. See, for example, Polkinghorne, *The Faith of a Physicist*, 49; and Niels Henrik Gregersen, 'A Contextual-Coherence Theory for the Theology–Science Dialogue', in *Rethinking Theology and Science: Six Models for the Current Dialogue*, ed. by Niels Henrik, Gregersen and J. Wentzel van Huyssteen (Grand Rapids, MI: Eerdmans, 1998), 205–12, esp. 208–9. For a substantive critique of the claim that discernment can yield novel facts, see Drees, *Religion, Science and Naturalism*, 143–4.

46. Philip Clayton, *Explanation from Physics to Theology: An Essay in Rationality and Religion* (New Haven, CN: Yale University Press, 1989).

47. Nancey Murphy, 'Response to Review by Philip Clayton of "Theology in the Age of Scientific Reasoning" by Nancey Murphy', *CTNS Bulletin*, 11:1 (Winter 1991), 31; Philip Clayton, 'Review of "Theology in the Age of Scientific Reasoning" by Nancey Murphy,' *CTNS Bulletin*, 11:1 (Winter 1991), 29–31. See also Mary Hesse, 'Review of "Explanation from Physics to Theology" by Philip Clayton', *CTNS Bulletin*, 11:2 (Spring 1991), 39–40. See also the responses to Murphy in the September 1998 issue of *Zygon: Journal of Religion and Science*.

48. Philip Hefner, *The Human Factor: Evolution, Culture, and Religion*, Theology and the Sciences Series (Minneapolis: Fortress Press, 1993).

49. Karl E. Peters, 'Storytellers and Scenario Spinners: Some Reflections on Religion and Science in Light of a Pragmatic, Evolutionary Theory of Knowledge', *Zygon*, 32:4 (December 1997), 465–89.

50. Robert John Russell, 'Finite Creation Without a Beginning: The Doctrine of Creation in Relation to Big Bang and Quantum Cosmologies,' in *Quantum Cosmology and the Laws of Nature: Scientific Perspectives on Divine Action*, ed. by Robert J. Russell, Nancey C. Murphy, and Chris J. Isham, Scientific Perspectives on Divine Action Series (Vatican City State; Berkeley, CA: Vatican Observatory Publications; Center for Theology and the Natural Sciences, 1993), 293–329; Nancey Murphy and George F. Ellis, *On the Moral Nature of the Universe: Theology, Cosmology, and Ethics,* Theology and the Sciences Series (Minneapolis: Fortress Press, 1996).

51. For additional discussion, see Philip Clayton and Steven Knapp, 'Rationality and Christian Self-Conception', in *Religion and Science: History, Method, Dialogue*, ed. by W. Mark Richardson and Wesley J. Wildman (New York: Routledge, 1996), 131–44; Nicholas Wolterstorff, 'Entitled Christian Belief', in *Religion and Science*, ed. Richardson and Wildman, 145–50; Nancey Murphy, 'On the Nature of Theology', in *Religion and Science*, ed. Richardson and Wildman, 151–60; Philip Clayton and Steven Knapp, 'Is Holistic Justification Enough?' in *Religion and Science*, ed. Richardson and Wildman, 161–9; Gregory Peterson, 'The Scientific Status of Theology: Imre Lakatos, Method and Demarcation', *Perspectives on Science and Christian Faith*, 50:1 (March 1998), 22–31.

52. Barbour, *Religion in an Age of Science*, 74–6.

53. See D. Bloor, *Knowledge and Social Imagery* (London: Routledge & Kegan Paul, 1976). For an insightful treatment of the strong program, see Martin Rudwick, 'Senses of the Natural World and Senses of God: Another Look at the Historical Relation of Science and Religion', in *The Sciences and Theology in the Twentieth Century*, ed. by A.R. Peacocke (Notre Dame: University of Notre Dame Press, 1981), 241–61. For a helpful analysis, see Mary Hesse, 'Socializing Epistemology', in *Construction and Constraint: The Shaping of Scientific Rationality*, ed. by Ernan McMullin (Notre Dame: University of Notre Dame Press, 1988), 97–122.

54. Realists include Hiliary Putnam, Ian Hacking, and Jarrett Leplin. Antirealists include Bas C. van Fraassen, Larry Laudan, and Arthur Fine. For a helpful anthology see Ernan McMullin, ed. *Construction and Constraint: The Shaping of Scientific Rationality* (Notre Dame, IN: University of Notre Dame Press, 1988).

55. Ernan McMullin, 'How Should Cosmology Relate to Theology?' in *The Sciences and Theology in the Twentieth Century*, ed. by A.R. Peacocke (Notre Dame, IN: University of Notre Dame Press, 1981), 26.

56. Evelyn Fox Keller and Helen E. Longino (eds), *Feminism and Science* (Oxford: Oxford University Press, 1996). Prior major works on feminism and science include Sandra Harding, *The Science*

Question in Feminism (Ithaca: Cornell University Press, 1986); Evelyn Fox Keller, *Reflections on Gender and Science* (New Haven: Yale University Press, 1985); and Helen Longino, *Science as Social Knowledge: Values and Objectivity in Scientific Inquiry* (Princeton: Princeton University Press, 1990).

57. Sandra Harding, 'Why Has the Sex/Gender System Become Visible Only Now?' in *Discovering Reality: Feminist Perspectives on Epistemology, Metaphysics, Methodology, and Philosophy of Science*, ed. by Sandra Harding and Merrill B. Hintikka (Dordrecht, Holland: D. Reidel Publishing Company, 1983), esp. Introduction, ix–x and pp. 312–13; Carolyn Merchant, *The Death of Nature: Women, Ecology, and the Scientific Revolution* (New York: Harper & Row, 1980). See also Mary Midgley, *The Ethical Primate: Humans, Freedom, and Morality* (New York: Routledge, 1994), esp. chs. 7, 8; Helen E. Longino and Ruth Doell, 'Body, Bias, and Behaviour: A Comparative Analysis of Reasoning in Two Areas of Biological Science', in *Feminism and Science*, ed. by Evelyn Fox Keller and Helen E. Longino (Oxford: Oxford University Press, 1996), 73–90.

58. Donna J. Haraway, *Simians, Cyborgs, and Women: The Reinvention of Nature* (New York: Routledge, 1991), 187.

59. Barbour, *Religion in an Age of Science*, 75–81.

60. Early landmark publications of a systematic feminist theology include Rosemary Radford Ruether, *Sexism and God-Talk: Toward a Feminist Theology* (Boston: Beacon Press, 1983); and Elizabeth Schüssler Fiorenza, *In Memory of Her: A Feminist Theological Reconstruction of Christian Origins* (New York: Crossroad, 1984). A much older textual source would be *The Women's Bible* dating back to 1895. For additional references see Fiorenza, *In Memory of Her*, esp. ch. 1.

61. Ann Pederson and Mary Solberg, 'CyberFlesh: An Embodied Feminist Pedagogy for Science and Religion', paper presented at the American Academy of Religion Annual Meeting, 1999.

62. Lisa L. Stenmark, 'Seeing the Log in Our Own Eye: The Social Location of the Science and Religion Discourse', paper presented at the American Academy of Religion Annual Meeting, 1999. See also: Winnifred A. Tomm, 'Sexuality, Rationality, and Spirituality', *Zygon*, 25:2 (June 1990); William Grassie, 'Donna Haraway's Metatheory of Science and Religion: Cyborgs, Trickster, and Hermes,' *Zygon*, 31:2 (June 1996), 285–304.

63. Margaret Wertheim, *Pythagoras' Trousers: God, Physics, and the Gender Wars* (New York: Times Books, 1995); see also Margaret Wertheim, 'Faith, Physics, and Feminism: The 1995–96 J.K. Russell Fellowship Lecture', *CTNS Bulletin*, 16.2 (Spring 1996); Margaret Wertheim, 'God of the Quantum Vacuum', *New Scientist*, 150, no. 2102 (4 October 1997), 28–31.

64. Wertheim, *Pythagoras' Trousers*, 8–9, 15; see also David F. Noble, *A World Without Women: The Christian Clerical Culture of Western Science* (Oxford: Oxford University Press, 1992), Introduction.

65. See for example C.S.J. Anne M. Clifford, 'Feminist Perspectives on Science: Implications for an Ecological Theology of Creation,' *Journal of Feminist Studies in Religion*, 8.2 (Fall 1992), 65–90. For a related but distinct claim, see the chapter by Judith Scoville in this text (Chapter 13).

66. Michael Foster, 'The Christian Doctrine of Creation and the Rise of Modern Science,' in *Creation: The Impact of an Idea*, ed. by Daniel O'Connor and Francis Oakley (New York: Charles Scribner's Sons, 1969); Eugene M. Klaaren, *Religious Origins of Modern Science: Belief in Creation in Seventeenth-Century Thought* (Grand Rapids: William B. Eerdmans, 1977); David C. Lindberg and Ronald L. Numbers (eds), *God and Nature: Historical Essays on the Encounter Between Christianity and Science* (Berkeley: University of California Press, 1986); Gary B. Deason, 'Protestant Theology and the Rise of Modern Science: Criticism and Review of the Strong Thesis,' *CTNS Bulletin*, 6:4 (Autumn 1986): 1–8; Amos Funkenstein, *Theology and the Scientific Imagination: From the Middle Ages to the Seventeenth Century* (Princeton, NJ: Princeton University Press, 1986); I. Bernard Cohen (ed.), *Puritanism and the Rise of Modern Science: The Merton Thesis* (New Brunswick: Rutgers University Press, 1990); Roy A. Clouser, *The Myth of Religious Neutrality: An Essay on the Hidden Role of Religious Belief in Theories* (Notre Dame: University of Notre Dame Press, 1991); John H. Brooke, *Science and Religion: Some Historical Perspectives* (Cambridge: Cambridge University Press, 1991).

67. James T. Cushing, *Quantum Mechanics: Historical Contingency and the Copenhagen Hegemony* (Chicago: University of Chicago Press, 1994); Henry J. Folse, *The Philosophy of Niels Bohr: The Framework of Complementarity* (Amsterdam: North Holland, 1985); Max Jammer, *The Philosophy of Quantum Mechanics: The Interpretations of Quantum Mechanics in Historical Perspective* (New York: John Wiley & Sons, 1974); Helge Kragh, *Cosmology and Controversy: The Historical Development of Two Theories of the Universe* (Princeton: Princeton University Press, 1996).

68. Robert John Russell, 'The Revevance of Tillich for the Theology/Science Dialogus,' in *Paul Tillich Annual Meeting Conference Proceedings*, ed. by Paul Carr (North American Tillich Society, 1999), 269–308; Robert John Russell, 'Eschatology and Physical Cosmology: A Preliminary Reflection,' in *The Far Future: Eschatology from a Cosmic Perspective*, ed. by George F.R. Ellis (Philadelphia: Templeton Foundation Press, 2002), 266–315; Robert John Russell, 'Bodily Resurrection, Eschatology and Scientific Cosmology: The Mutual Interaction of Christian Theology and Science,' in *Resurrection: Theological and Scientific Assessments*, ed. by Ted Peters, Robert John Russell, and Michael Welker (Grand Rapids: Eerdmans Publishing Company, 2002), 3–30.

69. Murphy argues that the term 'critical realism' is strictly an epistemic theory defending a correspondence theory of truth and should not be used for the entire set of elements described here.

70. Robert John Russell, 'Whitehead, Einstein and the Newtonian Legacy,' in *Newton and the New Direction in Science*, ed. by S.J.G.V. Coyne, M. Heller (Citta del Vaticano: Specola Vaticana, 1988); see also, for example, Robert John Russell, 'A Critical Appraisal of Peacocke's Thought on Religion and Science,' in *Religion and Intellectual Life*, II:4 (New Rochelle: College of New Rochelle, 1985).

71. Drees, *Religion, Science and Naturalism*, 143.

72. Peacocke, *Theology for a Scientific Age*, 12. See Leplin, *Scientific Realism*.

73. Bloor, *Knowledge and Social Imagery*. See Peacocke, *Intimations of Reality*, 19–22, for helpful references and counterarguments.

74. Mikael Stenmark, *Rationality in Science, Religion, and Everyday Life: A Critical Evaluation of Four Models of Rationality* (Notre Dame, IN: University of Notre Dame Press, 1995).

75. Wesley Wildman, 'Similarities and Differences in the Practice of Science and Theology,' *CTNS Bulletin*, 14:4 (Fall 1994), 1–14.

76. Clayton, *Explanation*.

77. Nancey Murphy, *Beyond Liberalism and Fundamentalism: How Modern and Postmodern Philosophy Set the Theological Agenda* (Valley Forge, PA: Trinity Press International, 1996).

78. Barbour, *Religion and Science*; Charles and John B. Cobb Birch, Jr, *The Liberation of Life* (Cambridge: Cambridge University Press, 1981); John F. Haught, *Science and Religion: From Conflict to Conversion* (New York: Paulist Press, 1995); David Ray Griffin (ed.), *The Reenchantment of Science: Postmodern Proposals,* SUNY Series in Constructive Postmodern Thought (Albany, NY: State University of New York Press, 1988).

79. Polkinghorne, *The Faith of a Physicist*.

80. Drees, *Religion, Science and Naturalism*, esp. ch. 5.

Chapter 3

Barbour's Way(s) of Relating Science and Theology[1]

Christian Berg

Ian Barbour is well known as one the founding fathers of today's dialogue between science and theology. He has contributed to this field probably much longer than any other scholar who is still writing today. Ever since his earliest writings Barbour has been concerned about the precise nature of the relationship between science and theology. Time and again he came back to this question. Surely the best-known example for this is his famous typology, in which he suggests four categories for ways of relating science and theology:[2] Conflict, Independence, Dialogue, and Integration.[3] In the following, I will first point to the development in Barbour's thoughts since his earliest writings in the 1950s. Secondly, I will argue that Barbour's fourfold typology reflects cornerstones of this development. I will then discuss, thirdly, some questions this typology raises. Finally, I will point out how some of these problems can be avoided if one chooses a different way of categorizing the relationship of science and theology.

Development of Barbour's Way of Relating Science and Theology

One can distinguish, roughly, three periods in Barbour's work: an early period from the early 1950s to the early 1960s; a middle period from then to the middle of the 1980s; and a late period following Barbour's retirement in 1986.

Outset – Early Period: Early 1950s to Early 1960s

During his first decade in science and theology, between the early 1950s and the early 1960s, Barbour discusses several issues at their interface, although not as comprehensively as in later writings. Typical features of this period are his argument against positivism and against a conflict between science and religion, his interest in existential questions, and his view of science and religion as complementary.

Arguing against positivism   'Why is it that the mention of a Christian view is often criticized, whereas a logical positivist may be dogmatic and even militant in the expression of his faith?'[4] Barbour questions positivism for its exclusive use of the scientific method. 'Is it valid to use the methods of the natural sciences as an exclusive pattern for all fields, for dealing with all aspects of reality?'[5] This was written in 1953, the year in which Barbour enrolled at Yale Divinity School. Three years later he reviewed a book of Karl Heim, where he found an explicit answer to that earlier question. Heim distinguishes the I–Thou encounter with another subject from the I–It relations to objective things, with which science deals. The self 'belongs to a different order, which cannot be evaluated in quantitative terms.'[6] Therefore, 'the all-sufficiency of the methods of science has been challenged in the claim to an area with which scientific investigation cannot deal.'[7]

Although Barbour opposed positivism he could not totally withdraw from its influence. Since a positivist environment values empirical validation, Barbour pointed out that there are basic similarities between science and religion, 'especially in regard to the interaction of experience and interpretation in both areas.'[8] According to him, in religion the 'process of experiential testing is not altogether unlike the empirical component of science, though here the laboratory is the individual's life.'[9] Similarly, Barbour speaks of 'methods of religion.'[10] Such expressions have to be seen as a tribute to an empiricist environment. In his later writings, Barbour became more cautious about speaking of such direct parallels between science and religion.[11] However, even in *When Science Meets Religion* he speaks of the 'data of religion' in parallel to the 'data of science,' and of religious 'models' in parallel to scientific models and so on.[12]

Interest in the existential dimension   A second characteristic of Barbour's early writings is his interest in existential questions. 'God acts primarily through historical events and human communities, and He is revealed *through persons* ... Though physics is a very human enterprise, it centers on 'I–It' rather than 'I–Thou' relations.'[13] Again, his book *Christianity and the Scientist* wants to look 'at persons and their existential lives. It is concerned with the scientist himself, the man with two areas of loyalty: dedication to science and commitment to God. How do these loyalties interact?'[14] This interest in existential questions not only reflects the spirit of those days. Barbour took up certain elements of religious existentialism also to reach the independence of religion from science and to avoid conflicts between them.

No conflict between science and theology   Barbour repeatedly argued against a conflict between science and religion in his early period. 'If the intelligent citizen can move beyond popular misconceptions of both science and religion, he need feel no conflict between their methods.'[15] Such a conflict can be avoided because science and religion ask essentially different questions: science is concerned about I–It relations, while religion is concerned about the I–Thou encounter.[16] There is no conflict regarding either the methods or the contents of science. 'Theologians will be interested in developments in several areas of science but I can see *no point at which Christian beliefs are at stake.*'[17]

Complementarity between science and religion   As a result of Barbour's investigation of the precise nature of the relationship between science and religion

in this early period one could say that 'no *conflict* is possible' but also that science
and religion 'provide complementary modes of description of reality', just as wave
and particle are representations for light.[18] If complementary modes of description
are necessary even in physics, this will be even more so between different fields.
'Despite the desirability of unity, alternative constructs may be necessary to do
justice to the total situation.'[19] Barbour argues that science and religion ask different
types of question and refer to different aspects of experience, hence they provide
complementary modes of description of reality.[20]

First typology for the relation between science and religion   Barbour's fourfold
typology, which we mentioned above, has some predecessors in his earlier writings.
In *Christianity and the Scientist* Barbour refers to a typology, which H. Richard
Niebuhr uses in his book *Christ and Culture*. Barbour paraphrases and extends
Niebuhr's classifications 'as they might apply to the interpretation of contemporary
technology by the church'.[21] Barbour's five categories are: Religion *against* (1),
under (2), *above* (3), and *separate from* science (4), and religion *transforming*
science (5). Obviously, this early typology shows similarities to the later one we
mentioned.[22] However, interestingly, this early typology is used in an ethical
context, which deals with the responsibility of scientists and Christians, while the
later typology has no ethical categories at all. We will come back to this later.

   In sum, the dominance of positivism in the second third of the twentieth century
seemed to threaten religious faith. Arguing against this background, Barbour
emphasized that there need not be a conflict between science and religion, for
neither the theories nor the methods of science conflict with religious faith. Science
and religion provide complementary modes of description of reality.

Elaboration – Middle Period: Mid-1960s to Mid-1980s

In the two decades from the middle of the 1960s to the middle of the 1980s, starting
with his encyclopedic book *Issues in Science and Religion* (1966) Barbour
elaborated many ideas and concepts he had touched earlier, and he revised some of
them.

Critical realism questions 'complementarity'   The notion of complementarity
allows an efficient separation of science and religion but Barbour began to see
problematic aspects of such a position. Although he still sees the concept of two
'complementary languages' as a 'valid starting point' in *Issues in Science and
Religion*,[23] he is now aware that the 'complementary language view' of the analytic
tradition gives up realist claims. Such an instrumentalist interpretation of religion
would imply that 'all cognitive functions of religious language are dismissed.'[24] In
Issues in Science and Religion Barbour elaborates his concept of critical realism for
the first time and he concludes: '"Critical realism" will not allow us to be content
with two unrelated languages.'[25] We live in *one* world described by both science and
religion, and therefore we cannot be content with two unrelated languages. Later, in

Myths, Models, and Paradigms (1973), Barbour is even more sceptical about the notion of complementarity. Without mentioning his own previous thoughts on this concept he says that 'some authors ... speak of the complementarity of science and religion.'[26] Now he is 'somewhat dubious about such extended usage of the term if it is intended to convey some parallel with complementarity in physics'.[27]

Growing interest in metaphysics   A second difference to the early period is that Barbour's interest has now shifted from existential to metaphysical questions. Among others, one can see a biographical and a systematic reason for his growing interest in metaphysics. In 1965 George Brown Barbour, Ian's father, published a book describing his experiences during his paleontological research with Teilhard de Chardin in China.[28] Perhaps stimulated by this family connection, one year later Ian Barbour entered into a dialogue with Teilhard's writings for the first time. However, Barbour's interest in metaphysical issues was also motivated by the conviction of the unity of the world we live in. Ultimately a unity of scientific and religious knowledge is to be sought because both science and religion describe aspects of the same reality. Teilhard is aiming at such a unity in his writings. He is striving for a unified worldview, which 'provides a standing criticism of complacency in settling too readily for a plurality of unrelated languages.'[29] Consequently, Barbour also started discussing Whitehead's philosophy, for '[b]oth Teilhard and Whitehead ... are convinced of the unity of human experience and both are epistemological realists; they would insist that if alternative languages refer to a single world, they must ultimately be seen in relation to each other and incorporated into a single system of thought.'[30]

    In sum, seeing science and religion in an instrumentalist way just as two complementary languages without any realist claim is not an option for a critical realist like Barbour. Science and religion do not conflict, but they do make truth claims about reality. Hence their separation is not convincing and their relation has to be mediated by metaphysical categories. Barbour's criticism of the unrelated-language-view, his interest in critical realism as well as in metaphysics are all aspects of the same development.

Yield – Late Period: From 1986 On

In his late period, starting with his retirement in 1986, Barbour pulled together many of his earlier ideas and concepts and presented them in comprehensive ways. In doing so he extensively drew on previous publications, as can easily be seen in the two volumes of his Gifford Lectures.[31] Moreover, while Barbour had already published different typologies for the relationship of science and religion before,[32] there is basically just one typology in his late writings. Over more than a decade he published this typology at least six times in more or less the same form.[33] This indicates that he continued to see this typology as a useful categorization. Moreover, twelve years after its first publication, Barbour spelled out this typology in his book *When Science Meets Religion* (2000), and he defends this typology against criticism even in 2002.[34]

Barbour's Typology Reflects His Own Development

It is not surprising that Barbour is continuously suggesting the above-mentioned typology in his late period, for it reflects, as we will soon see, cornerstones of his own development throughout the past 50 years. The results of each phase of his own development are represented by a category of his typology. Barbour is following a dialectical movement, both in his own development and in his typology. He has always been opposing a conflict between science and religion, particularly in his early period. Hence 'conflict' can be seen, as we said above, as a background against which Barbour's own position evolves.[35] Conflicts will be avoided if science and religion are independent from each other. Therefore, in his early years Barbour stressed religion's own right against the dominance of science. He used the notion of complementarity to describe the relationship between science and religion, and he took up existentialist elements to point out the independence of religion from science. Consequently, Barbour's typology continues with Independence, which can be seen as an antithesis to Conflict.

In his dialectical move Barbour wants to keep the strengths of each position; he wants to 'do justice to what is valid in the *Independence* position'[36] – leaving out the weaknesses and taking them up into a third position (synthesis). However, as we saw above, already in his middle period Barbour realized difficulties of the Independence positions: because the analytic view of unrelated languages, for instance, gives up cognitive claims, the independence of science and religion would not be satisfactory. Barbour's paradigm for avoiding both Conflict and Independence is thus Dialogue, which shall overcome the separation of science and religion. Dialogue can be seen as a synthesis of the first two categories.

Yet for some reason Barbour restricts the Dialogue position to 'general characteristics of science and of nature'.[37] Since these kinds of issues only lead to rather preliminary, introductory questions, they should be followed by more substantial exchanges over the contents of science and religion. According to Barbour, this is being done in the fourth category, *Integration*. If one follows realist assumptions for both religion and science one cannot avoid metaphysical categories. This is the reason for Barbour's interest in Whitehead's process metaphysics and a *Systematic Synthesis* of science and religion, the last of three ways of *Integration*, with which Barbour is sympathetic himself.

Barbour's Typology Revisited

Barbour's typology is easily comprehensible, intuitively accessible, and follows an internal logic. A closer look, however, does also pose some questions.

Conflict or Foundationalism?

Scientific materialists oppose almost any religious assertion and see a conflict between science and religion, to be sure. But what about biblical literalists? Many biblical literalists propose a 'creation science' and would argue that a 'true' or a 'revealed' science would not contradict the scriptural witness. Ted Peters argues against subsuming scientific creationists under Conflict, for 'they see themselves in conflict with scientism but not with science itself.'[38] Furthermore, one could also argue that biblical literalists would not only be in conflict with science (or scientism) but also with (the mainstream of) theology, since a literal understanding of the Bible is surely rejected by the majority of theologians. In other words, what 'scientific materialists' and 'biblical literalists' respectively understand as 'science' or 'religion' differs considerably, and one might wonder whether it would be appropriate to speak of a 'conflict between science and religion' as the common denominator of these positions. Notwithstanding, I would agree with Barbour in grouping 'scientific materialists' and 'biblical literalists' in the same category – yet I would not call this conflict, but foundationalism. Barbour rightly points out that both positions share an important view. The scientific materialist sees logic and sense data as providing such foundations, while the biblical literalist finds them in infallible scripture.[39] In other words, *it is the epistemological position* which biblical literalists and scientific materialists share. They both have a foundationalist epistemology, they both claim that there is an indubitable foundation for knowledge.[40]

Independence or Separation?

Barbour is right in preserving the autonomy of science and keeping it independent from theology. Yet why should 'independence' mean being totally unrelated? I submit that Barbour is erroneously equating independence and total separation or isolation. Although I agree with Barbour's criticism of the Independence positions, I do not think that independence as such is a questionable concept. The independence of science and theology does not preclude that one discipline constructively reflects upon and/or utilizes methods of the other. Neither does it preclude a dialogue between them – unless one restricts dialogue to Barbour's narrow meaning of it.[41]

Dialogue 'On General Characteristics' Alone?

According to Barbour, Dialogue focuses on general features of nature while advocates of *Integration* stress particular scientific theories.[42] But surely 'dialogue' is often used in a much broader sense (cf. the whole science and religion *dialogue*). Moreover, when Barbour discusses 'methodological parallels,' one form of Dialogue, he criticizes that these are 'important but preliminary.'[43] Barbour criticizes the Dialogue position because it would not lead to more substantial forms of exchange between the contents of science and theology. But this is rather a critique of his own categorization, which restricts Dialogue to 'general characteristics of science and of nature,' and leaves the discussion of 'particular scientific theories' to the Integration position. Yet why should it not be possible to dialogue on particular scientific theories and/or theological concepts? Why does Barbour restrict Dialogue to this narrow sense?

Barbour's definition of Dialogue leaves out important areas in which dialogue between science and religion is actually taking place. It is remarkable, for instance, that he does not consider ethical issues as a starting point for a dialogue between science and religion.[44] Ted Peters suggests the category of 'ethical overlap' in his own typology.[45] However, Barbour is arguing, as we have already noted, that his typology 'was developed for fundamental science as a form of knowledge, not for applied science in its impact on society and nature.'[46] This distinction also has to be questioned, even from within Barbour's own framework, for the following reasons. Firstly, Barbour states elsewhere that one cannot separate science from ethics. In *Ethics in an Age of Technology* he quotes Loren Graham, who argues that there is no value-free science. Barbour thus concludes: 'These interpretations suggest that science and ethical values interact and cannot be totally isolated from each other.'[47] Secondly, Barbour also argues that one cannot separate science from technology. He proposes a contextual understanding, in which science, technology and society interact,[48] and in which there is a 'diversity of science-technology interactions.'[49] Such an understanding will question any sharp line between 'fundamental' and 'applied' science. Thirdly, one cannot separate theology from ethics, either, and I assume Barbour is aware of this. In *Science and Secularity* he writes, 'the absence of an adequate theology of nature is one of the roots of our ecological crisis.'[50] In *Religion and Science* he asks: 'Can religious traditions contribute to a new environmental ethic?'[51] In addition, even though his later typology might not have been developed for that, it does have roots in a similar typology for an ethical context, which Barbour uses in *Christianity and the Scientist*. Finally, there is already a considerable dialogue going on between science and religion about ethical issues, these days especially with regard to biotechnology and environmental ethics.

In sum, Barbour unnecessarily restricts Dialogue to a narrow sense, leaving out important possibilities for a fruitful interaction between science and theology.

Integration?

For Barbour, integration is a very typical word. In 1952 he had already called for an 'integration of knowledge.'[52] Although Barbour rightly emphasizes that metaphysical categories are needed to relate science and religion, his concept of Integration nevertheless poses several questions. To begin with, Barbour's definition is rather vague, for Integration describes those authors who 'hold that some sort of integration is possible between the content of theology and the content of science'. They focus on relations between doctrines in theology and theories in science which they see as much more direct than do supporters of Dialogue.[53] This broad definition gives rise to ambiguity, and Barbour himself is not always consistent in his use of the categories Dialogue and Integration.[54] Apart from this, the three positions, which Barbour subsumes under Integration (Natural Theology, Theology of Nature, and Systematic Synthesis) raise several questions, too.

Natural theology as integration? One particularly wonders about Barbour's first sub-category, natural theology. Barbour states, 'here arguments for the existence of God are based entirely on human reason rather than on historical revelation or religious experience.'[55] Later he criticizes this position, arguing that this 'would not lead to the personal, active God of the Bible ... but only to an intelligent designer.'[56] However, this critique does not hold for natural theology in general, it only implies that natural theology should not and cannot *replace* revealed theology. According to many medieval scholars, for example, revealed theology was not competing with natural theology, but, as it were, completing it. *Fides quaerens intellectum* – faith seeking understanding was the agenda. In an earlier article Barbour himself wrote that 'Catholic thought has had a long tradition of natural theology, but always as a preamble to revealed theology rather than as a self-sufficient basis for religious beliefs.'[57] *Insofar* that natural theology is seen only as a 'preamble to revealed theology,' one cannot criticize that it is only leading to an intelligent designer. Neither should one suggest natural theology as a way of *integrating* science and theology because it only includes one aspect of theological reasoning. Of course Barbour is right that an intelligent designer would not be a satisfying concept of God but his critique of natural theology barely applies to this position as such. Rather, it reveals the problems of subsuming natural theology under *Integration*, that is, it reveals the problems of Barbour's own categorization![58]

Theology of nature and systematic synthesis?   Barbour's second and third sub-categories (Theology of Nature and Systematic Synthesis) are those positions, which Barbour also proposes as his own view. He is 'in basic agreement with the "Theology of Nature" position, coupled with a cautious use of process philosophy.'[59] Theology of Nature starts with 'religious experience and historical revelation' and then reformulates traditional doctrines in the light of scientific insights.[60] I submit this is an appropriate concept for religious faith in an age of science, for the credibility of Christian faith is bound to the condition of the possibility of integrating the scientific account of the world into the Christian understanding of the world as God's creation.[61] However, I'm not so sure whether this should be called 'integration' of science and theology. 'Integration' runs the risk of neglecting the special features of each discipline. As I see it, in Barbour's kind of integration the theological contribution is indeed sometimes underrepresented. For instance, when Barbour speaks of 'God as the leader of a cosmic community,'[62] he neglects the difference between God and world, between Creator and creation as it has been seen by a long theological tradition. Again, Barbour views Christ as 'representing a new stage in evolution,' and he sees 'a basic continuity of creation and redemption.'[63] Yet Barbour does not say anything about any *dis*continuity between creation and redemption. Such *dis*continuity, however, has been central in Christian theology ever since Paul's letter to the Romans (see chapter 8, in particular), and certainly since Paul of Samosata in the third century and Arius in the fourth. I would not go as far as Thomas Settle who says that 'Barbour offers criticisms of the theology of process "from the standpoint of theology" without at any time making it clear that the views of Whitehead and Hartshorne on the one hand, and traditional theology, on the other, are logically incompatible.'[64] But I do think that Barbour's integration of science and theology might sometimes be too ambitious, at theology's cost.[65]

Outline for an Alternative Structuring of the Relationship of Science and Theology

It is always easier to criticize someone else than to propose an alternative, and I cannot present anything nearly as elaborate as Barbour's typology. However, I will outline an alternative way of categorizing the relation between science and theology, which, in my view, avoids some of the problems we noted above.

The Importance of Epistemology

We could see that both positions subsumed under Conflict advocate a foundationalist epistemology. It is this epistemological foundationalism, which is the common denominator between scientific materialists and biblical literalists, more than any 'conflict between science and religion' because those positions have different concepts of science and religion. Similarly, Barbour's critique of the notion of complementarity as well as his critique of the Independence position was also motivated by an epistemological position, namely epistemological realism. As Barbour says, 'we cannot remain content with a plurality of languages if they are languages about the same world.'[66] Barbour does not say, however, that this implies that instrumentalists need not go along with him in progressing from Independence to Dialogue, they can indeed be content with unrelated languages and thus see independence as an appropriate relation. The movement Barbour's typology suggests does therefore already presuppose a certain epistemological position. Obviously, the question of which epistemology one holds is more fundamental than any of the relational categories of conflict, independence, or else.

Different Dimensions in the Relation of Science and Theology

Because of the importance of epistemology for determining the relationship of science and theology, I suggest as a first category 'epistemology' instead of 'conflict,' and I will call this one 'dimension' of the dialogue of science and theology. As a second dimension of the relationship between science and theology I suggest metaphysics, as a third dimension ethics. These three dimensions derive from three key questions about ultimate reality: How do we understand the process of knowing? How do we understand the nature of reality and the nature of humans? How do we understand humanity's' role and obligations in this world?[67]

In my view, structuring diverse ways of relating science and theology according to these three dimensions provides more fundamental and better-defined categories than the ones Barbour uses.

First dimension: epistemology If one starts discussing the relation of science and theology with respect to the epistemological dimension, a first distinction for structuring the field could be between realist and non-realist positions. Since most non-realists would reject discussions of metaphysical questions as meaningless speculation, it will not be necessary any more to discuss metaphysical issues with them, that is, the discussion of metaphysics can focus on different realist positions.

However, this does not preclude that non-realists (for example, constructivists) investigate the process of acquiring knowledge and so on in both science and theology. A constructivist might well be interested in a dialogue between science and theology in order to learn about familiarities and differences between those two endeavours, which both claim to be rational.

In the remaining group of realist positions one can then continue the discussion in greater detail. A next distinction could then be between foundationalist and nonfoundationalist epistemologies. Both scientific materialists and biblical literalists should realize and acknowledge the results the philosophy of science has produced in the second half of the twentieth century. There is no indubitable basis for our knowledge, neither in science nor in theology. Therefore, foundationalism is not an option, neither in science nor in theology.

Second dimension: metaphysics   The second category I suggest for structuring the relationship between science and theology is metaphysics. Since the non-realist positions need not be discussed here any more, the field will be easier to survey. Among others, fundamental metaphysical alternatives would be substance ontology versus relational ontology. In both cases consonance with the scientific account as well as with theological convictions were to be sought. Since our current view of nature seems to suggest relational categories, it would be a special challenge for a substance ontology to give a convincing account of the process character of nature. A relational ontology, in turn, would have to express theological convictions, such as the Trinitarian dogma (that is, God as three persons but one substance), which have traditionally been formulated in terms of substances, in relational terms.

Another metaphysical distinction could be made regarding different concepts for the relationship of God and the world. Theism, pantheism, and panentheism will be three important approaches. Here the specific task would be to portray the relation between God and the world in a way that accounts for God's independence from the world, creation's (relative) autonomy, as well as their mutual interaction in general and God's action in the world in particular.

Third dimension: ethics   As a third and final category I suggest ethics. This category is different from the former insofar as no epistemological or metaphysical position is precluded from ethical reflection. Regardless of their differing epistemological or metaphysical convictions, scholars can engage in a dialogue over ethical issues. Instrumentalists as well as realists, naturalists and materialists as well as believers can contribute to the ethical discourse at the interface of science and theology.[68] Among others, one could distinguish here between deontological and teleological concepts. Is the ultimate criterion of what is morally right or wrong the non-moral value that is brought into being by an action (for example, happiness, well-being, and so on), or is the criterion rather the fulfilment of one or more rules or duties? Modern biotechnology especially raises difficult ethical problems at the interface of science and theology. The (in-)adequacy of utilitarianism as the most important teleological concept and the need for deontological concepts are hotly debated.

Of course the ethical discourse will also refer to epistemological and metaphysical issues. How do we, for instance, understand the nature of human beings; how do we understand the beginning and the end of human life?

Dimensions Instead of Relational Categories

The strategy of categorizing the relationship of science and theology I have suggested starts with structuring that relationship according to the three different dimensions of epistemology, metaphysics, and ethics, followed by a closer look at their interface in each of these dimensions. Compared to the relational categories Barbour (as well as many others) uses – conflict, dialogue, consonance, and so on – these more systematic categories have the additional advantage that they are more observer-independent than relational categories: as the case of creation scientists demonstrated, whether or not one sees a conflict depends on one's own standpoint. The question which epistemological, metaphysical or ethical viewpoint one holds, however, can be answered more neutrally. In addition, the proposal made here can distinguish different views of the relationship of science and theology for different dimensions – even within the same person. This allows a more accurate assessment of different positions (which is, of course, more complicated, too). For example, someone could advocate an existentialist approach regarding the epistemological dimension – which would imply Barbour's *Independence* position – while seeing nevertheless the need for *integrating* the scientific account of the world into one's own Christian worldview and metaphysics. Again, an (epistemological) instrumentalist could argue for a *dialogue* of science and theology for ethical reasons, despite the fact that he would reject any realist claims and would therefore fall under Barbour's *Independence* category. An instrumentalist could argue that, although scientific and theological concepts are nothing but useful fictions, it would still be useful for them to engage in a dialogue in order to meet the ethical challenges of the day.

Barbour's Position as a Test Case for the Three Dimensions

That there may be different views of the relation of science and theology within the same subject makes it even more difficult to give an overview of the positions of many scholars in the field than is the case with Barbour's typology. Only by a detailed analysis will it be possible to subsume individual authors under the suggested categories, simply because this requires exploring their approaches in three different respects or dimensions. In closing, I will, however, at least try to put Barbour's own position into this new frame as a test case. In doing so, I will also make use of relational categories, but only in a second step – after determining Barbour's position with regard to the three dimensions mentioned above.

Barbour advocates some kinship of science and theology in epistemological respects. Both science and theology make 'truth claims about reality,' in both cases there is an interaction between experience and interpretation, both have an empirical component, both are open to rational argumentation. Although science is more objective and more rational, and so on, these characteristics are not totally absent in religion. There is kinship and familiarity, but also differences in degree. One could perhaps say that, according to Barbour, science and theology are, as it were, cousins in epistemological respects.

In metaphysical respects, it is Barbour's agenda to elaborate an integrated worldview, to which both science and theology contribute. Barbour uses Whitehead's process thought and his relational ontology for expressing theological doctrines. Conflicts are excluded, since theological concepts have to be reformulated in the light of scientific insights. On the other hand, Barbour says that religion asks totally different questions, is concerned about questions of meaning, about ultimate reality. In other words, religious faith raises questions going beyond science. One could therefore suggest that science and theology contribute complementary aspects to an integrated view of reality. They contribute quite different, but ultimately coherent aspects to an inclusive description of reality. If one does not restrict integration to the narrow sense in which Barbour uses it, one could say that, in metaphysical respects, Barbour's own approach is aiming at integrating scientific and theological concepts into a coherent view of reality.

Finally, in ethical respects, Barbour's position could be considered as calling for a dialogue, allowing a broader concept of dialogue than Barbour's own. The ethical problems of today transgress the borders of our academic disciplines, and they are too complex to be solved by ethicists or scientists alone. Barbour has repeatedly argued for an interdisciplinary ethical discourse on technology. Therefore, only in true dialogue, in which both sides learn from one another, theologians and ethicists on the one side, scientists and engineers on the other, will we be able to meet the ethical challenges of today.

In sum, in terms of the categories suggested here, Barbour's view of science and theology could be summarized as the following. With regard to epistemology, there is some kinship between science and theology; with regard to metaphysics, both contribute complementary aspects to an integrated description of reality; with regard to ethics, they should engage in a true dialogue.

Notes

1. I want to thank both Bob Russell and Adrian Lane for reading earlier versions of this paper and for their helpful comments.
2. Barbour is not always consistent in his usage of the terms theology and religion and often he uses them synonymically. He published this typology, for instance, both as 'Ways of relating science and *theology*' and 'Ways of relating science and *religion*' (see note 33 for a complete list of publications of this typology). Since we cannot discuss the distinction between the science–religion and the science–theology dialogues here we have to adopt Barbour's usage. For a critique of Barbour's usage, however, see Christian Berg, *Theologie im technologischen Zeitalter. Das Werk Ian Barbours als Beitrag zu Verhältnisbestimmung von Theologie zu Naturwissenschaft und Technik* (Stuttgart: Kohlhammer, 2002).
3. Since I assume that most readers will be familiar with Barbour's typology, I will only briefly mention the categories and sub-categories here. Barbour's Conflict category (1) includes 'Biblical Literalism' and 'Scientific Materialism'; his Independence category (2) includes 'Contrasting Methods' (including existentialism and neo-orthodoxy) and 'Differing Languages' (i.e. analytic traditions); Dialogue (3) contains 'Presuppositions and Limit Questions' and 'Methodological Parallels' (and in *Religion and Science. Historical and Contemporary Issues,* a Revised and

Expanded Edition of *Religion in an Age of Science* (San Francisco CA: HarperSan Francisco, 1997), also 'Nature Centered Spirituality'); Integration (4) consists of the three sub-categories 'Natural Theology', 'Theology of Nature', and 'Systematic Synthesis' (which is indebted to Whitehead's process theology).

4. Barbour, 'The Faculty Christian Fellowship', *Christian Century*, 70 (March 25, 1953), 348.
5. Ibid., 348f.
6. Barbour, 'Karl Heim on Christian Faith and Natural Science', *The Christian Scholar*, 39 (1956), 231.
7. Ibid. In the following years Barbour gets increasingly explicit in his criticism of positivism; cf. Barbour's 'The Methods of Science and Religion', in *Science Ponders Religion*, ed. by Harlow Shapley (New York: Appleton-Century-Crofts, Inc. 1960), 213.
8. Ibid., 211.
9. Barbour, *Christianity and the Scientist* (New York: Association Press, 1960), 113f.
10. Idem, 'The Methods of Science and Religion'.
11. Cf. *Myths, Models, and Paradigms. A Comparative Study in Science and Religion*, 2nd edn (New York: Harper, 1976), 129ff.
12. Barbour, *When Science Meets Religion* (San Francisco: HarperSanFrancisco, 2000), 25; cf. also *Religion and Science*, ch. 5, esp. 110.
13. Idem, 'On the Contribution of Physics to Theology', *Religious Education*, 52 (1957), 335.
14. Idem, *Christianity and the Scientist*, 12. This book might therefore be seen as an answer to a question Barbour himself posed earlier: 'What is the Christian vocation of a professor?' (Barbour, 'The Faculty Christian Fellowship', 348).
15. Idem, 'The Methods of Science and Religion', 215.
16. Ibid., 206.
17. Barbour, 'On the Contribution of Physics to Theology', 334 (Barbour's emphasis).
18. 'Are There Religious Perspectives in the Physical Sciences?' *Religion in Life*, 26 (1957), 523f.
19. Ibid.
20. Barbour determines the relationship between science and religion in the same way at several other occasions during this period. See, for instance, Barbour, 'Are There Religious Perspectives in the Physical Sciences?', 524; 'On the Contribution of Physics to Theology', 336; 'The Methods of Science and Religion', 214f.; and *Christianity and the Scientist*, 115f.
21. Barbour, *Christianity and the Scientist*, 86.
22. While the first two categories, for instance, religion 'against' and 'under' science, will in one way or another lead to a *Conflict* between science and religion, 'religion separate from science' is reflected by what will later be the *Independence* position.
23. Barbour, *Issues in Science and Religion*, 3rd edn (New York: Harper, 1972), 4.
24. Ibid., 247.
25. Ibid., 454.
26. Barbour, *Myths, Models, and Paradigms*, 76.
27. Ibid., 77.
28. George Brown Barbour, *In the Field with Teilhard* (New York: Herder, 1965).
29. Barbour, 'Five Ways of Reading Teilhard', *The Teilhard Review*, 3 (1968), 18. See also 'The Significance of Teilhard. His greatest contribution was his concern for the synthesis of evolutionary and Christian thought', *Christian Century*, 84 (30 August 1967), 1101.
30. Barbour, 'Five Ways of Reading Teilhard,' 18.
31. The two editions of the first Gifford Lecture, *Religion in an Age of Science* (1990) and *Religion and Science* (1998) are strongly indebted to *Issues in Science and Religion* (1966) and *Myths, Models, and Paradigms* (1973), while *Ethics in an Age of Technology* (1993) draws on *Technology, Environment, and Human Values* (1980), on *Earth Might Be Fair* (1972), and on *Science and Secularity* (1970).

32. In the 1960s he had presented two more typologies: in *Issues in Science and Religion* he suggested three categories of 'Science and Religion in the Twentieth Century' (115ff.), in *Science and Religion* (1968) he named the three categories: 1. The 'Conflicts' of the Past, 2. Three Ways of Isolating Science and Religion, 3. Some Areas of Recent Dialogue. This is already in outline what Barbour presents as his well-known fourfold typology some 20 years later.

33. This typology was published with no or only minimal revisions as I.G. Barbour, 'Ways of Relating Science and Theology', in *Physics, Philosophy, and Theology. A Common Quest for Understanding*, ed. by Robert J. Russell, William R. Stoeger and George V. Coyne (Vatican City State; Berkeley, CA: Vatican Observatory Publications; Center for Theology and the Natural Sciences, 1988), 21–48; as 'Surveying the Possibilities. Ways of Relating Science and Religion' in *Religion and the Natural Sciences*, ed. by James E. Huchingson (Orlando, 1993), 6–34; as 'Ways of Relating Science and Religion' in the first chapter of his first Gifford Lecture, pp. 3–30 (similarly in the revised version of that book, pp. 77–105). In only slightly different form he published the same article as 'Consultation Summation' in *The Church and Contemporary Cosmology*, ed. by James Miller (Pittsburgh, 1990) and in the earliest form of that late typology as 'The Relationship between Science and Religion' in *Religion, Science, and the Search for Wisdom. Proceedings of a Conference on Religion and Science*, ed. by David M. Byers (Washington, DC, 1987), 166–91. In different format but with similar content this typology can also be found in his book *When Science Meets Religion* (2000).

34. Barbour, 'On typologies for relating science and religion', *Zygon*, 37 (2002), 345–59.

35. In this respect I agree with Cantor and Kenny, who say, 'the conflict thesis has set Barbour's agenda for categorizing the ways in which science and religion interrelate' (Geoffrey Cantor/Chris Kenny, 'Barbour's fourfold way: problems with his taxonomy of science-religion relationships', *Zygon*, 36 [2001], 768).

36. Barbour, *Religion and Science*, 105.

37. Ibid., 90.

38. Ted Peters, 'Theology and Natural Science', in *The Modern Theologians*, ed. by David F. Ford, 2nd edn (Cambridge, MA)/ Oxford, UK: Blackwell, 1997), 665.

39. Barbour, *Religion and Science*, 78.

40. In Wentzel van Huyssteen's words foundationalism is 'the thesis that all our beliefs can be justified by appealing to some item of knowledge that is self-evident or indubitable' (Wentzel van Huyssteen, *Essays in Postfoundationalist Theology* [Grand Rapids, MI/ Cambridge, UK: Eerdmans, 1997], 2).

41. Besides, one could argue that not only is science independent from theology but that Christian faith, and thus theology is also independent from science in the first place, insofar neither the ground nor the subject matter of faith depend upon science. Rather, they depend upon God's revelation in Christ (cf. Eilert Herms, 'Die Lehre im Leben der Kirche', in *Zeitschrift für Theologie und Kirche*, 82: 2 (1990). However, since today's understanding of God's revelation in Christ reflects the categories and concepts of a scientific age, it will inevitably include those categories and concepts. I submit that only and precisely in this indirect way theology depends upon science.

42. Barbour, *Religion and Science*, 90.

43. Ibid., 95.

44. Of the several times he published his typology, only in the revised version of the Gifford Lecture, *Religion and Science*, does he add a third subcategory, Nature-centered Spirituality, which is at least related to environmental ethics. However, this is neither systematically developed in the book nor does Barbour refer to this category subsequently (he omits it again, for instance, in his later book *When Science Meets Religion*). Therefore, the overall impression is that his typology lacks the ethical dimension.

45. Peters, 'Theology and Natural Science', 653.

46. Barbour, 'On Typologies for relating science and religion', 352.

47. Idem, *Ethics in an Age of Technology*, 28.

48. Ibid., 20.

49. Ibid., 21.
50. Barbour, *Science and Secularity. The Ethics of Technology* (New York: Harper & Row, 1970), 5.
51. Idem, *Religion and Science*, xv.
52. Idem, 'Integration as an Objective in the Physical Sciences', *American Journal of Physics*, 20 (1952), 568.
53. Idem, *Religion and Science*, 98.
54. For instance, discussing cosmological questions that 'constitute topics of *Dialogue* between scientists and theologians' he first mentions the Anthropic Principle (Ibid., 204). In closing that section Barbour then writes that he finds this principle 'quite consistent with a *theology of nature* (an alternative form of the *Integration* model)' (Ibid., 205). Elsewhere Barbour concedes that 'there is no clear line between Dialogue and Integration' (*When Science Meets Religion*, 170; cf. also 'On Typologies for Relating Science and Religion' in *Zygon*, 37 [2002], 352).
55. *Religion in an Age of Science*, 24.
56. Ibid., 26.
57. 'Science and Religion Today', in *Science and Religion. New Perspectives on the Dialogue*, ed. by Ian Barbour (London: SCM Press, 1968), 8.
58. Why did Barbour, then, put natural theology here? By discussing this view first, which would be based 'entirely on human reason rather than on historical revelation or religious experience,' he can then in a second step move on dialectically to 'the opposite', namely theology of nature, which starts from 'historical revelation and religious experience' (*Religion in an Age of Science*, 26). The third step, the synthesis of the former, would then be his 'Systematic Synthesis,' a 'more systematic integration can occur if both science and religion contribute to a coherent world view elaborated in a comprehensive metaphysics' (ibid., 28).
59. Barbour, *Religion and Science*, 105.
60. Ibid., 100.
61. This is paraphrasing Wolfhart Pannenberg; cf. his second volume of *Systematische Theologie* (Göttingen: Vandenhoeck & Ruprecht, 1991), 78.
62. Barbour, *Religion and Science*, 322.
63. Ibid., 247f.
64. Thomas W. Settle, 'A Prolegommenon to Intellectually Honest Theology', *Philosophical Forum*, vol. 1, (1968), 136–70, 141.
65. For further details on Barbour's Integration position, see C. Berg, *Theologie im technologischen Zeitalter*, particularly ch. 4; cf. also C. Berg, 'Dimensions of order. Some comments on Barbour's way of relating science and religion and his doctrine of creation' in *Studies in Science and Theology* 8, ed. by Niels H. Gregersen, Ulf Görman, and Hubert Meisinger (Denmark: University of Aarhus, 2002), 263–76.
66. Barbour, *Religion and Science*, 89.
67. The concept of dimensions has already been used for categorizing the relationship of science and theology, but in slightly different ways. For instance, taking up a suggestion made by Arthur Peacocke, Robert J. Russell views the relation of science and theology as a 'four-dimensional space,' each dimension of which stands for one of the categories approaches, languages, attitudes, and objects (Robert J. Russell, 'A critical appraisal of Peacocke's thought on religion and science', *Religion and Intellectual Life*, 2 [1985], 50). Peacocke replies to this view in his *Theology for a Scientific Age*, Enlarged edition, (London: SCM Press, 1993), 20–21.
68. In my view, 'theology' must always include theological ethics as well.

Chapter 4

Critical Realism and Other Realisms

Niels Henrik Gregersen

The Current Status of Critical Realism (CR)

Since the mid-1960s, critical realism (CR) has been a majority position in the Anglo-American science–religion dialogue. Introduced by Ian Barbour and further developed by Arthur Peacocke and John Polkinghorne,[1] CR has for decades been the 'orthodox' position in the field of science and religion.

Its basic ideas are as follows. First we have the realist thesis: scientists presuppose that the world existed well before we – its human interpreters – came into being. Similarly ordinary believers think that God's Being is prior to themselves and independent of human recognition. Therefore it is natural to regard both science and religion as making cognitive claims about reality. Committed to 'realism' scientists and believers are co-discoverers of the world, albeit investigating reality from different angles.

Second, the 'critical' guards the realist from being a 'naive' representationalist who believes that our ideas simply mirror reality. Science and theology are activities, which take place within epistemic communities shaped by metaphors, models, and paradigms. As such, theories in science and theology have to be taken 'seriously but not literally'. CR can thus present itself as the balanced view between a naive realism and a purely constructionist view of knowledge. CR only articulates the working assumptions of a majority of practicing scientists and believers. For just as scientists believe that atoms are real, though beyond picturability, so religious people believe that God is real, even though 'nobody has ever seen God' (1 John 4:16).[2] Moreover, theories about atoms and God can be challenged by data and experiences, and are thus open to revision and improvement; in this sense both science and theology can be said to 'approximate reality'.

CR is thus a suggestive position, which furthermore offers theology a sort of epistemic parity with science. More recently, however, the idea of critical realism has been criticized within science–religion scholarship. Already in 1985 the philosopher of science Ernan McMullin argued that the idea of 'approximating reality' in a cumulative sense rightly applies only to some of the mature sciences (for example, physics, chemistry, and geology). Scientific realism (SCR) cannot be justified as a global theory of science, nor can a corresponding argument be made for theology. McMullin accepts the parallel that the objects of science and religion lie beyond the range of literal descriptions, but he warns that 'it would be unwise to push the parallels any further, or suggest that what enables the realism of science to be self-critical and progressive may somehow be transferred to the domain of religious belief'.[3] Willem B. Drees and Kees van Kooten Niekerk have followed McMullin's line by embracing elements of SCR, while being skeptic about CR in theology. Drees finds that CR misinterprets lived religion which is more a way of life than a theory about the way things are.[4] Niekerk takes a more positive stance towards CR but he argues that the cognitive claims of CR can only be validated within the framework of a religious community: 'a critical realist view of theology, or rather of particular theological propositions about God, is only a viable option within the context of faith.'[5] Thus, also committed realists notice the difficulties in holding to CR as an overarching theory for the science–religion dialogue.

Others have offered a more principled critique of CR. Nancey Murphy argues that CR remains committed to modernity's referential view of language, which in postmodern epistemology has been replaced by theory networks; the real issue is explanatory progress, not reality as it is in itself.[6] Wentzel van Huyssteen originally defended CR: theological models are 'reality depicting' and even testable by comparing the explanatory power of theological theories.[7] In his later work, however, van Huyssteen has changed his focus from discussing the explanatory status of *theories* in science and religion to the *epistemic values* of rational persons who may share both religious and scientific convictions: 'On a postfoundationalist view no generic, universal claims for realism (or even critical realism) can be made for the domains of our intellectual inquiry in general.' Even though van Huyssteen still defends the possibility of a modest realism, he redefines realism in a pragmatic way: 'realism here is a practical postulate justified by its utility.'[8] If one follows this line of thought to its very end, however, realist claims do not appear to be very stable. Wesley Robbins has thus commended a turn to pragmaticism as the gateway to a full-blown parity between science and religion. Robbins finds that CR presupposes a Cartesian dualism between knower and known, and is bound to negotiate the borderlines between subjectivity and objectivity in indeterminate ways. For cognitive claims always emerge out of the dynamic interactions between our diverse cognitive systems and a world which cannot be investigated under abstraction from our cognitive schemes.[9]

As for my own position of a 'contextual coherence theory', I see cognitive claims as built into the tasks of science as well as those of theology. However, making claims about realness is not the same as redeeming one's cognitive claims; the hard work lies in the justification of the claims of realism, and this justification can only be made in the horizontal game of coherence between different theoretical truth-candidates. Accordingly, the role of theology is not primarily to 'explain' the data in competition with the sciences, but to redescribe a world already described and (partially) explained by the sciences. The construction of theology in analogy to an empirical research program is only viable to a very limited degree.[10] In what follows I hope to specify my position a bit further with respect to CR. As will appear, my own coherentist position is realist concerning *metaphysical realism* (MR) and *semantic realism* (SR), but more skeptic about the idea of a *theoretical-explanatory realism* (TER).

Tenets of a Scientific Realism (SCR)

Let me first clarify the distinction between MR, SR, and TER. In his robust defense of scientific realism (SCR), philosopher Stathis Psillos argues that SCR incorporates the following three forms of realism:

1   The metaphysical stance [MR] asserts that the world has a definite and mind-independent natural-kind structure.
2   The semantic stance [SR] takes scientific theories at face-value, seeing them as truth-conditioned descriptions of their intended domain, both observable and unobservable. Hence they are capable of being true or false … The theoretical terms featuring in theories have putative factual reference. So, if scientific theories are true, the unobservable entities they posit populate the world.
3   The epistemic stance [TER] regards mature and predictive successful scientific theories as well-confirmed and approximately true of the world. So, the entities posited by them, or, at any rate, entities very similar to those posited, do inhabit the world.[11]

Psillos's definition provides a helpful overview of the different stances or tenets of SCR, and anyone familiar with the idea of CR will immediately recognize the structural similarities between SCR and CR. However, a careful distinction should be made. For whereas the former designates a specific movement in the philosophy of science since the 1960s, the latter holds to the tenets of MR, SR, and TER at the highest level of generality and applies them to rather diverse forms of knowledge.

SCR, for example, makes a specific appeal to scientific experiments. Its standard argument has been pointedly phrased by the early Hilary Putnam in his saying that the explanatory success of the sciences would seem to be nothing but a miracle if the theories of science are not at least 'partially true accounts' of the way in which the world actually behaves.[12] However, the claim of SCR goes far beyond the accumulation of empirical knowledge. Richard N. Boyd and others made an explanationist version (TER) of the No Miracle Argument. This position can be defined as follows:

Theoretical-Explanatory Realism
TER takes the stance that unless the theoretical entities employed by scientific theories really existed, the evident success of science (in terms of empirical predictions and technical applications) cannot be explained.

In addition to the postulates of realism, reference, and empirical success, Boyd also made a *progress postulate* by saying that '[t]he historical progress of the mature sciences is largely a matter of successively more accurate approximations to the truth about both observable and unobservable phenomena. Later theories typically build upon the (observational and theoretical) knowledge embodied in previous theories.'[13]

Thus the progress postulate involves a historical thesis about the *continuity between scientific theories*: later theories (such as quantum theory) are able to incorporate earlier theories (such as classical mechanics) via translation rules, some of which are mathematical, while others merely hermeneutical (as when we interpret Mendel's theory of heredity as adumbrating the later gene theory).

As is well known, this idea of *convergent realism* has been severely challenged by historians of science such as Paul Feuerabend, Larry Laudan, and the later Putnam. Space does not allow me to discuss this debate here,[14] but suffice it to say that *not even the strongest proponents of SCR raise the claims of TER as a global theory about science*. The claims of TER can only be made piecemeal, on a case-by-case basis, expressed by the repeated qualifier that SCR only applies to 'mature and predictive successful sciences.' In these cases TER can be justified. But the claim should not be extended to the natural sciences in general. How, for example, can we justify the claim that 'the nature of time' has been progressively unveiled via cosmology, thermodynamics, evolutionary theory, and neuroscience? Certainly, we know today a lot more now than before about basic physical processes (some of which point to an arrow of time), but scientific theories do not seem to converge on a common referent – 'time.'[15] Or put differently, if we were serious realists about scientific theories of time, we would soon overpopulate the world with a variety of 'time realities,' some of which would be in conflict with one another. 'Science,' after all, is a shorthand for a patchwork of theories which do not always synthesize.

Such examples of cognitive pluralism are of course much more prevalent within the social and human sciences. Accordingly, claims of progress and convergence are here harder to substantiate. Can we justify the claim that we have unveiled more and more the true nature of World War II? Certainly, history knows much more today than earlier, but probably also less. Or can we justify the view that the history of theology evermore unveils the true nature of God? Probably in some respects, say in the general thrust towards universalism in religious thought. But it might be true as well that theology has also lost quite significant insights from the past, say from Meister Eckhart, in the process of refining theology's methodology.

Please note that my point is not that there have not been *elements* of progress in the scientific understanding of time, of World War II, or of God theology. However, I am increasingly skeptic about a TER which makes the generalized claim that our theories – *grosso modo* – unveil one and the same reality progressively. First, we have not justified our truth-claims by claiming to have approximated reality; one often observes a certain tautology in claiming in a realist meta-theory what we already take for granted in our first-order theorizing.

Secondly, 'prediction' is hardly the best clue to measure or even understand the rationality of theology. Rather, I believe that the rationality of theology lies in its capacity to *redescribe and re-order* relevant data of the world (while acknowledging that data remain open to different descriptions and ways of ordering). A theology of creation which is able to give meaning to the fact of evolution and to take account of biological explanations of evolution in a precise and consistent way is certainly better off than a theology of creation which is not able to do so. Reaching a rich internal coherence coupled with contextual sensitivity seems the best available guide for choosing between truth-candidates.

Thus, my own contextual coherence theory of the science–religion dialogue endorses MR and SR but is critical of the overemphasis on TER in theology. Even if we all hope to be steadily attuned to the reality of God in our theological ventures, we are not in a position to justify this claim. The only way towards progress is to make clear how our choices between different theological truth candidates are guided by rational criteria such as *comprehensiveness* with respect to relevant data, *intelligibility* in terms of ordering capacity, *sensitivity* to the relevant contexts (here science), and *authenticity* with respect to representing the core assumptions of the interpreted religious tradition. Thus in what follows I hope to show that coherentism is able to preserve the ontological commitments of CR while locating the rational justification of theological theories in their ability to specify their relation to everything else that we believe is true within a network of beliefs which comprises both theological and scientific reality assumptions.

Rescuing Metaphysical Realism (MR) and Semantic Realism (SR)

Metaphysical realism is the simple view that things and relations exist objectively, and are what they are like, independent of our knowledge about them. Most ordinary people are realists in this sense. My sight of the stars of the heavens depends on their existence and the light they send out, but their existence and characteristics – the way they are chemically composed and physically interact with one another – are independent of the spark of satisfaction or gloom that I feel by looking at them. We here arrive at the following definition:

Metaphysical Realism
MR takes the stance that the world consists of a variety of mind-independent entities and/or objective relations.

The world is thus a given, not a pure, creation of our mental operations or cultural constructions. Some pragmaticists have rightly pointed out that MR is a presupposition that we *make* in the practice of our knowledge. The paradox of metaphysical realism, in other words, is that it is a *taken* position, not a given position, but with regard to a reality that we understand to be *given*, not taken.[16] However, this only gives the impression of a contradiction, for the position of MR includes the fact that our cognitive processes are part of reality as well. For also our imaginations, beliefs, and cognitive schemes grow out of the interaction with a world that is experienced as prior to us.[17]

It seems natural for believers to understand the reality of God and religious awareness in a similar way.[18] God exists and has some objective characteristics whether or not I acknowledge and honor the reality of God. For sure, God does not exist in the sense that empirical mail-boxes or human qualities like love and hate do. But granting this, and understanding God with Paul Tillich to be 'the power to be in and above everything that exists', does not imply an anti-realist stance toward God. This would only be the case if we deprive God of any ontological functions as creator, and see God merely as a symbol of our way of seeing and taking up the world. However, the point that God – as genuinely infinity – in a sense includes the reality of the world. Or to be more precise: the God-world relation is certainly objective, even though our language about God is symbolic as soon as it transcends the objective relation between Being-Itself and the derived beings: the creatures.[19]

Now, for things to be real, they don't need to be fully independent of us.[20] My old Volvo is fabricated somewhere in Sweden and is by no means unaffected by the

320,000 kilometers of use; anyway, the entity called 'Volvo' in my garage is still a mind-independent entity. Also in this 'mixed' case there may be analogies to the reality of God. Even if we believe that God is actually affected by human misery and prayers, God is still taken to be real in a mind-independent sense. God must *be* in a certain way, in order to be receptive to the world that is created and upheld by God. This reality claim is reflected in the classic distinction between the essential characteristics of God (such as God's ontological aseity), and attributes which are related to the world (God as creator, providence, redeemer, and so on).

So far MR is a natural ontological attitude at work in everyday life as well as in religion. However, not all things that we normally count as real can be said to be mind-independent realities in the two meanings indicated above. A global version of MR is not tenable, and my definition of MR is therefore confined to 'a variety' of entities and relations, rather than to all things *tout court*. For example, the little green flat piece of paper in my pocket certainly exists as much as the stars do, but to say that I have 'really' $100 in my pocket is to adopt a social stance towards it. This stance is evidently not mind-independent. It's only within the perspective of a monetary system that the little green flat thing is a $100 note. A currency is a social fact which supervenes on physical things (coins or paper) which in themselves are mind-independent entities, even if they are fabricated by human hands. Similarly a joke is not mind-independent, even though it supervenes on a physically embodied story. It would hardly be appropriate to say that a story is 'really' funny, if no one ever laughed.

Even in this stronger case of mind-dependence, there are analogies to religion. For instance, it seems meaningless to say, 'This is really a gospel', if the message brings no good news to anybody. The gospel is only a gospel by eliciting faith, and by being received in trust. Similarly, a 'revelation' cannot be a mind-independent thing, since a revelation, by definition, is revealing something to *somebody* in a given situation.[21] Revelations don't *exist* as entities; revelations *occur*; and when they occur, they are real ('objective-relational') events.

These examples show us two things. First, MR is not a game of all or nothing. One can be a realist in one sense concerning stars, Volvos, and God, without being a realist in quite the same sense concerning dollars, jokes, and revelations. Second, one can be a realist concerning entities as well as about relations, concerning natural-kind entities (such as H_2O) and relations (such as fluid or frozen water). As we shall see below, an MR concerning structures and relations is pivotal to the theological project of Ian Barbour.

There is, however, yet another indeterminacy concerning MR. For saying 'that' something exists is not the same thing as saying 'what' it is that exists. Thus I can be an unqualified metaphysical realist concerning the 'thing called Volvo' in my garage, without saying very much *specific* about 'that thing called Volvo': 'it is a majestic car,' 'a useful vehicle,' 'a write-off,' and so on. Thus in order to specify the cognitive claims involved in metaphysical realism (MR) we have to assume a semantic realism (SR):

Semantic Realism

SR takes a cognitive stance to the world that involves assertions that say something specific about something (which is assumed to exist prior to our cognition).

Assertions that specify the nature of God seem to be basic to Christian faith. In the case of a theological realism, however, the semantic specification of what the idea of God *means* has implications for the unique being of God to which theology aims to *refer*. Since God, as defined by the Abrahamic faiths, is the creative source of all that exists, God cannot be imagined as an isolated entity 'out there'; God must be creatively present in, through, and above all that exists. 'Where God is not, nothing is,' as expressed by Anselm of Canterbury (*Monologion* 14). By implication God is not only the source of being, but also the source of all knowledge about God; accordingly, all true knowledge about God happens through divine self-revelation. On this view, 'revelation' is not a provincial category that can be appended to a 'natural knowledge of God' derived from human rationality 'apart from God,' for no such epistemic stance is possible via-à-vis God. On a monotheistic ontology, no human reasoning is imaginable, to which God is not intimately present as the 'light of all people' (John 1:4). There is no true knowledge of God, which is not revealed by God, even where this knowledge is mediated through so-called ordinary human experiences. The logic involved in the very meaning of 'God' thus assumes that, even though God exists ontologically 'prior' to the world of creation and 'prior' to divine self-revelation, God does not exist as a spatial or temporal being separated from the creatures in space and time. Expressed in Trinitarian terms, God is the 'whence' of all that exists in space and time ('the Father'), God is the source of intelligibility of all cognitive beings (the 'Son' or Logos/Light), and God is the energy and future *telos* of all created beings ('the Spirit'). In this way, God's 'reality' is an all-inclusive infinity to whom we cannot take distance. But distance is exactly what we assume in the subject–object logic of our ordinary propositional thinking. Our 'subjective' knowing is here contrasted to the 'objects' out there. In the case of knowing God, however, this propositional logic implodes. *God, by definition, is not only the object, but also the subject of human thinking. At this point all analogies between common sense realism and theological realism break down.* This hiatus between the logic of finite beings, and the logic of God's infinity must be borne in mind whenever a critical realism is transported from science into theology.

   In twentieth-century theology this logic of infinity has been worked out in the wake of Hegel's concept of genuine infinity.[22] However, the logic of infinity goes way back into patristic theology. While the idea of a principled theological anti-realism is of relatively new date, the idea that God exceeds all positive characterizations informs the theology of the Greek Fathers. In his highly influential work, *On the Divine Names*, Pseudo-Dionysios makes the twofold point that God in the holy scriptures has indeed revealed Godself to human beings in and through divine names such as love, light, beauty, wisdom, peace. However, the fullness of divine being exceeds any positive characterization, and God is thus 'beyond intellect' (*huper noun*) and even 'beyond being' (*huperousía*). Positively speaking,

God is the Cause of all that is, and hence 'the being immanent in and underlying the things which are, however they are.' But God cannot be thought of as a being in analogy to other objective beings:

> God is not some kind of being. No. But in a way that is simple and undefinable he gathers into himself and anticipates every existence. So he is called 'King of the ages' [1 Tim. 1:17], for in him and around him all being is and subsists. He was not. He will not be. He did not come to be. He is not in the midst of becoming. He will not come to be. No. He is not. He is the essence of being for the things which have being.[23]

Pseudo-Dionysius is an interesting case by affirming a MR while questioning a straightforward SR. In the end, says Pseudo-Dionysius, one has to give up all preconceived notions of God in the pure praise of the heart to God. However, the patristic idea of negative theology is never dissociated from a positive theology based on God's self-revelation in the holy scripture and in the world of creation. Accordingly one can also hold to a theological realism which emphasizes SR while just presupposing a MR as a basic ontological assumption. One can interpret the theology of Karl Barth, and more recently of Michael Welker, as working on this line.[24] What a human person is, for example, can only be abstractly and provisionally described by, say, the neurosciences and human psychology. A fuller description of human personhood is only viable by including the human person's relationship to God, and by thinking of God's prior election of the human being as God's partner. Here a theological realism is devoted to a rich semantic description of reality, a description of reality which assumes that no part of reality is utterly godless. In order to be relevant to the science–religion dialogue, however, this program of a semantic theological realism must be able to interpret, in theological terms, the same world that is also referred to in scientific theories.

It is here that the idea of theology as a *redescription of a world already provisionally described and partially explained by the sciences* comes into play. Causal explanations cannot be removed from theology (we found it even in the negative theology of Pseudo-Dionysius). Theology can rightly be said to explain, for example, the prescientific fact that the world is rather than is not ('the world is because God created the world'). Theology may also be able to explain characteristic features of our scientifically described universe, such as the fact that the laws of nature are fine-tuned for life, or that evolution seems to produce evermore complex creatures ('God coordinated the laws of nature with the purpose of nurturing life and complexity'). What I want to argue, however, is that the *causal explanations* in which a theory of God serves as the *explanans*, do not have the status of empirically testable, predictive theories. In fact, much of theology's enterprise has the form of *post hoc* explanations of facts previously known, though perhaps not previously used for theological purposes. Theology doesn't usually make predictions, but neither are theological explanations simply *ad hoc* explanations, since they explain persistent features of the universe.[25] But I contend that most theological explanations are *semantic explanations*, which offer a coherent picture about how things relate to one another (without necessarily being able to explain the causal route from the creative power of God to the particulars of the created world). As I hope to show now, this view is not at all foreign to the theological proponents of TER among critical realists. But it seems that the difference between causal and semantic explanations has not always been made sufficiently clear.

Introducing CR in Science and Religion: Ian Barbour

When the history of the new science–religion dialogue is eventually written, Ian Barbour will probably be credited for introducing the idea of CR into the science–religion dialogue. He did so in the influential textbook, *Issues in Science and Religion* from 1966, where he also laid out the demarcation lines of realism over against positivism, instrumentalism, and idealism:

> Against the positivist, the realist asserts that the real is not the observable. Against the instrumentalist, he affirms that valid concepts are true as well as useful. Against the idealist, he maintains that concepts represent the structure of events in the world. The patterns in the data are not imposed by us, but originate at least in part in *objective relationships in nature.*[26]

Barbour here followed a trend of the 1960s in which the idea of a scientific realism was revived – even before Putnam's No Miracle Argument. Earlier in the century there had been strong internal divisions within the scientific community about the realness of the scientific referents. In the wake of the success of the statistical mechanics of thermodynamics and the strength of relativity theory, Max Planck and Albert Einstein turned the tide for realism, but in the philosophical climate of logical positivism the interpretation of quantum mechanics by Niels Bohr and Werner Heisenberg settled on a more empiricist program, according to which the main task of science was to save the phenomena while being agnostic about the ontology behind the scene of data. This agnosticism about the particular nature of quantum realities is today defended also by prominent quantum philosophers such as Bas van Fraasen.[27] In the view of scientific realism, however, 'atoms are as real as tables, though their modes of behavior are quite different.'[28]

Among the main proponents for the new wave of realism in the philosophy of science was J.J.C. Smart whose *Philosophic and Scientific Realism* (1963) influenced Barbour, as did Normann Campbell's *What is Science?*, one of the early realist proposals of the 1920s. For some reason or other, Barbour does not mention the work *Critical Realism* (1916) by Roy Wood Sellars, nor the work of his son Wilfred Sellars, whose *Science, Perception, and Reality* (1963) today is recognized as perhaps the most nuanced argument for CR.[29] Barbour's early embrace of CR, however, was informed partly by the realist movements of the 1920s (which include Whitehead), partly by the movement of SCR which was still in its infancy in the 1960s. Hereby Barbour also acknowledges his basic consonance with the realist epistemology of Thomism.[30]

Thus CR has been used as an umbrella term for different epistemologies. But even though CR has occupied the reigning position in the science–religion community, it should be noted that CR is largely absent in today's philosophy of science. While SCR is still a live option (with all the qualifications and criticisms noted above), CR is virtually nonexistent in today's philosophy of science.[31]

Since CR has several meanings, it is worth attending to the place of the term in the writings of Ian Barbour. As far as I can see, Barbour's argument can be reconstructed as follows. (1) Barbour *presupposes* MR on the basis of common sense, which is backed up by the first-order assumptions of practicing scientists and believers. (2) Barbour finds it necessary to *defend* SR both in science and in religion, over against proponents of anti-realism in second-order reflections on science and religion (philosophy of science respecting philosophy of religion). (3) This defense takes place by *extending* the elements of TER into the field of religion, in particular to theological models and theories. What is crucial then for the validation of Barbour's construction of a meaningful dialogue between science and religion is the extent to which he succeeds in substantiating the sufficient analogies between SCR and a theological realism (TR).

Thus, Barbour's first step in *Issues in Science and Religion* is that the real is more than *just* the observable world. In this first step lies the departure from a positivistic phenomenalism which argues that all knowledge can be reduced to either observation sentences or to mere analytical clarification of language usages. Instead we have a triangle of (a) *theories*, (b) *data* and, (c) *reality*. Theories intend to transcend observable data into the objective relations of the world behind the scene of data. The real is 'not [only] the observable.' So far Barbour endorses MR.

In a second move, Barbour supports SR in so far as he claims that theories are more than useful fictions, since they raise truth-claims about the presupposed reality. His criticism of instrumentalism as well as idealism serves to safeguard the referential nature of scientific as well as the religious knowledge-claims – 'valid concepts are true as well as useful;' 'concepts represent the structure of events in the world.'

Before we go on and see how Barbour, in his third move, substantiates these tenets of MR and SR, it is worth analyzing the kind of realism he supports. Remember that against the background of SCR the realism defended is mostly an *entity-realism*, that is, the claim that atoms, electrons and so on, actually exist in the world prior to our knowledge about them. We also find elements of an entity-realism in Barbour, but his interest gravitates around the 'objective relationships of reality.' This is probably a reflex of Barbour's influence from Whitehead's relational metaphysics. But Barbour also allies himself with Ernst Nagel who actually stands in the positivist tradition. With Nagel Barbour argues that it is not the sensory qualities of objects that stand in the foreground in science but aspects of reality that are 'not directly apprehensible'. Accordingly also religious models deal with non-observables. However, here another feature of Barbour's version of CR comes to the fore. The reason for positing the realness of molecules is the fact that they make up 'pervasive structural patterns' that have a law-like nature (so E. Nagel). In standard philosophical parlance this is called an *explanatory realism*. Thus alongside the relational ontology that Barbour supports, he also emphasizes 'the relational character of scientific terms'. When testing scientific truth-claims, we are not testing separate concepts but networks of theories that make intelligible what really happens 'out there' in the world. 'For many realists, intelligibility rather than observability is the hallmark of the real,' says Barbour.[32]

What is not quite clear, however, is the congruence between the different authors that Barbour uses to stabilize TER in theology. For Nagel, the realness of theoretical notions finally depends on their ability to subsume events under testable laws (according to the Hempel–Oppenheimer model of scientific explanation). It seems that there is here some tension with Whitehead's realist epistemology which centers on the networks of relations which 'include both the knower and the known', and where knowledge arises from the 'mutual interaction' between subjectivity and objectivity.[33] In short, whereas Nagel's sort of realism presupposes a split between the *explanans* (the law) and the *explanandum* (the events and relations), and uses a formalistic model of causal explanation, process thinkers would argue that abstract explanations grow out of the primary relation between the knower and known: 'knowledge is ultimate,' said Whitehead, for the Cartesian split between subject and object leads to an unrealistic bifurcation of nature.[34] Thus, what is common between Nagel and Whitehead is their insistence that relations are as real as isolated entities. But Whitehead's emphasis – and Barbour's, I surmise – on the inseparability of knowledge and reality presupposes a much broader notion of explanation, namely an intelligible ordering of otherwise disparate entities. In my terminology, *it is not so much the causal explanation as the semantic explanation that stands in the foreground of Barbour's version of CR*. But if this is the case, the route from an explanatory realism in SCR to CR in religion may be longer than explicitly recognized by Barbour.

In his helpful analysis of different concepts of explanation, Philip Clayton has pointed to the 'contextual shift' within philosophy of science beginning around 1970 with a few forerunners. Stephen Toulmin is quoted for stating that '[s]cience progresses, not by recognizing the truth of new observations alone, but by *making sense* of them.' In his investigation of religious explanations Clayton also observes the co-presence of explanation and understanding:

> Paralleling the contextual shift in natural science, then, the analysis of religious explanations shows them to be characterized more by the quest for coherence than by some universal structure. Unlike the natural sciences, though, they are concerned with *semantic* coherence, the meaningfulness of a coherently constructed world-picture that constitutes its personal disclosure value.[35]

Interestingly Clayton also understands the work of Barbour as demonstrating the methodological fruitfulness of the contextual shift in science and religion.[36] If Clayton is right, Barbour is a contextualist, not a formalist.

With this distinction between causal and semantic explanations in mind, let us proceed to the third step in Barbour's argument: the analogies in explanatory realism (TER) between scientific and theological modes of knowledge. Similarities and differences are most fully worked out in Barbour's *Myths, Models, and Paradigms* (1974). In both cases, models are analogies that can be applied outside their original context and understood as coherent unities. They are neither literal nor fictional terms. Instead they are partial representations of what is real though unobservable, symbolizing aspects of the world that are inaccessible to us. They provide order and organization for observations in science and for the religious experience of persons and groups.[37]

The similarity with SCR is here the qualified realism of 'partial and inadequate ways;' the entities employed by models and theories are not directly accessible. However, we seem to be far away from the explanatory realism of SCR-proponents such as Richard Boyd or Stathis Psillos. What is important for Barbour is the 'ordering' of scientific observations respecting religious experiences. This is in fact, in my terminology, a plea for coherence as the arbiter of truth-claims. Correspondingly Barbour shows a keen awareness of the differences between scientific and religious models. These differences include the non-cognitive role of religious models and their eliciting of personal involvement. They tend to be more influential than formal structures such as theological doctrine. Religious models are more directly related to experience, such as worship, ethics, and discipleship.[38] These careful qualifications in fact anticipate later criticisms raised against CR. Indeed, religion is more than cognitive; religious language is self-involving; and the emotional functions of religions are not always tied up with religious beliefs. Could it be the case that more similarities appear if we compare science and theology rather than science and religion?

Developing the CR Program: Arthur Peacocke

The work of Arthur Peacocke may be understood as an attempt in this direction. In his early writings Peacocke referred to 'a skeptical and qualified realism', and quoted *in extenso* the passages just cited from Barbour above.[39] Later on, *In Intimations of Reality*, Peacocke developed his own position further but still in close communication with Ian Barbour. Both authors underline that not only natural-kind entities are real (as in SCR), but also processes and relations. Furthermore, also emergent higher-order entities (such as organisms) are as real as are their constituents (such as the molecules).[40] However, Peacocke also added new perspectives to CR, which have later been adopted by Barbour. First, Peacocke defines from the outset the theological enterprise as 'the reflective and intellectual analysis of the religious experience of mankind and, in particular, of the Christian experience',[41] that is, as a second-order reflection on religious life. Second, Peacocke uses the insights of Thomas Kuhn (and the theologian Janet Soskice) to stress the importance of research groups and communities for the stability of cognitive claims. The continuity of reference thus presupposes stable interpretative communities, and in this sense both science and religion can be said to embody *traditions* of rational enquiry:

> The continuous linguistic community is vital to social reference in science, to the introducing events that named its entities and terms. Similarly, in the Christian community, key words and concepts go back to events and disclosures in the biblical sources or to church councils that resolved and formulated the outcome of often intensive debate and controversies about valid interpretation and theological language – and so about the appropriateness of various models … Furthermore, experiences of God continue to occur, and the interpretation of both these and past such experiences are communicated to, and many endure to be meaningful in, that continuing community.[42]

This emphasis on linguistic communities means that not isolated statements and theories, but social groups are the carriers of propositions. In line with Janet Soskice's *Metaphor and Religious Language* Peacocke can say that 'to be a realist about the referent is to be a fallibilist about knowledge of the referent.'[43] However, both Soskice and Peacocke contend that claims of reference can be made and justified, provided the evidential *and* social conditions are right.

Peacocke does so by a theory of reference in religion in which he distinguishes between direct and mediated experiences of God. Similar to the way in which science moves between first-time discoveries and subsequent repeated experiments, religions move between 'seminal initiating experiences of individuals and communities' and the 'continuous reinterpretation ("development of doctrine").' Thus theology presupposes immediate God-experiences but constitutes in itself a reinterpretation of tradition in the light of novel insights such as those provided by religion. In this process, the 'general assent continues in strength only if current experiences of at least *some* members of the community continue to be congruent with the earlier ones.'[44] If I am right, Peacocke's position can be laid out as follows: (1) the identity of reference (what we *mean* to refer to) can only be clarified in the context of a tradition, and (2) the validation of knowledge-claims presupposes some sort of repeatability of experience.

Certainly Peacocke at this stage claimed that religious experiences ('the direct experience of God of humankind') provides the anchorage for theology as their first-order interpreter and second-order arbiter. However, there is some ambiguity here, for Peacocke would not be satisfied by saying that theology simply has to 'save the phenomena' of religious experiences. The claim is that experiences are pointers to God. The CR *theory* thus assumes that religious experiences function as *data* providing the initial access to the *reality* of God. CR here appears as a rather complex position, involving a variety of claims. In his *Theology in the Age of Science*, Peacocke points to different aspects of CR. First, theology and science are said to each have their data and realities – with 'realities' in plural. After a while theology and science are seen as 'mutually interacting approaches to reality' – with 'reality' in singular. In the end Peacocke suggests the role of theology to be a fundamental and integrative discipline, 'the study of humanity-nature-God'.[45] Let us take a closer look at these three aspects of CR.

In the first case, critical realism proposes a *parallelism* between science and theology, each of which are supposed to have separate domains. Doctrine is about religious experience, which forms the raw material for theology, its *data*. The data of a Christian theology can then be enlarged so as to encompass not only individual religious experiences but also scripture, the tradition, and reason.[46] We might say that while experience, scripture, tradition, and reason constitute the *proximate referent* of theology, the reality of God is the *ultimate referent* of theology.

In the second case, we have the picture of two interacting approaches to one and the same reality. Let us call this the *convergent version* of critical realism. However, the only way to warrant the notion of a common referent of science and theology is by reinterpreting science in the light of theology, and theology in the light of science. Notice that it is this integrative aim which also stands at the center of the contextual coherence theory.

In the third case, we face the *synthetic version* of critical realism. The role of theology is here neither confined to the specialized study of religion, nor to a reinterpretation of science. The aim of theology is here nothing less than all-encompassing. Peacocke speaks here of theology as a 'constitutional monarch,' Polkinghorne speaks about theology as 'the great integrative discipline,' Barbour about 'systematic synthesis.'[47] Not that theology is able to answer all questions. Scientific questions are to be answered scientifically. But what theology can do for science is to provide answers to those questions that arise from science but are not themselves scientific in character. In this case theology and science meet on the extra-disciplinary field of a metaphysics, which is able to formulate a coherent worldview. Ian Barbour refers to process philosophy as a promising candidate for such a synthesis. But whether based on theology or on philosophy, the synthetic version of CR argues for an all-encompassing worldview.

The three versions of critical realism seem to presuppose what Hilary Putnam – somewhat disrespectfully but still quite illuminatingly – has called the *Cookie Cutter Metaphor*.[48] The world is like a cake. We can't say everything about that world at once but only about certain aspects of it; hence the 'plurality' of data and approaches. There are different slices of the cake (parallelist CR). But in any slice of the cake the higher layers presuppose the basic layers (convergent CR). And yet again, the world can also be investigated as a whole. The cake as a whole is then purviewed from above, as it were (synthetic CR). Theology, then, proposes itself to be that overarching discipline, which reflects on human existence and the universe as a whole, and uses 'God' as the overarching explanation of the world.

Can CR be Justified in Science and Theology?

If the analysis above holds true, the idea of CR in science and religion has several independent theses built into it: (1) an *epistemic thesis* of similarities between science and theology, (2) an *ontological thesis* of the realness of higher-order levels, and (3) a *theological thesis* of God as explanation of the unity of the world at all levels. Accordingly theology and science are sometimes presented as cousins and comrades, sometimes as regent and subjects. In all cases MR and SR are presupposed. But what about TER, the idea that an approximation to reality is warranted by the progress of theoretical explanations?

John Polkinghorne is an interesting case, since he – being a physicist – is acutely aware of the differences between science and religion. He argues that metaphors are 'poetic revelatory devices' which play no corresponding role in science (though perhaps in the popularization of science). Likewise he understands models as 'exploratory devises,' and he quotes with approval Barbour for saying that a model is 'an imaginative tool for ordering experience, rather than a description of the world.'[49] Thus, it is primarily at the level of theories, and in their experiential attitudes, that science and religion meet.

Polkinghorne is at once the most cautious and the most audacious of the three CR proponents discussed here. He is cautious in so far as he reverts to Barbour's original program where the rationalizing power of religion, as we saw, was found mainly in theology's capacity of organizing experiences so that we can structure and interpret patterns of events in the world as well as in our personal lives. This is, as a matter of fact, an argument for a semantic rather than a causal explanation. In Polkinghorne's most recent defense for CR, we find the same insistence that 'intelligibility is the reliable guide to ontology.'[50] Substantially this is a plea for coherentism. Polkinghorne is nonetheless prepared to extend his realist stance from SCR to a generalized CR, and it is here that he is audacious. Polkinghorne points to the development of the Christological dogma from the Son of God Christology of Paul in Romans 1 to the Logos Christology of John 1 and forward to the Chalcedonian dogma (451) of the two natures of Christ, human and divine. Polkinghorne understands this development of dogma as an approximation to the reality of Jesus Christ. He finds 'a gradation within this sequence of passages, both in relation to the strength of the claims to status being made and also with respect to the sophistication with which they are expressed.' I am prepared to grant that, but the crucial question remains: Can we infer from the development of dogma to an ever increasing approximation to the reality of Christ? Polkinghorne makes this claim by appealing to the 'analogies' with physical explanations, in which we, according to Polkinghorne, have to do with 'the actual uncovering of a more accurate (verisimilitudinous) account of the nature of the physical world.'[51] But is this analogy justifiable? Can one argue for a theological realism (the verisimilitude of dogma to Christ) by virtue of the analogy to the development of quantum theory? I do not find this analogy compelling, and it seems to me that a TER in SCR cannot be legitimately extended to a TER in theology. In the case of Christology, it might well be that the sophistication of dogma eclipses the reality of Jesus, both as a historical figure and as part of divine nature.

The same problem appears in other uses of TER in theology. Suppose that the current Harvard study of the efficacy of long-distance intercessory prayers to God for sick people (who do not know that they are prayed for) turns out to show a positive correlation between intercessory prayers and the well-being of the patients. Given the way the experiment is set up, a religious placebo effect ('self-suggestion') is ruled out from the outset. However, the causal efficacy of intercessions would still not evidence a religious explanation ('God grants prayers'), since there is also the other possibility, namely, that the mental activities of those who pray have a causal effect still unknown to us ('mind-waves are causally significant'). We would still have the intellectual choice between a purely mentalistic account ('what matters is *only* the positive thoughts of other people') or a theological account in which God is claimed to be active in, with and under the natural as well as mental networks of God's creation ('God acts through the activity of prayers'). My point here is that theological explanation would be the same, whether or not mental causality could be evidenced, but the semantic explanation would differ perhaps, significantly. In the end, what makes theology a rational enterprise is its power to order, in an intelligible manner, a vast variety of findings and to put the theological truth-claims in a specific relation to the relevant empirical findings.

To summarize what I have intended to show in this essay:

1 CR articulates in a helpful way the reality-claims involved in Christian belief.
2 A theological realism involves both a metaphysical realism (MR) and a semantic realism (SR).
3 In both cases a common sense realism breaks down, since the metaphysical reality of God is not a separable entity, but the infinite origin all that exists, and since all that can be said in finite categories about the infinite God is asserted about the God–world relations, not about God solo.
4 The extension from a scientific realism to a theological realism via a theoretical-explanatory realism (TER) has not been sufficiently clarified.
5 A clarification in terms of distinguishing between causal and semantic explanations in theology and science.
6 Even if one cannot ultimately justify a truth-claim by causal knock-out arguments, one should not give up the rationality of the truth-candidate as a means for ordering reality and making the world intelligible.
7 Even though 'correspondence with reality' is certainly an appropriate *definition of truth* and a pointer to the sort of theoretical knowledge we would like to have, it seems that 'coherence with contextually relevant data and theories' is the only available *criterion of truth* by which we can justify the assertability of religious explanations in the context of other theoretical frameworks.

Both as discoverers of truth and as adventurers in faith, hope and love we are bound to stay in the mundane horizons of that which is accessible to us: experiences always encoded in networks of imagination, language and theorizing.

Notes

1. Ian Barbour, *Issues in Science and Religion* (New York: Harper, 1966), 156–74, 216–18; Arthur Peacocke, *Intimations of Reality: Critical Realism in Science and Religion* (Notre Dame: University of Notre Dame Press, 1984); John Polkinghorne, *Scientists as Theologians: A Comparison of the Writings of Ian Barbour, Arthur Peacocke and John Polkinghorne* (London: SPCK, 1996), 11–25, and *Belief in God in an Age of Science* (Yale: Yale University Press, 1998), 25–47.
2. Cf. Barbour, *Issues*, 218.
3. Ernan McMullin, 'Realism in Theology and Science: A Response to Peacocke', *Religion and Intellectual Life*, 2:4 (1985): 39–47; 43 and 47.
4. Willem B. Drees, *Religion, Science and Naturalism* (Cambridge: Cambridge University Press, 1996), 130–50; and 'A 3 x 3 Classification of Science-and-Religion' in *The Concept of Nature in Science and Theology Part II*, Studies in Science and Theology 4, ed. by N.H. Gregersen, M.W.S. Parsons, and C. Wassermann (Geneva: Labor et Fides, 1996), 18–32.
5. Kees van Kooten Niekerk, 'Critical Realism', in *Encyclopedia of Science and Religion* (New York: MacMillan Reference, 2003). See also Niekerk, 'A Critical Realist Perspective on the Dialogue between Theology and Science' in *Rethinking Theology and Science: Six Models for the Current Dialogue*, ed. by Niels Henrik Gregersen and J. Wentzel van Huyssteen (Grand Rapids: Eerdmans, 1998), 51–86, esp. 73–8.
6. Nancey C. Murphy, 'From Critical Realism to Methodological Approach: Response to Robbins, van Huyssteen, and Hefner', *Zygon*, 23:3, 287–90; and *Anglo-American Postmodernity* (Boulder, CO: Westview Press), 39–48.
7. J. Wentzel van Huyssteen, *Theology and the Justification of Faith* (Grand Rapids, MI: Eerdmans, 1989), 147–52, esp. 161.

8. J. Wentzel van Huyssteen, *The Shaping of Rationality: Toward Interdisciplinarity in Theology of Science* (Grand Rapids: Eerdmans, 1999), 213–21; quotations 213 and 216.

9. J. Wesley Robbins, 'Pragmatism, Critical Realism, and the Cognitive Value of Religion and Science', *Zygon*, 34:4 (1999): 655–66.

10. Niels Henrik Gregersen, 'A Contextual Coherence Theory for the Science–Theology Dialogue' in *Rethinking Theology and Science*, 181–231, esp. 227f.

11. Stathis Psillos, *Scientific Realism: How Science Tracks the Truth* (London: Routledge, 1999), xix.

12. Hilary Putnam, 'What is Realism?' [1975], in *Scientific Realism*, ed. by Jarrett Leplin (Berkeley: University of California Press, 1984), 140–153; 140f.

13. Richard Boyd, 'On the Current Status of Scientific Realism' [1983], in *The Philosophy of Science*, ed. by Richard Boyd et al. (Cambridge MA: MIT Press, 1991), 195–222, 195.

14. See the essays in Jarrett Leplin (ed.), *Scientific Realism* (Berkeley: University of California Press, 1984); cf. *Rethinking Theology and Science*, 200–204.

15. See the survey by Dirk Evers on the different concepts of time in the physical sciences and in human activities, *Raum – Materie – Zeit: Schöpfungstheologie im Dialog mit naturwissenschaftlicher Kosmologie* (Tübingen: Mohr-Siebeck, 2000), 283–360.

16. Nicholas Rescher, *A System of Pragmatic Idealism vol 1, Human Knowledge in Idealistic Perspective* (Princeton: Princeton University Press, 1992), 275. I have discussed the difference between Rescher's pragmatic realism and Hilary Putnam's 'internal realism' in *Rethinking Theology and Science*, 198–200.

17. It seems to me that this point is not adequately reflected in Wesley Robbins' allegation (see note 9 above) that CR proponents are born to be Cartesians. On this problem, see George Lakoff and Mark John Johnson, *Philosophy in the Flesh: The Embodied Mind and Its Challenge to Western Thought* (New York: Basicbooks, 1999), 89–91, who speak of an 'embodied scientific realism' as a consequence of cognitive science.

18. See Niels Henrik Gregersen, 'Religious Imagination and the Idea of Revelation', *Ars Disputandi*, 1:3 (2002), 1–14.

19. In his article, 'Realism and antirealism' in *The Oxford Companion to Christian Thought* (ed. by Adrian Hastings (Oxford: Oxford University Press, 2000), 593–4), William P. Alston interprets Tillich as an anti-realist. This only holds true, however, if we by 'God' understand separate a-cosmic reality, not if we understand God as the ever-creating source of all that exists in the world.

20. Edward Craig, 'Realism and Antirealism', in *Routledge Encyclopedia of Philosophy*, ed. by Edward Craig, vol. 8 (London, New York: Routledge, 1998) 115–19, 116.

21. I am aware that this is a controversial issue in theology. To Karl Barth, Christ is the revelation of God prior to, and even independent of, the human recognition. To Paul Tillich, revelation implies that something is revealed to somebody. I here follow the latter's phenomenological understanding.

22. G.W.F. Hegel, *Wissenschaft der Logik I* (Hamburg: Felix Meiner, 1968), 125–35. Hegel's fundamental insight informed Karl Barth's work from its beginnings (see his commentary to Romans 7:1 in *Der Römerbrief* [Munich: Chr. Kaiser, 1922], 213), and is – through Barth – a cornerstone also in the theological realism of T.F. Torrance, see his *Reality and Scientific Theology* (Edinburgh: Scottish Academic Press, 1982). On the fundamental role of the concept of infinity as a minimal criterion for any ontological doctrine of God, see Wolfhart Pannenberg, *Metaphysics and the Idea of God* (Edinburgh: T. & T. Clark, 1990), ch. 2.

23. *The Divine Names* 5.4 (Patrologia Graeca 3, 817D). Translation after Pseudo-Dionysius, *The Complete Works* (New York: Paulist Press, 1987), 98.

24. See Michael Welker, 'Theological Realism and Eschatological Symbol Systems' in, *Resurrection: Theological and Scientific Assessments*, ed. by Ted Peters, Robert John Russell, and Michael Welker (Grand Rapids: Eerdmans, 2002), 31–42.

25. Cf. my critique of Nancey Murphy's concept of theology as an empirical research program in *Rethinking Theology and Science*, 205–12.

26. Barbour, *Issues in Science and Religion*, 168 (Barbour's italics). See the helpful overview in Christian Berg, *Theologie im technologischen Zeitalter: Das Werk Ian Barbours als Beitrag zur Verhältnisbestimmung von Theologie zu Naturwissenschaft und Technik* (Stuttgart: Verlag Kohlhammer, 2002), ch. 3.3–4.

27. Bas van Fraasen, 'To Save the Phenomena', *Journal of Philosophy*, 73:18 (1976), 623–32.

28. Barbour, *Issues in Science and Religion*, 169.

29. See Thomas Vinci, 'Sellars, Wilfred' in *The Cambridge Dictionary of Philosophy*, ed. by Robert Audi (Cambridge: Cambridge University Press, 1975), 722–4, and the corresponding entries on 'Critical Realism', 'New Realism', and 'Scientific Realism'.

30. There seems no corresponding influence on Barbour coming from the Neo-Kantian tradition, in which the term *kritischer Realismus* was used by some of the Neo-Kantians at the end of the nineteenth century and the beginning of the twentieth. *Kritischer Realismus* was here meant to be a position which largely accepted the Kantian epistemology while at the same time avoiding the idealist tendencies inherent in the Kantian premises. See Wilhelm Wundt, 'Über naiven und kritischen Realismus', *Philosophische Studien* (*PS*) 12, (1895/96): 307–408; and *PS* 13 (1896/97): 1–105, 323–433; cf. M. Grünewald et al., 'Realismus' in *Historisches Wörterbuch der Philosophie*, Band 8, 148–78, 159f.

31. It is difficult to verify a claim of absence, but note that there is no entry on Critical Realism in the *Routledge Encyclopedia of Philosophy* (10 vols, 1998), neither is the term indexed in the aforementioned 800-page reader, *The Philosophy of Science*, edited by Richard Boyd et al. The term appears, however, in sociological literature, mainly connected to the Marxist social philosopher Roy Bhaskar, and in theology books, such as Bruce McCormack's *Karl Barth's Critical Realistic Dialectical Theology* (1995), and Sue Patterson's, *Realist Christian Theology in a Postmodern Age*, (Cambridge: Cambridge University Press, 1999).

32. Barbour, *Issues in Science and Religion*, 170.

33. Ibid., 171.

34. Alfred North Whitehead, *The Concept of Nature* (Cambridge: Cambridge University Press, 1920), 29–32.

35. Philip Clayton, Explanation from Physics to Theology: An Essay in Rationality and Religion (New Haven: Yale University Press, 1989), 36.

36. Ibid., 146.

37. Ian Barbour, *Myth, Models, and Paradigms: A Comparative Study in Science and Religion* (New York: Harper & Row, 1974), 69.

38. Ibid., 69.

39. Arthur Peacocke, *Creation and the World of Science: The Bampton Lectures 1978* (Oxford: Clarendon Press, 1979), 40f.

40. Compare Arthur Peacocke, *Intimations of Reality: Critical Realism in Science and Religion* (Notre Dame, IN: Notre Dame University Press, 1984), 34–7 and 41–5, with Barbour, *Issues*, 416–18 and esp. *Myths, Models, and Paradigms*, 69.

41. Peacocke, *Intimations to Reality*, 37.

42. Ibid., 42f; cf. Ian Barbour, *Religion in an Age of Science* (San Francisco: Harper & Row, 1990), 267: 'The context of theology is always the worshiping community.'

43. Peacocke, *Intimations*, 45: quoting Janet Soskice, *Metaphor and Religious Language* (Oxford: Oxford University Press, 1985).

44. Peacocke *Intimations*, 47.

45. A. Peacocke, *Theology for a Scientific Age* (London: SCM Press, 1990), 19f and 22.

46. As suggested by John Polkinghorne, *One World: The Interaction of Science and Theology* (London: SPCK, 1986), 30–33.

47. Peacocke, *Intimations*, 37; Polkinghorne, *Scientists as Theologians*, 12; Barbour, *Religion in an Age of Science*, 28.

48. Putnam, *The Many Faces of Realism*, 34.

49. J. Polkinghorne, *Scientists as Theologians*, 19: quoting from Barbour, *Myth, Models and Paradigms*, 6.
50. J. Polkinghorne, *Belief in God in an Age of Science*, 110. A similar move can be traced in Arthur Peacocke's later work, see his appeal to coherence and comprehensiveness in 'Science and the Future of Theology: Critical Issues', *Zygon*, 35:1, 119–40.
51. Polkinghorne, *Belief in God in an Age of Science*, 30 and 32.

Chapter 5

Religion, Theology, and the Philosophy of Science: An Appreciation of the Work of Ian Barbour

Nancey Murphy

Introduction

Ian Barbour is not merely one among many authors in the field of theology and science; not even one among the few *notable* scholars in the field. Rather he has the distinction of being one of the founders of this new and growing scholarly community. My judgment is based on the fact that on every topic I have had occasion to pursue, it has been necessary to check first to see what Ian has written and to pick up the discussion from there.

Barbour's primacy is due both to the historical fact that he began to write on religion and science early on, before many others joined in, and to the encyclopedic style of his work: he tends to canvass a topic thoroughly, treating all of its related aspects and surveying the range of positions on each issue before setting forth his own views. This style of scholarship makes a summary of his books difficult; they are already summaries of a vast literature. Nonetheless, I owe my readers a brief overview of the work I intend to appraise here: Part One of Volume 1 of his Gifford Lectures, titled *Religion in an Age of Science*.[1] The book as a whole incorporates the best from his two earlier books, *Issues in Science and Religion* and *Myths, Models, and Paradigms*,[2] bringing the discussion of those earlier topics up to date, but also delving into new areas.

Chapter 1 of Part One provides a typology of ways of relating Christianity and science: conflict, independence, dialogue, and integration. The least attractive options, as Barbour sees them, are the conflict model and, at the opposite extreme, the independence model – the view that religion and science are so different that they cannot possibly conflict. I believe some change can be noted in Barbour's views here. I believe he has moved from a primary emphasis on dialogue between religion and science to a greater interest in a systematic synthesis of science and Christian theology, using process thought as a medium.

Chapter 2, 'Models and Paradigms,' chiefly updates Barbour's earlier book on these topics, but incorporates into the discussion the recent emphasis on narrative, which has been furthered by theologians such as James McClendon and Michael Goldberg. This discussion replaces his earlier focus on the anthropological category of *myth*, which has often been misunderstood.

Chapter 3, 'Similarities and Differences,' examines some new areas: the historical character of both science and Christianity; the question of objectivism versus relativism; and the problem of religious pluralism.

Barbour's Style: *Via Media*

I have already characterized Barbour's style of scholarship as encyclopedic. He has a gift for surveying the body of literature on a contested topic, sorting the positions into categories, and presenting brief, clear accounts of the scholarship on both sides. I believe Ian's irenic style of scholarship reflects his personal character, as he strives to appreciate the varied points of view and establish a position of his own – a *via media* – that takes into account the strengths and weaknesses of all of the contenders. He does this, for instance, in taking a stand on religious truth between absolutism and relativism. However, I do *not* mean to suggest that in his attempt to find moderate positions, Barbour is simply a compromiser, with no significant positions of his own. As I read this recent work and think of how to position Barbour in the field, two characteristics stand out in Part One and give definitive shape to his work.

First, Barbour continues to argue for a 'critical realist' position on the truth and language of both science and religion. He sees this as a middle position between what is now termed 'naive realism' and relativistic interpretations of all sorts.

The second significant issue has to do with the sort of parallels Barbour pursues between Christianity and science. In my own writing I have argued that if one wants to find close parallels with science one needs to look not at religion as a whole but rather at the academic discipline of theology.[3] I have also argued that a more useful account of the structure and progress of science than Kuhn's paradigm analysis is Imre Lakatos's account of competing research programs. Thus, I was gratified to see Barbour's continuing attention to Lakatos in the present volume,[4] and also to the question of the proper level of analysis for relating Christianity to science. After his having raised these issues, however, his decisive return to a consideration of religion as a whole (as opposed to the narrower focus on theology) must be seen as a significant characteristic of his approach. This focus on religion as a whole will be one of the objects of my reflections in what follows; another will be what I have called his irenic style of scholarship, and in particular its result in his position on critical realism.

Religion versus Theology

Barbour raises a question, at several points, regarding the scale at which we ought to seek parallels between religion and science. 'Would it be illuminating,' he asks, 'to consider all of Christianity as one paradigm and refer to "the Christian paradigm"?'[5] Or, in connection with his discussion of my work. Barbour considers alternative candidates for what should be thought of in Lakatosian terms as a theological program: a single doctine (e.g., the atonement), a school of Christian thought (e.g., Thomism), or perhaps even Christianity as a whole in comparison with other religions. He cites Gary Gutting as even viewing belief in a personal God as constituting a Lakatosian core, although here Barbour thinks we have generalized the idea too far.[6]

The ongoing disagreement between Barbour and myself, as well as Barbour's own questions regarding the issue of scale, suggest that we have found an area that requires further clarification. We need a more detailed account of the structure of religious thought than that provided either by Barbour's suggestion in *Myths, Models, and Paradigms* that whole religions are akin to paradigms, or my earlier suggestion that theological schools be construed as scientific research programs.

Continuing in his Gifford Lectures (just cited) Barbour tends to speak not of Christianity as a paradigm, but of the Christian tradition as containing paradigms (see pp. 61–2). This seems to me to be an improvement. However, Kuhn has been criticized from the beginning for the lack of precision in his definition of a scientific paradigm. Despite his later distinction between a disciplinary matrix and an exemplar, I believe his terms are still difficult to apply. Thus, rather than attempt to push the analogies between religions[7] and paradigms, I suggest that we use the concept of a *tradition*, as explicated by Alasdair MacIntyre, for describing the structure of a religion and for developing an account of parallels between science and religion as well.

MacIntyre developed his account of traditions in order to make sense of the history of ethics. However, he has contributed to issues in the philosophy of science as well.[8] According to MacIntyre, traditions always begin with an authority of some sort, usually with an authoritative text or set of texts. As examples, MacIntyre includes the Homeric epics as formative texts for the virtue tradition is ethics, and Newton's *Principia* for the Newtonian tradition. Of course the Hebrew and Christian scriptures are formative texts as well. A tradition can be defined as a historically extended, socially embodied argument about how best to interpret and apply a set of formative texts.

I wish to highlight several aspects of this definition of a tradition and comment on their bearing on the present discussion. First, a tradition is socially embodied. That is, it provides the basis for a community's way of life. This means that academic theology alone is not, in this sense, a tradition; a religion is, of course, being by its very nature socially embodied.

Second, a tradition is defined as an *argument* about how to interpret and embody the texts. Thus, a tradition should not be expected to manifest the agreement on fundamental issues that characterizes a Kuhnian paradigm – quite the contrary, in fact. So it seems clear that MacIntyre's definition of a tradition fits religions better than does Kuhn's definition of a paradigm.

A third point that becomes apparent, not from MacIntyre's definition of a tradition but from his use of the term, is that traditions can be contained within other traditions. Among the cases that MacIntyre has discussed, the Thomist tradition is part of the Augustinian tradition, which in turn is part of the Christian tradition. But the containment relation is not a simple one like a set of Russian dolls. Thomas and his followers also constitute a subtradition within the moral tradition that takes the concept of virtue as its starting point, and which traces its origin to the Homeric texts.

So a large-scale tradition will be made up of a variety of entangled subtraditions, and there will be a variety of ways to cut those tangled streams of thought into discrete entities.

Now, within Christian subtraditions, working toward an even finer scale, we find theological schools with a great deal of agreement on fundamentals. At this fine scale, the concept of a tradition no longer applies, since the *differentia* between two theological schools are generally not socially embodied. For example, process theologians do not form a distinct community in any other sense than that of an intellectual community, and have no way of life that distinguishes them from, say, Schleiermacherians.

However, I have argued that Lakatos's concept of a research program applies quite well here.[9] A research program is a network of theories, unified by a central theory that is quite resistant to change and is therefore called the hard core. The rest of the network is composed of auxiliary hypotheses, which are subject to change in order to adjust the whole to a growing body of data. The data for Christian theology would come from scripture, experience, history, and elsewhere. A research program has a positive heuristic, that is, a plan for the development of the program. I have suggested that the positive heuristic for a theological research program would be, for instance, the plan to treat all of the standard Christian doctrines from the point of view of the writings of Martin Luther, or from the perspective of existentialist philosophy. Finally, research programs in science incorporate theories of instrumentation that explain what the relevant instruments do and why data they produce should be reliable. I have argued that the equivalent in theology are theories of *interpretation*: historiographical principles, hermeneutic theories, and a 'theory of discernment' to allow for recognition of religious experiences that have some degree of intersubjective consensus and genuine theological import.[10]

So it appears necessary and useful to have both concepts, that of a *tradition* and that of a *research program* in order to describe the large- and fine-scale structures, respectively, of religious thought. And while the two concepts are distinct, there will be borderline cases where it is not clear which applies. For example, Thomism has certainly grown into a full-fledged tradition, even containing a variety of its own subtraditions. But early in its history it would have lacked the social embodiment and diversity that characterize a tradition, and would better have been considered a theological research program.

Notice that research programs, like traditions, admit containment. For instance, we might locate Whiteheadian process theology within the broader program of process theology; and there might also be a research program in process Christology contained within Whiteheadian process theology. Speaking metaphorically, then, we can say that both traditions and research programs have a 'fractal' structure. That is, when we examine the parts of a research program we find that the part also has the 'shape' of a research program. Thus we do not need to decide among some of the alternatives Barbour presents; for example, we do not need to decide whether the term 'research program' should be applied to sustained treatments of a single doctrine or only to entire systematic theologies. It may well be both.

The point of the foregoing is that it is only with this complex account of the structure of religious thought that we can describe parallels between religion and science without the danger of making category mistakes. It is probably clear enough, now, where I am heading with all of this. Apt comparisons will be either between research programs in science and research programs in theology, or if one wishes to compare a religion as a whole to science, the correct scale on the scientific side will be something like the Aristotelian tradition, with its social embodiment in the *polis*, or the whole of Newtonian science along with its related worldview. When we look at science on this large scale, it bears a closer resemblance to religion than Barbour admits. Newtonian science 'writ large' has indeed been socially embodied – it is quite remarkable to see the extent to which Newtonian physics has served as a source of ideas for modern psychology, ethics, and political thought.[11]

Rational Adjudication

A final and highly significant reason for preferring an account of theology and religion in terms of the works of Lakatos and MacIntyre over one based on Kuhn's philosophy is that Kuhn is so often taken to have presented an irrationalist account of science – indeed, likening paradigm change to religious conversion![12] Lakatos and MacIntyre have both written accounts intended to pick out criteria by which intellectual changes could sometimes be recognized as rational. While there are some who believe that the acceptance of Christian teaching must be by means of a leap of faith, other Christians throughout the centuries have seen a role for rational judgment. My own appreciation for Lakatos's work came about as a result of my recognition that his theory of choice could be used in theology. My current advocacy of MacIntyre's work is due to my perception that he is the only contemporary philosopher who appreciates all of the complexities involved in rational adjudication between competing large-scale traditions and yet does not advocate some sort of relativism.

MacIntyre's account of rational adjudication between competing traditions involves the construction of a narrative account of each tradition: of the crises it has encountered (incoherence, new experience that cannot be explained, and so on) and how it has or has not overcome these crises. Has it been possible to reformulate the tradition in such a way that it overcomes its crises without losing its identity? Comparison of these narratives may show that one tradition is clearly superior to another: it may become apparent that one tradition is making progress while its rival has become sterile.

In addition, if there are participants within the traditions with enough empathy and imagination to understand the rival tradition's point of view in its own terms, then

> protagonists of each tradition, having considered in what ways their own tradition has by its own standards of achievement in enquiry found it difficult to develop its enquiries beyond a certain point, or has produced in some area insoluble antinomies, ask whether the alternative and rival tradition may not be able to provide resources to characterize and to explain the failings and defects of their own tradition more adequately than they, using the resources of that tradition, have been able to do.[13]

MacIntyre's epistemological prescriptions would sound unrealistic were they not worked out in conjunction with detailed historical and constructive arguments that they serve to describe. A major goal is to show the superiority of his rejuvenated form of the Aristotelian-Thomist tradition to its most significant current rival, the Enlightenment tradition. To do this he has to show three things: (1) that the Enlightenment tradition of 'traditionless reason' is incapable of solving its own most pressing intellectual problems – in particular, the problem of the tradition-ladenness of standards of rationality; (2) that his own version of the Aristotelian-Thomist tradition has a good chance of solving the problem; and (3) why we could have been so misled by the tradition that claimed to reject all tradition. He makes his argument by assuming the standpoint of tradition-constituted reason and by then using that perspective to diagnose the mistakes of his predecessors: the Enlightenment tradition cannot tell its own story intelligibly because its own standards of rationality require such standards to be universal and not historically conditioned. His own account is vindicated by the extent to which it sheds new light on this aspect of intellectual history.

So MacIntyre's work provides a model for the philosophical theologian:[14] it requires the identification and clarification of one's own tradition (for example, the Aristotelian-Thomist subtradition within Christianity); constructive contributions to overcoming its own internal incoherence (for example, redefining 'virtue' in such a way that it is not dependent on Aristotle's metaphysical biology); recounting the past crises within the tradition and how these have been overcome (for example, the clash between Augustinianism and Aristotelianism, and how Thomas reconciled them). Finally, it requires identification of the most serious current rivals and an attempt not only to give formulation to their own internal problems in ways persuasive to their adherents, but also to explain why things look as they do from the rival standpoint, why the rival was destined to fail just at the point where it does fail, and why insiders could not be expected to recognize that tragic flaw. While this is a critical evaluation, it is important to stress that it depends on a fair and knowledgeable account of the rival point of view.

In light of MacIntyre's account of the process of defending a tradition against rivals, we see the relevance of the theological disciplines, understood as *practices* partially constitutive of the tradition.[15] Biblical studies is the ongoing social practice whose aim is increasingly adequate interpretation of Christians' formative texts. Practical theology and theological ethics investigate proper applications of the texts. Systematic theology seeks coherence in the tradition's self-understanding. On this view, historical theology and church history are particularly important disciplines, for they not only seek to illuminate the coherence of the tradition over time, but also narrate the story of the tradition's epistemological crises and how they have been overcome.

Philosophy of religion, on this account, does not bring objective, timeless standards of rationality to bear on Christian belief. Philosophers themselves will always be partisan: 'To be outside all traditions is to be a stranger to enquiry; it is to be in a state of intellectual and moral destitution.'[16] Philosophers of religion can participate in the immense task of attempting to compare rival traditions on the basis of how well each has met its own internal standards.

Some philosohpers have argued for a 'presumption of atheism.' That is, the theist bears the burden of proof, and if that burden cannot be discharged then atheism wins by default. Not so if MacIntyre is correct. Traditions with nontheistic accounts of ultimate reality require the same sort of scrutiny and evaluation as religious traditions and there are no special problems to be faced by a theistic tradition. Theistic and atheistic traditions compete on equal footing.

While a central value of MacIntyre's work is that it applies to traditions as communal 'property', he does provide some valuable resources for addressing the relation between individual religious convictions and theological programs. For the individual, the presence of rival traditions (with their interpretive schemata) puts one's own interpretations in question. I suspect that true intellectual crises result not so much from pure rational reflection, but autobiographically: How have I understood my own life as a believer, and can I make of it a coherent narrative? For example, can I continue to see myself as a descendant of Adam and Eve while I devote myself to the study of evolutionary biology? Can I continue to participate in re-enactment of the Last Supper when I identify myself as a feminist and note that there are no women mentioned in this high point of the Jesus story?

So the question is not, Can I justify the existence of God? but rather, Can I identify myself as a rational person and continue to live out my own life using the interpretive resources of the Christian tradition (or my particular Christian subtradition)?[17] But no individual should be expected to be able to answer this question without the resources provided by others, including scholars.

So this last question returns our focus from the level of individual epistemic crisis to that of the conflict of large-scale traditions. I suggest that the two most significant crises for the Christian tradition in the modern period have been occasioned by epistemological changes early in the period and by the rise of modern science. Jeffrey Stout has well described the first of these. There was a shift from an epistemology that recognized authority as an important means of showing a belief to be 'probable' – that is, approvable – to one where 'probability' means supported by the preponderance of (empirical) evidence. He sees the whole of modern theology to have been an unsuccessful attempt to come to terms with the new epistemology.[18] However, this crisis is now resolving itself; the epistemological tradition of modernity is now in at least as deep a crisis as Christian theology has ever been.

The rise of modern science has created crises in the modern period comparable to the rediscovery of Aristotle in the Middle Ages. The liberal strategy of defining theology or religion in such a way that conflict was ruled out a priori may have been a Pyhrric victory, leaving theology too empty of cognitive content to be interesting. The fundamentalist strategy of attempting to resist scientific progress has been a disaster. If Christianity is to compete effectively against scientific materialism, it needs to learn to make as good use of science for its own purposes as do the Sagans and Monods.

So the current challenge to Christian scholars is to use the new epistemological resources available today to come to terms with, among other things, contemporary science. This brings us back to where we started – to an appreciation for the great contributions Ian Barbour has made to this project.

Critique of Barbour's *Via Media*

I return now to the issue of Barbour's style of scholarship. While I always appreciate the irenic spirit of Ian's work, I am sometimes uneasy about the results to which it leads. I am taking the opportunity of this essay to try to get clear on the source of the uneasiness. I believe it can be expressed this way: in some instances (and I want to emphasize that this is only sometimes) I believe that Ian is seeking a midpoint between positions that are not in any sense on a spectrum. To illustrate, consider the position that he takes vis-à-vis the objectivity of science versus its social conditioning. I suspect that it is a mistake to treat claims for the objectivity of science and claims that science can be explained sociologically as opposing positions – and then to seek to find a compromise between them, as Ian does. For instance, after describing the strong program in the sociology of science, he says that while extrascientific factors serve to correct the 'internalistic' view of science, scholars in the strong program drift towards relativism and minimize the way data constrain scientific theories. Moreover they cannot adequately account for the predictive power and technological fertility of science. Although Barbour admits that ideologies are a factor, their effects can be minimized by an appeal to data and other criteria.[19] So here Barbour is attempting to give the sociologists their due, but to 'lean back' in the other direction toward the internalist account.

We can tell that there is something wrong with this way of setting up the opposition, for Barbour goes on to say of the sociologists that they fail to recognize the inconsistency in arguing for the universality of cultural relativism, since such relativism should then apply to and subvert their own claims as well.[20] Now, this charge may be true of some of the thinkers that Barbour has in mind here, but David Bloor, one of the foremost proponents of the 'strong programme', states explicitly that his analysis does apply to his own position; Bloor is at some pains to explain that social conditioning does not invalidate either his own theories or anyone else's.[21] So what is going on here?

I suggest that we look at Bloor's analysis not as a position opposed to accounts of science in terms of truth, objectivity, and so on, but rather as a position pertaining to a different level of analysis. It is the answer to a different set of questions. To understand Bloor's position it is helpful to contrast it with Lakatos's views on explanation in the history of science. Lakatos argues that his methodology can be used to reconstruct the *rational* episodes in the history of science, but episodes that do not fit his account of scientific reasoning are *eo ipso* irrational and need to be explained by other factors such as sociology. Thus there is internal history and external history. What Bloor means in calling his work the 'strong programme' in the sociology of scientific knowledge is that it is not content to provide causal accounts only of the irrational moves in science or of scientific theories that are taken to be false. It attempts causal (sociological) accounts of *all* science.

Now, if one is convinced of a dichotomy 'true (or justified) versus caused' then Bloor will appear to be calling *all* knowledge into question. But this is *not* Bloor's point. All knowledge is underdetermined by purely rational considerations. Thus it always makes sense to ask why a person or group believes X *despite lack of rational compulsion*. And it can often be illuminating to trace the social utility of belief in X.

A further complication, of course, is that beliefs regarding what counts as justification of knowledge are also underdetermined. So what causes an individual philosopher or a group to opt for one epistemological theory rather than another? See Stephen Toulmin's fascinating account of the social factors that motivated Descartes and his followers to develop an epistemology that rejected tradition and sought absolute certitude in his *Cosmopolis*.[22] As an example of the role of sociological factors in epistemology itself, Bloor argues that the differences between Popper's and Kuhn's methodologies can be traced to a difference between Enlightenment and Romantic ideologies.[23] Rather than repeat Bloor's example, though, I shall try my hand at a sociological analysis of my own and Ian's work.

Let us return to the issues I raised above in Section 3, 'Religion versus Theology'. Barbour claims that religions are like scientific paradigms. Why does he make this claim, rather than saying that it is academic theology that is like science? If he made the latter move he would not have to devote so much attention to how religions differ from science. For example, summing up he notes that religion is a way of life and that religious language serves a variety of functions that have no parallel in science. There is the affective dimension of religion; religions offer salvation; religions require more total involvement than does science; religions fulfill psychological needs.

The question can be sharpened by noting that there is a scientific culture that has grown up around science proper. Barbour himself notes the religious trappings of science advocated by the likes of Carl Sagan in *Cosmos*: 'Sitting at the instrument panel from which he shows us the wonders of the universe, he is a new kind of high priest, not only revealing the mysteries to us but telling us how we should live'. Scientific language is used by Sagan to express awe and reverence for the ultimate, Nature with a capital N. Scientific knowledge offers salvation from our self-destructive urges. So, more specifically, why does Barbour choose to focus on religion in the *broad* sense (that is, as opposed to professional theology) but to focus on science in the *narrow* sense, as opposed to the penumbra of scientistic culture?

I propose some hypotheses. First, Barbour developed his ideas while teaching in a college religious studies department. There is presently a great deal of bias against theology in religious studies departments. I am not attributing any such bias to Ian; just noting that a concentration on religion is appropriate in some social locations, a concentration on theology in others. Second, Barbour is a physicist. The world of science is strongly influenced by atheism. These two factors together may well have caused Ian to be concerned about an *apologia* for religion. Third, since the scientistic culture is thoroughly atheistic, it stands to reason that he should seek to avoid legitimizing it by comparing it with the venerable religions of the world.

Notice what I have done. I have given a causal explanation for Barbour's position over against my own, based on his social location. Now, does that mean his position is wrong? (I now take off my sociologist's hat and put on my philosopher's hat.) No. His position is wrong for the reasons I have given in Section 3 above!

Then is my position undermined by the fact that I accept causal explanations of beliefs? Or am I going to claim that my position is somehow exempt from social conditioning because it happens to be *true*? No. I am as socially located as the next person. When I did my work on Lakatos, my location was the Graduate *Theological*

Union, a multi-denominational consortium of Christian seminaries; my interest was to argue for the cognitive content of theology over against what George Lindbeck has called the experiential-expressivist account.

The moral of this little story is that because knowledge is underdetermined there is no necessary opposition between sociological accounts and more traditional epistemological accounts. They are analyses on different levels, looking at different kinds of motivating factors, and thus there is no place halfway between them, such as critical realism intends to fill. It is important to distinguish the different questions each is intended to answer, rather than seeing them as opposing answers to a single question.

Conclusion

I conclude by saying what a pleasure and honor it has been to have the opportunity to respond to Ian's Gifford Lectures. But I also want to end with a *complaint* about how difficult it is to criticize his work. This is for a variety of reasons. I have already mentioned the difficulty of summarizing an encyclopedic work such as Ian's. I hope it is also clear from what I have said or implied that I agree with much of what he has written, and in fact see his work as setting the parameters within which the discussion of theology and science must take place; thus I have had to hunt diligently for points of disagreement.

Yet another difficulty for the reviewer is the irenic style of scholarship that I have focused on above. This feature makes it hard to criticize Barbour's work, since any complaint to the effect that he has not given enough attention to one side of an issue will almost inevitably make the reviewer come across as an extremist. For example, had I argued directly that Barbour gives too little to the historical conditioning of knowledge it would have made me appear more of a ranting relativist than in fact I am. So it has seemed appropriate not to engage issues *within* the scope of Barbour's work, but rather to attempt to step back and place his work as a whole against a broader range of possibilities. I have commented on two features, his general style of scholarship, and the question of how to describe the structure of religious thought when attempting to compare it to science. I hope in so doing I have made a positive contribution to the scholarly endeavor that Ian has done so much to establish.[24]

Notes

1.   Ian G. Barbour, *Religion in an Age of Science: The Gifford Lectures, 1989–1991, Volume 1* (San Francisco: Harper & Row, 1990).

2.   Barbour, *Issues in Science and Religion* (Englewood Cliffs, NJ: Prentice Hall, 1966); and *Myths, Models, and Paradigms* (New York: Harper & Row, 1974).

3.   Barbour has replied that his decision to focus on religious beliefs rather than theology is so as not to exclude Buddhists and other nontheistic religions. My point, though, is that it is appropriate to compare academic discipline to academic discipline, not academic discipline to the individual lay person's beliefs. James W. McClendon, Jr and James M. Smith propose the term 'theoretics' for the rigorous academic study of religious convictions in cases where the predominantly Christian word

'theology' might be objectionable. See their *Convictions: Defusing Religious Relativism* (Valley Forge, PA: Trinity Press International, 1994).

4. He compared Lakatos's work to Kuhn's at a number of points in *Myths, Models, and Paradigms.*

5. Barbour, *Religion in an Age of Science*, 57.

6. Ibid., 61–2.

7. Or theological schools; see Hans Küng, 'Paradigm Change in Theology' in *Paradigm Change in Theology*, ed. by Hans Küng and David Tracy (Edinburgh: T. & T. Clark, 1989).

8. Alasdair MacIntyre, 'Epistemological Crises, Dramatic Narrative, and the Philosophy of Science', *Monist*, 60:4 (October 1977), 453–72; reprinted in *Paradigms and Revolutions*, ed. by Gary Gutting (Notre Dame: University of Notre Dame Press, 1980), 54–74; and in *Why Narrative? Readings in Narrative Theology*, ed. by Stanley Hauerwas and L. Gregory Jones (Grand Rapids, MI: Eerdmans, 1989), 138–57.

9. Imre Lakatos, 'Falsification and the Methodology of Scientific Research Programmes', in *The Methodology of Scientific Research Programmes: Philosophical Papers, Volume One*, ed. by John Worrall and Gregory Currie (Cambridge: Cambridge University Press, 1978), 8–101.

10. Nancey Murphy, *Theology in the Age of Scientific Reasoning* (Ithaca: Cornell University Press, 1990).

11. See my discussion of the extension of atomism to a variety of spheres of life in my *Anglo-American Postmodernity: Philosophical Perspectives on Science, Religion, and Ethics* (Boulder, CO: Westview Press, 1997), ch. 1.

12. Barbour is to be commended for *not* having drawn this conclusion from Kuhn's work. If anything, I believe he presents Kuhn as more of a rationalist than is actually the case. The issue here is not whether Kuhn does or does not describe science as a rational enterprise, but whether he offers any guidance for theory choice. He does not, whereas both Lakatos and MacIntyre do.

13. Alasdair MacIntyre, *Whose Justice? Which Rationality?* (Notre Dame: University of Notre Dame Press, 1988), 166–7. See also his *Three Rival Versions of Moral Enquiry: Encyclopaedia, Genealogy, and Tradition* (Notre Dame, IN: University of Notre Dame Press, 1990) in which he criticizes the 'genealogical tradition' as well.

14. It should be noted that this is my own application of MacIntyre's work, not a project toward which he himself is favorably disposed.

15. For an account of doctrinal theology as a practice, see James W. McClendon, Jr, *Doctrine: Systematic Theology, Volume II* (Nashville, TN: Abingdon Press, 1994), ch. 1.

16. MacIntyre, *Whose Justice?*, 367.

17. Paul Feyerabend described 'reason' itself as a tradition, interacting with the many others in Western history. So the question might be phrased, Can I live out a coherent life story while participating in both traditions?

18. Jeffrey Stout, *The Flight from Authority: Religion, Morality, and the Quest for Autonomy* (Notre Dame, IN: University of Notre Dame Press, 1981).

19. Barbour, *Religion in an Age of Science*, 75.

20. Ibid., 75.

21. See David Bloor, *Knowledge and Social Imagery*, 2nd edn (Chicago: University of Chicago Press, 1991), 17–18.

22. Stephen Toulmin, *Cosmopolis: The Hidden Agenda of Modernity* (Chicago: University of Chicago Press, 1990).

23. Bloor, *Knowledge and Social Imagery*, ch. 4.

24. This essay is a revision and amplification of a paper titled 'Ian Barbour on Religion and the Methods of Science: An Appreciation', presented at the American Academy of Religion theology and science group in November 1994 and published in *Zygon*, 31:1 (March, 1996), 11–19.

III

BARBOUR'S CONTRIBUTIONS TO THEOLOGICAL AND ETHICAL ISSUES

A

God and Nature

Chapter 6

Barbour's Panentheistic Metaphysic

Philip Clayton

A Brief Acknowledgment

Other authors in this volume will have praised Ian Barbour's role as a founder of the religion–science dialogue, as an encyclopedic author, as a clear describer of complicated scientific theories, as an organizer and administrator, and as an authority over a vast range of academic fields.

For my part, I would like to bring to the table his abilities as summarizer of complex, multi-day conferences, such as the 'Science and the Spiritual Quest' (SSQ) conferences at Harvard, in Paris, and in Spain. I will never forget looking up at Ian frequently as he sat in the choir loft of Harvard's Memorial Church during the Harvard SSQ conference. Hour after hour he sat taking notes, calmly but intensely, as the twenty-some speakers presented their twenty-some diverse and not always crystal-clear perspectives. When I walked up to check in with him well into the final day, Ian did not complain, as many might have, 'This is a morass of confusion and equivocation; *no one* could ever summarize this conference coherently!' Instead he said merely, 'Philip, it's a lot of material; could I have an extra minute or two at the end in order to tie everything together?' Those who heard Ian's brilliant synthetic lecture at the end of the Harvard conference recognized the work of a master, bringing together an incredible variety of scientific and religious viewpoints under succinct headings, summarizing them in trenchant formulations, and probing each with critical though always humble questions. On these and similar occasions I was privileged to watch the consummate scholar at work. It is a lesson not soon forgotten.

Barbour as Metaphysician

Many of Ian Barbour's contributions have been amply acknowledged. Less frequently, however, do commentators examine Barbour's role as a metaphysician. Thus it is to this aspect of his work that the bulk of the chapter will be devoted. When metaphysics is mentioned one thinks immediately of Barbour's advocacy of process thought, which (I would like to show) undergirds his constructive theology, his orientation in the science–religion debate, and his ethical and political views.

Just how important is process metaphysics in Barbour's publications? Almost invariably the constructive sections of Barbour's essays end with a segment on process thought. In *When Science Meets Religion,*[1] for example, four of the six sections on 'integration' are devoted to process thought as an apparently successful means for integrating science and religion. In the very important third part of *Religion in an Age of Science*,[2] 'Philosophical and Theological Reflections,' process philosophy dominates the presentation. Looking across the various articles and books, one finds process thought used, in one form or another, as the basis for Barbour's answers to the doctrine of God, the God-world relation, the doctrine of creation, the theory of divine action, the problem of evil, anthropology, the nature and work of Christ, the mind-body problem, emergence, ethics (for example, kenosis), epistemology, feminist philosophy, environmentalism, and eschatology. As he summarizes triumphantly: 'Process thought represents God's action as Creator and Redeemer within a single conceptual scheme.'[3] Given the argumentative weight it bears, it's no overstatement to say that process thought is pervasive in Barbour's opus.

Why Metaphysics?

First of all, what's the significance of the fact that the founding father of the scholarly religion–science dialogue is so deeply committed to process metaphysics? Before one shifts to the details of his position, one should note what it means to ascribe such a role to metaphysical reflection. Three central features of Barbour's overall approach depend directly on this methodological commitment. In each case, I believe, the broader religion–science discussion would do well to follow his example.

- First, starting with metaphysics means that Barbour does not place his own religious faith into unmediated contact with the science he summarizes, but rather seeks conceptual mediation between them.
- Second, this starting point means that the conceptual mediation he offers is not occasionalist or opportunist. Instead of pulling in random analogies and metaphors as might be helpful for each new topic, Barbour has sought to use mediating principles that form a consistent, systematic whole.
- Third, this methodology has (rightly) caused Barbour at different points to question or alter both the science that he summarizes and the theological conclusions that he works with.

Let us reflect on this third feature for a moment. It is the direct source, I suggest, of two fundamental principles that Barbour has brought to the religion–science debate and that together may represent his greatest contribution to the field.

1   Interpreted Science

The primary discussion partner for religion is not the scientific data or results, or even the sum total of physical theories; rather, it includes those theories *as interpreted*. That is, religion–science discussion actually begins with the multiple ways in which scientific theories have been construed philosophically. Barbour recognized this fact as early as his 1974 *Myths, Models, and Paradigms*, which showed how both science and religion actually depend on the choice between competing paradigms and models. What provides fuel for constructive theology is not 'raw' scientific theory in physics or biology but rather the philosophical implications of these theories. It is, if you will, the philosophy of physics or the philosophy of biology that matters most to theologians.

Barbour seems to define metaphysics as the project of deciding among the various philosophical interpretations of science, with special attention to the sorts of philosophical and theological issues that have been central in the religion–science debate. For in evaluating the contending options in the philosophy of science, one encounters the metaphysical positions that will either open the door to theological truth claims or exclude them. Only science as metaphysically interpreted, not 'raw science' or scientific data alone, can serve this function.

2   The Role of Philosophical Theology

For its part, theology may initiate dialogue with the sciences using level-one discourse (for example, immediate statements about faith, ritual, and religious practice) in the sense of the 'first order descriptions' that were the focus of Hans Frei's theology.[4] But if full-fledged dialogue is to entail genuine *interaction* with the sciences, this means that theology will be touched and probed as well. The theology that is capable of stepping outside of the vocabulary of its faith commitments and engaging in this sort of dialogue – and this is Barbour's great insight, which too few of his commentators have recognized – is philosophical theology: theology expressed in terms of a unified metaphysical system. The real discussion partner with the sciences, at least in Barbour's case, is actually Christian metaphysical theism.

By emphasizing these two principles I do not mean to deny that Barbour sometimes, and rightly, suggests more direct connections between scientific practice and religious practice. In fact, his early work on this topic, *Myths, Models, and Paradigms*, offers a number of direct connections of this sort. Still, *Myths* is primarily an essay in the epistemology and methodology of the science–religion dialogue. As Barbour turns to constructive theology, metaphysics increasingly provides the level playing field on which the scientific and theological players can meet and interact. Thus, I suggest, the metaphysical dimension of Barbour's work represents his deeper long-term contribution to the field.

Barbour's Panentheism

As an example of Barbour's methodological commitments, consider his advocacy of panentheism. Studying this example, even briefly, reveals principles of his work as a scientist-theologian that underlie his contributions in most, if not all, of the fields in which he has worked. My core thesis is that Barbour's panentheism relies centrally on the metaphysics of Whitehead and Hartshorne, even though he has modified and extended their metaphysics in interesting ways in order to adapt it to the needs of the religion–science dialogue.

Barbour does not use the word 'panentheism' as frequently in his presentations of process thought as one might expect, but his advocacy of the position is clear by implication. Let me thus first reconstruct the argument that lies behind Barbour's panentheism. In every passage where he addresses the doctrine of God, he clearly accepts a process view of God. For him this means in the first place a doctrine of God inspired by Whitehead's *Process and Reality*.[5] God is 'the primordial ground of order' who 'structures the potential forms of relationship before they are actualized.' But God is also 'the ground of novelty' who presents 'new possibilities among which alternatives are left open.' God influences all events (actual occasions) in the world by providing 'distinctive possibilities to each new entity,' and God is also pervasively influenced by events in the world.[6]

Repeatedly, Barbour endorses the modifications to Whitehead's doctrine of God made by later process thinkers, in particular Charles Hartshorne and David Griffin. Generally, he grants divine transcendence a larger role than Whitehead granted it.[7] This means that Barbour breaks with Whitehead's doctrine of symmetrical co-relation, as expressed in the famous sentences from *Process and Reality*:

> It is as true to say that God is permanent and the World fluent as that the World is permanent and God is fluent.
>
> It is as true to say that God is one and the World many, as that the World is one and God many …
>
> It is as true to say that the World is immanent in God, as that God is immanent in the World.
>
> It is as true to say that God transcends the World, as that the World transcends God.
>
> It is as true to say that God creates the World, as that the World creates God.[8]

Instead, Barbour stands closer to Charles Hartshorne, following him on most of his major modifications of Whitehead's doctrine of God. Thus Barbour comes to accept Hartshorne's view that 'the world is in God (*panentheism*), a view that neither identifies God with the world (*pantheism*) nor separates God from the world (*theism*). "God includes the world but is more than the world."'[9]

Like many other Hartshorne-inspired panentheists, Barbour is willing to speak of God's relationship to the universe as partially analogous to our relation to our bodies. Unlike God's knowledge of the world, which is complete and everlasting, we have only a limited awareness of many aspects of our bodies and only partial memory of the past. Barbour follows Hartshorne in extending the mind-body analogy as a way to conceive God's internal relatedness to the world. Like a mind that embraces every aspect of the body with which it is associated and cares infinitely about every part, God is present to every event in the universe at every moment.[10]

Barbour, in accord with Hartshorne, wants to understand this mind-body analogy as itself 'social in character,' rather than in a reductionistically biological sense. But he breaks with Hartshorne in that he prefers 'interpersonal social models.' This process panentheism, Barbour asserts, is able to offer adequate answers to all six of the major problems faced by the monarchical model of God: the problems of human freedom; evil and suffering; masculine and feminine attributes of the divine; interreligious dialogue; an evolutionary and ecological world; and chance and law.[11]

Entering into Dialogue with Barbour

I strongly endorse all of Barbour's premises so far formulated, both methodological and substantive. His reliance on theistic metaphysics, too seldom recognized, provides a much-needed corrective to theologians as well as to science–religion scholars. But praise alone makes for thin reading. In the latter half of this contribution I suggest we enter into constructive dialogue with Barbour, looking to see how his own project might be extended and completed in a consistent fashion. Three areas of his thought in particular beg for further elaboration and reflection.

1 How Emergentist can Process Thought be?

One encounters a certain tension between the Whiteheadian metaphysics of actual occasions and the doctrine of emergence that Barbour endorses. Following Whitehead, Barbour writes: 'A unified entity at any level contributes something of its own in the way it appropriates its past, relates itself to various possibilities, and produces a novel synthesis that is not strictly deducible from the antecedents.'[12] The strength of Whitehead's process philosophy is that it defines reality in precisely the same sense at every level. All reality consists of moments of experience or 'actual occasions.' Actual occasions 'prehend' previous occasions as their data and become data for later occasions; moreover God offers 'aims' (roughly, a set of possibilities ordered according to their value for the individual actual occasion) to each of these units of experience. True, not all types of experience are identical; human experience is more complex than the experience of amoebas. But, true to its inspiration in the atemporal philosophy of Leibniz (and perhaps to Whitehead's training in logic and physics), Whitehead's philosophy is much more about process than it is about emergence.

By contrast, emergence theories argue for a real change in the nature of the things as they come to exist over the course of evolutionary history. The particles of macrophysics are different from those of subatomic physics; primitive cells exhibit different types of organizational structure than one finds in the molecules of physical chemistry; continual differences in structure and function define the gradations that constitute the plant and animal kingdoms; and differences in types of behavior, self-expression, and awareness of self are crucial in distinguishing between humans and other higher primates. The defining principle of emergence is that these differences at the various levels determine what it is for each type of entity to exist. An ontology of emergence defines the process of evolution, whereas for Whitehead the evolutionary process is a result of the actions of entities called actual occasions, which are fundamentally (ontologically) the same from the beginning of cosmic evolution to the present.

It is not strange that Barbour would want to advocate both emergence and Whitehead's philosophy: emergence is powerfully supported by recent studies across the physical sciences, and the strengths of process thought have already become clear. But that two separate conceptual resources are attractive does not imply that they are conceptually consistent. The question is: Does Barbour go far enough when he begins to concede the weaknesses in Whitehead's position? He writes, 'However, Whitehead himself was so intent on elaborating a set of metaphysical categories applicable to all events that I believe he gave insufficient attention to the radically different ways in which those categories are exemplified at different levels.'[13] As we saw above, Whitehead is committed to a unitary metaphysic of actual occasions, which is often labeled 'panexperientialism.' The followers of Whitehead whom Barbour mentions (Hartshorne and Griffin in particular) still retain this unitary metaphysic, even as they offer changes of emphasis. One faces here, I suggest, a clear decision: either to accept the core tenet of panexperientialism, or to reject it in favor of a genuinely emergentist metaphysics. It is either true or not true that reality is composed of moments of conscious experience 'all the way down,' as it were.

Thus Barbour may face a forced choice here. Although the unitary account of reality given by Whitehead is metaphysically more parsimonious, many scholars have found themselves forced to modify it based on the scientific data that increasingly support an emergentist interpretation of evolution. This leads us to take on the very difficult challenge of developing a metaphysics of emergence that is as sophisticated as Whitehead's metaphysics of process. But at least the challenges are clear. Barbour faces a similar challenge to declare where his primary allegiance rests, and to acknowledge the questions of integration that begin there.

In a famous letter to Samuel Alexander, R.G. Collingwood succinctly states the tensions between Whitehead and emergence theories, and the reasons for preferring the latter:

> There is still one point in which I think … [*Process and Reality*] fails to take up and develop a leading point in [*Space, Time, and Deity*]. Your world seems to me a world in which evolution and history have a real place: Whitehead's world is indeed all process, but I don't see that this process is in the same way productive or creative of new things (e.g., Life, Mind) arising on the old as on a foundation … I don't believe that matter is really alive, and all that business. I think it's only a dodge to evade the question, how does anything generically new come into existence?[14]

To do justice to the emergence of genuinely new types of entities at new levels, one will need to integrate Whitehead with an emergence-based metaphysics. Barbour's comments, it seems, commit him to this task, although he has not yet sufficiently acknowledged its urgency.

2   Problems with 'Dual-aspect' Theories of Mind

Barbour shows a particular attraction to 'two-aspect theories' as an answer to the mind-body problem. For example, in the CTNS volume *Neuroscience and the*

Person, he advocates a position he calls 'dipolar' or 'two-aspect' monism, which he derives (in part) from Whitehead. Thus he writes,

> The process view has much is common with two-language theories or a parallelism that takes mental and neural phenomena to be two aspects of the same events ... All integrated entities at any level have an inner reality and an outer reality, but these take very different forms at different levels.[15]

Barbour adds qualifications, to which we return in a moment. The question remains, however: are two-aspect theories consistent with traditional process thought, and are they consistent with the emergence concepts that he employs? Or does dual-aspect monism in fact reflect a third conceptual system, traceable back to Baruch de Spinoza, that stands in some tension with both of these recent schools of thought?

On Spinoza's view, there is one substance or reality which can be referred to either as 'God' or 'Nature' (*Deus sive Natura*). As Spinoza shows in Book I of his *Ethica more geometrico*, the one infinite substance must possess infinite attributes. Unfortunately, we are aware of only two of these attributes: Thought and Extension. Thought and extension represent two different ways of looking at the one reality, both accurate but neither complete. Hence, there can be no inconsistency between them, *but also no causal interaction*. They are not two separate things but only the one reality looked at in two separate ways. Applied to the mind-body problem, this means that the mental language of thought, wishes and experiences and the neurological language of neurons, synapses, and brain regions are just two different ways of describing the one reality. There is and can be no causal interaction between 'minds' and 'bodies'; they are merely two different paradigms, two different conceptual schemes. Like the proverbial pie, reality allows itself to be sliced in multiple ways. Depending on the context of interest, the one or the other will prove itself more useful.

In contrast to dual-aspect monism, Whitehead's thought clearly gives precedence to the mental as a more accurate description of ultimate reality – hence the standard labels 'panpsychism' or, more appropriately, 'panexperientialism.' Spinoza's dual-aspect theory is even more clearly in tension with emergence theories, which argue for a causal relationship between the central nervous system and the emergent mental phenomena that it produces. Emergence does not accept a 'thing' called soul or mind, but it does accept that certain highly complex physical systems manifest real emergent properties such as thought and volition, which constrain the neurophysiological systems out of which they arise through a sort of 'downward causation.'

Perhaps Barbour would respond that the famous position of Roger Sperry, which holds that 'mind' refers to the brain state as a whole, is both emergentist and an expression of dual-aspect theory. Could this be the view he means to endorse? But even if Sperry's view straddles the fence in this way (a claim that I would dispute if space allowed), it could represent at best only a variant of the 'weak emergence' thesis. Emergence theories today divide clearly into 'weak' and 'strong' theories of mental causation. According to weak emergentists like Sperry, mental states don't actually 'do' anything; all the real causal work is done by the physical states described by the relevant neurosciences. Such a view makes of thought an epiphenomenon, a by-product of physical systems that itself does not produce any actual changes. Although I find this a counter-intuitive position distant enough from our everyday experience as embodied thinkers to be unacceptable, it is no trivial matter to provide compelling reasons for abandoning it.[16] Strong emergence, by contrast, holds that emergent levels of reality like mind can in turn exercise downward causation on the lower levels that give rise to them. Although the downward causation in question must be carefully defined so as to avoid dualism, it is in the end, I think, the more satisfactory position. It is also the only one that is consistent with even a modified form of process thought. Process thought, after all, requires internal or subjective causation and not merely the external, efficient causal interactions between entities that typify physics and biology. For this reason, I (along with authors like Arthur Peacocke and George Ellis) have encouraged Barbour to endorse strong emergence. But if one is a strong emergentist, one cannot also be a dual-aspect monist.

Indeed, in other passages Barbour does actually defend a more robust view of the human self, one which stands closer to strong emergence (or even to weak dualism) than to Whitehead. As Barbour recognizes, 'Whitehead's analysis seems somewhat strained at the two ends of the spectrum,' namely at the level of electrons on the one hand and at the level of the human self on the other.[17] More particularly, he argues,

> I have also questioned whether Whitehead's understanding of the episodic character of moments of experience provides an adequate view of human selfhood. I would argue that we can accept more continuity and a stronger route of inheritance of personal identity without reverting to traditional categories of substance.[18]

Even within the essay that toys with dual-aspect theory, Barbour nuances his position. Thus he writes: 'Unlike many two-aspect theories, [the process view] defends interaction, downward causality, and the constraints that higher-level events exert on events at lower levels. At higher levels there are new events and entities and not just new relationships among lower-level events and entities.'[19] Later he notes that his own view 'is very similar to the emergent monism' that Arthur Peacocke and I defend in the same volume.

But then he adds, 'it would not be inconsistent for [emergent monists] to accept the Whiteheadian emphasis on momentary events and dynamic processes.'[20] This is where the difficulties arise and where more work needs to be done. I share Barbour's sense of the need to supplement process thought, which maintains the episodic character of moments of experience, with a theory of the time-bridging nature of the self. In order to make the needed modifications, however, one must draw on the resources of *other* metaphysical systems, such as German Idealism, which has provided the most sophisticated philosophical account of subjectivity to date. But this requires further constructive work of a sort that still remains to be undertaken.

3   Modified Panentheism

Finally, I suggest that the previous two modifications provide grounds for modifying Barbour's understanding of panentheism, and this in two specific directions. The first modification would strengthen the dimension of emergence, pulling Barbour's doctrine of God in the direction of the Panentheistic Analogy. Recall that the Panentheistic Analogy understands God's relation to the world as analogous in certain respects to the relationship of our mind and body.[21]

Join me in a brief thought experiment. Let us imagine that Barbour accepts strong emergence as described above. This means that the human mind is a higher level of reality, dependent upon the lower levels but also able to influence them in turn. If he then also allows some analogy between the human mind and the mind of God, as process thought requires, then notice what results. Process thinkers correctly realize that God responds not just to a *portion* of the universe as we do, insofar as we have privileged access only to that particular segment of the universe that we call our bodies. Instead, one has to say that the *entire universe* functions for God the way our bodies function for us – the entire universe has 'presentational immediacy' for God. In this respect, at least, God's relationship to the universe would be analogous to our relationship to our bodies. And indeed, Hartshorne's modification of Whitehead's metaphysics moves in precisely this direction. The 'consequent' nature of God is formed of God's response to every actual occasion in the universe at every moment. As the mind (the dominant actual occasion in the human being) unifies the diverse experiences of the body, so God unifies the diverse experiences of the universe into a unity. These sorts of conclusions are consistent with Barbour's opus as a whole and bring additional conceptual clarification to his position.

The second modification goes in a very different direction. It involves a clearer admission of the apparent limitations to metaphysical reflection, pointing toward a deeper element of mystery in all language about God. One possible result is to strengthen the dimension of faith in religious language.

Barbour's work sometimes gives the impression that process philosophy and process theology provide an adequate metaphysical basis for both scientific and religious practice. If this were true, we would presently possess a rational bridge between the two distant shores of science and religion, even if the bridge is still in the early stages of construction. But if, as I have argued, process thought, emergence theory, and dual-aspect monism represent three different conceptual worlds rather than one single metaphysical system, then we do *not* yet possess such a bridge. The pieces of the puzzle do not yet fit together; the final metaphysical account still eludes us; our efforts reveal mystery more than mastery. As Barbour himself writes at one point, 'Only in worship can we acknowledge the mystery of God and the pretensions of any system of thought claiming to have mapped out God's ways.'[22]

Paradoxically, were Ian Barbour to more fully acknowledge the present limitations of process thought – and for that matter, of all present attempts at 'integration' – the great champion of process metaphysics would have to leave a larger place for doctrinal considerations in his thought about God. Suppose, for example, that our metaphysical reflection about God leads us to the tentative conclusion that there is a divine Being who reveals something of his/her nature and values in cosmic evolution, in our intellectual activity, and in our ethical intuitions (Kant's 'the starry heavens above, the moral law within'). Then we might reasonably seek to enhance the limited conclusions of 'unaided human reason' by utilizing the confessional language found in one or more of the world's religious traditions as a possible repository of the divine self-revelation – all the while suspecting that neither they nor the metaphysicians have achieved an exhaustive and fully accurate description of the divine.

This line of argument, which I find plausible, might lead us in turn to begin to explore doctrinal formulations from one or more religious traditions to supplement metaphysical reflection. The result might be a style of doing 'panentheistic metaphysics' similar to Barbour's but divergent from it in certain important respects. It might, for example, give more prominent place to the voice of traditional systematic theology and present-day constructive doctrinal theology. If metaphysics and constructive theology could be integrated in this way, it might serve to supplement the sometimes 'thin' conclusions of the metaphysicians by the richer, 'thicker,' and deeper formulations of the systematic theologians through the ages.[23] Would not the resulting model of panentheism be more attractive and more useful, both for the religion–science debate and for the life of faith?

Notes

1. I.G. Barbour, *When Science Meets Religion* (San Francisco: HarperSanFrancisco, 2000).
2. Idem, *Religion in an Age of Science: The Gifford Lectures 1989–1991 Volume 1* (San Francisco: Harper & Row, 1990).
3. Ibid., 269.
4. See Hans W. Frei, *The Eclipse of Biblical Narrative: A Study in Eighteenth and Nineteenth Century Hermeneutics* (New Haven: Yale University Press, 1974); *The Identity of Jesus Christ: The Hermeneutical Bases of Dogmatic Theology* (Philadelphia: Fortress Press, 1975); *Types of Christian Theology*, ed. by George Hunsinger and William C. Placher (New Haven: Yale University Press, 1992); *Theology and Narrative: Selected Essays*, ed. by Hunsinger and Placher (New York: Oxford University Press, 1993); cf. also Garrett Green (ed.), *Scriptural Authority and Narrative Interpretation* (Philadelphia: Fortress Press, 1987).
5. See in particular Barbour, *Religion in an Age of Science*, ch. 8, esp. 232ff.
6. Barbour, *When Science Meets Religion*, 175–6.
7. Barbour, *Religion in an Age of Science*, 263ff.
8. Alfred North Whitehead, *Process and Reality*, corrected edn, ed. by David Ray Griffin and Donald W. Sherburne (New York: The Free Press, 1978), 348.
9. Quoting Charles Hartshorne, *The Divine Relativity: A Social Conception of God* (New Haven: Yale University Press, 1948), 90.
10. Barbour, *Religion in an Age of Science*, 260.
11. For Barbour's account of how process theism can answer each of these crucial issues in a more convincing way than the monarchical model can, see *Religion in an Age of Science*, 261f.
12. Barbour, *When Science Meets Religion*, 174f.
13. I.G. Barbour, 'Five Models of God and Evolution', in *Evolutionary and Molecular Biology: Scientific Perspectives on Divine Action*, ed. by Robert John Russell, William R. Stoeger, and Francisco J. Ayala (Vatican City State; Berkeley, CA: Vatican Observatory Publications; Center for Theology and the Natural Sciences, 1998), 441.
14. R.G. Collingwood, quoted in Dorothy Emmet's introductory essay to Samuel Alexander's *Space, Time, and Deity, The Gifford Lectures at Glasgow 1916–1918* (London: Macmillan, 1920), xvii f.

15. I.G. Barbour, 'Neuroscience, Artificial Intelligence, and Human Nature: Theological and Philosophical Reflections', in N*euroscience and the Person: Scientific Perspectives on Divine Action*, ed. by Robert John Russell et al. (Vatican City State; Berkeley: Vatican Observatory; Center for Theology and the Natural Sciences, 1999), 249–80, quotes pp. 276 and 275 respectively.

16. But see my *The Emergence of Spirit* (Oxford: Oxford University Press, forthcoming 2004), ch. 2.

17. Barbour, *Religion in an Age of Science*, 227.

18. Barbour, 'Five Models of God and Evolution', 441.

19. Barbour, 'Neuroscience, Artificial Intelligence, and Human Nature', 276.

20. Ibid., 278.

21. See Clayton, *God and Contemporary Science* (Grand Rapids, MI: Eerdmans, 1997), e.g. 233–42, 257–62.

22. Barbour, *Religion in an Age of Science*, 270.

23. Sometimes Barbour seems pulled in this direction, as when he writes, 'The role of God in process thought has much in common with the biblical understanding of the Holy Spirit' ('Five Models of God and Evolution', 440). At other points, however, process thought appears to serve as the touchstone and biblical theology as exemplification or illustration of that metaphysical foundation. Thus he writes in *Religion in an Age of Science*, 'I submit that it is in the biblical idea of *the Spirit* that we find the closest parallels to the process understanding of God's presence in the world and in Christ' (p. 236).

B

Physics and Cosmology

Chapter 7

What is 'the Universe' which Cosmology Studies?[1]

William R. Stoeger, SJ

Cosmology as a Scientific Discipline

What is cosmology? The standard answer is that cosmology is the branch of physics and astronomy which investigates the universe as a single object of study – its history, its structure, its dynamics and the processes which are or have been important in its evolution. And that is certainly correct. But this leads to a further, and in some ways more tricky, question: What is 'the universe' which cosmology studies? And, further, does it really exist? These questions are rarely answered or reflected upon in doing cosmology, nor even in philosophical considerations of its framework and its findings.

Many researchers have pointed out that the object of cosmology – the universe, or perhaps more correctly, the observable universe (see below) – is different from the object of any other science. The universe, they stress, is, first of all, unique – there is only one universe we can study and model.[2] Thus, we cannot investigate other instances of a 'universe' like we can of a star, a galaxy, an animal, a human being. As a result cosmology is, in some ways, more like history than a natural science. Secondly, we are immersed in 'the universe' we study. Not only do we have very limited access to it; we can not even see or examine the entire object we refer to as 'the universe'. Nor can we securely determine its extent. Certainly, we can characterize the extent and the age of our observable region of the universe – what I shall refer to as 'the observable universe' – since the Big Bang, granted the minimal adequacy of our theoretical models of it. But in cosmology we are in some definite way modeling more than the region of the universe we can directly observe. We are attempting to model the entire complex or system which is kinematically and dynamically connected with, and embraces, our observable universe. In fact, not only do we as cosmologists locate the observable universe within 'a more inclusive domain', but we also strive to locate it within, and link it with, the largest and most comprehensive system with which the theory at the moment provides us.[3] We refer to this as 'the universe as a whole'.[4] It is only by referring to this universe as a whole that we can make intelligible the observable universe.

But what is this universe which is unique, in which we are immersed and to which we have only very limited access? What is the object which cosmology claims to study? How can we characterize it? And does it really exist? Or is it just the motley collection of all objects in existence – or all objects we can or potentially will be able to see in the future? And finally, can the universe be infinite in spatial or in temporal extent? This is, I believe, an important question to try to answer and

127

clarify. In doing so, we shall be able to assess more precisely what cosmology is really about, what its limitations are, and what the status of its principal object, 'the universe', is.

This volume is dedicated to Ian Barbour, who pioneered the use of critical realism as a methodological bridge between science and theology. In this paper I examine how cosmology moves from a consideration of 'the observable universe' to the unobserved 'the universe as a whole' in the spirit of critical realism, emphasizing the role that retroduction plays in this process. Retroduction has been strongly emphasized by Ernan McMullin as 'the inference which makes science', and therefore as an important element in the critical-realist bridge. Though Barbour did not explicitly discuss retroduction in his work, he did rely on McMullin's account of critical realism in developing his ideas. In applying it in detail to cosmology, the most fundamental and extensive (one might even say 'extreme') of the natural sciences, I hope to stimulate the strengthening of the bridge which Barbour and McMullin have constructed.

The Universe as a Whole

When we gaze out into space with our telescopes, we discover planets and stars, clusters of stars, interstellar and circumstellar gas clouds, galaxies of various shapes and sizes, clusters of galaxies, and superclusters reaching out to the limits of our observations, and back in time to the cosmic microwave background radiation, which was formed before, and last scattered at, about 300,000 years after the Big Bang. But we do not see 'the universe' as such. There is no object we detect, or can observationally define, as 'the universe'. Not even the cosmic microwave background radiation, which is something like the afterglow of the Big Bang, originating from the hot primeval plasma long before there were stars, and galaxies or any other lumpy structures, and tells us so much about the early universe, specifies the boundaries of the observable universe.[5] And when we model the universe with Friedmann–Lemaître–Robertson–Walker (FLRW) space-times, there is no clear identification between the expanding spatial-sections of these models and an observationally defined object or objects. The identification is with 'the universe as a whole', but we cannot specify that observationally or even conceptually apart from the cosmological models themselves. Of course, what we are doing is considering that everything we see – to the limit of observations – and everything beyond the limit of our observations makes up this 'universe as a whole'. Thus there is no single object we see which we can identify as the universe. We conceive ourselves to be, instead, embedded in the vast physical system which enfolds all other systems, and which, at least in conception, is not subordinated or embraced by any larger system. It is this largest of all systems, which embraces the totality of all that is connected to us in any way whatsoever, that our cosmological models represent.

But how is this 'universe as a whole' – this largest and most comprehensive of all physical systems – described? And what is our justification for doing so? Our specification of 'the universe as a whole' is, as we have just emphasized, accomplished through the cosmological models we adopt. These involve a four-dimensional manifold (three spatial dimensions and one time dimension) with metric, whose curvature and dynamics are determined by the distribution of mass-energy within it through Einstein's general theory of relativity. The mass-energy distributions also obey the other (non-gravitational) laws of physics, and are partially constrained at least by present cosmological observations.[6] These basic models have been further elaborated under severe pressure of the horizon, flatness and inhomogeneity problems into models with very early inflationary phases. At almost the same time, enigmas relating to the need to set initial conditions just after the Big Bang, along with the dawning realization that the initial singularity itself (at "t = 0") demands an adequate quantum-gravity treatment which would unify all four fundamental forces, have led to conceptions or models of 'the universe as a whole' such as those which rely on the wavefunction of the universe and its emergence from a primordial spatial manifold with no boundary,[7] or those of the chaotic inflationary program which consist of a very large (if not infinite) number of horizon-size regions as the entire universe emerges from the Planck epoch,[8] almost immediately after the Big Bang.

Thus, as cosmology and physics develop, the suggested candidates for 'the universe as a whole' change – always becoming more comprehensive and inclusive. This is simply in response to the problems and inadequacies of earlier 'universe as a whole' candidates. Like all other theoretical scientists, cosmologists are continually striving to improve their models and theories, under the requirements new observations and the emerging appreciation of previously unforeseen issues, problems and insights place on them. Each new construction of 'the universe as a whole' is directed towards making reality as we know it – the observable universe as we come to appreciate it more fully, and in greater and greater detail – more intelligible, from the point of view of physics. Each new development attempts to explain aspects or features which earlier cosmological models failed to account for. It goes without saying, that this process will probably continue forever, and that we shall only achieve complete intelligibility – if such is realizable – when we broach the question of the ultimate origin of reality, and the regularities and processes which govern its behavior. This issue, I would maintain, takes us beyond the natural sciences – into the realms of philosophy and theology.

From this characterization of 'the universe', we clearly see that there is no way to identify uniquely 'the universe as a whole'. There is no previously defined and recognized physical system to which we can point and which we are trying to describe and explain. It is rather that that which we gradually come to know of physical reality in its vastness and profundity strongly points to a much more inclusive and comprehensive reality enfolding it and rendering it more intelligible than it is simply within the confines of our observable region. The existence and characteristics of our observable universe demand an explanation and invite our understanding, in terms of physics and philosophy. That inevitably leads us to some 'universe as a whole', whose provisional description evolves as we grow in our appreciation for the requirements which need to be met in order to observe what we observe. In other words, since we can certainly say more and more about what characterizes 'the observable universe', we can use these data to constrain to some degree what 'the universe as a whole' must be like. This is simply because the observable universe must be related to 'the universe as a whole', whatever that is, as a part to the whole, and the whole must be such that it can have a region within itself like the observable universe we experience.

We have reached the conclusion that the observable universe must be a region of a much more inclusive system primarily from the realization that, from the point of view of astronomy and physics, its intelligibility demands it. That is, we cannot understand the evolution and global characteristics of all that is accessible to our observation, much less its origin, say in quantum cosmological terms, in light of our present knowledge of physics, except as part of a larger overarching system which originated at the time of the Big Bang – or 'before' it. The need for this cosmic context of intelligibility is comparable to our need on a more local level for our solar system, and for our galaxy the Milky Way, in order to understand why the Earth exists and why we are here on it. (The difference is that we can observe and directly investigate these systems, whereas we cannot observe anything we can identify with 'the universe as a whole'.)

As a consequence, even the way we define the observable universe and describe its characteristics in terms of observations of the cosmic microwave background radiation and of the distribution of distant galaxies and clusters of galaxies depends crucially on our model of 'the universe as a whole'. This stems from our reliance on that model in interpreting those data. Observations of any sort – and cosmological observations are no exception – are very much theory laden. There are no model independent characteristics of our observable universe! This does not mean that the observational results are unreliable. It just means that they are provisional – as all scientific results are – as long as the model upon which their meaning and interpretation depends continues to be confirmed and supported. That will be the case provided that the model as it is developed continues to yield consistent and well-supported descriptions and interpretations of the observational results; leads to the solution of outstanding problems; and predicts phenomena which are eventually observed. These are the criteria which support the 'truth' of the model.[9]

This viewpoint is consonant with Ernan McMullin's emphasis[10] on the essential role retroduction plays in the natural sciences. Retroduction – which was first clearly distinguished by C.S. Peirce (he usually referred to it as 'abduction') – is the process by which the scientist uses his or her well-educated imagination to construct hypotheses concerning hidden realities, causes or relationships to explain observable phenomena, including regularities, processes, structures, correlations, and relationships. These hypotheses then undergo rigorous testing and modification over a period of time, until the resulting modified hypotheses reach a point where they are sufficiently well-confirmed to provide the basis for further scientific investigation and are accepted as the foundation for understanding the phenomena in question. The criterion for retroduction is its success and fertility. The actual entities hypothesized – such as, in our case, 'the universe as a whole' with certain definite characteristics – may continue to be hidden or directly inaccessible in many ways. But, if our employment in a scientific theory successfully and convincingly explains what we observe and provides a key to further knowledge and understanding, then this constitutes a compelling, but still provisional, warrant for affirming that those entities exist and have the characteristics the theory says they have. McMullin supports his emphasis on retroduction by demonstrating its importance in many key scientific discoveries of the distant and recent past, such as those of Galileo, Newton, Einstein, and Darwin.

In fact, McMullin specifically reflects on the application of retroduction to contemporary cosmology. In agreement with what we have already pointed out, he says that 'retroduction can ... establish the existence of structures and processes altogether different from any that lie within direct reach, and is limited only by the resources of the scientific imagination ... It is on this much more powerful pattern of inference that cosmology mainly relies.'[11] He goes on to indicate that the use of retroduction in cosmology enables us to affirm the existence of the universe as a single object of inquiry:

> When the spectra of distant stars, or the velocities of distant galaxies, continue to be interpretable by schemas derived from terrestrial processes, confidence quite properly grows in the assumption that these schemas are not just conventions imposed for convention's sake or because our minds cannot operate otherwise, but that all parts of the universe are united in a web of physical process which is accessible through coherent and ever-widening theoretical constructs created and continually modified by us.[12]

Throughout Munitz's philosophical analysis of cosmology he stresses the distinction between the 'grammatical rules' of a cosmological model, its meaning, and its truth value – 'how good is it when compared to other accounts in saying "how things are", "what the facts are".'[13] The primary 'grammatical rule' of a cosmological model, according to Munitz, is its leading idea. Examples of leading ideas would be: the steady state universe, the Big Bang universe, the inflationary scenario, Hawking and Hartle's wavefunction of the universe idea, Linde's chaotic cosmology scheme.[14] Other such rules consist in the laws, theories and mathematics which the model incorporates and uses in describing and elaborating its conception of the universe as a whole.[15]

Turning to the 'truth' of the cosmological model, in determining that in terms of the three general criteria we mentioned above – success in describing and interpreting observational data, providing solutions to key problems, and predicting phenomena which are eventually confirmed – Munitz relies on a pragmatic, rather than on a correspondent, concept of truth.[16] That means that the 'truth' of the model does not depend on there existing independently of our knowledge 'a universe as a whole' which has all the characteristics of 'the universe as a whole' given by the model. We have no way of determining that. Rather the truth of the model depends on 'the adequacy or success with which a given cosmological model performs the roles of description, explanation and prediction relative to other models'.[17] We really cannot go further than that.

However, this already means, even from a weakly critical-realist perspective – and certainly from the point of view of McMullin's stress on the importance and strength of retroduction – that 'the universe as whole' of which we are a part must be something vaguely like that given by the model. In particular that there must be such a largest, most comprehensive system which fulfils functions like those specified in the model, even though we cannot show that it is the unique or final explanation. Munitz would not agree with this move, but I would appeal to the recalcitrance of reality in support of it. We can rule out many competing models on the basis of our observations and experiments over a period of time. Only one or two survive – these are better models of the way things really are, though never a final, perfect or unique description (there will be further improvements and perhaps even conceptually different candidates), precisely because they represent reality more accurately than the other previously held models.

Uncertain Features of Cosmological Models

Our cosmological models will still always possess features which may not represent the reality of the cosmological situation accurately (we can say this of any model used in the sciences, with respect to the reality it is attempting to model). This is particularly the case with their reliance on the underlying model of the space-time manifold upon which they are based. It is this which supplies the global connectivity of 'the universe as a whole' which the cosmological represents – a connectivity which transcends that accomplished via light signals and which expresses the uniformity of physical laws within it. But we can always ask, 'Upon what basis can that connectivity and that uniformity of physical laws be explained?' It is presently impossible to give an adequate answer to this question. Another way of posing the issue is to recognize that there is a tendency to reify the spatial manifold and to conceive it, for example, as a spatial manifold (or membrane) expanding under the influence of the vacuum energy it 'contains' on scales which are larger than that of the causal horizons defined within it.[18] It is unclear whether such features really represent reality as it is, or are just auxiliary concepts which are necessary for successfully applying the model but are not representative of the actual 'universe as a whole'. This is a very compelling reason for stressing their provisional character and for adopting a pragmatic notion of truth in evaluating them.

Unfortunately, as I have pointed out above, at present there is no adequate way of uniquely specifying the extent and overall composition of the universe as a whole, nor the evolutionary interrelationship and physics of its largest subsystems, one of which surely embraces our 'observable universe'. And perhaps we never shall. There are, as most are aware, various scenarios which have been suggested, for example the chaotic inflationary scheme of Andrei Linde,[19] which envisions a vast number of sub-universes developing at the moment of the Big Bang, and even afterwards, as the whole complex of physical reality emerges from the Planck era. Some of these inflate, like ours; and some fail to inflate, remaining stillborn. Each one can reproduce at an early stage of its evolution, spawning large numbers of 'baby-universes'. Speculative detailed accounts such as this depend, of course, on the physics of primordially super-extreme situations, when it is likely that all four fundamental physical interactions were unified in a quantum-gravity framework. We do not yet possess an adequate complete model of such a framework. However, we can certainly begin to rule out many accounts and their corresponding models. Thus our characterizations of exactly what is necessary for complete intelligibility of our observational universe, even from the point of view of physics – much less philosophy – are very preliminary. As a result our ideas concerning the largest system, 'the universe', necessary for our existence are also preliminary, and very uncertain.

Observational Support for the Universe as a Single Object

Nevertheless, we are relatively certain about what characterizes our 'observable universe', and about some of the key cosmic requirements for its existence. Most importantly, we now realize that all that we see – to the very limit of our observations – shares the same evolutionary origin and history, and the same fundamental laws and constants. The observable universe is not a collection of objects having completely disparate origins and histories, and governed by different laws of nature. There is, instead, overwhelming evidence that everything in our observable universe is intimately interconnected, and shares the same fundamental physics. That is precisely why we can treat it as a single system. This is strongly indicated by the very existence of the cosmic microwave background radiation, which we now know has its origin in the hot, ionized primeval plasma which filled the universe before the galaxies were formed and which we encounter in every direction we look. It has the same temperature, to within one part of 100,000, and the same characteristics (most notably its almost perfect black-body spectrum) in every direction. This indicates that every region of the observable universe possessed the same features and had the same temperature several hundred thousand years after the Big Bang. Further, less startling support is provided by the similar large-scale features we see throughout the observable universe in every direction, and the mounting evidence that the laws of physics are uniform throughout all the vast regions so far accessible to our observations. Thus it seems that the observable universe must be a single connected manifold or system which has its own dynamics – it is now very clear that our observable universe has been expanding and cooling in a uniform way for at least 12 billion years.

If the observable universe has these characteristics, then it is a simple step to conclude that there is a much larger system, the universe as a whole, which also has similar properties. That step is simply moving from what we see – the observable universe is defined relative to our position as observers, considering the limits of what we can observe now or in the future from this spatial position – to what we cannot observe but which we have good reason to believe exists beyond those limits. Other observers within our observational horizon will have an observable universe which overlaps ours but extends beyond where we can see. And there is no clue of anything which would bound that patchwork of overlapping observational universes. Furthermore, as I have already emphasized, we need to have a much larger, more inclusive system which enfolds these nearby observable universes, in order to explain adequately the principal features they exhibit. The key reason for this is that, from a scientific point of view, there is no reason why our spatial position should be privileged (the cosmological principle) – in fact, we have every reason to believe (though we cannot observationally prove this) that it is similar to all other spatial positions. This is a foundational presupposition of contemporary scientific cosmology. It implies that our observable universe is not the only one – and that there are many other such regions, all of which require the larger universe to have properties consistent with the properties we see. This automatically compels us to derive the properties and characteristics of our observable universe from those of a much more comprehensive system. It is in light of such comprehensive models that the cosmologically relevant data such as galaxy number counts and the cosmic microwave background radiation spectral, temperature and anisotropy data have been interpreted. They have provided a consistent and a reliable foundation for further investigation, prediction, and observational testing. On the basis of this line of reasoning, not only must this more comprehensive 'universe as a whole' have features consistent with those of our observational universe. It must also be spatially unbounded (but not necessarily spatially infinite), enveloping all the regions to which our observable universe is in any way connected.

Infinite Space and Infinite Time?

The various models cosmologists develop of 'the universe as a whole' raise a subsidiary philosophical problem, which we should briefly discuss here, particularly because it comes up in our next section, where we discuss Stanley L. Jaki's argument for there being a definable object we can call 'the Universe'. It is the problem of realized infinity. There are two primary contexts in which it arises in cosmology. The first concerns the infinite spatial sections some standard cosmological models possess. The second is the issue whether or not a given universe as a whole could be without a beginning in time, that is, whether going back into the history of our universe as a whole could involve an infinite past time – or, what may not be equivalent, whether the universe as a whole has always existed in some form. There has been a long and significant strand of philosophical tradition going all the way back to Aristotle,[20] and recently finding resurgence in the analysis and reflections of the mathematician David Hilbert, maintaining that, though there are potentially infinite processes (for example, one can count forever without coming to an end, or can continue to divide and subdivide a line segment forever), there can be no physically actualized infinite sets of objects.[21] There are philosophers and mathematicians who maintain that an actualized infinity is possible, reflecting on the groundbreaking work of Georg Cantor on transfinite numbers. We cannot resolve this controversy here. But we can present the principal lines of argument on each side, show how they apply, or do not apply, to the cosmological models, and hazard some preliminary conclusions about actualized infinities in these contexts.

Before describing the two basic positions in the controversy, its relevance to both the spatial and the temporal extent of 'the universe as a whole' should be explained. The spatial issue is more easily understood, and less complicated. So we shall treat that first. When we model the observable universe, which is definitely of finite extent, some of the models which we find most compelling and adequate for 'the universe as a whole' which embraces our observable universe have infinite, unbounded spatial sections. This is the case with both the open and the flat Friedmann–Lemaître–Robertson–Walker (FLRW) cosmological models, which are used pervasively in contemporary cosmology. This means that at any moment in the history of such a model universe, its spatial extent is infinite and unbounded – it extends forever in every direction (in three dimensions), just like an infinite flat spatial plane in two dimensions. Neither the models themselves, nor other known physics or astronomy, provide a natural way of bounding its spatial extent, or preventing it from going on forever. That automatically means that such 'universes as a whole' contain an infinite amount of mass-energy, as well. The closed FLRW models, on the other hand, which represent universes which have a high enough mass-energy density so that they will eventually stop expanding and collapse, have finite spatial sections without boundary. Now, if it continues to be the case that the best models of the observable universe are open or flat FLRW models, does that necessarily mean that we must envision 'the universe as a whole' embracing it to be spatially infinite? Obviously not! It just means that the best available model of the finite observable universe suggests an infinite universe as whole, which may or may not be the case in reality itself. If we find, scientifically or philosophically, that an unbounded infinite spatial manifold is not realizable, then there must be some way of modifying these otherwise acceptable models so that they are finite.

In fact there is such a way to modify flat and open cosmological models, in order to make their spatial sections finite. It involves wrapping the spatial sections around to meet themselves 'on the other side'. For example, if we consider the universe a Euclidean cube, the top of the cube can be stretched and wrapped around to join smoothly onto the bottom of the cube, the left side wrapped around to join the right side, and the front side wrapped around to join the back side of the cube. This is referred to as a 3-torus, or three-dimensional donut. The two-dimensional version is simpler to visualize – involving the identification or joining of the top and bottom of a square, and then the identification of the left and right sides. This gives the two-dimensional surface of a donut or 2-torus.[22] The way in which space is connected globally is referred to as its 'topology'. By doing this we can keep the local structure and dynamics of the universe open or flat (expanding forever) while enabling the spatial sections to remain finite. In essense, there are infinitely many ways of effecting this for an open universe. Einstein's equations do not specify the global topology of the universe. The only way of determining that our universe has a multiply connected 'toplogy' like that of the 3-torus described above would be to make observations of distant galaxies or cosmic microwave background (CMB) fluctuations and show that there are multiple images of each galaxy or fluctuation – that is, the same galaxy or fluctuation is seen in different directions at different times.[23] To rule this out, we would have to show that none of the images we see at great distances in different directions is of the same galaxies or fluctuations. For the purposes of this paper, we shall not consider this possibility further, but rather focus on whether, philosophically speaking, there could in principle be infinite spatial sections, and an infinite temporal past.

As already indicated, the question of infinite past time, or whether or not the universe as a whole always existed, is more difficult and conceptually uncertain. The basic philosophical question is: Can there be, in principle, a series of moments extending backwards in time to infinity? That is, can there already have been, to this point in time, the elapse of an infinite amount of time – or the occurrence of an infinite number of events? This is, clearly, the question of whether or not there can be a realized, or an achieved, infinity. Aristotle, Hilbert,[24] and many others would say no. And we shall examine the argument for that position, as well as that for the opposing position. But, first, we must discuss whether or not such considerations are really relevant to contemporary cosmology. As we shall see, their applicability is not at all clear.

It is obvious, first of all, that all the FLRW models themselves as such have a finite past time. The 'beginning' of the universe in such models is at the initial singularity, or Big Bang, and the time elapsed from the Big Bang to the present moment is always finite. And it is quite easy to argue on other grounds that the time from the Big Bang until now must be finite. But the FLRW models, as we have discussed earlier, really do not adequately represent 'the universe as a whole.' If we have encompassed the FLRW model which most adequately represents our observable universe by something like Linde's chaotic inflationary model, then it is very clear that the FLRW Big Bang is not the beginning of everything, only the beginning of our part of the overall multiverse, or 'universe as a whole.' According to this overall scenario, there were billions upon billions of other universes – or universe domains – like ours which could have existed, and which may still exist in some form or another. And those may stretch back forever in some sort of 'time'. Or could they? Does such a cosmological multiverse model philosophically require some sort of 'beginning'? Do the philosophical and mathematical arguments against a realized infinity apply to this case?

A severely complicating aspect to this and other emerging quantum cosmological models of 'the universe as a whole' is the uncertain primordial status of time itself. Time, as it is presently conceived in physics, has no absolute character, but is a property which is defined relative to the internal dynamics of certain systems. And it is not clear that it can always be defined. It is very unlikely that anything like a meaningful time can be applied to the overall multiverse which is essential to Linde's chaotic inflationary paradigm – it may very well be that only for each separate universe which emerges from the overall initial cluster of universes can a meaningful time be assigned. Furthermore, there is at least some evidence that, even for our Big Bang, time may not have existed at 'the beginning' – that time as we know it only gradually emerged as our observable universe made its transition from the Planck era of total quantum unification into the era of a classical relativistic space-time manifold. If this continues to be confirmed, then the origin of time cannot be identified with a temporal origin of the physical universe, if there was one. And then, although past time itself, in any definable sense, would be finite, there would be a sense in which the universe had existed forever, in some sort of timeless quantum configuration, from which its temporal phase eventually emerged. If this turns out to be nearer the truth, then the argued prohibition against a realized past infinity of temporal instants or events would not apply. There would be an existent primordial quantum configuration without temporal instants or events. Thus, the only way in which we could argue against a universe as a whole without a temporal beginning would be, as I mentioned above, first to show that some meaningful more universal concept of time is applicable to these extreme and counter-intuitive quantum cosmological situations, and second to demonstrate that the arguments against a realized infinity could be applied to that extended temporal concept. This possibility, however, would have to be, at least partially, the product of quantum cosmological considerations themselves – not simply of a priori philosophical analysis.

And now let us look briefly at the controversy regarding actualized infinity. First with respect to the question of whether an infinite spatial extent can be realized, and then to the issue of whether there can be an infinite temporal past, prescinding from the important quantum cosmological considerations we just touched on.

As already discussed, the flat and open FLRW models of our universe as a whole so far provide the most reliable descriptions within which our observable universe can be understood. These models possess infinite spatial sections (for a simply connected topology, that is, one with no wrapping of space to meet itself) – the expanding spatial manifold given by the model is infinite. Obviously, the fact that the mathematical model has infinite spatial sections does not necessarily imply that the our real universe as a whole must have them. It just means that, given our present state of knowledge and understanding, these models provide the best description so far. Future observations may indicate that our universe is not simply connected, but rather multiply connected – so that it wraps around upon itself spatially, preventing the spatial sections from being infinite. This would require a simple and straightforward modification of our cosmological models, adding the specification of a multiply connected topology. Obviously, such a specification would be the most natural way of insuring the finitude of the spatial universe, without introducing any edges. But, returning to our principle question, the fact that infinite spatial sections, or infinite sets, are conceivable without mathematical contradiction does not imply that they are physically realizable. Thus our central question is: Is it logically or metaphysically possible for real, physical space containing a distribution of mass-energy to be infinite? More generally, as William Lane Craig poses the question,[25] can 'the infinite as a completed determinate whole' be physically realized or instantiated? Are there clear and compelling ways to show that this is not possible? If such infinite structures are conceivable without mathematical or logical contradiction, what would make their physical realization impossible?

As we shall see, in speaking about infinite time intervals, a number of philosophers, mathematicians, and physicists maintain that it is not physically possible to achieve an actually infinite collection of objects, events, or physically distinguishable entities. Their arguments seem to presuppose beginning with a finite collection and then attempting to add to it sequentially in order to arrive eventually at an infinite set of objects or events. Whether this can be done or not, whether this is logically or metaphysically possible or not, whether this is even meaningful or not, we shall consider below. But this is not the issue with the spatially infinite sections in these models, about whose concrete realization we are asking. They were never finite to begin within – they are given as infinite from the beginning, even at the Big Bang. Can a space of infinite extent, thus containing an infinite amount of mass-energy, exist in reality? Here, obviously, we are talking not just about mathematical existence – clearly, infinite sets and infinite spaces of all sorts can exist mathematically. We are speaking of concrete physical existence.

In the continuing controversy about the possibility of the existence of something actually infinite, even when given 'all at once', the bases for the objections are of two general types. The first stresses that the existence of the actually infinite inevitably leads to unresolvable contradictions or antinomies as well as the necessity of rejecting intuitively obvious principles, such as 'the whole is greater than any of its parts', or 'adding objects or space to any set or manifold, even an infinite one, makes the set or manifold larger', which are generally applicable in all finite situations. The antinomies and contradictions are those which afflict the foundations of naive set theory – such as Cantor's antinomy.[26] One of Cantor's theorems is that 'the set of all subsets of any given set has a cardinal number greater than the set itself'. But this means that the set of all sets has the set of all its subsets with a cardinal number that is greater than the set of all sets itself. This is contradictory, since the original set was postulated to be 'the set of all sets.' Some mathematicians have circumvented these contradictions by placing restrictions on the ways in which sets can be legitimately defined. However, these restrictions have been judged by others as *ad hoc* and inadequate.

The second type of basis for objecting to the existence of the actually infinite is the intuitionist critique. According to this point of view, only sets and structures should be admitted as mathematically legitimate which are constructible – and given in a complete and determinate way.[27] Actually infinite sets are not constructible, and therefore should not be considered legitimate. These can be admitted only as potentially infinite or indefinite (for example, forever extendible) sets or spaces, but not as actually infinite. And, if these are not admissible mathematically, then they are inadmissible in reality. A similar principle has been formulated by David Hilbert:

> Just as operations with the infinitely small were replaced by operations with the finite which yielded exactly the same results and led to exactly the same elegant formal relationships, so in general must deductive methods based on the infinite be replaced by finite procedures which yield exactly the same results …[28]

This would seem to rule out abandoning basic principles which apply to the finite in order to work with the actually infinite.

The fundamental rejoinder to these criticisms from those supporting the possibility of the actually infinite is either to stress that some of the logical principles for dealing with the actually infinite are different in some ways from those pertaining to the finite – for example, with respect to the relationship of a part to the whole – or to deny that what is strictly mathematically admissible according to certain interpretations and allowable procedures, actually infinite sets and structures, are incapable of being realized in physical reality. This might be called the 'Platonic' position.

Applying these considerations to the infinite spatial sections of open and flat FLRW models, it is certainly true that the spatial sections at later times will be 'larger' than those at earlier times, though all of them will be infinite. This is certainly valid, according the canons of Cantor's transfinite arithmetic, but not according to some intuitionist and more traditional (for example, Aristotelian and neo-Scholastic) philosophical critiques of it and its applications. Evaluating the arguments on each side of the debate, I believe that it is likely that we cannot deal with the actually infinite in mathematics or in philosophy in a well-defined and unambiguous way. Assuming that the concepts we have of the actually infinite are adequate and well-defined seems to lead to puzzles, contradictions, and counter-intuitive results which resist resolution. However, this does not mean, it seems to me, that the existence of an actually infinite space or set is logically or metaphysically impossible. That may be, but nothing in the arguments available demonstrates that – only that our conceptual apparatus for dealing with that possibility is not adequate. I suspect that our conceptual structures are really confined to the potentially infinite, and that we really are not able to deal with, or manipulate conceptually, actually infinite structures, if they exist. This is confirmed by the fact that we really do not have any model or way of dealing with 'the completion' of an infinite set or space – they are really never complete – they go on without limit or end, and without retracing any earlier points or elements. In that sense, they are really 'indefinitely large', and to refer to them as 'infinite' really does not specify them any more than that – it is really equivalent to the negative definition that it is simply 'without end.'

In moving to a consideration of the possibility of a realized infinite past time, the reflections above are also pertinent. But, there is an additional very important issue that is not relevant in the case of realized infinite space which has received much attention from mathematicians and philosophers and which casts doubt upon the possibility of realized infinite past time. That is the fact that time is not given all at once, as space generally is, but sequentially in a series of moments or events. Past time is therefore different from future time, in that for past time those events or moments have already happened, or have been 'completed', whereas future time consists of all those moments or events which have not yet happened, but which potentially will or can happen. Thus, an infinite past time represents a never-ending, limitless series of moments or events which has already been completed up to the present. We can certainly go backwards indefinitely into the past, by construction, but there is no way of beginning far enough in the past and ending up at the present moment, such that an infinite amount of time has elapsed. It is impossible to construct such a series or visualize how such a series could be actualized – and yet we would be maintaining that it has been completed. How could that ever have happened? It cannot have had a beginning. We cannot begin the construction of such an infinite completed series of moments without 'beginning' an infinite time ago, but then no matter how long we go, we never arrive at a point where we are at present infinitely far from the beginning, as required. Bertrand Russell pointed this out long ago – that classes or structures which are infinite have to be given 'all at once'. They cannot be given or completed by 'successive synthesis'.[29]

Defenders of an actual infinite past argue in reply that, though it is true that it is impossible to conceive constructing an infinite past by successive addition of moments, that is simply because we are still locked into thinking of doing it in a finite time. We need to realize that this is done only in an infinite time. This reply, however, still seems lame – simply because there is no way of definitely conceiving a *completed* infinite series of moments, even in an infinite time – we just do not have the capacity to model a completed infinite time. All we have is the concept of a series of moments which continues forever without end, and without definite completion, without ever reaching a point at which it has already been going on for an infinite amount of time. Thus, it appears that we run into another version of the ambiguities, indefiniteness and inescapable potentiality of any concept of the infinite as applied to what is physical or material.

This discussion, of course, prescinds from the separate more fundamental questions of whether time itself only emerged 'later' on from the eternally existing primordial universe – that is, whether the universe in some sense always existed, even though time emerged from the quantum cosmological substrate only a finite time ago – or whether there are applicable and meaningful concepts of time, according to which the quantum cosmological scenarios of ensembles of universes emerging from the primordial quantum foam can be ordered in some way according to 'before and after.' If there was a 'time' when there was no time, then it seems perfectly possible that the universe as a whole, in some quantum configuration, could have always existed, with time as we know it emerging 'later.'

In summary, I believe we can say that time as we conceive it philosophically and physically seems to exclude the possibility of an infinite past. However, it is at least possible, paradoxically speaking, that the universe as a whole of which we are a part always existed – that is, it never had a beginning in time. This could have been the case, as I have just mentioned, if there was a primordial quantum cosmological configuration which possessed no temporal characteristics, and from which time itself emerged, say, as the gravitational interaction separated from the other three non-gravitational forces. Furthermore, with regard to the space of our universe as a whole, though our concepts of infinite sets and spaces lead to certain contradictions and paradoxes, these seem to be the result of the inadequacy and limitations of the concepts themselves rather than an indication of the impossibility of an actually given infinite space or set. At a minimum, we must say that an actually infinite space, or spatial section, in the universe as a whole leads to no clear violation of logic or metaphysics.

Other Philosophical Reflections

We have been focusing on the observable universe and on 'the universe as a whole,' concepts which we derive from the practice of contemporary cosmology. The recognition of the differentiated interconnectedness of all things within our observable cosmic region along with the strong requirement for a largest inclusive and most comprehensive physical system to provide the observable universe's full scientific intelligibility must be carried over to philosophical considerations. Perhaps this scientific starting point can provide philosophy with a firmer basis for pursuing questions relating to creation and the laws of nature.

In fact, intertwined in the tortuous reflections of the philosophy of nature down through the centuries have been speculative clues that something like 'the universe as a whole' of contemporary cosmology exists. In his provocative little book *Is*

There a Universe?,[30] Stanley L. Jaki traces the history, development and implications of this idea, and ends by suggesting an outline for a philosophical proof that there is a universe, based on Aristotelian/Thomistic insights.[31] Though no rigorous proof is elaborated, its principal steps can be discerned from Jaki's reflections. The starting point is to recognize the existence of material things and their rationality. The fact that things exist and are understandable implies a certain unity of all things. Though one individual existing entity is not another individual existing entity, all of them are related, or connected, to one another, in various ways, via universal characteristics, laws of nature, systems. And we employ universals to understand and know them. Each thing is in some way ordered to the others. Thus, the multitude is a unity. Otherwise, it would not be knowable. Then Jaki goes on to emphasize that, since everything material that exists can be numbered, or represented and described using number, it must be bounded, not infinite. This is simply because, he maintains, an infinite number of objects cannot be realized. Thus, there exists a finite bounded unity of all that exists which is interconnected. Whether we see such a proof as compelling or not, it is interesting to see its relationship with what we have already discovered from our reflections on cosmology – in particular the connected character of reality as we experience and observe it. This is certainly an essential feature of what 'the universe as a whole' means. It is also somewhat surprising to see the role rationality, or intelligibility, plays in both the Aristotelian/Thomistic philosophical and the contemporary cosmological portrayal of 'the universe'. The one step of the philosophical argument outlined above with which cosmologists might well take issue is the countably finite characterization of the universe. As we have mentioned, some of the cosmological models of 'the universe as a whole' and the other (closed FLRW) models have infinite spatial sections without boundary. However, I doubt that this step is essential to the philosophical argument. What is essential is the interconnectedness, or interrelatedness, of the universe.

Conclusions

Cosmology and astrophysics have shown us that there is a reality we can meaningfully identify as 'the universe,' the largest of all systems which embraces our observable region and renders it intelligible. However, we cannot observationally study it as such, or adequately describe its extent and its characteristics. Nevertheless, we can securely investigate our observable region, which itself is incredibly vast in extent and compellingly argue to the profound and radical interconnectedness of all that it contains. From there we can also securely argue, as I have indicated, to the existence of some much larger, more comprehensive 'universe as a whole.' Only with that does our observable universe have adequate intelligibility.

Thus, there are at least three levels of 'universe.' There is the observable universe we have access to. There is the universe as a whole, to which we do not have direct access, but to whose existence – and to some of whose characteristics – we can infer, from what we know of the observable universe and what is needed for understanding it. And there is what might be called the 'totality of all that is', which may be coextensive with the universe as a whole, but also may be much larger than that. It refers to all that exists. This might be much larger than the universe as a whole, because it might include entities which fall outside what is physically discernible or describable, as well as physical entities or systems which are completely disconnected from us – are neither observable by us in principle, nor connected with our observable universe in any other way, nor necessary for its intelligibility. Neither philosophically nor scientifically can we rule out such entities and systems. But they cannot constitute 'the universe as a whole,' which cosmology attempts to describe and model.

Notes

1. This article (copyright 2001 by the Pachart Foundation) was originally published under the same title in *Philosophy in Science*, Volume 9, edited by William R. Stoeger, SJ, Michael Heller, and Józef M. Zyciński (Tucson, AZ: Pachart Publishing House, 2001), 9–28. It is being reprinted here with permission in modified form; Section 5 is new.
2. Cf. for instance William R. Stoeger, SJ, 'Contemporary Cosmology and Its Implications for the Science–Religion Dialogue', in *Physics, Philosophy and Theology: A Common Quest for Understanding*, ed. by Robert J. Russell, William R. Stoeger, SJ, and George V. Coyne, SJ, Scientific Perspectives on Divine Action Series (Vatican City State; Berkeley, CA: Vatican Observatory Publications; Center for Theology and the Natural Sciences, 1988), 220–47 (see page 228f).
3. Milton K. Munitz, *The Question of Reality* (Princeton: Princeton University Press, 1990), 189.
4. The first and only person I am aware who has discussed this clearly and carefully is Milton K. Munitz, *Cosmic Understanding: Philosophy and Science of the Universe* (Princeton: Princeton University Press, 1986), 51–7, 60–69, 150–73; *The Question of Reality*, 139–59, 173–91.
5. The boundary of the observable universe at any point in time can be strictly given by what is known as the visual horizon which is defined as the set of particle world-lines which are future-directed from the intersection of our past light cone with the surface of the last scattering, at which the universe first becomes transparent to radiation and where the photons of the cosmic microwave background radiation were on average last scattered before moving on towards us through the more recent transparent epochs of cosmic history. However, as is clear, the visual horizon is always expanding outward, simply because our past light cone is gradually including more and more of the universe. Thus, the observable universe might be roughly defined as all that which falls within the visual horizon at some distant future moment. The particle horizon is farther out, and is defined analogously, but in terms of the future-directed world lines emanating from the intersection of our light cone with the surface of the initial singularity (Big Bang). The particle horizon is the limit of causality in our region of the universe. It may be possible, eventually to acquire cosmologically relevant data from beyond the visual horizon (but never from beyond the particle horizon) via neutrinos or gravitational waves. Cf. G.F.R. Ellis and W.R. Stoeger, 'Horizons in Inflationary Universes', *Classical and Quantum Gravity*, 5 (1988), 207–20.
6. In principle, they can be completely constrained by observational data, arrayed along our past light cone. See, for instance, G.F.R. Ellis, D.M. Matravers, and W.R. Stoeger, 'Complementary Approaches to Cosmology: Relating Theory and Observations', *Quarterly Journal of the Royal Astronomical Society*, 36 (1995), 29–45, and references therein.
7. Stephen W. Hawking, 'The Boundary Conditions of the Universe', in *Astrophysical Cosmology*, ed. by H.A. Bruck, G.V. Coyne, and M.S. Longaire (Vatican City: Pontifical Academy of Sciences, 1982), 563–72; James B. Hartle and Stephen W. Hawking, 'Wave Function of the Universe',

Physical Review, D 28 (1983), 2960–75; cf. also C.J. Isham, 'Creation of the Universe as a Quantum Process', in *Physics, Philosophy and Theology*, 375–408.

8. The Planck epoch is defined as that extremely early stage of cosmic evolution, immediately after the Big Bang, during which quantum gravity completely dominates and all four interactions are unified into one 'superforce'. Presently available physics is not adequate to describe this regime. Work in quantum cosmology and on various quantum gravity programs (for example, superstrings) may eventually yield an adequate model of the physics at these extremely high temperatures T > 10^32 K.

9. Munitz, *The Question of Reality*, 168–73; 187–90.

10. Ernan McMullin, 'Structural Explanation', *American Philosophical Quarterly*, 15 (1978), 139–47; 'The Shaping of Scientific Rationality', in *Construction and Constraint: The Shaping of Scientific Rationality*, ed. by Ernan McMullin (Notre Dame, IN: University of Notre Dame Press, 1988), 1–47; *The Inference That Makes Science* (Milwaukee: Marquette University Press, 1992), 112.

11. McMullin, 'Is Philosophy Relevant to Cosmology?', *American Philosophical Quarterly*, 18 (1981),180.

12. Ibid., 181.

13. Cf., for instance, Munitz, *The Question of Reality*, 158–9.

14. Munitz, *The Question of Reality*, 159–67.

15. Ibid., 167–8.

16. Ibid., 188–9.

17. Ibid., 189.

18. Cf. Stoeger, in *Physics, Philosophy and Theology*, 230–31.

19. Andrei Linde, *Particle Physics and Inflationary Cosmology* (Chur, Switzerland: Harwood Academic Publishers, 1990), 245–332.

20. Aristotle, *Physics*, III.5.204^{b}1–206^{a}8.

21. I am indebted to Robert J. Spitzer, SJ for suggesting to me the importance of Hilbert's arguments in this context. For Spitzer's own well-developed treatment of the impossibility of achieved temperal infinity and spatial infinity, see Robert J. Spitzer, 'Definitions of Real Time and Ultimate Reality', in *Ultimate Reality and Meaning: Interdisciplinary Studies in the Philosophy of Understanding*, 23, 3: 2260–76, and Robert J. Spitzer, SJ, 'Indications of Creation in Contemporary Big Bang Cosmology', in *Philosophy in Science*, vol. 10, ed. by William R. Stoeger, SJ, Michael Heller, and Józef M. Zyciński (Tucson, AZ: Pachart Publishing House, 2003), 35–106.

22. Cf. Charles C. Dyer, 'An Introduction to Small Universe Models' and G.F.R. Ellis, 'Observational Properties of Small Universe', both in *Theory and Observational Limits in Cosmology*, ed. by William R. Stoeger (Vatican City State: Specola Vaticana/Vatican Observatory, 1987), 467–73 and 475–86, and references therein; Jean-Pierre Luminet, Glenn D. Starkman, and Jeffrey R. Weeks, 'Is Space Finite?', *Scientific American*, Special Edition (2002), 58–65, and references therein.

23. Cf. Ellis, 'Observational Properties', and Luminet et al., 'Is Space Finite?'.

24. David Hilbert, 'On the Infinite', in *Philosophy of Mathematics*, ed. by Paul Benacerraf and Hilary Putnam (Englewood Cliffs, NJ: Prentice Hall, 1964), 134–51.

25. William Lane Craig, 'Finitude of the Past and God's Existence', in *Theism, Atheism, and the Big Bang Cosmology*, ed. by William Lane Craig and Quentin Smith (Oxford: Clarendon Press, 1993), 3–76.

26. Cf. Craig, 'Finitude of the Past and God's Existence', 19.

27. Ibid., 20, 21–2.

28. Hilbert, 'On the Infinite', 135.

29. Bertrand Russell, *Our Knowledge of the External World* (New York: Mentor Books, 1960), as quoted in Quentin Smith, 'Infinity and the Past', in *Theism, Atheism, and the Big Bang Cosmology*, 88.

30. Stanley L. Jaki, *Is There a Universe?* (New York: Wethersfield Institute, 1993).

31. Ibid., 92–102.

Chapter 8

Barbour's Assessment of the Philosophical and Theological Implications of Physics and Cosmology

Robert John Russell

The purpose of this chapter,[1] like that of the volume as a whole, is to look backward at the impact of Ian Barbour's work on 'science and religion', and to look forward at the new vistas his work raises for us all. Here I shall focus on Ian Barbour's assessment of the philosophical and theological implications of three key areas in contemporary physics and cosmology: quantum mechanics (QM), special relativity (SR), and Big Bang cosmology. With what today seems almost like prescience, Barbour first probed to the heart of these issues long before any of the present scholars had emerged. As far back as the early 1960s, when the reigning interpretation of QM was positivist/empiricist and reductionist, Barbour recognized its profound implications for an ontology of indeterminism and holism, the role of subjectivity in epistemology, and importance of the search for unity beyond complementarity. He rejected relativity as entailing relativism and idealism while underscoring its challenge to a theology of God's temporal involvement with the world, and he pointed to the 'horizon' issues raised by Big Bang cosmology to a theology of creation.

I have chosen to focus primarily on Barbour's first Gifford Lectures, *Religion in an Age of Science*,[2] since it summarizes and extends much of his earlier writings, though I will augment this focus with material drawn from other sources such as *Issues in Science and Religion*.[3] I believe that this material offers us a highly illuminating overview of Barbour's approach to the relationship between theology and science: it is a splendid example of his methodology ('a theology of nature'), his development of what he would call 'critical realism' in dealing with both science and theology, and the key role of process philosophy in mediating between them. It also provides crucial insights into some of Barbour's fundamental theological commitments.

Quantum Theory[4]

I will briefly comment on three areas in QM – complementarity, parts and wholes, and Bell's Theorem – before discussing his treatment of indeterminacy and divine action in some detail.

Complementarity and Critical Realism

Barbour argues that modern physics has overthrown the classical view of nature as static, deterministic, and reductionistic and instead has underscored nature as temporal, indeterministic, and holistic. Moreover, in place of classical or naive realism, and against those who have adopted positivism, instrumentalism, or idealism, Barbour develops what he called 'critical realism,' with its stress on the correspondence between theoretical models and reality as limited and partial, and its understanding of language as both referential and inherently metaphorical. Most physicists, he admits, have adopted Bohr's principle of complementarity which seems to challenge realism through its use of both wave and particle models to describe quantum phenomena and its pointing to the conceptual limitations of human understanding. Incidentally, one of Barbour's most important stances then, in my opinion, was his caution about the often uncritical attempts to extend complementarity in other fields, such as biology or psychology, or to the relations between fields, such as between science and religion.[5] I agree with Barbour's concerns, though I do find promising those instances where analogies can be found with forms of complementarity that occur independently in other fields.[6] But the central issue posed to Barbour by complementarity is the status of theoretical terms in physics: Does complementarity undercut the possibility of giving a critical realist interpretation of quantum physics? If so, this result would have significant negative implications for Barbour's overall philosophy of nature, including his use of Whitehead.

In response, Barbour pointed out that, while Bohr is often taken as an instrumentalist, he can best be understood as a realist. In *Issues* he simply rejects what he takes as Bohr's Kantianism, arguing instead that 'the use of scientific concepts is always realist in intent'.[7] In the Gifford lectures he drew on the work of Henry Folse[8] to argue that, although Bohr rejected classical realism, he still believed in a 'real world' with which we interact in making measurements, a belief that is consistent with critical realism. Finally Barbour urged that, in spite of complementarity, we should not abandon the search for new unifying models in quantum physics.

I agree with the Barbour/Folse assessment that a minimal form of realism is present in at least some of Bohr's writings. A striking example is the way Bohr tried to convince Einstein, the ardent realist, about complementarity by arguing for an analogy between special relativity and quantum mechanics.[9] Still, in looking ahead at the agenda for future work, I want to stress the continuing challenge complementarity poses to realism. From his earliest writings on the subject, Bohr claimed that complementarity involves not only competing models, like wave and particle, but more importantly competing epistemic themes, like space time description and causal explanation – themes which were combined effortlessly in classical physics but which can no longer be interwoven.[10] How then are we to think of a reality whose causal explanation cannot be understood in the language of space and time? Moreover, in light of Bell's Theorem (1964, 1966) and its recent, intense scrutiny by philosophers of science, we now know that the problems raised by complementarity are much more serious than previously realized for a realist interpretation of quantum theory.[11] Finally, other developing interpretations of QM, such as 'many worlds' and even 'many minds', offer further challenges to a critical realist reading of QM.[12]

Parts and Wholes

Barbour sees quantum theory as posing a pivotal challenge to both epistemic and ontological reductionism as based in classical physics. In quantum theory, the description of complex systems (including even a helium atom) cannot be reduced to the description of its parts.[13] I agree with Barbour that quantum holism challenges reductionism, but only if quantum theory can be given a realist interpretation; from a positivist or instrumentalist position, the lack of epistemic reducibility carries no ontological implications per se.

Bell's Theorem[14]

Although its roots lie in the mid-1930s (EPR) debate between Einstein and Bohr, Bell's Theorem (and the experiments of Aspect and others) raises severe challenges to realism. We start with the observation of simultaneous (technically, spacelike or acausal) correlations found between highly separated systems which once were in a single, composite state. Such distant systems are said to be 'non-local': photons will not have time to move between the observations and produce the correlations. The correlations make it appear that these separated systems are still somehow a single integrated system: they are said to be 'entangled.' Moreover, these correlations are there in the data whether or not quantum theory is correct; it is only a secondary fact that quantum theory correctly predicts them.

There is almost universal agreement that non-local correlations force us to reject either special relativity, thus allowing for superluminal interactions ('tachyons') between them that account for the correlations, or classical realism in which systems are thought of as possessing definite properties whether or not they are being observed. According to Barbour, most physicists follow Bohr by giving up classical realism and retaining special relativity. Barbour then tentatively sides with Bohr and suggests that locality can be combined with critical realism and a limited form of holism.

In my opinion, Barbour's move does not solve the problem, but it might stimulate us to reconsider the alternatives of either locality or classical realism in slightly different form. Following other scholars, I believe we should explore a nonlocal form of realism in which quantum non-locality is an indication of an underlying 'non-separable' ontology. Here entangled (once bound) particles now at a (spacelike) distance remain part of an ontological whole. This in turn takes us to the edge of current research and points us ahead to the questions on the horizon: how are we to produce a conceptual framework, or another, through which a nonseparable ontology can be made intelligible? Whether Whitehead's metaphysics will provide such a framework is, in my opinion, an open question, particularly in light of the rather mixed assessment it received by Abner Shimony in relation to QM.[15]

In sum, I am grateful to Barbour for his pioneering analysis of quantum mechanics in *Issues* and its elaboration in the Gifford Lectures and beyond. It is really only in the light of Bell's Theorem that philosophers of science have now come to realize how truly severe are the challenges to realism posed not only from quantum theory but from the sheer phenomena of quantum correlations. In looking forward I suspect 'the game is truly afoot' regarding the viability of critical realism as we reflect on quantum theory and beyond that relativistic quantum mechanics and quantum field theory.

Detailed Discussion: Divine Action and Quantum Mechanics

A variety of scholars have written on quantum mechanics and divine action. My aim is to assess Barbour's contributions to the issue, to determine whether he and I differ in significant ways in our approaches to it, and what issues result for future exploration.

One of the perennial challenges for anyone seeking to explore any of the many philosophical and theological implications of quantum mechanics, including divine action, is the fact that there are a variety of competing interpretations of QM and to date there is no unequivocal experimental basis for deciding between them. The best one can do, as I have argued on several occasions, is to adopt a 'what if' strategy, exploring one interpretation for its theological implications while keeping clearly in mind that a very different interpretation may one day be vindicated.

As a critical realist, Barbour follows Bohr's Copenhagen interpretation, by interpreting the statistical character of quantum events and its representation in the Heisenberg Uncertainty Principle as a sign of objective, ontological indeterminacy in nature.[16] According to this interpretation, quantum chance is entirely different from chance in classical physics, where unpredictability is due merely to our epistemic ignorance of underlying deterministic natural processes. Instead quantum chance is due to the fundamental lack of such underlying processes. To be more precise, according to the Copenhagen interpretation the 'wave function ψ' provides a complete description of the physical state of a quantum system in terms of a superposition of possible states, ψ_i. Now ψ evolves deterministically in time according to the Schrödinger equation until the system interacts irreversibly with a larger system, typically one ranging in size from a dust mote to a classical object. At this point, often called a 'quantum event' or 'measurement process,' the wave function is said to 'collapse' to one of the states in the superposition. The 'collapse' is not governed by the Schrödinger equation or any other known natural law, and thus we have no way of specifying which, if any, efficient natural causes bring it about. All we can do is calculate the relative probability that ψ will collapse to a particular state ψ_i; we cannot predict precisely which state this will be. It is this unpredictability, and the apparent lack of an efficient natural cause here, that suggests that during a quantum event nature at the quantum level is ontologically indeterministic.

In recent work, Barbour used this interpretation of quantum mechanics to explore a non-interventionist account of divine action: 'Quantum events have necessary but not sufficient physical causes ... [T]heir final determination might be made directly by God. What appears to be chance … may be the very point at which God acts.'[17] I too have found it very helpful to work within the philosophical interpretation of quantum mechanics expressed so clearly here by Barbour and its theological appropriation for a non-interventionist approach to divine action.[18] If nature at the quantum level provides the necessary (formal, material) but not sufficient (efficient) causes to bring about a quantum event, then we can argue that God acts together with these necessary but insufficient natural causes to bring about a quantum event without violating the laws of nature or without becoming a natural cause. In short, quantum events occur in part because of divine causality, in part because of natural causality. This claim in turn raises a number of issues which I have sought to address elsewhere.

Do Barbour and I then differ in significant ways in our approaches to divine action and quantum level? First of all, I agree with Barbour regarding many of the advantages of this approach to divine action: God's action at the quantum level can in some circumstances be amplified and lead to macroscopic, large-scale phenomena (for example, the effect of quantum-based genetic mutations in biological evolution). It would not be 'detectable' by science as a 'skew' in routine data, nor open to scientific proof or refutation.[19] But Barbour also points to several problems with this approach, particularly with William Pollard's version in which God is thought of as controlling all quantum indeterminacies. The resulting position, which Barbour calls 'theological determinism' or predestination, seems to give God 'total control over the world,' undercuts human free will and makes God responsible for evil (that is, the problem of theodicy). Moreover, by restricting divine action to the quantum level, Pollard opens the door to a bottom-up 'implicit reductionism'. Finally, Barbour argues that without an elaborated metaphysics, which Pollard lacks, one is left to simply 'juxtapose divine causation, natural causation, and free human causation'.[20]

Nancey Murphy has also explored the idea that God acts in all quantum events and she claims that in her approach, unlike that of Pollard, this does not lead us to view God's action as undercutting free will.[21] She also sees her work as providing a new metaphysical theory of causation appropriate to quantum mechanics. Unlike the approach of Pollard/Murphy, George Ellis, Thomas Tracy, and I have explored an alternative in which God actualizes some but not all quantum events. In specific, I argue that God acts together with nature to determine all those events from 'just after' the cosmological beginning at 't = 0'[22] to all those on Earth (and elsewhere in the universe) which lead to and are involved in the evolution of sentience. However, once there are creatures capable of top-down, 'mind–brain' interaction, God refrains from acting in those 'basic acts', those specific somatic events at the quantum level in which 'mind' acts on 'body' to carry out sentient agency, thus allowing for the enactment of 'free will'.[23] This approach avoids Barbour's concern regarding theological determinism, and since it combines bottom-up and top-down approaches,[24] it also sidesteps any concessions to reductionist bottom-up only accounts. I will return to the problem of theodicy in closing this section.

Where, then, does the difference, if any, between Barbour and me lie? I believe it lies in our assessment of whether the inclusion of intrinsic novelty at the level of quantum mechanics is *necessary* to the case for non-interventionist divine action.

Since Barbour works within the framework of process philosophy, he claims there are three independent principles of causation at work in each actual occasion at every level in nature: (1) the causal past (each occasion prehends its unique set of past occasions, resulting in what we call efficient causality); (2) God's action, which provides the subjective lure or aim to each occasion but does not determine the outcome (God's lure is what Barbour calls 'final causation'); and (3) an element of irreducible and genuine novelty (or 'self-causation') as, during concrescence, the occasion experiences and shapes itself in light of the causal past and the divine subjective lure.[25] Thus God's subjective lure together with the causal past influence, but do not determine, the actual quantum concrescence. Instead intrinsic novelty is the key factor and it is the ultimate source of quantum indeterminism.

Instead I view novelty as an emergent property at higher levels of biological and neurophysiological complexity where sentience and consciousness arise and where it is associated with volition, but genuine novelty is not a factor at the level of quantum processes. Here, as already discussed, God acts together with the necessary but insufficient natural causes to determine that a specific quantum event occurs in all quantum events – with the proviso that for those somatic events in which 'mind' in a sentient organism acts on neurophysiology to carry out agency, God does not act to determine the specific outcome. In all other cases, what we take as quantum indeterminism is merely hidden divine action; there is no genuine novelty in subatomic nature, though there is genuine novelty at the level of sentience.

In short, then, the difference between Barbour and me seems to lie only in whether it is necessary to include novelty at the quantum level in order to defend a non-interventionist account of divine action. Meanwhile, for both of us several major problems loom on the horizon. One is the fact that quantum indeterminism is an 'interpretation-specific' feature of quantum mechanics. A more ubiquitous feature that occurs in many – possibly all? – interpretations is non-locality. What implications for divine action would these other interpretations and features raise and how would they, in turn, affect the significance of indeterminism for divine action? Another crucial area is the problem of theodicy. I believe that, with its many ramifications throughout a theology of nature that takes evolutionary history seriously, theodicy poses a truly profound challenge for a process approach *and* for my own. As we turn forward to the future discussions of quantum physics and divine action we must address these problems in their full details.[26]

Relativity and the Temporality of the World

Barbour's Rejection of Idealism and Relativism as Based on Relativity

For decades, Barbour has criticized two persistent claims regarding Einstein's special theory of relativity (SR): relativity supports idealism and relativism.[27] In the Gifford Lectures he argued that, while physical properties such as length and mass depend on the relative velocity of the observer, this does not suggest that the mind affects these properties since the 'observer' can be an inanimate device. To those who find support in SR for moral and religious relativism, he countered with the fact that SR discloses new features of the world which are, in fact, absolute: the speed of light, the spacetime interval between events, the laws of physics themselves. Instead of total relativism, Barbour recommends an emphasis on both diversity and underlying unity. Two decades earlier in *Issues*, Barbour had given an even sharper critique of idealist interpretations of physics, including purported evidence of the Holy Spirit in the equivalence of mass and energy and a mentalist ontology based on the role of mathematics in physics.[28] In a paradigmatic move, though, Barbour turned to the underlying issue: what legitimate reasons do we have for rejecting the mechanistic worldview of classical physics? His response: not only is classical physics outmoded, but science never does provide an unambiguous basis for a metaphysical system – mechanism, idealism, or any other. Thus the move to mechanism was 'an uncritical transition from physics to metaphysics'. Instead the primary lesson for us is to recognize 'the limitations of science' – the partiality and incompleteness of any scientific theory – and the error of 'misplaced concreteness' in taking the abstractions of any theory as an 'all-inclusive clue to reality.' I have always been indebted to Barbour's wisdom in drawing these conclusions, especially as they came in the period of the 1960s–1970s when the 'new age' hype surrounding physics was so ubiquitous in popular culture. His wisdom has clearly stood the test of time.

Barbour's Support of a 'Flowing Time' Interpretation of Relativity

I want to focus here on Barbour's critique of the 'block universe' interpretation of SR in favor of a 'flowing time' approach, since I believe this is precisely where the future conversations about the implications of SR lie. Here Barbour joins the perennial debate over two competing theories of time: the static theory, characterized by an ontology of being whose sources can be traced back to Parmenides, versus the dynamic theory, with its ontology of becoming rooted historically in the thought of Heraclitus. With the discovery of SR by Einstein in 1905 and its geometrical or 'spacetime' interpretation by Hermann Minkowski in 1907–08, the debate over the nature of time has intensified.[29] The spacetime or 'block universe' interpretation spatializes time as the fourth dimension of spacetime and accords past and future events the same ontological status as the present event. Einstein himself was an early convert to Minkowski's spacetime realism, and scholars from Costa de Beauregard to Chris Isham have defended it. Others, however, such as Milic Capek and John Polkinghorne, support a flowing time interpretation of SR.[30] Barbour endorses the latter, writing that 'dynamic events, not unchanging substances, are now taken to constitute reality,' and the universe is 'dynamic and interconnected ... a unified flux of interacting events.'[31] Moreover, given the unification of SR and QM in relativistic quantum mechanics, the 'flowing time' interpretation of SR and the indeterminacy interpretation of QM can be combined, depicting the future in which 'indeterminacies become determinate ... with the passage of time.'[32] But Barbour also notes that SR points to an underlying ontology of 'separateness and isolation' since we are 'momentarily alone in each present' and 'it takes time for connections to be effective.' On a truly cosmic scale, 'we are isolated from most of the universe for incredibly long stretches of time.'

Barbour's Novel Claim: Wholeness and Separateness as Based on Relativity

Once again I am indebted to Barbour for stressing a complex interpretation involving both *wholeness and separateness* in tension which is unique among scholars in the 'theology and science' community. My question, though, is how a flowing time interpretation, when stripped by SR of a unique, universal present, can support the wholeness Barbour insists on, since it inevitably seems to break up the world into ontologically isolated spacetime events or extended worldlines? Indeed, this problem of an 'isolated present' has frequently been seen as a severe challenge to a realist interpretation of SR.[33] Lawrence Sklar, for example, warns that 'we fall ... into solipsism of the present moment. Reality has now been reduced to a point!'[34] Yet Barbour counters this by speaking of both isolation and interconnectedness.

I believe that Barbour can succeed in maintaining both wholeness and separation, not because he offers a different *physical interpretation* of SR, but because he presupposes an alternative *metaphysical framework* which other scholars such as Sklar have overlooked. It seems clear to me that the 'default' metaphysical position is 'classical': that is, one in which only external relations (that is, light signals, finite-speed causal influences) are involved. Since this *externality* is undercut by SR, solipsism seems unavoidable. But Barbour begins with a Whiteheadian metaphysics in which relations arise between events through prehension, and these relations are *internal*. It is, I propose, because of Barbour's metaphysics that the 'geometric' and 'causal' isolation resulting from the physics of SR is not as catastrophic for Barbour as it is for those employing the standard metaphysics of strictly external relations.

So it would appear that Barbour's approach succeeds in incorporating SR into a metaphysical system which not only acknowledges but actually celebrates the event-like character of reality while overcoming the challenge of isolationism into which an external-relations event ontology is driven by deploying, in its place, an internal-relations event ontology.[35] I think this is an extremely important point. Nevertheless it leads to three subsequent, and very different, directions for further research: one from metaphysics back to physics, the other from physics to alternative metaphysical systems, and the third from physics to theology and the doctrine of God.

Three Critical Questions for Further Discussion

1   Does the advantage offered by process metaphysics, as suggested above, lead to new avenues of research in physics itself?   Chris Isham laid this before us over a decade ago in a debate over time in SR:[36] are the differences between the block universe and flowing time an example of an idle philosophical dispute lacking empirical paydirt or could they lead to genuinely new insights within physics proper? Cobb, in his article in this volume, has made the same point: '[Barbour] is not giving us an account of where science *should* go from the point of view of process theology. He is showing us that process theology is compatible with where science is already heading.' I find this a crucial question, and I hope to pursue it in future research.[37]

One appropriate direction would be to explore Whitehead's own use of SR in his construction of process metaphysics in the 1920s. Here he accepted the formalism of SR scientifically although he interpreted it differently from Einstein. As John Cobb points out,[38] Whitehead's interpretation of SR was based on multiple time systems in pseudo-Euclidean (flat) spacetime. In 1922, Whitehead[39] incorporated SR explicitly into his scientific work on a relativistic theory of gravity while retaining its pseudo-Euclidean framework. Einstein's 1915 general theory of relativity (GR), on the other hand, appropriated curved spacetime to account for gravity. Although Whitehead's gravitational theory included four distinct proposals for the effects of gravity, from a mathematical perspective, his theory and GR were quite similar in many ways: Whitehead incorporated a solution to GR's field equations (a modified form of the Schwarzschild solution), along with the free-space equations themselves ($R_{\mu\nu} = 0$), as two of his four proposals. Recent work by Christoph Wassermann and me has been aimed at understanding the physical and philosophical significance of the remaining two proposals.[40]

2   Are there other metaphysical systems which offer a more promising relational ontology than does process thought?   I am thinking specifically of that broad current of contemporary theology focused on what Catherine Mowry LaCugna called 'the recovery of the Trinity' and typified by such theologians as Karl Barth, Karl Rahner, Jürgen Moltmann, Wolfhart Pannenberg, Elizabeth Johnson, and Ted Peters.[41] Here, in short, the relationality of the Triune persons provides the basis, in varying ways, for the relationality of creation. Would these offer a more fruitful avenue to explore the philosophical implications of SR for Christian theology?

With these issues in mind, I turn briefly to a specific theological issue.

3.   How, in light of SR, are we to conceive of God's knowledge of and temporal influence on the universe?   We recall that Charles Hartshorne underscored the challenge relativity raises for process theology – and by implication, I would say, for any theology in which God is said to experience the world in time – given the downfall of the universal present through which God could be said to experience the world.[42] In response, Barbour, for example, suggests that since God is omnipresent and immanent in all events, God can know all events 'instantaneously' without regard to such restrictions as the speed of light. Moreover, God influences each event in terms of its unique, causal past.[43]

This issue leads directly into the perennial topic of 'time and eternity': how is the relation between eternity, as the divine mode of temporality, and our creaturely mode of temporality to be reinterpreted in light of SR and its various interpretations? These are fascinating suggestions worth pursuing further, and I believe that as we work through them we will discover whether a Whiteheadian form of relationality, such as Barbour adopts, or one based on Trinitarian theology, which I prefer, proves more fertile in interpreting our religious experience and in suggesting new ways of thinking scientifically about nature.

Cosmology and Creation[44]

Barbour, Gilkey, and the Strict Distinction between Ontological and Historical Origins

If science were to present compelling evidence that the universe has a finite past and began at 't = 0', should this be important to Christian theology? This question clearly involves issues of both methodology and content for the theology–science interaction. I believe we can learn a great deal about the kind of answers Barbour gave these issues by tracing his position in both *Issues* and the Gifford Lectures to Langdon Gilkey's famous book of 1959, *Maker of Heaven and Earth*.[45] The dependence of Barbour on Gilkey is crucial, I believe, to understanding Barbour's developing position on cosmology and creation.[46]

Barbour's pioneering text, *Issues in Science and Religion*, was written in the mid-1960s, during the competition between Big Bang cosmology, based on GR, and Fred Hoyle's steady state theory in which the universe expands forever with no beginning and no end. Here Barbour states that 'both theories are capable of either a naturalistic or a theistic interpretation … [T]he Christian need not favor either theory, for the doctrine of creation is not really about temporal beginnings but about the basic relationship between the world and God.'[47] Barbour attributes this argument to Gilkey, describing *Maker* as 'the best recent exposition of the doctrine by a Protestant theologian.'[48] Barbour admits that Neo-Orthodoxy, exemplified by Gilkey, leads to 'a radical separation of scientific and religious questions' but he agrees with Gilkey who 'emphasized that creation is a relationship, not an event; the doctrine deals with ontological dependence, not temporal history.'[49]

What then were Gilkey's arguments that Barbour appropriated? In *Maker* Gilkey tells us that the idea of an '"originating" activity of God' has taken two distinct forms historically: ontological origination, which means that '… God originates the *existence* of each creature out of nothing, whatever its position in the time scale,' and historical/empirical origination, which means 'originating' in the sense of founding and establishing at the beginning.[50] He attributes this distinction to Thomas Aquinas[51] and, in a move which casts long shadows over all that is to follow, he interprets it as a *strict dichotomy*. Gilkey then accepts the idea of ontological origination as theologically appropriate, but he rejects historical origination. Knowledge about a first moment of time cannot be a valid part of theology since theology does not contain *any* 'facts' about the natural order.[52] In my opinion, it is Gilkey's interpretation of Aquinas as urging a strict dichotomy that underlies Barbour's position in *Issues*, even though Barbour added to it the claim that the division in scientific opinion over Big Bang and steady state cosmologies provided an additional reason for not giving cosmology too large a role in theology.

When Barbour's first series of Gifford Lectures were given in 1989, more than two decades had passed since the demise of the steady state model and the commensurate strengthening of support for Big Bang cosmology. After succinctly describing Big Bang cosmology and its principle feature, the beginning of the universe some 15 billion years ago, Barbour summarizes several theological responses. On the one hand, Pope Pius XII in 1951 interprets t = 0 as supporting creation in time. On the other hand, Arthur Peacocke sees t = 0 as entirely irrelevant to theology. Barbour then cites four factors in preparing for a more mediating assessment: (1) We should be wary of 'gaps' arguments, although he admits that t = 0 would be a different sort of gap since it would be 'in principle inaccessible to science'; (2) The Big Bang might be only one of an infinite set of oscillations of the universe; (3) Scientific theories are replaced eventually; and (4) Both a finite and an infinite past 'start with an unexplained universe'. With this in mind, Barbour then offers his constructive position: while no 'major theological issues are at stake' here, if the Big Bang remains in place scientifically it can be seen by the theist as 'an instant of divine origination' though it is 'not the main concern expressed in the religious notion of creation.'[53] And with this, Barbour closes by returning to his much earlier position and its roots in Gilkey: '[Still] agree with the neo-orthodox authors who say that it is the sheer *existence* of the universe that is the datum of theology, and that the details of scientific cosmology are irrelevant here. [Creation *ex nihilo*] is an ontological and not a historical assertion.'[54]

In sum, then, Barbour's views on t = 0, as rooted in Gilkey's position in *Maker* and expressed in *Issues* and the Gifford Lectures, consist of three critical points: the sharp ontological/historical distinction proposed by Gilkey; the ontological interpretation as carrying the central meaning of *ex nihilo*; and the conclusion that t = 0, being empirical and scientifically uncertain plays no significant role in the *ex nihilo* tradition.

Moving Beyond the Gilkey/Barbour Position Using Lakatos

I believe we can move beyond the Gilkey/Barbour position by recognizing that Gilkey made an unnecessary and costly premise: that ontological and empirical origination form a sharp dichotomy. Instead I propose we reintegrate historical/empirical language into the broader context of ontological origination, thus giving a factual domain to which ontological origination can be related without literalization *or* equivocation. If science supports a universe with a finite age, as the Big Bang suggests, this can count as indirect empirical evidence in support of ontological origination. Ontological dependence is thus the *crucial*, but not the *exhaustive*, meaning of creation. To use a legal analogy, the Big Bang serves as a character witness but not an eyewitness for creation.

To make this case stronger, I recently sought to adopt the Lakatosian methodology of scientific research programs in this context.[55] Philosopher of science Imre Lakatos was first discussed by Barbour in *Myths, Models, and Paradigms*[56] and the theological use of his methodology has since been developed in detail by Nancey Murphy[57] and Philip Clayton.[58] Following them, I propose we structure the doctrine of creation *ex nihilo* and its relation to data drawn from cosmology in terms of a Lakatosian research program. This will include a central, or 'core', hypothesis, namely that '*creatio ex nihilo* means ontological origination', surrounded by a concentric circle or 'protective belt' of auxiliary hypotheses, namely that 'ontological origination entails finitude,' next that 'finitude includes temporal finitude,' and finally that 'temporal finitude includes past temporal finitude.' In this way evidence for empirical origination from contemporary science, such as the Big Bang offers in terms of t = 0, could be related to a core theological hypothesis, such as *creatio ex nihilo*, in such a way as to allow it to confirm the hypothesis without the evidence being directly connected with creation theology.

I want to emphasize, though, that this method allows for disconfirmation as well as confirmation. For example, the infinite size and the unending future of the open Big Bang scenario work against the finitude of creation, as does the infinite past entailed by some proposals in quantum gravity. Moreover, it would be more in keeping with Lakatosian methodology if we used it to compare several competing theological research programs, each of which attempts to relate *creatio ex nihilo* to cosmology in its own way, and comparatively assess which program is most progressive by the way it predicts novel facts and avoids *ad hoc* moves.

There is an additional advantage to the Lakatosian approach: it allows us to anticipate that both science and theology will undergo crucial changes, and it gives us a way to build change directly into the methodology. For example, standard Big Bang cosmology, and with it t = 0, have been replaced by the variety of inflationary (or 'hot') Big Bang cosmologies developed in the past several decades. Here the question of t = 0 is, in principle, undecideable.[59] Using a Lakatosian approach to the relations between theology and science, we can move with these changes in cosmology and continue to engage it theologically.[60] A similar scenario goes for moves to quantum cosmology. Thus I predict that a Lakatosian approach as discussed by Barbour, Murphy, and Clayton will continue to be fruitful in the future as we press forward for new insights into the creative mutual interaction between science and theology.

Conclusion

In this chapter I have reflected critically on the impact of Ian Barbour's work on 'science and religion' and on the new vistas his work raises. These reflections have, of necessity, been limited to a handful of topics in Barbour's assessment of the philosophical and theological implications of quantum mechanics, special relativity, and Big Bang cosmology. Even within these limitations, I believe we have traced key elements in Barbour's work: his methodology that incorporates the implications of science into Christian theology via a 'theology of nature,' his development of a philosophy of 'critical realism' in relation to both science and theology, and his exploration of the crucial role of process philosophy in mediating between them. In the process, I hope to have underscored the remarkable potential for future interdisciplinary research of the germinal and prophetic writings of Ian G. Barbour who five decades ago saw, splendidly and uniquely among his peers, the possibilities for genuine dialogue and interaction between physics, philosophy, and Christian theology.

Notes

1. This chapter is based in part on a previous publication, Robert John Russell, 'Religion and the Theories of Science: A Response to Barbour', *Zygon*, 31:1 (March 1996), 29–41.

2. Ian G. Barbour, *Religion in an Age of Science, The Gifford Lectures; 1989–1991, Volume 1* (San Francisco: Harper & Row, 1990).

3. I. G. Barbour, *Issues in Science and Religion* (New York: Harper & Row, 1971; originally published in 1966 by Prentice Hall).

4. Barbour, *Religion in an Age of Science*, ch. 4. For an early discussion, see Barbour, *Issues in Science and Religion*, ch. 10.

5. For a more detailed discussion, see Barbour, *Issues in Science and Religion*, ch. 10/II/3, and Ian G. Barbour, *Myths, Models, and Paradigms: A Comparative Study in Science and Religion* (New York: Harper & Row, 1974), ch. 5.

6. See for example Robert John Russell, 'Whitehead, Einstein and the Newtonian Legacy', in *Newton and the New Direction in Science*, ed. by S.J.G.V. Coyne and M. Heller (Citta del Vaticano: Specola Vaticana, 1988), 359–61.

7. Barbour, *Issues in Science and Religion*, 294. This is not a convincing argument since the intention of scientists does not count as philosophical evidence for or against realism.

8. Henry J. Folse, *The Philosophy of Niels Bohr: The Framework of Complementarity* (Amsterdam: North Holland, 1985).

9. Niels Bohr, 'Causality and Complementarity', in *Philosophical Writings, Vol. 4: Causality and Complementarity: Supplementary Papers*, ed. by Jan Faye and Henry J. Folse (Woodbridge, CT: Ox Bow Press, 1937), 83–91.

10. For an excellent source and analysis of Bohr's writings see Max Jammer, *The Philosophy of Quantum Mechanics: The Interpretations of Quantum Mechanics in Historical Perspective* (New York: John Wiley & Sons, 1974), chs. 4–6.

11. John Polkinghorne claims that quantum field theory (QFT) resolves the paradox of complementarity. While it is certainly true that the QFT provides more insight into the mathematical relation between wavelike and particlelike properties than does ordinary quantum mechanics, I do not believe that the paradox is entirely removed. One telling piece of evidence is the continuing failure to produce an adequate ontology for quantum phenomena. See John C. Polkinghorne, *Reason and Reality: The Relationship Between Science and Theology* (London: SPCK, 1991), 25–6; Michael Redhead, *Incompleteness, Nonlocality, and Realism: A Prolegomenon to the Philosophy of Quantum Mechanics* (Oxford: Clarendon Press, 1987); James T. Cushing and Ernan McMullin (eds), *Philosophical Consequences of Quantum Theory: Reflections on Bell's Theorem* (Notre Dame: University of Notre Dame Press, 1989); Paul Teller, *An Interpretive Introduction to Quantum Field Theory* (Princeton: Princeton University Press, 1995); Robert John Russell, Philip Clayton et al. (eds), *Quantum Mechanics: Scientific Perspectives on Divine Action* (Vatican City State; Berkeley, CA: Vatican Observatory Publications; Center for Theology and the Natural Sciences, 2001).

12. Russell, Clayton et al., *Quantum Mechanics*.

13. 'A bound electron in an atom has to be considered as a state of *the whole atom* rather than as a separate entity … The helium atom is a total pattern with *no distinguishable parts*' [Barbour's italics] (Barbour, *Religion in an Age of Science*, 105, cf. 104–5). For an early discussion see Barbour, *Issues in Science and Religion*, ch. 10/II/4. I think Barbour's claim regarding the lack of distinguishable parts may be overstated. For example, consider two electrons in a bound state with total spin zero (the >singlet state'). We know that the spins of the individual electrons are anticorrelated even though we cannot know which electron is 'spin up' or 'spin down'. Does this constitute at least partial knowledge of distinguishable parts?

14. For a readable and reliable introduction, see Nick Herbert, *Quantum Reality: Beyond the New Physics* (Garden City, NY: Anchor Press; Doubleday, 1985), chs. 10–13. For a more technical recent

discussion see the articles by Abner Shimony, Raymond Chiao, William Stoeger, James Cushing, Michael Redhead, John Polkinghorne, and me in Russell, Clayton et al., *Quantum Mechanics*.

15. Abner Shimony, 'Quantum Physics and the Philosophy of Whitehead', in *Search for a Naturalistic World View: Volume II, Natural Science and Metaphysics* (Cambridge: Cambridge University Press, 1993; first printed 1965). For further references and responses see Russell, Clayton et al., *Quantum Mechanics*.

16. Barbour, *Religion in an Age of Science*, 101–4, 123.

17. I.G. Barbour, 'Five Models of God and Evolution', in *Evolutionary and Molecular Biology: Scientific Perspectives on Divine Action*, ed. by Robert John Russell, William R. Stoeger, SJ, and Francisco J. Ayala (Vatican City State: Vatican Observatory Publications; Berkeley, CA: Center for Theology and the Natural Sciences, 1998), 432.

18. See Robert John Russell, 'The Physics of David Bohm and Its Relevance to Philosophy and Theology', *Zygon*, 20:2 (June 1985), 135–58; 'Contingency in Physics and Cosmology: A Critique of the Theology of Wolfhart Pannenberg', *Zygon*, 23:1 (March 1988), 23–43; 'Whitehead, Einstein and the Newtonian Legacy'; 'Special Providence and Genetic Mutation: A New Defense of Theistic Evolution', in *Evolutionary and Molecular Biology*; 'Divine Action and Quantum Mechanics: A Fresh Assessment', in *Quantum Mechanics*.

19. Barbour, 'Five Models of God and Evolution', 432.

20. Barbour's response to Pollard is found in slightly different versions in several sources including: Barbour, *Issues in Science and Religion*, 428–30; *Religion in an Age of Science*, 117–18; 'Five Models of God and Evolution', 432–3. I have cited the most significant ones here. The issue about 'gaps' in Barbour's earliest critique of Pollard seems to me to be more of a verbal than a substantive disagreement since Pollard is aware of the implications of ontological indeterminism for a 'gapless' form of divine action.

21. See in particular Nancey Murphy, 'Divine Action in the Natural Order: Buridan's Ass and Schrödinger's Cat', in *Chaos and Complexity: Scientific Perspectives on Divine Action*, ed. by Robert J. Russell, Nancey C. Murphy, and Arthur R. Peacocke, Scientific Perspectives on Divine Action Series (Vatican City State; Berkeley, CA: Vatican Observatory Publications; Center for Theology and the Natural Sciences, 1995), 325–58. I am not persuaded by Murphy's defense of these claims, but the underlying difference between us may be over compatibilism.

22. This statement must obviously be adjusted for inflationary cosmologies in which the existence of 't = 0' is in principle undecidable, or for quantum cosmologies in which the universe is eternally old.

23. When it comes to the problem of 'grace and free will', I do not work with a 'divine self-limitation' model to ensure free will, since I see grace and free will as compatible; indeed, it is God's grace that make the will truly free. My only concern, here, is the enactment of free will neurophysiologically; in this specific case, I do believe it necessary for God not to act in order that these somatic events are not overdetermined.

24. See for example R.J. Russell, 'Introduction', in *Chaos and Complexity*, 12; Russell, 'Special Providence and Genetic Mutation,' Sec. 4.3, 'Is a "Bottom-up" Approach to Divine Action Warranted and Does it Exclude Other Approaches?', 218–20; and R.J. Russell, *Quantum Mechanics*, sec 3: 'Methodological Issues', 300–301.

25. Barbour, *Religion in an Age of Science*, 222–4.

26. I believe it can best be addressed if we relocate the problem of suffering, disease, death and extinction in nature within a theology of the redemption and eschatological transformation of nature. For a preliminary discussion, see R.J. Russell, 'Eschatology and Physical Cosmology: A Preliminary Reflection', in *The Far Future: Eschatology from a Cosmic Perspective*, ed. by George F.R. Ellis (Philadelphia: Templeton Foundation Press, 2002); R.J. Russell, 'Bodily Resurrection, Eschatology and Scientific Cosmology: The Mutual Interaction of Christian Theology and Science', in *Resurrection: Theological and Scientific Assessments*, ed. by Ted Peters, Robert John Russell, and Michael Welker (Grand Rapids: Eerdmans Publishing Company, 2002).

27. Barbour, *Issues in Science and Religion*, ch. 10; Barbour, *Religion in an Age of Science*, 108–10.

28. Barbour, *Issues in Science and Religion*, 286–90.
29. A. Einstein, 'Zur Elektrodynamik Bewegter Korper', *Annalen der Physic*, 17 (1905), 891–921. Arthur I. Miller, *Albert Einstein's Special Theory of Relativity: Emergence (1905) and Early Interpretation (1905–1911)* (Reading, MA: Addison-Wesley Publishing Company, Inc., 1981), provides helpful background material.
30. Olivier Costa de Beauregard, 'Time in Relativity Theory: Arguments for a Philosophy of Being', in *The Voices of Time: A Cooperative Survey of Man's Views of Time as Expressed by the Sciences and by the Humanities*, ed. by J.T. Fraser (Amherst: The University of Massachusetts Press, 1966, 1981), 417–33. Milic Capek, 'Time in Relativity Theory: Arguments for a Philosophy of Being', in *The Voices of Time*, ed. Fraser, 434–54; Isham and Polkinghorne debate the problem in Chris J. Isham and John C. Polkinghorne, 'The Debate Over the Block Universe', in *Quantum Cosmology and the Laws of Nature: Scientific Perspectives on Divine Action*, ed. by Robert J. Russell, Nancey C. Murphy, and Chris J. Isham, Scientific Perspectives on Divine Action Series (Vatican City State; Berkeley, CA: Vatican Observatory Publications; Center for Theology and the Natural Sciences, 1993), 134–44.
31. Barbour, *Religion in an Age of Science*, 110.
32. For extended recent discussions of the compatibility of SR and QM see Russell, Clayton et al., *Quantum Mechanics*.
33. William Lane Craig, for example, argues that though there are three options for defining the 'present' in the context of SR, each leads to serious problems for the realist. See William Lane Craig, *Time and the Metaphysics of Relativity* (Dordrecht: Kluwer Academic Publishers, 2001), ch. 5, particularly 77–102. Craig himself adopts a different approach in support of flowing time. He rejects the assumption that Minkowskian spacetime is valid ontologically and argues instead for a neo-Lorentzian interpretation of SR similar to Einstein's original views. What is particularly important here is that Craig does so for theological reasons.
34. Lawrence Sklar, 'Time, Reality, and Relativity', in *Reduction, Time and Reality*, ed. by Richard Healey (Cambridge: Cambridge University Press, 1981), cited from Craig, *Time and the Metaphysics of Relativity*, 82, footnote 26.
35. For a very helpful discussion of the views of both process scholars and scientists including Ilya Prigogine and David Bohm on these issues, see David Ray Griffin, *Physics and the Ultimate Significance of Time: Bohm, Prigogine, and Process Philosophy* (Albany: State University of New York Press, 1986).
36. See the challenge to John Polkinghorne, who defends a 'flowing time' perspective, by Chris Isham, who defends a 'block universe' view, in Isham and Polkinghorne, 'The Block Universe'.
37. R.J. Russell, 'Time in Eternity', *Dialog*, 39:1 (March 2000); 'Eschatology and Physical Cosmology: A Preliminary Reflection'; 'Bodily Resurrection, Eschatology and Scientific Cosmology: The Mutual Interaction of Christian Theology and Science'. See also R.J. Russell, 'Nature and Creation in Modern Physics and Cosmology: A Trinitarian Approach' (1994), 5th European Conference on Science and Theology, 25. Again, Craig's exploration of a neo-Lorentzian approach is quite germane here.
38. See Cobb's paper in this volume (Chapter 15).
39. Alfred North Whitehead, *The Principle of Relativity with Applications to Physical Science* (Cambridge: Cambridge University Press, 1922).
40. Robert John Russell and Christoph Wassermann, 'Kerr Solution of Whitehead's Theory of Gravity', *Bulletin of the American Physical Society*, 32 (January 1987), 90; Russell, 'Whitehead, Einstein and the Newtonian Legacy'. This work was sponsored in part by the Center for Process Studies.
41. For an excellent overview and his own constructive approach, see Ted Peters, *God as Trinity: Relationality and Temporality in the Divine Life* (Louisville, KY: Westminster/John Knox Press, 1993).
42. Charles Hartshorne, *A Natural Theology for Our Time* (La Salle, IL: Open Court, 1967), ch. 4.
43. Barbour, *Religion in an Age of Science*, 112, note 29.

44. I want to mention briefly a very problematic point that is usually overlooked in process scholarship. Most discussions of cosmology and theology, including that of Barbour, are carried out entirely in the context of Einstein's Big Bang cosmology. Yet as early as 1922, Whitehead offered his own alternative scientific theory of gravity and thus at least potentially his own approach to a scientific cosmology – one that could be critically compared with Big Bang scenarios. Why, then, is Whitehead's approach overlooked? Clearly a brief review is in order.

   In 1922 Whitehead proposed a theory of gravity (see Whitehead, *The Principle of Relativity with Applications to Physical Science*). Here he accepted Einstein's free-space equations ($R_{\mu\upsilon} = 0$ which applies to the orbits of planets around the sun and the deflection of starlight by the sun) as consistent with his approach to nature, and then gave several additional equations as deserving consideration. Einstein, in contrast, in order to generate a physical cosmology, such as the Big Bang, gave us the full field equations, $R_{\mu\upsilon} - {}^1\!/_2\,Rg_{\mu\upsilon} = 8\pi\,T_{\mu\upsilon}$, where the stress-energy tensor $T_{\mu\upsilon}$ introduces the effects of matter into the field equation. The problem is that Whitehead, even in these additional equations, does not include the effects of matter; instead they are still free-space equations. My conclusion is that Whitehead's theory of gravity, as it currently stands, is intrinsically incapable of generating a physical cosmology which can be used as a scientific model of the expanding universe (see Russell, 'Whitehead, Einstein and the Newtonian Legacy'). If so, one should read the term 'cosmology' in process literature as referring to a metaphysical cosmology which has elegant and persuasive features but which lacks an empirically testable physical model. The upshot for this chapter is that, in focusing on Big Bang cosmology in relation to theology, process scholars in effect have already shifted out of a strictly Whiteheadian perspective on the universe. (In what I take to be a rare and very helpful move in the field, John Cobb, Jr, in Chapter 15 in this volume, offers a similar comment on the lack of attention to Whitehead's theory of gravity by process scholars.)

45. Langdon Gilkey, *Maker of Heaven and Earth: The Christian Doctrine of Creation in the Light of Modern Knowledge* (Lanham: University Press of America, 1959; originally published, Garden City: Doubleday, 1959).

46. This section is based in part on Robert John Russell, 'Finite Creation Without a Beginning: The Doctrine of Creation in Relation to Big Bang and Quantum Cosmologies', in *Quantum Cosmology and the Laws of Nature: Scientific Perspectives on Divine Action*, ed. by Robert J. Russell, Nancey C. Murphy, and Chris J. Isham, Scientific Perspectives on Divine Action Series (Vatican City State; Berkeley, CA: Vatican Observatory Publications; Center for Theology and the Natural Sciences, 1993).

47. Barbour, *Issues in Science and Religion*, 366–8.

48. Ibid., 377.

49. Ibid. 380. In the concluding section of Chapter 12 and again in his general conclusions to the entire book (Chapter 13) Barbour reiterates his agreement with Gilkey Barbour, *Issues in Science and Religion*, 458. Note: relying on Jarislov Pelikan's arguments, Barbour is also critical of the *ex nihilo* tradition since it has historically suppressed the tradition of continuing creation. He urges that we merge continuing creation with providence, and he deploys a number of arguments in support of this move. These arguments are worth pursuing, but not in the limited context of this paper.

50. Gilkey, *Maker of Heaven and Earth*, 310.

51. Ibid., 313. where he cites Aquinas's *Summa Theologica*, Part I, Question 46, Article 2.

52. In a curious twist to this story, Gilkey never argued to dismiss t = 0 as secondary to what is the 'real' theological meaning to the doctrine of creation. Instead he saw the issue of t = 0 as critically important, since it forces us to confront a *foundational* problem which governs and characterizes *every* major doctrine in Christian theology: the dialectic between 'the world of fact and experience' and 'the transcendent power and love of God' (*Maker*, 315–16) Given its importance, but unable to introduce empirical language into theology, Gilkey sought to resolve the problem by proposing we view religious language about historical/empirical origins and other empirical facts as *myth*. Hence, although I disagree with Gilkey's resolution of the problem, we owe him a great deal for his lucid insistence on its importance as such. If Gilkey is correct, the epistemological problems surrounding t = 0 are well worth *our* pursuing because they are *inherent* to the theological agenda as such.

53. Barbour, *Religion in an Age of Science*, 125–9.
54. Ibid., 144–5.
55. Imre Lakatos, 'Falsification and the Methodology of Scientific Research Programmes', in *The Methodology of Scientific Research Programmes: Philosophical Papers, Volume 1*, ed. by John Worrall and Gregory Currie (Cambridge: Cambridge University Press, 1978), 8–101.
56. Barbour, *Myths, Models, and Paradigms*, chs. 6, 7.
57. N. Murphy, *Theology in the Age of Scientific Reasoning* (Ithaca: Cornell University Press, 1990).
58. P. Clayton, *Explanation from Physics to Theology: An Essay in Rationality and Religion* (New Haven, CT: Yale University Press, 1989).
59. R.J. Russell, 'Did God Create Our Universe? Theological Reflections on the Big Bang, Inflation and Quantum Cosmologies', *Annals of the New York Academy of Sciences, 950: Cosmic Questions* (December 2001), ed. James B. Miller (New York Academy of Sciences).
60. Russell, 'Finite Creation Without a Beginning'.

C

Evolution, Anthropology, and Neuroscience

Case Studies in Barbour's Integrative Model: Liberal Anglo-Catholicism in the 1920s

W. Mark Richardson

Ian Barbour is widely recognized for having brought credibility to science–religion dialogue and interaction during years when much of intellectual culture was either hostile or indifferent to it. The context of science and religion dialogue today is dramatically different from the era of his first major publication, *Issues in Science and Religion*,[1] and to a large degree because of his influence.

One of the principal contributions of Ian Barbour is the capacity to synthesize vast ranges of historical, theoretical, and empirical knowledge, and to state succinctly the key issues residing at various points of the interface between science and religion. Clarity, accuracy, and perspective-giving are trademarks of his work.

Finally, he has contributed to the constructive development of the field by his application of Process philosophical principles to mediate the relation between the sciences and classic theological themes. Barbour affirms that no matter how important the interaction of religion and science, the relationship between them is not direct, but mediated by metaphysical frameworks for the interpretation of the whole of human experience and knowledge.[2]

In a recent collection titled *Neuroscience and the Person: Scientific Perspectives on Divine Action*,[3] Barbour's essay opens with Christian theological views of the human being, continues with a review of relevant data from the neurosciences and models of personhood from computational and informational systems, and closes with an exposition of the integrating power of process philosophy, bridging the conceptual distance between theology and the neurosciences. The form of the essay itself illustrates the kind of model for the field his career has provided.

This chapter consists of historical illustrations of Barbour's 'integrative' model, taking up an aspect of the same theme mentioned above: *the nature of the human being in theological perspective and the role of contemporary science in the revision of theological anthropology*. I offer case studies of Barbour's thesis that the relation of scientific data and theory to theology is mediated philosophically. I will consider three early twentieth-century Anglican theologians in whom evolutionary theory in broad outline caused theological reformulation on human origins. Whereas their revisions all depart from an Augustinian foundation in significant ways, their constructive proposals differ depending on philosophical commitments.

Opposing Theological Models of Human Origins

Today we are used to thinking about the human being as building genetically on the shoulders of millions of years of life. The process gives rise to the complex and fragile origins of the human being, who is regarded as unique but finite and continuous with natural history. We think of the human being as different in degree from other species, even if this difference is dramatic in effect.

No matter how familiar the story of evolution, we may not fully appreciate how new it is in the long history of theology, or agree on how complex the task of theological revision in light of its implications. Many continue to find meaning in the story of 'the fall', formalized by Augustine. Although we have long since let go of a *historical* reading of Augustine's scriptural source, the *symbolic* reading often follows the same pattern in its depiction of meaning. The tradition account has this form:

a   starting with the human being endowed with mature reason and will, and placed in an unobstructed relationship with God;
b   a subsequent willful disobedience against God, causing alienation from God, depravity or disorganization of human life, death, and damnation of humanity which shares in Adam's 'original guilt';
c   restored relationship with God (at least for some) through an atoning transaction centered in Christ's death, leading to salvation.[4]

Many symbolic accounts of this pattern treat 'Adam and Eve' as every person, but oftentimes without careful enough grounding in the biological, social, and larger environmental history. Thus, there is something inexplicable (a 'mystery') about the cataclysmic human turning from the good; something is 'lost'. A restored divine–human relationship is based in transaction in which Christ's death is not merely a consequence, but constitutive. At the very least, this pattern – original perfection, sin and alienation, restoration – lingers in our liturgies, and so I suspect it lingers deep within Christian self-understanding as well.

But in light of a radically different cosmological understanding today we should ask: *restoring* humanity to what? What is it that once existed, has been *lost*, and which needs to be *found*? What could the 'original righteousness' mean? Those who continue to resuscitate the 'fall' pattern through symbolic refinements increasingly strain to preserve meaning while avoiding rank inconsistencies. If the symbolic reading succeeds in overcoming the above questions by regarding true human identity, for example, in eschatological terms, then one must wonder whether the original intention of the 'fall' idea has been so changed as to be unrecognizable, and useless theologically.

Could it be that the evolutionary picture requires a more radical break from this pattern than our symbolic renderings of the story so far have offered? If 'original righteousness' and its restoration are no longer intelligible in an evolutionary worldview, then they could in fact distort the theological imagination, and the spiritual quest linked with a more realistic rendering of our created origins. In this sense, the sciences may be 'prophetic' from outside by forcing theology to be more aligned with our picture of the physical universe as a whole – its laws and conditions, its long history from initial conditions to human presence. In theological terms: knowledge from the sciences pressures us to see human origins within a wider scope of the doctrine of creation.

Barbour hints at the direction which needs developing. He notes that various sciences point to a holistic view of the mind–brain relationship, the significance of emotional underpinnings to human cognition, the embeddedness of human identity in social reality, and natural life preceding it. Because of the evolutionary worldview, he rejects the traditional meaning of original sin and sees the biblical account of Adam and Eve as referring to the universal human experience in which innocence is replaced by responsibility. In the process sin arises as self-centerdness and disobedienceto God.[5] The movement from 'innocence to responsibility', could imply the following. The equivalent of 'self-concern' in pre-moral species – the struggle to survive under conditions of scarcity – takes on a different quality with the emergence of human beings, whose moral and spiritual characteristics are constrained by these conditions and by finite perspective generally. The capacities we associate with 'mind' allow for a richness of meaning at the base of action, making moral being possible, placing natural self-assertion within a larger context and a greater good, and with this possibility comes the corollary possibility of moral failure.

This by no means diminishes the tragic dimension of *sin*. But the tone of the problem changes once we appreciate the biological constraints on finite freedom at its very origins built up from evolutionary processes, and extended within social-cultural systems.[6] Sin must be a feature of emergent capacities we associate with being human. Taking this seriously will mean that moral agency does indeed build on the 'free process' perspective, the costliness of which is striking enough in nature at simpler levels of organization, and more dramatic still at the level of human persons and societies.[7] This trajectory can no longer presuppose the origins of moral agency except as fragile, and its environment for appreciating the good, ambiguous. The world presents to the human being a context of violence, aggression, a competitive urge to survive, alongside self-giving and cooperative social behaviors – leading to valuations of good/bad, order/disorder, beauty/ugliness. Taken together these factors lead to error in judgment – a disparity in our finite judgments between apparent and real goods. If moral failure in human action, reinforced and habituated, is for all practical purposes inevitable, then it may also affect the way we understand natural phenomena with respect to their origins in God's goodness.

Among adherents to the broad outlines of evolutionary thinking, who would deny the constraints of the four basic drives which Konrad Lorenz describes – feeding, reproduction, flight, and aggression?[8] It is not necessary to regard our behavior as conforming lockstep to the dictates of instinct. All one needs to claim is that when humanity adds the new element of willful action (accounted for by powers of symbolic language, memory, anticipation of future, among other factors) it does so building upon the inherited biological and social materials, and building on the conditions of an environment, which together form the basis of intentional structuring of reality, and values to be realized. We inherit a system of drives, but differ in the capacity to plan, prioritize and order action in the pursuit of goals.

Moral existence is constrained from below but not sufficiently explained from below.

Two points must be made utterly clear in this challenge to 'fall' theory. First, giving up the language and concept of 'fall' does not mean giving up the notion of sin, or even original sin. The notions of 'fall' and 'original sin' have different and separable functions. Second, the effects of sin are far from trivial or unreal. In point of fact, the consequences of sin are horrendous, to use the language of Marilyn Adams; they are destructive of life and spirit; they are embedded in the social matrix so deeply that all individual self-understanding is shaped by it.[9]

One might ask, 'Isn't it just such a story as the human 'fall', as found in the former vision, which makes sense of the irrational violence of our own time?' One reply is that the 'fall' is not about the tragic consequence of sin, but about *the origins* of sin. And, in large measure, the theologians considered below take the view that evidence from the sciences, and the dominant worldview interpreting the science, do not favor this theological view of the origins. They give us differing pictures of this problem, but they each take the evolutionary context seriously.

So to summarize this section, much changes when we switch from imagining our species originating in a primordial paradise of mature will and reason, to imagining the species as 'in the making', and building up moral consciousness and agency from roots in pre-moral natural existence.[10] Evolutionary theory and its relation to theological perspectives on human origins is a good place to examine the importance of Barbour's integration model for the theology–science relationship. The two major strands regarding human nature and its origins can be labeled 'the fall from freedom' tradition, and the 'soul making' tradition, following generally terminology of John Hick in his influential work, *Evil and the God of Love*.[11] Each takes human sin seriously, but sees its effects on human constitution, its relation to the whole of nature, and its theological solution, differently.

The Theological Context for Discussing the Problem

I will consider theological reflections on human origins from the liberal Anglo-Catholic tradition in the 1920s. This particular context is chosen for a number of reasons. First, British theologians during this period have long been on the perimeter of the focus on liberal, neo-Reformed, and existential Protestant theologies in twentieth-century academic theology. No doubt these latter traditions were compelling and their dominance needs no justification. But it happens to be the case that British theology and philosophical theology in this era were prolific and of notable quality also, represented in such figures as Charles Gore, William Temple, Frederic Tennant, Lionel Thornton, Charles Raven, A.E. Taylor, Hastings Rashdall, and N.P. Williams, and still others. These figures did their work conscious of the changing scientific cultural climate, and usually with an explicit effort to integrate its effects into their theology.

Second, these figures represent a second or third round of refinements on theology after Darwin. What typified liberal Anglo-Catholicism was its commitment to classic creedal doctrine, centered in incarnation and trinity, coupled with openness to theological revision responsive to contemporary worldview. Far from resisting evolutionary ideas, some of the early liberals tended toward enthusiastic and uncritical absorption of them. Incarnation and trinity were now seen in the context of evolutionary dynamic, bottom-up perspective combined with themes of development in philosophical idealism. The impression at times, especially in late nineteenth-century writings, was of an uncritical rendering of natural and historical progress.[12] But the theology of the 1920s reflected the sobering impact of World War I. We may see it most dramatically in a Reformed figure such as Karl Barth, but it had an effect on liberal Anglo-Catholicism as well. N.P. Williams, one of the figures discussed below, wrote in his Bampton Lectures of 1924:

> It may have been possible, exactly ten years ago, at the beginning of the fateful year 1914, for men to dismiss the problem of its genesis with a light-hearted *solvitur ambulanda*, and to console themselves for the impossibility of accounting for the origin of evil by assurance ... of an irresistible upward trend of moral evolution assumed to be in automatic conformity with the ascending curve of material, mechanical and scientific advance. But the events through which humanity has lived since then have forever dispelled such a credulous optimism.[13]

However, a significant fact is that the postwar climate did not throw Anglican theology off its track of rethinking 'creation' and 'incarnation' from a scientifically informed point of view, at least in broad outline. And this may distinguish this 'minor' tradition more than anything else. The context led to a more critical theology; but it did not cause a retreat into insular traditionalism, nor abandonment of apologetics – the project of giving a persuasive account of the world's intelligibility in light of theism interpreted through the lens of evolution and philosophical idealism. Williams, for example, constructed an alternative to the Augustinian 'fall' which was deeply grounded in the history of traditions but sensitive to the contemporary worldview. We may find the constructive alternative (described below) strange in today's context, yet admire the motivation for pursuing revision.

One thesis of this essay is that liberal Anglo-Catholic theology in the 1920s offered a number of examples of Barbour's integrative way of approaching the science–religion relationship, forty years in advance of *Issues in Science and Religion*. This is especially evident in the appropriation of a scientific worldview influenced by evolutionary ideas. Popular examples of theology in this era usually represent 'conflict' (for example, the growing American Fundamentalist movement) or 'independence' (such as Barthian dialectical theology after *The Epistle to the Romans*). Some of the work in British theology and philosophy in the 1920s is strikingly integrative relative to the above examples, and reinforces the theme in recent histories of science and religion that the modern era is more complicated than the stereotypes of cultural attitudes admit.[14]

The figures below differ, at points considerably, in their constructive alternatives to classic treatments of 'fall' and 'original sin'. But they agree that a problem to be solved is the integration of evolutionary perspectives on the long and dynamic 'history of nature' into theological understanding of creation and of human origins. Some of the themes have no direct relation to formal evolutionary theory, and can be found in recognizable form in Schleiermacher. I think in particular of Schleiermacher's grounding of theological anthropology in embodied natural being, his tendency to see moral evil as resolved in a greater redemptive good, and his eschatological view of the human ideal. But, the mark of Hegel's philosophy of history is still greater than this. My point is that it is not evolutionary thinking *per se* which influences every aspect of their revision; it is among other major influences toward reform which originate in the nineteenth century.

What remains will be a survey of three theologians in the Anglican tradition in the 1920s, centering on their treatment of the topic of human origins in theology. Charles Gore's *The Reconstruction of Belief*, and William Temple's *Christus Veritas* and *Nature, Man and God* are examples of apologetic theology; N.P. Williams's *The Ideas of the Fall and of Original Sin* is, as the title indicates, a more specialized work on the very topic of this essay. I will attempt to show how the relationship developed between evolutionary worldview and theology is mediated by an interpretive framework in theology or philosophy.

Liberal Anglo-Catholicism in the 1920s: N.P. Williams

N.P. Williams was an Oxford philosophical theologian whose Bampton Lectures of 1924 were on the topic of the concepts of 'the fall' and of 'original sin'. The larger framework of his thought was the history of religions with special emphasis on the Semitic traditions. In his analysis of the topic we will see also that the early twentieth-century interest in depth psychology had greatly influenced his understanding of religious experience. Finally, he took notice of the philosophy of Henri Bergson, in *Creative Evolution*, and it contributed to his constructive thought. The influence of British idealism upon him is less marked than in Temple and Gore, but the three held to forms of emergent philosophy, synthesizing teleological and evolutionary principles.

We will see that Williams's approach appreciates the role of the evolutionary worldview in forcing theological revision, especially of 'fall' theology. I begin with Williams because he develops a framework which will be useful in placing Temple and Gore as well.

History of the Semitic Tradition

Williams places his study carefully in the context of a history of religions, identifying three major branches. He claims that virtually every understanding of human nature and human origins can fit in one of the three categories, each having an ancient history. The basic forms are:

- Derivatives of Indic traditions – *non-moral monism* – which see evil as appearance, non-reality. In some, especially modern, views of this, the 'experience' of evil is a necessary moment in the finite expression of the Absolute. This is 'non-moral monism'.

- Derivatives of Persian traditions – *dualism* – which see evil as a real force, opposed to the good, and having co-eternal status with the good. Both good and the evil have their manifestations in the created world and in the structures of reality. The human goal is future redemption experienced as release from the bondage of evil.
- Derivatives of Semitic traditions – *ethical monotheism* – which see creation as good; evil is a temporary and contingent phenomenon resulting from the creature's willful disaffection from God. The human goal is redemptive victory, and the fulfilment of divine image in this world and the next.

Sub-branches of this last type concern us because they represent diverging Christian understandings of human nature and the origin of sin. There is the softer Hellenistic version in which good survives in humanity, though it has been weakened by sin. And there is the North African tradition in which fallen humanity is constitutionally corrupted, legally condemned and alienated from God because of sin.

To round out the historical background, which sets up his own constructive position, Williams notes the relatively minor role of Genesis 3 in the history of Israel on the question of human origins and sin. Reflection on this topic was identified with Genesis 6 in early apocalyptic writings – the fallen angels (Watchers) who mate with human beings, and thus bring false desire, impurity, distortion into the human condition universally through biological inheritance. It was not until the second century BCE, the later apocalyptic era, that the Genesis 3 account gained popularity as scriptural foci on these themes. The Genesis 6 account reflects evil coming into human existence, preceding the creation of human beings.

Second, the still later rabbinic tradition of the *yecir ha-ra* sees opposing principles built into each person at conception by God. Contrary to Augustine's vision of a single act infecting humankind universally, in the *yecir ha-ra* tradition God implants the evil imagination in every person at conception, and has placed divine law over against it. Free will works within the tension established between evil imagination and law.

With these basic parts in the Semitic history in front of us, we now have the historical material from which Williams constructs his position. The interest of this essay is to show the effects of the contemporary intellectual culture as 'data' which shaped his constructive theology. As mentioned, three important elements will shape his somewhat synthetic theological perspective: the evolutionary worldview of his day, Freudian principles regarding drives conditioning human action, and Bergsonian philosophy. I will show the effects of each on his constructive thesis about the theology of human origins.

Theology of Origins and Evolutionary Worldview

Williams says about the Augustinian account that it conceptually runs aground on the facts of natural history, and the effects are spiritually dangerous as they 'over invest' in some original transgressive act:

> It follows from this exalted view of man's paradisal condition that the malice of
> the first sin was infinite in its demerit because it was the first ... All subsequent
> sins, indeed, have been due to the inordinate power of concupiscence and the
> corruption of man's nature engendered by the fall. [The first sin was] ... due to
> pure senseless perversity; it was ... committed not as a result of weakness or
> frailty, but against a settled habit of virtue.[15]

Based on the evolutionary-emergent picture of his day, Williams represents the
human being as 'born at the bottom of the mountain, refusing to follow that path
which led most directly to its summit, and preferring to follow a tortuous route of
his own devising'.[16] In spite of Williams's great appreciation for the depth of
Augustine's psychological and spiritual insight, his opposition to the Augustinian
'fall' tradition was quite passionate as the following remark attests:

> It should be beneath the dignity of theology to use a term of which the *prima
> facie* meaning has to be elaborately explained away on every occasion of its use;
> if our religion is to regain its ancient power in an age which demands
> remorseless clarity of thought and expression, it cannot afford to disregard a
> maxim dictated by common sense, namely, that if a term cannot be used in a
> given connexion without a non-natural interpretation, it had better not be used
> in that connexion at all.[17]

By a theological return to the picture of primitive humanity as sketched by Irenaeus,
Williams believed '... the conflict between fall and the evolutionary view of human
history would largely disappear.'[18]

The Influence of Depth Psychology

Williams was quite taken by the explanatory power of the Freudian psychology of
his day. Its function in the interpretation of religious experience affected the way he
conceived the relation between present religious life, ancient scriptures, and
tradition.[19] But the more important impact of Freud on Williams was on the
understanding of the origins of moral consciousness once the evolutionary context
is established. Williams accepted from Freud that the basic instinctual drives of
human existence can be understood in terms of the sex complex associated with
reproductive success, the self-preservation complex, and the 'herd' complex. These
correspond roughly to 'id', 'ego', and 'super-ego' respectively. As regards the last,
evolutionary success of group existence finds its highest form in the slow process
of evolution in human social systems and the laws which represent its highest aims
and values. The interplay of these motivational forces accounts in large part for
human behavior.[20]

Moral life emerges in the interiorization of the herd instinct, according to
Williams. The concrete content of morality, as it exists in any time or place is
defined by the exigencies of 'the herd', and mediated to consciousness through the
pressure of the herd. So the social complex is the source for the awakening of moral
life. We have many examples of human loyalties, self-sacrificing behavior, self-
transcending yearning for the Absolute in whom *eternal values* find their support.
But this interior power, according to Williams, 'is from the psychologist's point of

view an artificial and secondary construction upon *one* of the three primary ... complexes'.

Williams saw human free will as played out in the tension between the *herd instinct*, on the one hand, and the *ego instinct* and *sex instinct*, on the other hand. This is Williams's modern psychological rendering of the ancient rabbinic account, mentioned above, where freedom is played out between divine law and the 'evil imagination' implanted in each person.

But – and this leads us to the last piece of the Williams picture – in point of fact, the balance among the three basic complexes is not there, and this accounts for the experienced hopelessness of our condition:

> ... owing to the weakness of the herd instinct which feeds it ... the moral sentiment which is built upon it, does not possess anything like the amount of vital energy necessary to place it on equal terms with the two other primary complexes, so as to preserve that equilibrium of the empirical self ... which the transcendental self needs in order to be able to function with freedom.[21]

At some point along the way of temporal existence, balance has been compromised. Hence, the modern psychological interpretation of the rabbinic tradition is next placed into a still larger framework of universal history.

Bergson's Elan Vital, *and Fallen 'World-soul'*

Next, Williams draws upon the modern philosophy of Bergson regarding a life energy which gives purposive direction to the blind mechanisms of evolution and he thinks of this in conjunction with the stoic notion of *logos spermatikos* and the world-soul notion.[22] This vital energy which pre-exists the multiplicity of physical and natural systems, is part of God's 'good' creation. Williams then located the onset of evil in some mysterious primordial 'fall' of the world-soul, thus finding similarity between the world-soul philosophy and the early apocalypticists' reading of Genesis 6 – the angels who mate with humankind and bring heritable distortion into existence.[23]

One of the effects of this picture is to see evolutionary mechanisms as against God's original intention, not expressions of it. In deference to evolutionary thinking, 'disorganization' in nature is taken back before the emergence of humankind, but interpreted in a manner dangerously close to jeopardizing ethical monotheism and its conception of creation as 'good'.

> The cat which tortures the mouse by playing with it ... the insectivorous plant, which with cold and Mephistophelean ferocity disguises its death dealing petals ... to allure and entrap its unwary victims: all these perform functions which are evil in the sense that they rouse the detestation of the refined moral consciousness in man; but they are free from guilt, they commit no sin, because they are but blindly following the fundamental law of their being ...
>
> How then, shall that God ... whose love bears the same relation to our weak emotions of sympathy and fellow feeling as the infinity of his wisdom does to our ... limited knowledge, have done so? The answer can only be that he did not do so; that he did not create such a universe. ... To explain evil in nature, no less

than in man, we are compelled to assume ... A revolt against the will of the
Creator ... at a point before differentiation of life into its present multiplicity of
forms and the emergence of separate species.[24]

So in review, Williams allowed empirical science and its theoretical conclusions
both in psychology, and in evolutionary biology, to function as data for theology.
These disciplines are then mediated by a philosophical interpretive bridge taken
piecemeal from a number of sources. His theory deals with the collective experience
of flaw and moral failure, taking seriously psychology and spiritual experience of
the biased will, as well as its effects. On this point, the influence of St Paul and
Augustine remains prominent in Williams.

By placing an understanding of the existence of temporal evil in a deeper past,
Williams hoped to be true to an evolutionary framework while also preserving
ethical monotheism (that is, finding a temporal, contingent explanation for evil). He
pictures moral consciousness as emergent and its origins fragile. Here, Williams
believed that Augustine's theory is more wrong than right in spite of its *prima facie*
attractiveness in the understanding of the universal effects of sin.

But this evolutionary picture is mediated to theology through the complex
addition of world-soul philosophy. And here the problems begin. First, a notion of
something like a vital force, co-existent with matter-energy but unavailable to
science, was lively in his day but has none of the same credibility in today's
intellectual climate. Second, and more theological, to move the source of the
world's apparent broken state back to a pre-differentiated vital force may spare us
from the implausibility of finding sufficient cause for violence, suffering, and death
in primordial humanity. But it does not protect ethical monotheism to place the evil
agency in creation elsewhere. Third, the theory attempts to preserve a distinction
between what God *causes/intends* and what God *lets happen*, but it does so at a high
cost by its negative valuation of natural processes. This undercuts the ethical
monotheist view of creation and veers in the direction of dualism. In the end, if God
is the source of all there is then God must be part of any accounting for ill effects in
the world. In this respect Williams offers no improvement on the basic weakness of
freewill defense.

Liberal Anglo-Catholicism in the 1920s: William Temple

William Temple was trained philosophically under the influence of the British
Idealists, prominent in late nineteenth century and early twentieth century at
Oxford. One of his teachers was the personal idealist, Edward Caird. Owen Thomas
states that, later, Whitehead had significantly influenced his views of the world as
apprehended, the structure and relations of the world-process, mind, and value.[25]
Temple's interpretation of the evolutionary context occurred in this broader
metaphysical framework, attempting the always precarious task of holding together
of evolutionary mechanism and ultimate purpose. Most of his major works argue for
theism as the most persuasive ground for the intelligibility of the world and our
experience. The universe's slow evolutionary emergence in the direction of greater
complexity, eventually expressed in finite mind and spirit, makes most sense if there

is Mind as source of this bottom-up process, giving it direction and purpose. Temple states early in *Christus Veritas*:

> It [reality] consists of many grades, of which each presupposes those lower than itself, and of which each finds its own completion or perfect development only in so far as it is possessed or indwelt by that which is above it ... To make my present meaning clear it is enough to take the broad divisions: Matter, Life, Mind, Spirit ...
> Matter only reveals what it really is when Life supervenes upon it ... Similarly, Life only reveals what it really is when Mind supervenes upon it.[26]

At the heart of his philosophical theology is *value* theory. The universe is inscribed with value. There is no fact–value split, according to Temple, but rather intellectual, aesthetic and moral value are all present together in the universe. Consistent with his epistemic realism, he held that value is *in* the object, discovered and appreciated by the subject; it is not merely epiphenomenal. Again, a most succinct statement of Temple's theory of value comes from Thomas's study:

> He [Temple] claims that the identity of substance with value follows from the theistic hypothesis. The universe receives its existence from the Creative Will. But the correlative of will is good or value; will is always aimed at the realization of value. Therefore, ... the constitutive principle of every existent, is its value ... although value is logically prior to existence ... it must receive existence to be a part of reality. But nothing receives existence except as a realization of value or as a means to value.[27]

These commitments help us determine his perspective on the theology of human origins and sin. Sin will be construed as human participation in evil, and evil as 'negative value'.

How does the possibility of 'evil' originate, according to Temple? From his emergent perspective on the human being he saw that, 'Consciousness supervenes upon an organic existence which has already established a habitual routine. That routine includes a process in which one organism becomes food for another.'[28]

But this evolutionary history is no obstacle to theism. And here, Temple steers away from Williams. The predator–prey relation, exemplary of the interaction of energy systems in the biological world, is given a more positive face and clearly thought of as divine creative process:

> ... it seems clear from the accounts of naturalists that even for them [the smaller animals who are prey] enjoyment of life is the prevailing tone or color of experience ... there is reason to be satisfied [at this level] of a balance of good over evil. The violence of nature intrinsic to systems is not evil, rather, ... the best understanding we can frame of the animal world offers no obstacle to a reasonable theism.[29]

In his discourse on human moral action, Temple centers on the uniqueness of the imagination, its power to conceive and make associations among ideas derived from experience in the natural world. In a sense, imagination is a functional corollary with physical sensations:

> Imagination offers to desire the stimulus which the appropriate physical objects offer to appetite. Hence comes a great, and in principle unlimited, expansion of the life of desire, which in pre-human existence functions for the sake of vital needs of the organisms ... may take the form of aspiration or of lust.[30]

The point here is that self-consciousness allows the finite spirit to reach beyond immediate appetite to meaning as the framework of desire.

This capacity of mind, taken into action, turns potential value in the universe into actualized value. Other forms of life and mind may possess consciousness, but of a kind in which self-centeredness is not yet 'self-assertion' in the moral sense. However, given the human capacities mentioned above, in the distortion of desire and in the distortion of judgment, the person becomes not only the *subject* of his value judgments, but also the *center* and criterion of his own value system.

Sin, then, derives from a good and innate aspect of animal existence – desire – and consists in its exaggeration or misdirection. Because of the limits of finitude – the myriad of motivating forces on the springs of action, the constraint on discernment owing to limits of one's context – persons never grasp absolutely true proportion and perspective on the world. Discrepancies occur between the *apparent* good and the *real* good, and between the ordering of finite goods.

In Temple's view, it is a virtual inevitability that a divergence occurs between the apparent good and the actual good, and that these become reinforced in habits of action, and habits of self-perception. The origins of morality occur in an exploration of value under the finite and sometimes unstable conditions of emerging agency.[31]

Once tendencies of distortion edge their way into the human patterns of action, they reinforce the next phase of action. But now, within self-conscious agents, the habituation is raised to moral status. Says Temple:

> The human mind is a focus of appreciation. It has knowledge of good and evil ... which before he won it were merely instinctive reactions to environment, become through that knowledge sins against the light, they are done with a new degree of self-assertion ... because imagination is so potent to stimulate desire, there is additional impulse to those acts. Man in so far as he is evil is worse than any animal; and in every man there is the bias or tendency to evil.[32]

Temple, of course, addresses the social dimension of sin also within this framework of distorted values. Far from being 'exclusive atoms of consciousness' personal existence occurs in a social system of experience. The human being is partly self-determining and self-integrating, and yet inextricably this is derived from a context of meaning given by the social environment. It is best, therefore, to think of humans as 'reciprocally determining beings'. Therefore, the existence of one self-centered soul would spread an evil infection through all who come within its range of influence. Temple states:

> If A is self-centered, B tends to become so by imitation; but also B becomes so in self-defense ... A and B perpetually develop their own and one another's self-

centeredness. Actual human society is to a large extent ... that network of competing selfishness, all kept in check by each one's selfish fear of the others ....[33]

The thrust of Temple's position suggests that human sin is virtually given in the dawning of self-consciousness, and thus, inseparable from divine intention. He states: 'Human sin was not a necessary episode in the divine plan; but was always so closely implicated in the divine plan that it must be held to fall within the divine purpose.'[34]

If sin is so probable in the exploration of good by a finite will, that it is 'distinguishable from inevitability only in thought', then, as Temple suggested, in some sense one can say God intended a creation wherein the highest good is actualized as a consequence of negative value: 'A sinful world redeemed by the agony of love's self-sacrifice is a better world than the world that had never sinned.'[35] The whole idea here echoes a similar dialectic found in his mentor, the idealist philosopher Edward Caird, and is of course inspired by Hegel's dialectic of spirit.[36]

To summarize the comments on Temple, one can clearly see the impact of the idealistic philosophical framework for understanding the scientific evolutionary worldview. And together these influences affected his revision on the theology of human origins. In the three branches described by Williams, one sees in Temple a tendency to treat evil as a necessary element in the highest good; as part of the unity of existence. He holds out for the contingency of evil, but the line is very finely drawn.

Temple recognized negative value as a part of reality, but he did not associate it with the laws of nature or its outcomes as such, as Williams had done. He treated the thesis of the incarnation as the key to the unity and rationality of a world whose every feature – evil and suffering included – must make sense. So, whereas Williams erred in confusing the outcomes of nature's laws with a fallen world-soul, thus verging toward dualism, Temple tended toward – even if never conceding to it – seeing both value and its negation as necessary conditions in creation's movement to its highest good, which is the absolute value of self-giving love.

Liberal Anglo-Catholicism in the 1920s: Charles Gore

Charles Gore took it as a principle of Catholicism that divine purpose is worked out slowly through history, and that it involves all of creation. He envisioned a softer boundary between natural and revealed religion than supposed by either the more conservative Anglo-Catholics and neo-orthodox Protestants. In one of his few references to Karl Barth he states his disagreement with him on this matter. Nevertheless, he also saw Israel's history and its prophets as having a special vocation historically in view of the centrality of Christ in creation and redemption.

Theologically, Gore was a true liberal Anglo-Catholic with keen insight into the challenges of coherence with intellectual culture on the one hand, and faithfulness to creedal Christianity on the other hand. Philosophically, he too had been influenced by the British Personal Idealists, especially T.H. Green. As with Temple, this became part of the metaphysical framework for interpreting the evolutionary worldview. Gore synthesized this philosophical tradition with the Alexandrian Patristic emphasis on *logos*. The Personalist vision of a purposive universe stood in sharp contrast to the more mechanistic reading of Darwin in interpreters such as Huxley and Spencer. But Gore took evolution quite seriously as data to motivate theological reconstruction.[37]

Gore's understanding of the story of human origins in Genesis 3 breaks cleanly from a historical reading. He stated hypothetically that, had Darwin's theory been presented in the fourth century and Genesis 3 interpreted in light of it, it would have caused little concern since the ante-Nicene Fathers were skilled in the symbolic reading of texts.[38]

It seemed clear to Gore that evolutionary theory destroyed the basis for 'design arguments' as formulated through the eighteenth century.[39] But the same evolutionary grounds opened the possibility for a more powerful view of 'design'. The best way to make sense of evolutionary tendencies is through 'presiding purposive mind', a theme which we found in Temple as well.[40]

Gore viewed humanity within an organic unity, and interpreted this to mean that human beings are not personally responsible for the *roots* of sin, which are present before the birth of personal consciousness. *Original* sin makes perfect sense in the worldview of the organic unity of the species and the deeply social nature of the human being. Nevertheless, Gore places great stock in the notion of personal freedom and moral agency:

> Adam and Eve stand for all human beings, and the story of the 'fall' is the story of humanity and of every individual case. The lawlessness of the race conditions each person's lawlessness, but each person is responsible only for his own acquiescence in it.[41]

It was critical to Christian theism that, no matter how conditioned or predisposed, human moral agency exists and does real work.

Gore had a view similar to Williams and Temple on the emergence of the human being, but was perhaps even more advanced in thinking through the implications of this. He saw theological acceptance of emergence as susceptible to reductionism, but with care this alternative could be avoided. He also cautioned the theologian against finding God in the gaps of scientific knowledge, indicating a keen sense of the challenges posed to integrative outlooks:

> We shall not if we are wise, lay stress on the gaps in the scientific story of creation, or build on the conviction that living matter could not have been evolved out of what had no life ... but what we shall claim is that the fact that living beings and spiritual beings emerged in an age-long process out of a world which was lifeless and without any spiritual consciousness in itself, does not mean that life and spirit can be interpreted in terms of material force and chemical change as if they were nothing more ...[42]

In the context of emergence, to discover the divine intent for the human being is not to look backward but forward through Christ, and eschatologically. In a footnote in his section on the 'fall' he states, 'God sees things not as they are but as they are becoming. This is the *real* way to see things.'[43]

Gore took to task the caricature of his day (which lingers in our own) about the opposition between traditional theology and the new evolutionary worldview.[44] The opposition consisted, in his mind, between Augustine and his Calvinist descendants, and the 'modernist' interpretation of evolution which does not take seriously enough the notion of sin. He sought a middle ground to soften the contrast. The biblical account (Genesis 3) portrays humankind as in 'the complete ignorance as well as the innocence of childhood.' But this story makes almost no impression on the Old Testament as a whole, which is 'throughout the story of a divine purpose for man pursuing its gradual way to its goal, but constantly thwarted and baffled by sin.' Gore interpreted the biblical view as a human advance toward the realization of a God-given heritage impeded from what it might have been by constant and renewed disloyalty to God.

But in Gore's interpretation, sin is always a 'fall,' a perversion and loss, even if one of its consequences is progress. Progress could have occurred without it, and sin need not have been.[45] This is a different picture from Temple, for whom sin is contingent but, for all practical purposes, inevitable and thus traceable to God's purposes. It was crucial to Gore that one accept the idea of human origins in innocence, even fragileness, but at the same time, the experience and reality of 'disobedience' which is experienced as 'fall.' Unless this latter notion is honored, the relational key to Christian theism is lost, and the goodness of God is jeopardized.[46] One wonders what the 'lost birthright' is, which he spoke of, or what it is which once existed but now is lost.

The puzzle here is sharp in light of Gore's apparent appreciation for the evolutionary conditions of human origins. He placed emphasis on the biological and cultural roots of an individual's experience of sin. And this is the chief point of 'original' sin.[47] He invoked modern psychology to reinforce the Christian view of the individual and corporate aspects of personhood:

> In the unconscious mind he carries instincts and memories which are racial and not personal. If this is so, it would be very bold to deny that there may be, or must be, some inheritance of sin, in its weakening and perverting effect upon the spiritual nature, in those roots of our being which lie below the beginnings of personal consciousness.[48]

These claims accent the constraints on individual freedom, but an insistence nonetheless on freedom's importance theologically.

So the middle ground he created seems to be this: we are inextricably linked with nature and it has its effects on the roots of moral awakening. However, the higher capacities which constitute our humanity – intelligence, conscience, moral and spiritual capacities – change the status of creaturely action. The instability of moral beginnings, due to biological and environmental factors, are real and significant markers of our finitude. But freedom, however limited, means that action can go wrong, and ironically, this marks off human life as a very high stature indeed: '… the glory and dignity of humanity depend upon, and are bound up with, the recognition of the supremacy of the moral ideal or law … It cannot be interpreted as merely a human quality.'

So how do we place Gore with respect to the other two figures, above? He attempts to hold the classic view of ethical monotheism – that creation is good and an expression of God's goodness.[49] In response to the nagging problem of suffering in the world prior to human beings, he went so far as to challenge the characterization. He anticipated some of the present reassessment of group behaviors in higher mammals. As such he especially distances himself from Williams as the following remark will indicate:

> the estimate of nature as a 'gladiator show' which was fashionable in Huxley's day, has been greatly modified, and almost reversed by the emphasis which recent biology lays on the capacity for sociality, cooperation and unselfishness as chief among the conditions which throughout the animal kingdom make for success.[50]

He is careful to keep a distance between evil and divine purpose, and to retain the view that willful disobedience of moral creatures is the source of evil. Ultimately, Gore pleaded ignorance about how to interpret in detail the fact of pain and suffering incident to physical evolution. But he did not see it posing a fundamental threat to theism.

Conclusions

On the whole, I think that the positions of Gore and Temple fall much closer together than either of them to Williams. They avoid an interpretation of nature's laws as markers of a fallen world-soul – a heavenly rebellion. Williams's strategy to overcome the Augustinian vision of 'fall' is not acceptable to them. I have claimed that Temple's position veers toward an evil as necessary consequence (perhaps taking the implications of evolutionary conditions of agency more seriously), and that Gore holds a more classic view of ethical monotheism.

The examples in this essay from liberal Anglo-Catholicism of the 1920s indicate there are differences which remain among those who revise their theological view of human origins and sin based on evolutionary principles. There are still other mediating commitments which determine the interpretation of the evolutionary data. Thus, evolutionary worldview as such was far from determining the whole of the theological picture. Nevertheless, the data of evolution indeed made a significant difference.

Regarding Anglican theology in the 1920s, I have argued that a major shift occurred away from themes associated with Augustinian 'fall' theology, and toward what has later been referred to as 'soul-making' theology. Their views of soteriology, I believe, reflect this change.

Indeed I think it can be shown that the redemptive theories of the above theologians, and others in that period we have not discussed, shifted in accordance with the shifts in their view of origins. And the revisions vary in ways which align with the degrees of difference we have detected in the theologies of origins and the human condition.

This essay has a modest function of simply reinforcing Barbour's outlook on theology of nature in the integrative framework. Science and religion remain independent sources, with overlap of concerns. But the relation is not direct, 'and we need philosophical categories to help us unify scientific and theological assertions in a more systematic way'.[51]

Notes

1. I.G. Barbour, *Issues in Science and Religion* (New York: Harper & Row, 1971; originally published in 1966 by Prentice Hall).
2. Idem, *Religion and Science: Historical and Contemporary Issues* (SanFranscisco: HarperSanFranscisco, 1997), 98–105. On the topic of this present essay, Marilyn McCord Adams reinforces this thesis in her work *Horrendous Evils* (Ithaca: Cornell University Press, 1999).
3. Idem, 'Neuroscience, Artificial Intelligence, and Human Nature: Theological and Philosophical Reflections', in *Neuroscience and the Person: Scientific Perspectives on Divine Action*, ed. by Robert John Russell (Vatican City State; Berkeley: Vatican Observatory; Center for Theology and the Natural Sciences, 1999), 249–80.
4. St Augustine, *City of God*, trans. Henry Bettenson (New York: Penguin, 1984), Bk. 12, ch 22, 502; Bk 13, ch 15, 523; and Bk. 14, ch 11, 569.
5. I.G. Barbour, *Religion and Science*, 269.
6. On this point we may find Rene Girard's thesis about memesis and distorted desire useful.
7. This is explained in several of John Polkinghorne's works.
8. Leslie Stevenson and David L. Haberman, *Ten Theories of Human Nature*, 3rd edn (New York: Oxford University Press, 1998), 207–22.
9. Adams, *Horrendous Evils and the Goodness of God*.
10. Theology in its pursuit of coherence links this vision of origins to an interpretation of what salvation consists in. For this reason, speculations about the origins of human moral existence are not trivial. Different visions of the Cosmological-scale problem – *What went wrong?* – lead to different visions of the remedy – *How will it get fixed?*; and different soteriologies lead to different spiritualities. This is the topic of another paper, but it is extremely important to examine this correlation between theories of origins and theories of soteriology.
11. John Hick, *Evil and the God of Love* (San Francisco: Harper & Row, 1966).
12. There are tinges of this in Aubrey Moore's 'The Christian Doctrine of God', but it is full blown in J.R. Illingworth's 'The Incarnation in Relation to Development', both essays in *Lux Mundi*, ed. by Charles Gore (1889).
13. N.P. Williams, *The Ideas of The Fall and of Original Sin*, Bampton Lectures of 1924 (London: Longmans, Green & Co., 1927), 3–4. The view expressed here is echoed in the views of Charles Gore in *The Reconstruction of Belief* (London: Murray, 1926) 25–6.
14. This fact would be no surprise to Barbour himself, as one of his exemplars of 'integration' is the process philosopher A.N. Whitehead. However, I suspect that Barbour himself would look more to the late twentieth century for examples of integrative projects in theology.
15. Williams, *The Ideas of The Fall and of Original Sin*, 364.
16. Ibid., 454.
17. Ibid., 457–8.
18. Williams, *The Ideas of The Fall and of Original Sin*.
19. Ibid., 34, 47–8, 85–91.
20. Ibid., 474.
21. Ibid., 491–2.

22. 'If we can assume that there was a pre-cosmic vitiation of the whole "life-force", when it was still one and simple, at a point of time prior to its bifurcation and ramification into a manifold of distinct individuals or entelechies, we shall be in possession of a conception which should explain, so far as explanation is possible, the continuity and homogeneity ... from the bacillus up to Man' (Williams, *The Ideas of the Fall and of Original Sin*, 523).

23. '... this interior self-perversion, which we have hypothetically attributed to the collective Life-force which was God's primal creature – this orientation away from God and in the direction of ruthless self-assertion – would necessarily manifest itself in a development of organic life permeated through and through with the spirit of selfishness, competition, and blood-thirsty struggle for existence' (ibid., 527).

24. Ibid., 522–3.

25. See Owen Thomas, *William Temple's Philosophy of Religion* (London: SPCK, 1961) for an excellent introduction to the thought of Temple. It is an especially helpful analysis of Temple's dialectical method, and of the intellectual context of his thought. Also classic as a secondary source is F.A. Iremonger (ed.), *William Temple, Archbishop of Canterbury: His Life and Letters* (New York: Oxford University Press, 1948). An essay in this volume by Dorothy Emmet, 'The Philosopher', is especially noteworthy.

26. William Temple, *Christus Veritas*, (London: Macmillan, 1924), 4–5.

27. Thomas, *William Temple's Philosophy of Religion*, 55.

28. William Temple, *Nature, Man and God: The Gifford Lectures 1932, 1933* (London: Macmillan, 1935; hereafter *NMG*), 359.

29. *NMG*, 360.

30. *NMG*, 361.

31. *NMG*, 365.

32. Ibid.

33. *NMG*, 367. Here we have an intriguing anticipation of James Alison's theological thesis, based on Rene Girard's mimesis theory, of the reciprocity of distorted desire. It is useful background since Alison does not establish his theology well in the evolutionary context, but only in a social systems context. See James Alison, *Raising Abel: The Recovery of Eschatological Imagination* (New York: Crossroads Publishing, 1996).

34. *NMG*, 366. In a letter written to Dorothy Emmet, Temple stated: 'Evil, therefore, must be held not to be directly willed by God, but to fall within the divine purpose, both because it is an occasion for evoking greater resources of good, and because God produced in man a being who sins, not perhaps inevitably, but with an overwhelming degree of probability. Presumably God knew that this would be the case, and knew what he was about in so creating him. Here Temple gives us what has been described as a theory of a "fall upwards"' (Dorothy Emmet's essay 'The Philosopher', in *William Temple, Archbishop of Canterbury*, ed. Iremonger, 530).

35. Temple, *Christus Veritas*, ch. 4.

36. Edward Caird, *The Evolution of Religion*, Gifford Lectures of 1890–92 (Glasgow: Maclehose and Sons, 1893), 257.

37. See Carpenter's study for a very useful introduction to the influences on Gore's thought.

38. Charles Gore, *The Reconstruction of Belief* (London: John Murray, 1926), 10.

39. Ibid., 6–9.

40. Gore, *The Philosophy of the Good Life* (London: John Murray, 1930), 244–5. Also Gore, *Reconstruction*, 60.

41. Carpenter, *Gore: A Study*, 193.

42. Gore, *Reconstruction*, 58–9.

43. Ibid., 568, footnote 2.

44. Ibid., 569.

45. Ibid., 572.

46. Charles Gore, 'The Fall of Man', an address in Balliol College Chapel; 30 January 1921.

47. Gore, *Reconstruction*, 572.
48. Ibid., 573.
49. Ibid., 46.
50. Ibid., 161.
51. Barbour, *Religion and Science*, 101.

Chapter 10

DNA, Darwin, and Doxology: A Contemporary Conversation between Biology and Faith

Martinez J. Hewlett

The twenty-first century opened with major announcements related to human biology. In February of 2001, the Human Genome Project reported in *Nature* that the sequencing of human DNA was essentially complete.[1] In this same issue of the journal, an initial analysis of that sequence revealed that the number of genes that constitutes the human genome was reduced from the original estimate of 100,000 to a new estimate of 30,000 to 40,000, or about twice the number of the fruit fly.[2] The first of these milestones represents a major vindication for the molecular biological orientation of the neo-Darwinian synthesis. On the other hand, the second report highlights the difficulty of the presumption by some biologists that the complete sequence of human DNA will be synonymous with what it means to be human. The philosophical tension that underlies these two advances in biology dramatizes the current status of this discipline and frames Ian Barbour's critique of it.

Twenty-first century Biology

Now that a working draft of a sequence for at least a representative human DNA chromosomal complement is finished, biology is moving into a new and dramatic phase. What some believe to be the culmination of a program of research that began in the nineteenth century with Darwin, Mendel, and Miescher may be at hand.

The 'modern synthesis' (so named by Julian Huxley in 1942[3]) resulted from the fusing of Darwinian evolutionary theory and Mendelian genetics. When, in 1943, DNA, the substance that Miescher had found in the nucleus of cells, was identified as the chemical that constitutes the gene, the stage was set for the program that has dominated much of biology for the last 60 years.

At the heart of Darwin's model is the idea of selection of characteristics and the reproductive survival of those that best fit the environmental circumstances. This force of natural selection then drives the evolutionary history of life. In 1859 there was no idea about the 'thing' upon which this force would act. However, after the rediscovery of Mendel, the thing at least had a theoretical shape: the unit of inheritance called the gene. Once the chemical identity of the gene was established as DNA, the thing upon which selection acts took physical form. More importantly, the work of Luria and Delbrück demonstrated that genetic variations arise by chance or random events (mutations) that change the sequence of the DNA.[4] Thus, the source of variation in the population that is so essential to the evolutionary model was discovered.

It could be easily demonstrated in model systems such as the bacterium *Escherichia coli* and the bacterial virus phage T4 that a one-to-one correspondence exists between the sequence of DNA (the genotype) and the product of the gene as it acts in the organism (the phenotype). This seminal observation spurred the search for ways to read the entire sequence of A's, G's, C's, and T's that constitute the genome of an organism, including humans. Thus the technology and terminology of molecular biology, born, in part, within the cybernetic community of post-World War II, began to permeate all of the subdisciplines of the life sciences.

As a methodology, molecular biology is, by its very nature, reductive. One cannot examine the structure of the macromolecules that constitute the cell without taking that cell apart and examining the DNA '... right down to the atomic level.'[5] The method is powerful and seductive. Vast arrays of data have been obtained for a number of organisms, ranging from bacteria to plants, from worms to man. The mining of this database is just beginning and is already yielding astonishing conclusions about the nature of genes and their expression. The reductive method does, indeed, work to give molecular-level information about the gene.

However, as Ian Barbour points out, there are three forms of reduction.[6] The first form, the methodology described above, is a research strategy. The second and third forms are philosophical statements. When, in addition, a biologist claims that the principles at one level of organization can be completely connected to and derived from the principles in effect at a lower level of organization, an epistemological argument is being set forth. The third form of reduction is, in fact, an ontological position. Materialism or atomism, as a metaphysical position, claims that organisms are 'nothing but atoms', and that this lowest, atomic level manifests an organism's 'true nature'.[7]

It might be sufficient if the differences between these levels were recognized by those scientists engaged in the discipline of biology. However, it is all too often the case that conclusions are drawn which are either uncritical or ignorant of the philosophical assumptions that are being made. Barbour indicts the writings of evolutionary biologists and commentators such as Daniel Dennett, Richard Dawkins, and Edward Wilson. First they conflate topics lying within science and philosophical positions external to science, and then they draw on the authority of science, particularly in their more popular writings, to validate these philosophical positions.[8]

Ian Barbour's Contributions to the Dialogue with the Life Sciences

Before any kind of productive encounter between two disciplines can take place, some sort of roadmap or set of guidelines is essential. Ian Barbour has provided an immense service to science and theology by describing the typologies of interaction between these two seemingly unrelated areas. He uses the following four categories: conflict, independence, dialogue, and integration.[9] By detailing, with specific examples, how each of these categories of interaction work, he offers a way out of the simplistic mode of seeing science and religion at war. Certainly the conflict model can be thought of as 'warfare', as it is generally characterized in the popular press. However, this can hardly be called an interaction, since both sides in the conflict are fundamentally fixed and not truly open to intellectual exchange.

The independence category of Barbour is most clearly represented in biology by the late Stephen Jay Gould's concept of non-overlapping magisteria (NOMA).[10] Gould's analysis of the situation is nicely summarized in the first paragraph of his article:

> No supposed 'conflict' between science and religion should exist because each subject has a legitimate magisterium, or domain of teaching authority – and these magisteria do not overlap (nor do they encompass all inquiry). But the two magisteria bump right up against each other, interdigitating in wondrously complex ways along their joint border.

Without the Barbour categories at hand, it is easy to be confused about this statement. Was Gould defending a religious viewpoint, as many of his critics contended? Or was he, instead, carving out clear boundaries that allowed religion to be tucked away, out of sight of scientific inquiry? By using Barbour's categories, we can see that this is a plea for independence and not for dialogue or integration, even given Gould's hand-to-hand metaphor. Thus, we have an important tool for negotiating the exchange between the life sciences and theology.

Beyond describing the landscape of the conversation, however, Ian Barbour has provided several key critiques of the biological enterprise as it is represented by the strict reductionist philosophical approach.

To begin with, his use of process philosophy and the Whiteheadian categories and levels of experience provide a way out of the conundrum into which the philosophy of science has fallen since the end of the Enlightenment in the middle of the twentieth century. Instead of focusing on descriptions that are inherently reductionistic and deterministic positions, process thought allows a metaphysics that is at once consistent with the methodology of biology but avoids the philosophic traps that plague some modern commentators. According to Barbour, chance and indeterminism as well as lawful regularities are part of process metaphysics. For considering higher-level wholes in biology, process thought points to irreducible properties even while acknowledging the limited importance of reductionistic and mechanistic methodologies in lower-level, molecular biology.[11]

How then to think about the results of modern biology and the view of the living world that they represent? Barbour argues for a critical realist position with respect to all scientific investigation. His definition of critical realism, as an intermediate position between classical realism and instrumentalism, is that science deals with 'models and theories [that] inadequately and selectively represent particular aspects of the world for specific purposes'.[12] This is, after all, how most practicing scientists carry out their work.

Barbour supports a typology of integration between theology and science, focusing in particular on a theology of nature in which some doctrines are reformulated in light of science even when the primary basis of such a theology is religious experience and historical revelation.[13] This kind of two-way reflection between science and theology is a characteristic of Barbour's thesis and has had a profound influence on those who have entered this field. It is this particular emphasis that, I believe, opens the future of this discourse in the most productive and beneficial manner possible.

Contemporary Issues and New Directions

The Human Genome Project is moving to exploit the database of information derived from the human DNA sequence. A major project will be the International Haplotype Map, or HapMap. Blood samples collected from around the globe will be used to characterize individual genetic differences, using the database sequence as a key for the comparison. The goal of this project is to allow a precise determination of genetic contributions to disease and even permit drug design based upon a person's unique genetic make-up. There is another side to this, however. The HapMap can also be used to highlight the slight differences among various groups of the human population. Herein lies the danger. If human nature is viewed simply as the sum of the base pairs, then such differences can be used to justify a variety of ill-conceived agendas. Already, the field of evolutionary psychology seeks to characterize human behavior in genetic terms. The combination of these two approaches could result in serious social justice issues.

It is here that Ian Barbour's critique of the materialism inherent in some human biological models becomes all important. Rather than dismissing the sociobiology of Edward Wilson out of hand, Barbour shows how that work embraces a 'sweeping epistemological reductionism that makes all academic disciplines into branches of biology'.[14] He then points out the importance of cultural factors in human evolution and comes ultimately to a process philosophy model that views human nature as multi-level entities.

Most importantly, he addresses the nature of consciousness using process thinking. He agrees with Roger Sperry[15] and ultimately with Philip Clayton[16] that 'mental states are higher level emergent properties of the brain' and that 'mental activity supervenes on neural activity without violating physiological laws'.[17] This reflection is important for both theologians and biologists as we move into an even more detailed view of human genetic data.

A new development that suggests a powerful approach for understanding living systems is the science of networks. The ideas of complexity theory combined with a model of how linkages between entities arise and influence the higher order functioning of systems leads to a very different view of biology. Network thinking can be applied to everything from the spread of disease to an analysis of river estuaries.[18] In a recent paper, Zoltán Oltvai and Albert-László Barabási discuss the science of networks as applied to the inner biochemical workings of cells.[19] This view of biological control mechanisms that go beyond the genome level speaks directly to the process philosophy that Barbour espouses when he speaks of 'multi-leveled systems and wholes' and of things that are 'relational and interdependent'.

As these kinds of models become increasingly important, the approach to reality that they represent will likely change the way in which human biology is done.

Doxology: In Celebration of Life

At some time in the career of every biologist there comes a moment of wonder and awe as she or he encounters yet another seeming miracle of life. This decidedly human reaction is what Barbour might call a 'religious experience', a numinous sense of the richness and complexity of creation. Indeed, even scientists that Barbour criticizes for their philosophical assumptions, such as Richard Dawkins and Edward Wilson, are deeply moved by the beauty and order that they see in nature.

But modern science has no method to describe this event, no words that are permitted to speak about this emotion. In fact, these qualitative properties are relegated to the level of epiphenomena, not truly 'real', since they are not quantifiable. This stand, coupled with the flight into materialism that has characterized the scientific program since David Hume in the eighteenth century, leads to a veneration of Nature rather than any deity, and a rejection of any inkling of purpose or design.

In Barbour's typology, if integration could truly occur between theology and science, this situation might be altered. Process philosophy coupled with the science of networks could lead to an appreciation of the various levels of experience present in the natural world. Rather than relying on the bottom-up causality model of the reductionist paradigm, the emergence of truly new properties of systems could be recognized. This would liberate both science and theology from the assumptions that have kept them apart. Theology could be open to scientific models that are not based entirely on materialist presumptions. Science could be comfortable with the limits of its methodology and models and with the possibility of levels of experience that are outside of those limits.

In this new order, the experience of the Divine inherent in the scientific enterprise could be freed for expression. A hymn of praise to the Creator, writ in the A's, G's, C's, and T's of the genetic language, may someday rise up in harmony with the *Te Deum*.

Notes

1. The International Human Genome Mapping Consortium, 'A Physical Map of the Human Genome', *Nature*, 409 (2001), 934–41.
2. The International Human Genome Mapping Consortium, 'Initial Sequencing and Analysis of the Human Genome,' *Nature*, 409 (2001): 860–921.
3. Julian Huxley, *Evolution: The Modern Synthesis* (London: Allen and Unwin, 1942).
4. Salvador Luria and Hans Delbrück, 'Mutations of Bacteria from Virus Sensitivity to Virus Resistance', *Genetics*, 28 (1943), 491–511.
5. Francis Crick, *Of Molecules and Men* (Seattle: University of Washington Press, 1966).
6. Ian Barbour, *Religion and Science: Historical and Contemporary Issues* (San Francisco: HarperSanFrancisco, 1997), 230–33.

7. Ibid., 232.
8. Ibid., 81.
9. Ibid., 77ff.
10. Stephen Jay Gould, 'Non-overlapping Magisteria', *The Skeptical Inquirer*, 24 (1999).
11. Barbour, *Religion and Science*, 291.
12. Ibid., 359.
13. Ibid., 100.
14. Ibid., 257.
15. Roger Sperry, *Science and the Moral Priority* (New York: Columbia University Press, 1983), 92.
16. Philip Clayton, *God and Contemporary Science* (Grand Rapids, MI: W. B. Eerdmans, 1997).
17. Barbour, *Religion and Science*, 262.
18. Mark Buchanan, *Nexus: Small Worlds and the Groundbreaking Science of Networks* (New York: W.W. Norton, 2002).
19. Zoltán N. Oltvai and Albert-László Barabási, 'Systems Biology: Life's Complexity Pyramid', *Science*, 298 (2002), 763–4.

Chapter 11

Selfish Genes and Loving Persons

Ted Peters

Ian Barbour is a person who hopes. 'Hope arises from visions of the future and convictions about the possibility of change, but it also rests on *faith*,' he writes; 'ultimately my hope derives from a religious faith in the power of reconciliation to overcome alienation, specifically, a biblical conviction that love and forgiveness can transform self-centeredness and isolation. In each case, faith can be realistic about the present and yet remain open to creative new potentialities.'[1]

Barbour's hope relies on a number of related assumptions: first, things change; second, the precedents of the past need not determine the future; third, the future is open to new potentialities; fourth, love and forgiveness can transform human self-centeredness; and fifth, we human beings are thereby capable of making wholesome changes to bring about new realities in the future. Barbour assumes that the natural world will permit significant change; and he assumes that inspired by God's transformatory power we can be guided to change things on behalf of a vision of what is good. We are not fated. Nature's past has not preprogrammed our future. This is Barbour's belief about the future.

Curiously yet understandably, he gets this belief from studying the past, in particular, studying Darwinian evolution. The dramatic impact of Charles Darwin's work on the Western worldview is the now well-founded conviction that things change. Natural forms such as distinct species are not material instantiations of fixed ideals or eternal essences, as Westerners had believed from Plato and Aristotle onward. 'It took Darwin's work to convince the scientific community that all of nature is in a state of flux.'[2] The implications for philosophy and theology are clear to Barbour: 'An evolutionary metaphysics will give an important place to temporality and change in its characterization of all entities.'[3]

Change liberates the future from the past. Yet, we need to ask: How much future change lies within the reach of human resolve? What limits does our evolutionary past place on the human desire to reconstitute our reality? Which envisioned possibilities are realistic potentialities, and which are merely wish dreams well beyond our finite reach? Finally, might God anticipate an eschatological future that transcends the precedents of our biological past?

In this chapter, I would like to jump from Barbour's springboard to a number of questions with specific reference to the Christian notion of *agape* love: if from our evolutionary past we human beings have inherited a propensity to selfishness, are we as persons able to experience or engage in neighborly love, in love for someone who is genuinely other? Are we able to love without self-regard, without reciprocity, without dependence on the drive for reproductive fitness? In pursuing answers to such questions, I would like to take advantage of some previous discussions of altruism in nonhuman and human societies as depicted in debates over the theory put forth by sociobiology; and I would like to draw upon theological discussions of the mandate to love our neighbor, one who is other to us. Taking advantage of distinctively theological resources will be necessary to appreciate a dimension invisible to science alone, namely, self-sacrificial love has never been considered a mere phenomenon of human culture – let alone of our biology – but rather an individual person's goal to be striven for; and, furthermore, it is a goal that requires the impartation of divine grace to achieve it.

Are Genes in the Evolutionary Driver's Seat?

The debate surrounding the possible connection between Darwinian natural selection and human social ethics employs vocabulary that differs somewhat from Christian theological vocabulary. The axial term around which the debate revolves is *altruism*.[4] In common parlance, altruism is the disposition to act with unselfish concern or devotion on behalf of the welfare of others. Decisive here theologically is that it is the welfare of someone who is *other*. In the current debate regarding evolution, altruism refers to actions that seem on the surface to reduce the prospect of passing one's genes on to future generations – that is, altruism is action that reduces one's own reproductive fitness. Below the surface appearance, however, we are told, altruism refers to the sacrifice of an individual organism on behalf of other organisms sharing a common gene pool; so individual sacrifice still serves the reproductive fitness of the kin group. Precluded is the concept of the genuinely *other*, if *other* refers to a life form outside a proximate genetic kin group – that is, outside a family or a species.

For Charles Darwin the key principle of evolution is 'natural selection' or 'survival of the fittest', referring *post hoc* to the evolutionary success of those species now in existence compared to those species that have become extinct.[5] When the wide variety of individual differences within a species become factors in adapting to environmental pressures, and when some adaptations are selected for and others selected against, large scale die-offs in the Malthusian sense occur; and the surviving remainder define the emerging new species.

The last half of the twentieth century brought us the neo-Darwinian synthesis, the synthesis of natural selection with genetic mutation. Mutating genes followed by environmental adaptation have refined our understanding of natural selection. DNA has become the factor of focus. The DNA that survives is considered a competitive success, the victor in nature's relentless and impersonal struggle to determine who will be more fit.

Enter the concept of the *selfish gene*. The emerging fields of sociobiology and evolutionary psychology have introduced a theory explicitly asserting that evolution is driven – by what Darwin had thought might be a force – by the gene's drive to replicate itself. Every coding segment of our DNA seeks its own immortality, and the reproductivity of the organism is the mechanism whereby DNA makes more DNA. Genes are selfish in that they want to replicate themselves, even if this means eliminating other genes in the competitive process.

It is important to note that, according to the selfish gene theory, the drive to replicate is inherent in DNA as DNA. The selfishness is not the product of a single gene or single genetic configuration. All genes are selfish in the sense that all genes are willing to compete with one another to survive unto the next generation. Every sexual connection provides a war zone as genes battle for hegemony.

What has happened here is that genes have become the subjects of activity, the protagonists in the drama of evolution. The agent of action is not the individual organism or the species; it is the gene. 'They [genes] are in you and me;' writes Richard Dawkins, 'they created us, body and mind; and their preservation is the ultimate rationale for our existence.'[6] Plants, animals, and even we human beings have been developed for the purpose of replicating genes. That is all we are, survival transportation for genes driving the evolutionary highway. 'We are survival machines – robot vehicles blindly programmed to preserve the selfish molecules known as genes.'[7] Whereas we may have thought that we as persons sit in the driver's seat of human responsibility, now it appears that our genes are doing the steering.

Selfishness in the Genotype with Altruism in the Phenotype

In the sociobiological scheme, the quality of selfishness has been removed from the moral sphere within human culture and attributed to pre-personal molecules, genes. Selfishness is simply assumed as given here; it is neither demonstrated empirically nor argued for philosophically. Yet, it has become the cardinal doctrine of sociobiology and its derivatives. Because the theory wears the cloak of science, it can claim moral neutrality for both its assertions and for the phenomenon it describes.

'This gene selfishness will usually give rise to selfishness in individual behavior,' writes Dawkins. 'Much as we might wish to believe otherwise, universal love and the welfare of the species as a whole are concepts that simply do not make evolutionary sense.'[8] This approaches the fallacy of composition, a fallacy committed when a property of a part is attributed to the composite whole. It does not necessarily follow that because genes are selfish that organisms or persons who possess genes are themselves selfish. In order to leave an opening for caring morality, Dawkins allows us as persons to counteract the influence of our genes. 'Our genes may instruct us to be selfish, but we are not necessarily compelled to obey them all of our lives.'[9]

Despite the startling moral shock of the term 'selfish', this judgment about human nature appears to be a scientific confirmation of the Augustinian notion of original sin. We are curved in upon ourselves; or, at least, our genes are curved in upon themselves. The effect is that we are unable by our own reason or strength to devote ourselves in love toward someone who is other, to love our neighbor as we love ourselves. It appears that we now have a scientific explanation for what Western Christians have believed all along regarding an inherited 'original' sin. 'The roots of all evil can be seen in natural selection,' writes Robert Wright; 'the enemy of justice and decency does indeed lie in our genes.'[10]

Yet, despite our state of sin or even because of our state of sin, Christians have held up love as our ethical mandate and goal; and the highest form of this love is self-sacrificial love. Is this precluded entirely by sociobiological theory? Perhaps, or perhaps not. Sociobiology makes room for limited manifestations of such love by formulating an auxiliary doctrine, cooperation on behalf of reproductive fitness. Cooperation within a species becomes a means for the selfish gene to insure its future. E.O. Wilson puts it this way: 'cooperative individuals generally survive longer and leave more offspring.'[11] Within a community of cooperation, the individual behaves altruistically toward others. The theological question is this: does such biologically based altruism constitute what Christians mean by *agape* love for someone who is other?

Relevant here to the question of otherness is a sociobiological correlate to the selfish gene doctrine, namely, the concept of kin preference. We can expect a certain amount of cooperation within a kin group, according to this theory, because every individual within a wider kin group shares the genes that drive for perpetuation. The literature in the field includes formulas purporting to measure degrees of kinship and, thereby, degrees of kin loyalty and service. Because each parent contributes half of the genes that constitute the genome of his or her children, a 50 per cent chance exists that a given child will bear a given parental gene, making the ratio 1:2. Between siblings sharing both parents the ratio is the same, 1:2. Nephews and nieces share genes at a ratio of 1:4; and it is 1:8 for first cousins.[12] The implication here is that we can expect a corresponding degree of cooperation and shared efforts at survival. As the number of shared genes increases so does love and shared defense; as the number of shared genes decreases, the potential for becoming an enemy rises. What appears to be family love is actually kin altruism promulgated by genetic determinism. 'The theory of kin selection has taken most of the good will out of altruism. When altruism is conceived of as the mechanism by which DNA multiplies itself through a network of relatives, spirituality becomes just one more Darwinian enabling device.'[13]

Preferential kin selection solves the sociobiologist's puzzle. The fundamental puzzle, as E.O. Wilson formulates it, is that altruism should not exist; yet it does. The central theoretical problem of sociobiology is this: 'how can altruism, which by definition reduces personal fitness, possibly evolve by natural selection?'[14] The answer is that what appears to be altruism is actually a form of reciprocity within a kin group, a reciprocity that indirectly contributes to reproductive fitness and hence to the ongoing life of the genes in question. What has become a virtual doctrine, *reciprocal altruism*, asserts that risk to an organism's own safety – risk to an organism's individual reproductive fitness – may very well appear to be altruistic; yet it should be seen in a larger perspective as insuring the survival of certain genes. In nature, survival of the individual can be sacrificed in the service of the survival of the gene.

What about trans-kin altruism – that is, service or equal treatment by an organism or a person toward someone who appears not to share the same gene pool? Patricia Williams explores the possibility of trans-kin altruism in the form charity (*agape*) as an extension to non-kin of what nature has provided among kin. 'The sociobiological reason for thinking our nature has some capacity for charity is the existence of altruism. We already behave self-sacrificially for the benefit of our close kin. Our reason and symbolic language force us to extend our altruism to those in our group who are not close kin.' Yet, despite the precedent of reciprocal altruism, charity to non-kin marks such a significant leap beyond where our genetic nature has left us that it may not fit within the scope of sociobiological theory:

> Altruism is not charity because altruism is nepotistic and ethnic. Reciprocity is not charity because reciprocity is egocentric. Perhaps the doctrines of original sin are correct when they claim that human nature lacks charity ... Our charity is not natural in the sense altruism is. Nepotism must be fought, charity nurtured.[15]

Theologian Philip Hefner accepts the restrictive scope of standard sociobiology; so to get to the self-sacrificial property of love he appeals to culture beyond genetic influence. Thinking of culture as epigenesis, he lengthens Wilson's leash (see below) so that culture permits extra-kin altruism. 'Culture is the stream of information that enables trans-kin altruism.'[16]

Such an appeal to culture may be less than adequate, however, because the theory in question claims it can explain even culture by appeal to genetic hegemony. Nothing escapes the leash of the selfish gene. According to sociobiology, morality like other aspects of human culture is an epigenetic manifestation of genetic activity. 'The genes hold culture on a leash,' argues E.O. Wilson; and human values are 'constrained in accordance with their effects on the human gene pool.'[17] The genes so manipulate human culture as to make us believe that certain behaviors are 'good' in themselves; yet, these behaviors in fact are good for the perpetuation of the genes. Although it is not apparent to the gene bearer, the genes employ human morality for their own long-range benefit.[18] Thus, apparent altruism at the level of the phenotype is a mask covering a relentless selfishness at the level of the genotype.[19]

Essential here is the element of illusion, or perhaps even deceit. The genes, now in the active driver's seat, employ culture to create an illusion as a means for persuading the human organism to strive for reproductive fitness. Michael Ruse along with E.O. Wilson put it this way:

> Morality, or more strictly, our belief in morality, is merely an adaptation put in place to further our reproductive ends. Hence the basis of ethics does not lie in God's will ... or any other part of the framework of the universe. In an important sense, ethics ... is an illusion fobbed off on us by our genes to get us to cooperate.[20]

If this turns out to be the case, then the most noble of ethical ideals becomes a mere camouflage covering selfish genetic aggression. It has become axiomatic to the field to say: 'Scratch an "altruist" and watch a "hypocrite" bleed.'[21]

Briefly summarized, the situation looks like this. Applying to insects, birds, and animals including human beings, sociobiological theory discerns three levels of an organism's selfish behavior. The first level is overt self-interest – that is, seeking reproduction of its own kind in direct service to genetic perpetuation. The second level is the mechanism of kin selection – that is, directly protecting kin with close genetic ties in competition for survival against organisms more genetically distant. The third level is reciprocal altruism – that is, apparently unselfish behavior on the part of an individual organism pressed indirectly into the service of genetic immortality. The conclusion drawn by such a theory is that, ethically speaking, instances of altruism bolster an illusion. Reciprocal altruism is reducible to a hidden but ever operative genetic selfishness. No matter what happens at the personal or social level, sophisticated moral activity is subject to puppet determinism at the more primary biological level.[22]

If such a theory holds, then the grounds for Ian Barbour's faith and hope would be washed away. Barbour believes love and forgiveness can transform self-centeredness and that religious faith has the power of reconciliation, the power to overcome alienation. What is untransformable, according to sociobiological theory, however, is the self-centeredness of the genes and the drive propelled through human culture for us to pursue reproductive fitness. The overcoming of alienation between persons in one genetically determined kin group with those outside the kin group or even outside the species would be impossible. Whether we believe it or not, we are biologically fated. If sociobiology can be considered science, then science will appear to have dashed the hopes lifted up by religious faith.

Beyond Biology?

Is the leash on human culture that short? Is it so short that genetic selfishness is the direct cause of cultural preferences including the moral behavior of persons? Is biological determinism so exhaustive that genuine love of someone who is other is ineluctably reducible to reproductive fitness, thereby rendering *agape* a mere fiction of the theological imagination?

The leash has been lengthened a trifle by the field of evolutionary psychology. 'Evolutionary psychology is psychology informed by the fact that the inherited architecture of the human mind is the product of the evolutionary process.'[23] Key here is that the focus is not limited to the gene but includes the mind; and the mind is adapted – that is, today's human mind is viewed as having adapted previously to environmental challenges; and through natural selection it has acquired its present characteristics. The adaptive problems previously solved have determined the design of the mind, a mind designed to function appropriately to its environment. One implication of this is that today's mind is not reducible to ancient genetic forces. Complex mental functions are due to more than selfish gene expression.

This means that psychology cannot be reduced to molecular biology. The assumption made by sociobiologists that the drive of the selfish gene is a relentless constant implies an agnosticism regarding the role of the evolutionary history of adaptation. This leads Donald Symons to demur by suggesting that sociobiology is insufficiently Darwinian. Darwinism relies upon adaptation through natural selection; and sociobiology – called 'Darwinian Social Science' or DSS by Symons – bypasses the role played by an organism's functional design produced through evolutionary adaptation. Symons argues that we human beings today strive for *specific* goals, not the *general* goal of maximizing reproduction. We are not merely subject to a generalized reproduction-maximizing mechanism. Our psychologies, then, are not the sole product of the drive toward reproductive fitness. Claiming to be the true heir to Darwin, Symons writes, 'Darwin's theory of natural selection is a theory of adaptation, a *historical* account of the origin and maintenance of phenotypic design ... Reproduction mindedness, however, is not a conceptual magic carpet, capable of soaring over questions of adaptation.'[24] One implication here is that evolutionary psychology would provide modest support for Barbour's hope for creative new potentialities; everything was not predetermined at the beginning by the selfish gene.

The lengthening of the leash here is liberating, but only minimally. Biological determinism remains tight even if the dialectic between gene expression and functional adaptation is loosened.

Further Beyond Biology?

The leash is lengthened further by Francisco Ayala's account of the appearance of human ethical thinking within evolutionary history. To endosomatic or organic systems of heredity he adds exosomatic or cultural inheritance. He defines culture as:

> [a] set of nonstrictly biological human activities and creations. Culture includes social and political institutions, religious and ethical traditions, language, common sense and scientific knowledge, art and literature, technology, and in general all the creations of the human mind. The advent of culture has brought with it cultural evolution, a superorganic mode of evolution superimposed on the organic mode, and that has in the last few millennia become the dominant mode of human evolution.[25]

In addition to passing genes on to future generations biologically, through the teaching-learning process we pass on information 'independent of biological parentage'.[26]

Although culture remains tied to the genes, the leash is lengthened. Natural selection remains firmly in force, to be sure; yet nonadaptive elements within culture are free to emerge. The general principle of natural selection is insufficient to explain every specific adaptive or nonadaptive trait:

> Literature, art, science, and technology, are among the behavioral features that may have come about not because they were adaptively favored in human evolution, but because they are expressions of the high intellectual abilities present in modern human beings; what was favored by natural selection (its target) was an increase in intellectual ability rather than each one of those particular activities.[27]

The import of this is that ethical values could emerge that would transcend the determinism of the selfish gene.

Ayala relies upon the appearance of human intelligence. With intelligence comes tool making. With tool making comes the ability to alter the environment. The ability to alter the environment combined with intelligence leads to thoughts about the future, to anticipations of today's behavior that would have an effect on tomorrow's reality. Planning becomes possible. Distinguishing means and ends becomes possible. So does comparative valuing, valuing which mode of action would be better than an alternative. This situation gives rise to speculations about what is good and bad, right and wrong. This valuing of actions as either good or evil Ayala calls 'ethical behavior'. He argues that 'ethical behavior (the proclivity to judge human actions as either good or evil) has evolved as a consequence of natural selection, not because it was adaptive in itself, but rather as a pleiotropic consequence of the high intelligence characteristic of human beings.' He continues: 'My thesis is that: (1) the capacity for ethics is a necessary attribute of human nature, and thus a product of biological evolution; but (2) moral norms are products of cultural evolution, not biological evolution.'[28]

Key here is that Ayala avoids reducing the contents of ethics to genetic determinism or even to adaptive functionalism. We make moral judgments because our intellectual inheritance makes it possible; not because ethics is an innate way for achieving biological gain. 'Ethical behavior is an attribute of the biological make-up of human beings and, hence, is a product of biological evolution. But I see no evidence that ethical behavior developed because it was adaptive in itself.'[29] This implies that ethical valuing and moral behavior cannot be reduced to an expression of the selfish gene.

The ethical behavior of which Ayala speaks here is strictly that of valuing, of judging. Our biologically inherited intelligence has made this possible; but our evolutionary history has not dictated which values should be judged as good. Even if we have natural dispositions to selfishness and aggression against those with competing genes, we as human persons 'have the power to rise above these tendencies ... The commandment of charity, "Love thy neighbor as thyself", often runs contrary to the fitness of the genes, even though it promotes social cooperation and peace of mind.'[30]

The temptation sociobiology leads us into would encourage us to adopt nature's values as our own:

> [T]he sociobiologists' position may be interpreted as calling for the supposition that those *norms* of morality should be considered supreme that achieve the most biological (genetic) gain (because that is, in their view, why the moral sense evolved at all). This, in turn, would justify social preferences, including racism and even genocide.[31]

Racism and genocide are the kind of human behavior that *agape* love repudiates; they are the kind of alienating behavior Barbour believes should be overcome with reconciliation. Ayala lengthens the leash to make this possible: 'Moral codes must be consistent with biological nature, but biology is insufficient for determining which moral codes are, or should be, accepted.'[32]

No one in these discussions doubts the comprehensive context of biological evolution or the significance of natural selection. No attempt is being made here to arrest the human soul from its body, or even to ground ethical striving in a metaphysical spirit. The task is much more modest, namely, to account for the contemporary human experience of an apparently nonadaptive phenomenon, that is, promulgating the value of love, especially love for someone who is genetically other.

Love, as Theologians Understand It

What is startling to a Christian theologian confronted with the claims of sociobiology is the apparent lack of consonance between fated selfish genes and free neighbor love. This raises questions. If we human beings are organisms driven by selfish genes, is it possible to love our neighbor who is other from us? If not, then is the Christian ideal of *agape* love merely that, an ideal? Or worse, is it just one more cultural mask hiding a genetic plot to persuade us to serve reproductive fitness? Is the best that the human race can accomplish reciprocal altruism? Is the value lifted up by theologians we know as *agape* love only one more 'illusion fobbed off on us by our genes to get us to cooperate'?

More specifically, let us speculate on alternatives. If sociobiology can be considered a scientific description of the natural reality, then perhaps the Christian ideal of neighbor love should be rendered dissonant by affirming that such love is not natural, that it carries us beyond our nature. However, if sociobiology is not a scientific *description* but rather an ideological *prescription* advocating a human ethic that mimics evolutionary values such as kin preference and reciprocal altruism, then Christian theology will find itself in flat contradiction to such an ideology. Determining which path to follow may hinge on defining precisely what Christian theologians intend by the term, *agape*.

Just what do we mean by the theological concept of *agape* love? Already in the New Testament, self-giving love is revered as indicative of the heart of God and the model for human striving; and saints through the centuries have elaborated on love as an exalted human virtue. With this background, a more careful delineation of love in terms of *agape* was worked out in the middle of the twentieth century primarily by neo-orthodox theologians such as Anders Nygren, Gustaf Aulen, Karl Barth, Emil Brunner, Reinhold Niebuhr, Paul Tillich, and others. Here we will let Karl Barth speak for the field.

The first and distinctive characteristic of *agape* love is that it is directed toward someone who is *other*. No quality or attribute in the beloved or even expectation of reciprocal action qualifies this type of love. 'Christian love turns to the other purely for the sake of the other,' writes Karl Barth. 'It does not desire it for itself. It loves it simply because it is there as this other, with all its value or lack of value. It loves freely.'[33] Gene Outka spells out the implication with the principle of 'unalterable regard', according to which 'the other is held to be irreducibly valuable'.[34] Such loving would be incompatible and irreconcilable with sociobiological doctrines such as kin preference and reciprocal altruism. The presence of preferred genes in the beloved would be excluded as a factor, thereby rendering kin closeness irrelevant. *Agape* love is frequently called 'neighbor love', not because it prefers to love neighbors who are proximate rather than strangers who are distant; rather, because the act of loving turns strangers into neighbors. Similarly, reciprocal altruism becomes a nonfactor when such loving requires no reciprocity, no return. The benefit of the beloved is the sole objective.

The second characteristic of *agape* love is that it originates in God's love. Human love of this type is prompted and made possible by God's love. Our loving 'has its primary and ultimate foundation … in the being and nature of God Himself'.[35] Key here is the trinitarian understanding of God indicative of Christian theology, wherein the dynamic of one person loving the other is operative in eternity. Love within God spreads to love within the creation:

> When He loves us, what comes on us to our benefit is an inconceivable overflowing of His eternal love which we can only acknowledge, recognize and confess in its actual occurrence ... [O]ur Christian love arises and takes place as the human act which answers and corresponds to His act.[36]

Significant for our discussion here is that theologians have not commonly sought to ground *agape* in our natural endowments. Rather, such love in the stream of human experience is an overflow of love from the divine fountain. This means theologians need not find precedents or propensities or potentialities within the genes or natural selection or adaptation.

The third characteristic is that *agape* love is closely associated with faith. 'Faith working through love' (Galatians 5:6b) became the motto for evangelical ethics already in the Protestant Reformation. 'Since faith brings the Holy Spirit and produces a new life in our hearts,' writes Philip Melanchthon, 'we also begin to love our neighbor because our hearts have spiritual and holy impulses.'[37] Karl Barth follows this lead:

> *Agape* consists in the orientation of human nature on God in a movement which does not merely express it but means that it is transcended, since in it man gives himself up to be genuinely freed by and for God, and therefore to be free from self-concern and free for the service of God.[38]

What Barth says here leads us to the fourth characteristic: freedom. Neighbor love that is disinterested – that is, not bound to self-interest – is made possible by freedom. Specifically, it is freedom from selfish impulses. Augustine described the natural human disposition as one in which the self is curved in upon itself (*homo incurvatus in se*), a state ascribed by sociobiologists now to genes. In order for the self to love someone who is other, added Augustine, the self needs to be liberated from itself; and God's grace provides that liberation.[39] Martin Luther followed by adding that by God's grace received in faith as forgiveness, a human being need not pursue virtue in order to pursue a right relationship with God. This frees the human heart to concentrate solely on the practical needs of the neighbor being loved. Therefore, we should be guided in all our works by 'this thought and contemplate this one thing alone ... [to] serve and benefit others' in all that we do, 'considering nothing except the need and the advantage' of our neighbor.[40] These two go together: freedom and focus on the needs of the beloved. Not only is the person of faith freed *from* self-focus, he or she is freed *for* creative focus on the flowering and fulfillment of others. 'The loving man has given up control of himself to place himself under the control of the other, the object of his love,' writes Barth. 'He is free to do this. It is in this freedom that the one who loves as a Christian loves.'[41]

Grace Perfects Nature?

No possibility of consonance between this understanding of love and the anthropology promulgated by sociobiology seems to present itself. Yet, some have tried heroically to reconcile the two. Roman Catholic ethicist Stephen Pope, for example, seeks to overcome the disparity and to absorb the sociobiological commitment to kin preference into Christian family ethics. Pope rightly distinguishes the moral agent; it is the self or person, not the gene, that is responsible for non-egoistic love. 'Some version of genetic selfishness examined by sociobiologists may be compatible with moral altruism as long as the distinction between self and genes is carefully maintained.'[42] The conscious motives of the self transcend the unconscious impulses of our biology, including gene expression. By shifting moral agency to the self or the person rather than the gene, Pope gains some ethical breathing room. I applaud Pope for making this move.

Next, Pope redefines *agape* love. He excises the radical devotion to the other as articulated by Barth. Pope incorporates into *agape* two things – self-love and mutuality; and this move makes room for including kin preference. Pope's view of 'agape rejects the primacy of both self-sacrifice and equal regard and instead understands agape as most fundamentally a form of mutuality and friendship. Mutuality includes reciprocity.'[43] By appealing to the scholastic doctrine that grace perfects nature, and by accepting the sociobiological description as a valid picture of nature, Pope's constructive proposal is that Christian love should build upon genetic selfishness rather than repudiate it. This leads to an 'order of love' that includes self-love and preference for those in one's family. 'Regarding the arena of the necessities of life, first priority is given to one's children, spouse, and parents.'[44]

Pope does not intend to bless tribalism, racism, or genocide. Priority to one's family in the order of love does not exclude love for those outside the circle of kin preference. Pope is well aware that Christian love is 'not simply indifferent to the suffering of others who are non-kin and non-reciprocators.'[45] Pope wants both, but he wants them in order. 'Kin preference, if properly balanced with concern for non-kin, is of course, valuable for families, but it is also valuable for their communities, their societies and the human species as a whole.'[46] What Pope is articulating here is the medieval understanding of love as *caritas*, an order of charity.[47] What is confusing is that by calling it *agape*, he so alters the definition of *agape* as to make it unrecognizable. He has gutted neighbor love of its radicality; and in its truncated version he has made it compatible with sociobiology. This method introduces confusion into the theological side of the discussion. A more straightforward approach would have led Pope to simply reject the theological concept of *agape* and substitute *caritas*.

To Pope's credit, he tries to avoid both the Scylla of the naturalistic fallacy and the Charybdis of the valuational fallacy. The peril to society posed by sociobiology is the naturalistic fallacy, basing an *ought* on an *is* – that is, suggesting that if kin preference exists in nature that it must be good and must be the guide for human ethics. It is a fallacy because a factual description does not warrant a moral prescription.

The opposite peril is risked when we falsely believe we can proceed with an ethical ideal that disregards our biological reality. If natural science provides an accurate description of the nature that we are, then biological constraints must be incorporated into ethical thinking. Colin Grant argues this point forcefully:

> Just as it is fallacious to seek to derive any kind of moral prescription from a purely factual description, so too it must surely be tenuous to the point of absurdity to think that we can affirm values in complete disregard of the way things are. We might call this the 'valuational fallacy' ... Thus the plea for a totally unnatural altruism in defiance of the totally selfish determinations of the natural order is not finally a repudiation of the modern self-centered perspective, but a further instance of it.[48]

Then, as if to corroborate Pope on grace perfecting nature, Grant builds on descriptions of reciprocal altruism to add: 'Far from an anomaly invented by humans, human altruism rather represents a refinement of a tendency evident to some extent in the wider natural order.'[49]

Just what direction should theologians follow at this point? One possible direction, in light of what Pope and Grant have said, would be to search for precedents or openings for genuine neighbor love in the history of nature. Grant maps the road. 'If God is characterized by *agape*, by transparent love, as the Christian gospel claims, then that reality must be expected to permeate life, rather than being confined to a latter day development peculiar to our own species.'[50] Does this mean gathering new evidence that contravenes the evidence massed by the sociobiologists? No. Rather, it is a matter of hermeneutics, of interpreting the existing evidence. In Grant's view, the theologian has an opportunity to provide:

> ... a formative vision of life through which the evidence is read ... The problem is that sociobiology does not recognize the apparent altruism that exists in the natural order ... How different our present prospects might be, if sociobiologists were to relinquish their obsession with selfishness and give sufficient scope to the cooperation and apparent altruism that they themselves are constrained to mention![51]

The implications for the theological task would be to review activities of differing species to point out altruistic or cooperative phenomena wherever it might be found; and then this will count as support for the Christian belief in *agape*.[52] Or, to push the analysis back behind species' behavior, a theologian might look for signs of divine *agape* in the creation as a whole. This is the path followed by the kenotic theologians.

Kenotic Creation?

If we step back from theological anthropology and ethics for a moment and place our discussion within the more inclusive locus of creation, we find some kenotic theists searching for continuity between natural selection and divine creation. Rather than consign nature to the hegemony of the selfish gene, they seek signs that nature is influenced if not ruled by self-sacrificial love. Arthur Peacocke, for example, argues that evolutionary history has a direction toward greater complexity, a direction built in by God *ab initio*, from the beginning. Although reluctant to dub this direction a purpose in the strong sense, he asserts that the large evolutionary story leads to the chapter wherein *homo sapiens* emerge. The emergence of intelligent compassionate beings such as ourselves is made possible only by the sacrifice of earlier stages of life, which become food for later stages. 'Plants feed on inorganic materials and animals have to feed on plants and some animals on other animals. The structured logic is inescapable: new forms of matter arise only through incorporating, imbibing, the old.'[53]

This means that even God cannot avoid the struggle between predator and prey in developing new species. This means that suffering and death are necessary for new life forms with complex information-processing systems to evolve, and that pain and death serve divine creativity in the grand epic of evolution. 'Hence, biological death of the individual is the prerequisite of the creativity of the biological order.'[54]

What kind of a God would create in this fashion? Peacocke's answer: a kenotic God – that is, a God who empties part of the divine self in order to permit creation to be self-creative. This kenotic God is also a God who suffers with the creatures who suffer and, further, this participation by God in creaturely suffering contributes to the creative process of evolution:

> We can perhaps dare to say that there is a creative self-emptying and self-offering (a *kenosis*) of *God*, a sharing in the suffering of God's creatures, in the very creative, evolutionary processes of the world. Such a perception now enriches the Christian affirmation of God's nature as best understood as inherently that of Love ... [We] affirm that God, in exercising divine creativity, is self-limiting, vulnerable, self-emptying, and self-giving – that is, supremely Love in creative action.[55]

The Peacocke scheme affirms with Barth that God creates out of divine love, even a self-sacrificing love.[56] One would expect from Peacocke's application of divine kenosis to creation that the creation would somehow exhibit or reflect the love of the creator. Yet, it does not. Essential for Peacocke is that the independent processes of nature remain intact, unaltered by special divine providence, so that descriptions of nature such as those offered by natural selection and the selfish gene remain intact. Nature to be nature does not need to reflect or exhibit God's love. This leaves the attribution of kenotic love to God and God alone. According to the Peacocke scheme, kenotic love describes the self-removal of divine omnipotence in order to allow the natural world the freedom to create suffering and to create through suffering. Peacocke's notion of kenosis fails to provide a warrant for saying that God participates in creaturely suffering or how this divine suffering is creatively efficacious.

Ian Barbour takes a position on divine suffering similar to that of Peacocke, but Barbour's view of God is different. For Peacocke, the divine kenosis is due to a voluntary, self-limiting love within God. For Barbour, no such voluntary self-limiting is necessary or possible because God is metaphysically limited from the outset. Following Whitehead's process panentheism, Barbour holds that God suffers with the world out of metaphysical necessity. 'Process thought is distinctive in holding that limitations of divine knowledge and power rise from metaphysical necessity rather than from voluntary self-limitation.'[57] Like Peacocke, Barbour acknowledges that suffering is an inescapable byproduct of evolutionary advance. 'Pain and suffering are widespread in nonhuman nature. In evolutionary history, increased capacity for pain was apparently a concomitant of increased sentience and was selected for its adaptive value in providing warning of danger and bodily harm.'[58]

Peacocke and Barbour are willing to find footprints of divine love on the long road to evolutionary advance; and they hint that creaturely suffering counts as a footprint because God suffers. Holmes Rolston turns the hint into an assertion. By adopting an interpretation of nature as 'cruciform', Rolston uses the suffering and death of Jesus as a lens through which to view the selfish gene and natural selection.

Rolston understands the problem we are dealing with here. A stubborn conflict exists between selfish genes and suffering love. 'All of biological nature can be seen to run counter to what Jesus teaches: that one ought to lay down one's life for others. In nature, there is no altruism, much less kenosis.'[59] Nature and Jesus seem irreconcilable. How can we reconcile them? Rolston's answer: change our interpretation of nature so that it looks kenotic, looks like a history of sacrificial loving. The sacrifice of victims in the struggle of prey when being devoured by their predators becomes an offering on the altar of evolutionary advance. The death of an individual for the perpetuation of genes through the family is a sacrifice of the part for the good of the whole species. Death serves what Rolston calls the 'creative upflow' leading to 'more diverse and more complex forms of life. The whole evolutionary upslope is a calling in which renewed life comes by blasting the old ... a blessed tragedy.'[60] With the eloquence of religious allusion, Rolston apotheosizes the very wasteful suffering that gave rise to our theodicy problem.

In order to reinterpret nature in these terms, Peacocke, Barbour, and Rolston have imported an element of purpose if not progress into the evolutionary scheme. Natural selection, they say, has a direction that leads to more complex forms of life. En route to this increased complexity, sentience arose as an adaptation, and the price of sentience is suffering. The price of suffering is a price God is willing to exact on creatures to accomplish the implied divine end, namely, complex and compassionate beings such as *homo sapiens*. Even though evolutionary biologists since Darwin's era have explicitly expunged purpose and direction and progress from their understanding of natural selection, these theologians reinsert it so as to make sense of what would otherwise be senseless and meaningless suffering.

In sum, this method of reinterpreting nature so as to make natural suffering divine requires a mild violation of scientific principles; it requires the importing of *telos* into evolutionary biology so that nature orients itself toward complexity as its final cause. It also risks violating theological principles regarding self-sacrificial love. The kenotic love ascribed to Christ in the New Testament (Philippians 2:1–11) refers to a divine love that is willing to absorb sacrifice in order to work to overcome suffering. It does not refer to the exacting of suffering through predation and extinction in order to accomplish some further divine end or goal.

Four Directions for Theological Response

The original challenge to *agape* theologians, recall, arises from the apparent incompatibility of the selfish gene in nature with commitment to *agape* love in the life of faith. This incompatibility takes a subtle form. In its surface form, sociobiology poses a challenge because it appears to make impossible genuine neighbor love for someone who is other. *Agape* appears to be contrary to nature. However, the incompatibility occurs at two different levels. Selfishness is ascribed to the genetic level; altruism is ascribed to the cultural level where we live as persons and societies. Sociobiologists tend to be reductionists, reducing the cultural to the genetic.

Any theological response is likely to start by repudiating reductionism and plead for a distinction between the genes, on the one hand, and the self or person, on the other. From this point of departure the theologian could then go one of four directions. First, the theologian could let nature be the way the sociobiologists describe it and then, with Philip Melanchthon cited above, appeal to the divine intervention of the Holy Spirit that reorients our impulses at the level of the self beyond what our genetic inheritance would otherwise make possible. Significant here is that *agape* love is affirmed to be an overflow into human personhood of divine love. Appealing to a supranatural intervention by the Holy Spirit imparting the grace to rise above our biological endowment has an additional advantage; it permits the theologian to leave the apparent scientific description intact. This kind of theology adds something unavailable to what science can investigate. The weakness in this position is that contemporary theologians find supranatural interventionism to be a worrisome shortcut; it risks assuming that God abandons the natural sphere and works simply in the supranatural sphere.

With Stephen Pope, the theologian could follow a second direction by redefining neighbor love in terms of kin preference so as to shrink *agape* sufficiently to enclose it within the sociobiological orbit. The advantage here is that no appeal is made to supranaturalism, and the principle of grace perfecting nature is affirmed. The disadvantage is that the concept of neighborly love is so truncated that its sharp edge – love for someone who is genetically other even to the point of self-sacrifice – is itself sacrificed in haste to make Christian virtue conform to the constraints of what appears to be our biological limits.

A third direction veers off from the second. Here the theologian would reinterpret nature, not by appealing to different evidence but by reinterpreting existing evidence so as to discern divine creativity and providence embedded in the evolutionary principle of natural selection. Taking this direction requires marking an evolutionary road on the map, a road toward growth in complexity. It requires the importation of a *telos*. Increased complexity permitting sentience and suffering becomes a way station en route to a divine destination. Kenotic theologians prefer taking this road, because it makes belief in God fully compatible with what is observed in nature through the eyes of science. Theology here justifies if not celebrates genetic competition and its accompanying suffering on the part of sentient beings by appeal to divine permission for natural contingency and freedom. The disadvantage in this position was already flagged by Darwin, who found the massive extent of sentient suffering so wasteful that it could not be compatible with a loving God. Indeed, if *agape* is essential to the God whom Christians proclaim, then attempts to render this love compatible with genetic selfishness, kin preference, predator devouring prey, species extinction, and human culture replete with racism and genocide becomes tendentious at best.

Although I applaud the courage to take science seriously as this third route does, it is my judgment that this method is not likely to serve the theologian well. It leans too closely to the naturalistic fallacy. Although to its credit this position begins with a theological vision rather than a mere description of nature as the scientist describes it, nevertheless, the present state of nature remains the arbiter. The apparently ineluctable cruelty of natural selection remains intact, semi-blessed by divine kenosis. Genetic selfishness and cooperation in kin preference remain the final court of appeal. This method precludes the possibility that God's will transcends nature, and that God may be calling the human race similarly to transcend our natural histories.

Because of the inadequacy of the above theological directions for response, I sense the need to identify a fourth option, namely, eschatology. Although I do not recommend that we adopt fallacious reasoning in any form, I would prefer leaning slightly in the valuational direction. If *agape* love in human life appears as an overflow of such love in the divine life, it may not require exhaustive precedents in the order of nature. Rather than appeal to the past, theologians can appeal to the future. Rather than thinking of our human potential for loving as strictly archonic – that is, co-present with genetic selfishness at the beginning of life's history on earth – *agape* love may be thought to be eschatological – that is, God may be calling humanity and all of nature toward a transformed future.[61] The theologian may wish to follow the footsteps of Barbour's faith and 'be realistic about the present yet remain open to creative new potentialities'.

In conclusion, the challenge posed to Christian anthropology by sociobiology is formidable. If in the future claims made by sociobiologists find confirmation through empirical experimentation, and if we must agree that human culture is driven by selfish genes, then it will be clear that theologians cannot appeal to culture for the vision and energy to support *agape* love. Belief in a love capable of devotion to the welfare of an other – and we need to specify that we mean an other who is not secretly advancing our own gene pool – will require belief in a potential for transcending our biological inheritance. It will require initially belief that who we are as persons are more than the sum of our genes, more than products of our biological and cultural evolution.[62] In addition, we may find ourselves looking toward the power of God to draw us forward to a future that is more than our past; a future that transcends our inherited propensity for dedication to reproductive fitness. Love for someone who is decidedly other is an eschatological call toward eternal life in the kingdom of God.

Notes

1.   Ian G. Barbour, *Technology, Environment, and Human Values* (Westport CT: Praeger, 1980), 314.
2.   Idem, *Issues in Science and Religion* (San Francisco: HarperSanFrancisco, 1966), 86.

3. Idem, *Religion in an Age of Science, The Gifford Lectures 1989–1991 Volume I* (San Francisco: Harper & Row, 1990), 184.

4. The term, *altruism*, goes back to Auguste Comte, wherein placing the welfare of others above the self stands in contrast to its opposite, egoism. Yet, in sociobiology it refers specifically to the role of cooperation to enhance reproductive fitness so that genes can proceed to the next generation. 'Altruistic behavior enhances another organism's prospects for reproduction while diminishing the altruist's own reproductive potential. This technical, biological term has a different meaning from the common term, *altruism*. The common term refers to human psychology. People are altruistic if motivated by concern for another's welfare. Much confusion in sociobiology results from combining these two separate and distinct uses of the word' (Patricia A. Williams, *Doing Without Adam and Eve: Sociobiology and Original Sin* [Minneapolis: Fortress Press, 2001], 126).

5. Charles Darwin, *The Origin of Species by Means of Natural Selection* (Chicago and London: Encyclopedia Britannica, 1952), ch. 4.

6. Richard Dawkins, *The Selfish Gene* (London: Granada, 1978), 21.

7. Ibid., 'Preface', x.

8. Ibid., 2.

9. Ibid., 3.

10. Robert Wright, *The Moral Animal* (New York: Pantheon Books, 1994), 151; see 13, 368.

11. Edward O. Wilson, *Consilience* (New York: Alfred A. Knopf, 1998), 253.

12. See W.D. Hamilton, 'The General Theory of Social Behavior', *The Journal of Theoretical Biology*, 7 (1964), Part I: 1–16; Part II: 17–32. See other early literature developing kin altruism: R.D. Alexander, 'The Search for an Evolutionary Philosophy', *Proceedings of the Royal Society, Victoria Australia*, 24 (1971), 177; R.L. Trivers, 'The Evolution of Reciprocal Altruism', *Quarterly Review of Biology*, 46 (1971): 35–57.

13. Edward O. Wilson, *Sociobiology: The New Synthesis* (Cambridge, MA: Harvard University Press, 1975), 120.

14. Ibid., 3.

15. Patricia Williams, *Doing Without Adam and Eve*, 153–4.

16. Philip Hefner, *The Human Factor* (Minneapolis: Fortress, 1993), 200.

17. Edward O. Wilson, *On Human Nature* (Cambridge, MA: Harvard University Press, 1978), 167. Ian Barbour comments that '*reductionism* … runs through Wilson's writing' (*Religion in an Age of Science*, 192).

18. See Michael Ruse and Edward O. Wilson, 'Evolutionary Ethics: A Phoenix Arisen', *Zygon*, 21 (1986), 95–112; Michael Ruse and Edward O. Wilson, 'Moral Philosophy as Applied Science', *Philosophy: Journal of the Royal Institute of Philosophy*, 61 (1986), 173–92.

19. Might we exploit the contrast between genotype and phenotype, and contend that morality at the phenotypical level alone provides a sufficient ethical foundation? Might we acknowledge the different levels while avoiding reductionism to the genetic level? Perhaps. Michael Ruse says, 'To talk of selfish genes is to talk metaphorically, and the whole point is that the phenotypes they promote are anything but selfish' (*Sociobiology: Sense or Nonsense?* [Dodrecht, Holland: Reidel Publishing Co., 1979], 198).

20. Michael Ruse and Edward O. Wilson, 'The Evolution of Ethics', *New Scientist*, 108:1478 (17 October 1985), 50–52.

21. M.T. Ghiselin, *The Economy of Nature and the Evolution of Sex* (Berkeley, CA: University of California Press, 1974), 247.

22. For descriptions of the cultural role played by *puppet determinism* and its complement, *promethean determinism*, proffered by contemporary genetics, see Ted Peters, *Playing God? Genetic Determinism and Human Freedom*, 2nd edn (New York: Routledge, 2002).

23. Jerome H. Barkow, Leda Cosmides, and John Tooby, 'Introduction', in *The Adapted Mind: Evolutionary Psychology and the Generation of Culture* (Oxford and New York: Oxford University Press, 1992), 7.

24. Donald Symons, 'On the Use and Misuse of Darwinism in the Study of Human Behavior', in *The Adapted Mind*, 150–51.
25. Francisco Ayala, 'So Human an Animal: Evolution and Ethics', in *Science and Theology: The New Consonance*, ed. by Ted Peters (Boulder, CO: Westview Press, 1998), 125.
26. Ibid.
27. Ibid., 127.
28. Ibid., 128.
29. Ibid., 130–31.
30. Ibid., 133.
31. Ibid., 132–3.
32. Ibid., 133.
33. Karl Barth, *Church Dogmatics*, volume IV, trans. by Geoffrey Bromiley (Edinburgh: T. & T. Clark, 1936–62), 2:733.
34. Gene Outka, *Agape: An Ethical Analysis* (New Haven: Yale University Press, 1972), 12. See Paul R. Sponheim, *Faith and the Other* (Minneapolis: Fortress Press, 1993).
35. Barth, *Church Dogmatics*, IV:2:754.
36. Ibid., 760.
37. Philip Melanchthon, 'Apology to the Augsburg Confession', *The Book of Concord*, ed. by Theodore Tappert (Minneapolis: Fortress, 1959), 124.
38. Barth, *Church Dogmatics*, IV:2:744.
39. For Augustine, the Holy Spirit enters directly into the human will, making possible what would otherwise be impossible by nature alone. '[O]ur will itself, without which we cannot do the good, is aided and uplifted by the imparting of the Spirit of grace' ('The Spirit and the Letter', in *Augustine: Later Works*, ed. by John Burnaby, Volume VIII of *The Library of Christian Classics* (Louisville: Westminster/John Knox, 1955), 209.
40. Martin Luther, 'The Freedom of a Christian', *Luther's Works*, American edn, 55 volumes (St Louis and Minneapolis: Concordia and Fortress, 1955–67), 31:365.
41. Barth, *Church Dogmatics*, IV:2:733.
42. Stephen J. Pope, 'Agape and Human Nature: Contributions from Neo-Darwinism', in *An Evolving Dialogue*, ed. by James B. Miller (Washington: American Association for the Advancement of Science, 1998), 425.
43. Ibid., 428.
44. Ibid., 429.
45. Ibid., 424.
46. Ibid., 431.
47. 'The *caritas* which the Middle Ages had learned decisively from Augustine was a synthesis of biblical *agape* and antique or hellenistic *eros*' (Barth, *Church Dogmatics*, IV:2:737). Neo-orthodox theologians of the mid-twentieth century sought to sunder the synthesis and extricate *agape* in its purified form. Stephen Pope, it seems, prefers the synthetic medieval version of Christian love.
48. Colin Grant, 'The Odds Against Altruism: The Sociobiology Agenda', in *An Evolving Dialogue*, 536.
49. Ibid., 537.
50. Grant, *An Evolving Dialogue*, 538.
51. Ibid., 538–9.
52. 'As contemporary evolutionary science is bringing out more clearly all the time, the story of life on Earth is less one of competition among species and more one of their cooperation and interdependence than we used to think' (John Haught, *God After Darwin* [Boulder: Westview, 2002], 45).
53. Arthur Peacocke, 'The Cost of New Life', in *The Work of Love: Creation as Kenosis*, ed. by John Polkinghorne (Grand Rapids, MI and Cambridge, UK: Eerdmans and SPCK, 2001), 35.
54. Ibid.

55. Ibid., 38, 41–2.
56. 'The love of God is the *causa finalis* of the Creation' (Arthur Peacocke, *Creation and the World of Science* [Oxford: Clarendon Press, 1979], 235). 'This self-limitation is the precondition for the coming into existence of free self-conscious human beings, that is, human experience as such. This act of self-limitation on behalf of the good and well-being, indeed the existence, of another being can properly be designated as being consistent with, and so exemplifying the ultimate character of *God as Love*'(idem, *Theology for a Scientific Age* [Minneapolis: Fortress, 1993], 123; Peacocke's italics.
57. Ian Barbour, 'God's Power: A Process View', *The Work of Love*, 12.
58. Ibid., 4.
59. Holmes Rolston, III, 'Kenosis and Nature', *The Work of Love*, 43.
60. Ibid., 50.
61. This eschatological orientation is conceptually developed in Ted Peters, *GOD – The World's Future*, 2nd edn (Minneapolis: Fortress, 2000) and applied to evolutionary biology in Ted Peters and Martinez Hewlett, *Evolution from Creation to New Creation* (Nashville: Abingdon, 2003).
62. Some degree of transcending our genes is permitted by Dawkins, *Selfish Gene*, 3; and Edward O. Wilson, 'Human Decency is Animal', *New York Times Magazine* (12 October 1975), 50.

D

Technology and the Environment

Chapter 12

Technology Requires Ethical Decisions

Roger L. Shinn

The events of September 11, 2001 jolted even the most sluggish minds to realize that technology is a powerful force, as perilous as it is promising, in our world. This recognition has for centuries barely slumbered in the minds of the world's great thinkers. Now it is awake, with burning urgency.

The Historical and Cultural Context

I begin with attention to the broad historical context of thought and activity. Consciously and unconsciously we inherit both insights and cumbersome baggage from the past. Read the classics of literature, philosophy, and theology, East and West, and you will find little attention to technology. Often there is deliberate condescension. In the West the Platonic and Aristotelian traditions adored the life of the mind, as it rose above the material world (Plato's cave) into the realm of pure contemplation (Aristotle's deity). The neglect of labor and economic production was related to a class structure, in which slaves or workers did the dreary work, freeing 'superior' people to speculate about nobler truths. In the East, the Hindu caste system and *maya* tradition and Confucian hierarchical structures devalued the toil that kept life going. All the while, technology shaped cultures – military, economic, and political – more than the great thinkers knew.

Christian theology, when not captivated by its Hellenic heritage, sometimes corrected this. Although Hebrew scriptures showed suspicion of the military and economic technologies of surrounding societies, the prophets, historians, and psalmists knew that human life is rooted in soil and the gifts of nature. Think of the attention to milk and honey, flocks, vineyards, hunger and famine, exploitation by greedy landlords, slavery and freedom, sycamore trees, the lives of fishermen and a tent-maker and the Son of a carpenter.

Morris Cohen, that tough-minded philosopher of a recent past, recalled a conversation with the Hindu philosopher Ramanathan, about the meaning of the Hebrew exodus from Egypt. Ramanathan was looking for 'an allegory of the relation of the soul to God'. Cohen insisted on the plain meaning: a people escaped from slavery to freedom. Ramanathan thought that only 'the eternal spiritual meaning' was worth attention. He could not be persuaded that a holy scripture was concerned with the 'carnal' stuff of material history.[1]

Christians, although they often yielded to excessive spiritualization of history, could not forget that commonplace work is a service of God. The Dominican monks practiced a daily discipline, not only of prayer and meditation, but of physical labor. As economist Kenneth Boulding used to say, they were the first intellectuals to get dirt under their fingernails. A primary innovator of modern science was the monk Gregor Mendel, who in a monastic garden made the first great genetic discoveries. A pioneer of the modern physical sciences, who saw how to relate intellectual imagination to empirical measurements, was Blaise Pascal, the fervent Jansenist.

Historians and philosophers often point out a contribution of Christianity to the development of science. Christian monotheism, rejecting pagan deities and spirits who inhabit nature, secularized the world, wiping out taboos that forbade the scientific exploration of nature. Yet the same monotheism meant that a unity underlies the obvious chaos of the world and makes possible the quest for scientific truth. Theologians, envying the prestige of science, sometimes sought to coopt that prestige to give respectability to the affirmations of faith. An extravagant example was the immense popularity of Harvey Cox's *The Secular City*. Cox himself was wise enough to become an incisive critic of his early work.[2]

Even during the peak of prestige of science and its technologies, modern warfare gave convincing evidence of the destructive power of scientific technologies. Soon came the explosion of ecological sensitivities to the dangers threatening societies that had trusted technologies to save the world from poverty and despair. Historian Lynn White called the bluff of the Christians who had so eagerly sought credit for hi-tech achievements. In his famous address in 1966 to the American Association for the Advancement of Science (AAAS), White blamed Christianity, 'especially in its Western form,' for 'the psychic revolution' that has wrought ecological destructiveness. A little later Arnold Toynbee, who had once acclaimed Christianity, decided that biblical monotheism had 'removed the age-old restraint that was once placed on man's greed by his awe.' Now, he said, 'nature is taking her revenge on us unmistakably.'[3]

White saw resources in Christianity for reform and, in a serious witticism, suggested that St Francis of Assissi, with his belief in 'a democracy of all creatures', become 'a patron saint for ecologists'. The AAAS, to no one's surprise, did not act on that proposal. But, sure enough, Pope John Paul II formally declared St Francis the patron saint of ecology on April 6, 1980.

Toynbee asked for a return to the 'once universal' pre-monotheistic pantheism. Neither White nor Toynbee explained how to feed a world population of six billion people. But both evoked praise from the 'Greens' who became highly visible at the turn of the millennium. In this context of technological messianism and its critics Ian Barbour has made his searching studies of technology and religion.

Some Themes from Barbour[4]

Ian Barbour is surely one of our most thoughtful explorers of the relation of religion (primarily but not solely Christianity) to science and technology. He commands amazing information of the physical sciences, the biological sciences, and the history of philosophy and theology. To this knowledge he brings powerful discernment of its intellectual and practical impact. He takes up controversial issues, surveying proposed options with remarkable fairness, then gives his own opinion and offers his readers the opportunity to agree or disagree.

For a decade or so he and I were part of a small group of scientists (primarily physicists) and theologians who met twice a year for two days of mutual education and discussion. Physicist Harold Schilling, our instigator and elder statesman, dedicated his book, *The New Consciousness in Science and Religion*,[5] to the group. Barbour, with his track record in both science and theology, was our most diligent member, our assiduous volunteer recorder. We started working on the intellectual relations between contemporary science and theology. Then, as ecological issues became more prominent, we turned to practical issues – a welcome turn for me, a social ethicist. I thought, perhaps too blithely, that issues of science and religion might be debated endlessly, but technology required decisions that must be made (or avoided, with fateful consequences) now.

Several of us wrote books stimulated by our discussion. Barbour edited one book of our collected papers: *Earth Might Be Fair: Reflections on Ethics, Religion, and Ecology* (1972).[6] He was our obvious choice; he had published works dealing with science, ecology, and theology, and he was already at work on further books that would constitute distinguished corpus.

Here I select five themes for comment. I am giving my own opinions, as they have evolved, often in conversation with Barbour. Usually we agree. I indicate some points on which I suspect that we differ.

The Relation Between Science and Technology

Barbour sees both the difference and the intimate relation between science and technology, without that condescension toward technology that I have mentioned. Science aims at understanding; technology, at activity. The criterion of scientific validity is verifiability – to use a term now disdained by many postmodernists but still important to scientists. Another criterion is esthetic, as theories are preferred because of their simplicity and elegance. The criterion of technology is effectiveness. In the ancient West that difference was often stark. Think of the contrast between Aristotle and Archimedes, only a century apart in time but far more distant in outlook. Modern colloquial conversation distinguished between 'long-hairs and slipstick boys,' until long hair became modish among many males and computers displaced slide rules. Science often precedes technology: Euclid's geometry has useful applications in practice. But technology may precede science: the lever was used practically before its scientific laws were discovered, as today children enjoy the see-saw long before they learn its laws in school.

Over the years science and technology have grown closer. Einstein's science leads to nuclear energy and weapons. And much science depends upon technology: the Hubble telescope is a stupendous technological achievement in the interests of scientific discovery. In philosophic pragmatism the difference between science and technology almost disappears. John Dewey described logic as 'the theory of inquiry' and saw the main function of thought to be problem-solving.[7] The test of validity was practice.

Technology, Power, and Ethics

Technology is an exercise of power – the power of human beings over non-human nature and the power of some people over others. As such, it shares the moral ambivalence of all human powers. Power surely is not evil; nobody wants to be powerless. Yet inevitably we think of Lord Acton's saying of 1887: 'Power tends to corrupt and absolute power corrupts absolutely.'[8] Unchecked power, whether military or economic or technological, is commonly misused.

I believe that Barbour is right in rejecting both the messianism that expects a 'technological fix' to make everybody happy and the demonizing of technology as an alien force that overrides conscious purpose. He also rejects, especially in his later writings, a third belief: that technology is innocently neutral, subject to human will, which directs it for good or bad purposes. Granted, technology is partially neutral: a laser can be used for healing or for weaponry. But technology, in general, is ambivalent rather than neutral. It is a social construction, incorporating the values of its designers. A surgeon's scalpel may in a rare situation become a weapon, and a switchblade may in an emergency enable surgery. But the design, manufacture, and sale of both has a purpose.

Military power has been a major force in the development of technology. Technologies do not lie around, waiting to be discovered and then applied. They are purposefully developed, usually to enhance the power of the powerful.

Barbour writes that technology 'often seems to be a power beyond our control, endangering social patterns and the environment on a scale previously unimaginable.' What weight should be given to that term, 'seems too be'? Ralph Waldo Emerson in 1847 wrote: 'Things are in the saddle, and ride mankind.' In our time Jacques Ellul has reified 'technique' – not quite the same as technology, but pretty close – as an enslaving power, to the degree that 'in the present social situation there is not even the beginning of a solution, no breach in the system of technical necessity.' Twenty-three years later he intensified his argument: 'Man can no longer be a subject. For the system implies that, at least in regard to itself, man must always be treated as an object.' Langdon Winner has analyzed 'techniques-out-of-control' as a theme in political thought.[9]

Margaret Mead sternly opposed such thinking. During several years we collaborated closely in studies of the World Council of Churches and (in the USA) of the National Council of Churches.[10] As I drafted position papers, she repeatedly forbade me to use the word technology as the subject of any transitive verb. Technology, she insisted, does not act; people act, using technology. She showed invincible faith in the power of people to change systems.

I *want* to side with Mead against Ellul. But I disobey her in the title of this essay. Technology is people in action, and it sometimes takes on a momentum of its own, sweeping its creators into situations they did not expect. Technology has shaped modern cities, industries, and wars, often contrary to human intention, even though it was people who exercised its power.

I resist the demonizing of technology. Ivan Illich, while arguing that often 'machines enslave men,' nevertheless described 'tools of conviviality' that enrich human life. As an example, he used the telephone that 'lets anybody say what he wants to the person of his choice; he can conduct business, express love, or pick a quarrel.'[11] I might note that Illich in 1973 did not know about cell phones that interrupt the beauty or the silence of an opera or an occasion of worship. I also remind myself that Socrates was not underprivileged because he could not phone Protagoras; maybe he was better off conversing in the marketplace, where Plato could listen in.

So I fight Ellul without winning decisively enough to stop fighting. Barbour, responding to my earlier comments on Ellul, writes: 'I still retain a faith that when enough people are concerned in a democracy they can be politically effective.'[12] I share that faith and struggle to maintain it. When I look at the forces of war, terrorism, and ecological destructiveness, I know the struggle will be long and arduous, with some wins and some losses along the way.

Exploratory Ethics in a High-tech Society

The advances of technology confront us with *new* decisions. I agree with Barbour: 'We face unprecedented choices for which traditional ethics give us little guidance. The evaluation of technology today must be global, anticipatory, and interdisciplinary.'[13] No Bible or Qur'an or Sutra tells us: 'Thou shalt, or shalt not, clone.' No Plato or Kant or Mill says anything about that.

This is not to disdain ethical and religious tradition. The cries for justice of the Hebrew prophets are as scorching now as when they were first uttered. But the specific prescriptions of biblical law for feeding the hungry and defending people against wicked kings are not much help today. We need scientific skills to produce and distribute food to a world on its way to eight billion people. The genetic foolishness of Plato is utterly inadequate to our perplexities about gene splicing. The traditional ethics of war and violence do not mention terrorism at the World Trade Center, nuclear proliferation, or biological warfare. Technology has changed our options. Yet science and technology cannot of themselves prescribe ethically sound decisions. Think of a few technological achievements of our time: supersonic aircraft, nuclear weapons, manipulation of DNA, cloning of animals and perhaps soon of human beings, easy abortions, mailing of anthrax, possibly the release of smallpox. The existence of new human powers does not certify their desirability. We – I mean all humanity – are learning, case by case with many risks along the way, to relate high-tech to human purposes.

Technology and Politics

As technology impinges on public policy, politics becomes the arena of decision. That raises a perplexing problem: are the electorate and their representatives in government competent to make decisions about the uses of high-tech?

The new 'age of information' might seem, at first glance, to fulfill ancient hopes of an informed citizenry. But the impression is delusory. When James Madison and his colleagues drafted the constitution, they assumed that geographical representation would give expression to the varied interests of the whole nation. They assumed also that elected senators and representatives would understand the proposals on which they vote. Now many interests clamoring for political attention are national or international, not local. And legislators often vote on matters they do not understand.

One consequence is that decision-making increasingly shifts from the floors of Congress to committees and their staffs. Today we are likely to smirk at the traditional description of the Senate as 'the greatest deliberative body of history.' Excessive power moves through arcane channels where conniving is easily concealed. Technical expertise is provided in abundance by lobbies, lavishly paid by corporations and interest groups. There is some help from the National Academy of Sciences, a federally chartered but independent association of scientists, which chooses panels qualified to evaluate technical proposals. Barbour has reminded me also of the activities of 'the Office of Technology Assessment, universities, and public interest groups.'[14]

Think of the current debate about human cloning. A panel of the National Academy of Sciences opposes President Bush's desire to ban cloning of human stem cells because, they believe, the procedure may lead to valuable human therapies. But the panel says: 'Human reproductive cloning should not now be practiced. It is dangerous and likely to fail.' It recommends, for the present, a legislative ban on reproductive cloning. But because the risk and danger may diminish with scientific progress, the panel asks for a review of the ban within five years, after 'a broad national dialogue.'[15] Here the National Academy rightly distinguishes between two kinds of judgment: risk assessment, on which they can speak with scientific skill, and 'the societal, religious and ethical issues,' which require 'a broad national dialogue.' Scientists have every right and responsibility to participate in that dialogue. So do the rest of us.

We must then ask whether the public and government are competent to carry out that dialogue. No oligarchy is likely to do better. We remember Winston Churchill's well-known quip of 1947 that 'democracy is the worst form of Government except all those other forms that have been tried from time to time.' That remark, though not directed against technology, becomes increasingly persuasive when esoteric technologies impinge on public ethical concerns.

In American society distrust of politics is endemic. If we seek scientific advice, we quickly realize that scientists are not disinterested referees when they evaluate proposals dear to their own hearts and purses. In one of the early debates about the proposed Intercontinental Ballistic Missile, Senator Fulbright pointed out that all the scientists testifying in favor of the system were employed by the Defense Department or by corporations that stood to profit from the missiles.[16] The panels of the National Academy of Sciences are at least a few steps removed from the partisanship of lobbies. However, the average citizen does not know that the Academy exists. The same citizen has heard about the tobacco and armaments lobbies. That citizen may know that Congress has appropriated large sums for armaments that even the Defense Department, usually greedy for all the money it can get, does not want. Why? The money is to be spent in the districts of one or two politicians on key committees.

One portentous case of the influence of lobbies became evident in the fiasco over health care legislation in 1994. According to *Newsweek* (September 19, 1994, 28), 'the interest groups spent at least $300 million – more than the Democratic and Republican 1988 and 1992 presidential nominees combined – to defeat health care. Much of this money was spent on blatantly untrue advertisements designed to scare the public.' Technology did not do that, but monied interests knew how to take advantage of technology.

Health care is a beautifully clear – or notoriously muddy – example of the complexities of establishing justice in an 'age of technology,' to pluck a phrase from one of Barbour's titles. High-tech medicine is expensive, and I have little ability to judge my needs. The journal *Consumer Reports*, for all its merits, cannot tell me whether I need another CAT scan or MRI. I am sure that I have received treatments that were excessive, but I lacked the skill or courage to reject the advice of the doctor who billed Medicare for the treatments. Beyond such questions, there is the issue of distributive justice. What demands have I a moral right to make on the public treasury, when I have already exceeded my biblical three score years and ten? The ethical issues are momentous, even apart from the confusion deliberately spread by high-spending interest groups.

Need and Greed

Here I start from Barbour's statement: 'Provided that population growth is curbed [a big proviso!], global resources are sufficient for every need, but not for every greed.'[17] I think it was Mahatma Gandhi who first coined that neat contrast between need and greed. I applaud that stab at the moral offense of lavish luxury in a world of desperate privation.

Then the skeptic within me speaks up. What precisely is the difference between need and greed? Part of the uniqueness of humanity is the elusiveness of human needs. Among animals sexual desire is pretty well governed by instincts relating to times and seasons. Human freedom expands vastly the scope and variety – and, of course, the marketing – of sexual activity. It is said that humans are the only species that make love all the year round, that only among humans does the female engage in sexual intercourse after menopause. I cannot verify those claims in detail, but the general idea is clear. Human need is expansive, not easy to define. To take another example, many people give their dogs a healthier diet than they enjoy themselves. Why? People eat for many reasons beyond maintenance of health – for enjoyment, conviviality, and ritual expression. They want – and think they need – a variety of delectable foods.

Are symphonies and operas an expression of need or greed? What about flower gardens and golf courses? If planting flowers rather than beans causes the death of one child from starvation, I certainly favor the child and the beans. But do I want a world with no flowers? Barbour has answered my question: 'No, but I can get along without carnations grown for export on land used for subsistence agriculture in Columbia.'[18] I fervently agree. My point is that need is a social construction and in high-tech society luxuries quickly become needs.

Is it need or greed that demands electrical refrigeration? Moses and Socrates, Confucius and Gautama Buddha, Croesus and Julius Caesar, along with the vast majority of the human race, got along without refrigeration. Electrical refrigerators have been known for maybe one hundredth of a percent of human history, not the most glorious hundredth of a percent. My family got along without one throughout my boyhood. Electrical refrigeration has become a virtual need by human social construction. Certainly I do not want to tell mothers in Mexico City or Harlem that they are greedy if they want electrical refrigerators. For better and worse, modern societies convert luxuries into necessities. Vast systems of water purification and waste disposal, unknown throughout most of history, have become needs. Sometimes an age of technology creates needs faster than it satisfies needs.

I must add one further twist to this discussion. It comes from Fred Hirsch's brilliant and disturbing book *Social Limits to Growth* (1977). Hirsch published about five years after *The Limits to Growth* (1972), written by Donella Meadows and her colleagues. The earlier volume was the most dramatic of several books that emphasized the physical limits to the carrying capacity of the earth, considered in terms of population, resources, and pollution. Hirsch, while aware of physical restraints, chose to emphasize the social limits.[19] He joined an observation about human nature to a simple matter of logic. What most people want, said Hirsch, is more than their neighbors have. And there is no way – this side of Garrison Keillor's Lake Wobegon – that everybody can have more than the average. Technology neither makes nor solves that issue. The problem comes home to human nature and justice and the nontechnological issues that Barbour fully recognizes. The redefinition of need in an age of ecological sensitivity becomes an immense task of social reconstruction.

Modernization, Westernization, and Globalization

The editor of this volume, I am glad to say, has invited me to do some 'projection of the goals and tasks that now lie ahead.' I can do that in terms of three words that are prominent in current discussions and polemics: *modernization*, *Westernization*, and *globalization*.

Most of the world wants *modernization* – or some of it. Even when modernization wrecks cherished traditions, people crave rising economic production, relief from backbreaking toil and life-threatening poverty, and medical advances that extend health and life.

The West with its technologies has led the world in modernization. There were past centuries when China was the leader, but for complex reasons the West has come to produce most of the innovations of modernization. Now much of the world wants modernization but resists *Westernization*. It accuses the West of decadence, reckless sexual excesses, drug addictions that it tries to solve by punishing the sources of drugs rather than by self-discipline. It resents the way Western television dangles before the world its lavish lifestyles. It rejects the rampant individualism that threatens cherished structures of community.

Globalization is the new buzzword that incites both idealism and fierce resentment. To some it means the triumph of world loyalty over tribal and national parochialism. To others it is a thin disguise for the pernicious effects of Westernization. Is the Security Council of the United Nations an elevation of world concerns over bitter nationalisms, or is it a clique of the rich and powerful determined to extend their domain? Do the World Bank (WB) and the International Monetary Fund (IMF) relieve poverty and help needy nations through emergencies or do they extend Western hegemony, enslave poor nations with intolerable debt, and force on them painful economic policies?

Complaints about globalization erupt explosively. Public riots confront summit conferences of the Americas and of the G-8 (the seven foremost industrial powers plus Russia), comparable gatherings of non-governmental groups, meetings of the WB and the IMF. Some of these meetings change their location in order to escape protestors. Others massively deploy local police. The principals try to project an image of concern for the whole world; the protestors shriek with the pain of the exploited.

The issues are too vast and complex to sort out here, but a few comments are possible. Certainly globalization is a mixed phenomenon. Some attacks on it are ironic. Condemnations often heard in the World Council of Churches seem unaware that ecumenism is linguistically a rough equivalent of globalism and the WCC is itself a multinational corporation, dependent on global networks of communication and travel. Among the accomplishments of globalization are the extinction (permanent, we wistfully hope) of smallpox, reduction of infant mortality in many societies, world-wide air travel, rise of food production per capita on most continents (excepting Africa), multinational actions to counter the life-threatening 'hole' in the ozone blanket above the earth. Among its perils are the growing gap between rich and poor nations, the pain of workers who lose jobs as corporations swiftly move capital and production around the world, frustrations of nations whose economies depend on decisions out of their control, actions that neglect the welfare of distant societies or that deliberately exploit them.

Militarily the massive power of high-tech societies evokes the counter-power of terrorism. Technology was expected to increase security by redundant defenses against perils. But in 1949 E.B. White, in a slender book that was almost a love song to New York, wrote of the destructibility of the city: 'A single flight of planes no bigger than a wedge of geese can quickly end this island fantasy, burn the towers, crumble the bridges, turn the underground passages into lethal chambers, cremate the millions.'[20] Now the events of 9/11 have brought a hint of what can happen. Perhaps even worse, weaponry may escalate to include biological terror.

It was once possible to believe that progress of technology assures progress of civilization. Edward Gibbon made this argument in his famous *Decline and Fall of the Roman Empire* (1840). Explaining that barbarians could never again destroy a powerful civilization, he wrote:

> Europe is secure from any future irruption of barbarians; since in order to conquer, they must cease to be barbarians. Their gradual advances in the science of war would always be accompanied, as we may learn from the example of Russia, with a proportionable improvement in the arts of peace and civil policy; and they themselves must deserve a place among the polished nations whom they subdue.

So he cheerfully concluded:

> We may therefore acquiesce in the pleasing conclusion that every age of the world has increased and still increases the real wealth, the happiness, the knowledge, and perhaps the virtue, of the human race.[21]

I first read that amazing opinion in the aftermath of World War II and the Shoah, and its absurdity has stuck in my mind. But it is still argued that technological advance encourages the advance of freedom and peace.

One example is the debate, which currently fascinates the chattering classes, between Francis Fukuyama and Samuel P. Huntington. Fukuyama, in his book *The End of History and the Last Man*, argues that the progress of liberal democracy and moderated capitalism is so convincing that it will overcome the despotic regimes and the ideological conflicts that have marked history. It is in that sense, not in some apocalyptic catastrophe, that he expects the 'end of history.' Huntington, by contrast, says that despotisms can appropriate Western technologies without conversion to the values of liberal democracy. So he calls his provocative book *The Clash of Civilizations and the Remaking of World Order*. He sees a world of seven or eight rival civilizations, each rooted in its own ideology or religion. The greatest clash, for us, is between the West and Islamic societies.[22]

The events of 9/11 for some people confirmed Huntington's thesis. Fukuyama, reporting that 'a stream of commentators' are now claiming that he was 'utterly wrong,' replies that 9/11 was part of 'a series of rearguard actions' and that 'time and resources are on the side of modernity.' Huntington reaffirms his case, saying that the fact that the terrorists were 'intelligent, ambitious young people' supports his contention that appropriation of Western technologies need not mean adoption of the values of liberal democracy.[23]

I might need a volume to state my disagreements with both Fukuyama and Huntington, although both have stretched my mind. For the present it is enough to say that I see convincing evidence that technological achievements do not invariably mean advance in 'the arts of peace and civil policy.' Fukuyama's confidence requires a leap of faith beyond my capacity. At the same time, I won't give up my hope and efforts for an expansion of liberal democracy, repentant of its own ecological extravagance and far more concerned than ours for justice. I expect tumultuous transformations if our world is to move toward a more just and sustainable world society. The changes will be resisted by those who see their interests threatened. For one example among many, think of the current binge in petroleum consumption in the United States, stupid militarily and ecologically, but urged onward by politicians, corporations, labor unions, and millions of consumers. The longer we delay changes, the more severe will be the conflicts.

Barbour and I share forebodings about this future. Curiously each of us has occasionally thought the other was not sufficiently alarmist. If we have a difference worth exploring, it may be – I am not entirely sure – that my world is a little more jumbled than Barbour's, with conflicts more intractable and problems more insoluble. If so, I hope he is right.

We both prefer pragmatic, exploratory investigations to doctrinaire assertions and programs. We both urge purposeful action. We are not utopians, but neither are we futilitarians. So we make our efforts to redirect the vast human powers inherent in technology, even though we know the obstacles are great. One classical way of putting this is to say that we are justified by faith, not works, but that faith without works is dead.

Notes

1. Morris Cohen, *The Meaning of History* (LaSalle, IL: Open Court, 1947), 9–10.
2. Harvey Cox, *The Secular City* (New York: Macmillan, 1965); *Religion in the Secular City* (New York: Simon & Schuster, 1984); 'The Secular City 25 Years Later', *The Christian Century*, 7 November 1990.
3. Lynn White, Jr, 'The Historical Roots of Our Ecologic Crisis', *Science*, 155 (March 19, 1967), 1203–7; reprinted in many collections. Arnold Toynbee, 'The Religious Background of the Present Environmental Crisis', *International Journal of Environmental Studies*, 3 (1972), 141–6.
4. This section of this chapter, at the suggestion of the editor, includes some paragraphs from my paper prepared for the Theology and Science Group of the American Academy of Religion, Chicago, November 20, 1994, and later published in *Zygon*, 31:1 (March 1996), 67–74. Section 3 of this chapter also includes a few sentences from that paper. Here I use these with permission of the editor of *Zygon*. I have reworked these excerpts in the light of Barbour's response to me at the meeting and in *Zygon*, 31, 102–4.
5. Harold Schilling, *The New Consciousness in Science and Religion* (Philadelphia: United Church Press, 1973).
6. Ian G. Barbour (ed.), *Earth Might Be Fair: Reflections on Ethics, Religion, and Ecology* (Englewood Cliffs, NJ: Prentice Hall, 1972).
7. John Dewey, *Logic: The Theory of Inquiry* (New York: Henry Holt, 1934).
8. John Emerich Edward Dahlberg Acton, Letter to Mandel Creighton, in *Essays on Freedom and Power*, ed. by Gertrude Himmelfarb (New York: Meridian, 1955), 335.
9. I.G. Barbour, *Religion and Science: Historical and Contemporary Issues* (San Francisco: HarperSanFrancisco, 1997), xiii. Jacques Ellul, *The Technological Society* (New York: Random House Vintage, 1964; original French edn, 1954), xxxi. *The Technological System* (New York: Continuum, 1980, original French edn, 1977), 12. Langdon Winner, *Autonomous Technology: Technics-out-of-Control as a Theme in Political Thought* (Cambridge, MA: MIT Press, 1977).
10. Margaret Mead, Roger L. Shinn et al., *To Love or to Perish: The Technological Crisis and the Churches* (New York: Friendship, 1972).
11. Ivan Illich, *Tools for Conviviality* (New York: Harper & Row, 1973), 22.
12. I.G. Barbour, 'Response to Roger L. Shinn', *Zygon*, 31:1 (March 1996), 104.
13. Idem, *Ethics in an Age of Technology: The Gifford Lectures 1989–1991 Volume 2* (San Francisco: HarperSanFrancisco, 1993), xvi.
14. Idem, *Zygon*, 31:1 (March 1996), 104.
15. Sheryl Gay Stolberg, 'Science Academy Supports Cloning to Treat Disease', *The New York Times*, 19 January 2002, A1.
16. Daniel D. McCracken, *Public Policy and the Expert: Ethical Problems of the Witness* (New York: Council on Religion and International Affairs, Special Studies #212, 1971), 44–7.
17. Barbour, *Ethics in an Age of Technology*, xvii. Barbour repeats this theme even more strongly in the final paragraph of his most recent book, *Nature, Human Nature, and God* (Minneapolis MN: Fortress Press, 2002), 140: 'There is enough for every need but not for every greed.'
18. Barbour, *Zygon*, 31:1 (March 1996), 103.

19. Donella Meadows et al., *The Limits to Growth* (New York: Universe, 1972). Cf. Donella Meadows et al., *Beyond the Limits: Confronting Global Collapse, Envisioning a Sustainable Future* (White River Junction, VT: Chelsea Green, 1992). The second book updates the first and includes answers to critics. Fred Hirsch, *Social Limits to Growth* (London: Routledge & Kegan Paul, 1977).

20. E.B. White, *Here Is New York* (New York: Harper & Brothers, 1949), 51.

21. Edward Gibbon, *Decline and Fall of the Roman Empire* (first published 1840; then in many later editions), Vol. II, end of ch. 38.

22. Francis Fukuyama, *The End of History and the Last Man* (New York: Simon & Schuster, 1992). Samuel P. Huntington, *The Clash of Civilizations and the Remaking of World Order* (New York: Simon & Schuster, 1996).

23. Fukuyama, 'History Is Still Going Our Way', *The Wall Street Journal*, 5 October 2001, op-ed page. Huntington, interviewed by Michael Steinberger, *The New York Times*, 20 October 2001, A13.

Chapter 13

Ethics, Technology, and Environment

Judith N. Scoville

Ian Barbour provides a unique contribution to 'the science and religion' dialogue: his is the only comprehensive set of writings that connects Christian theology and its engagement with the natural sciences, on the one hand, and Christian ethics and its concerns over technology and the environment on the other. Even within the latter focus, his inclusion of the environment distinguishes his writings from most works on Christian ethics and technology, which largely focus on medical and reproductive technologies. Of particular importance is the attention he gives to social ethics and to values such as justice and participation in discussions of ethics, technology, and the environment. The division of Barbour's Gifford Lectures into two volumes, however, has tended to obscure the important connections between the science and religion side of his scholarship and the ethics and technology side. Furthermore, most scholars in religion and science have given relatively little attention to environmental ethics, while many ecotheologians have given inadequate attention to the important work being done in religion and science. Yet, as Barbour states, there is a critical connection between science and religion and environmental ethics. Our theological models, particularly those of God's relation to nature, will be modified by our understanding of nature. Today's understanding highlights nature as dynamic and evolutionary, laced with emergent novelty and characterized by both chance and law. It is an ecological view of nature stressing interdependence between multiple levels. The modifications in our theological models will, in turn, affect the attitudes we hold about nature, leading to practical ramifications for environmental ethics.[1]

My objective is to suggest avenues for scholarly work that will more fully connect environmental ethics, the study of technology, and the field of science and religion. In particular, I will cross the division of Barbour's work into science and religion, on the one hand, and technology and ethics, on the other, by inquiring into ways of relating science and ethics, a relationship that has great significance for environmental ethics. I will use Barbour's four-part typology for relating religion and science to illuminate the different ways in which environmental ethics can relate to science. To make the discussion more concrete, I will conclude by evaluating Barbour's treatment of agriculture.

Technology and Values

In 1980 Barbour produced a unique work, *Technology, Environment, and Human Values*, in which he brought together environmental concern, a careful study of technology, and Christian ethics.[2] The book built on his earlier book on technology and ethics, *Science and Secularity* (1970),[3] and on his active participation in early discussions of the environmental crisis by scientists, theologians, and ethicists. His environmental interests led him to edit and contribute essays to two important anthologies dealing with religious and philosophical environmental ethics, *Earth Might Be Fair* (1972) and *Western Man and Environmental Ethics* (1973).[4] As Director of the Science, Ethics, and Public Policy program at Carleton College, he organized a symposium, 'Responses to Global Scarcities,' and edited the essays from it into *Finite Resources and the Human Future* (1976).[5] In addition, he co-authored a study of energy policy, *Energy and American Values* (1982).[6] Thus Barbour brings to Christian environmental ethics an extraordinary and unmatched set of qualifications. He comes to the topic as a scientist and theologian, as the 'father' of the field of science and religion, as one who has done a careful philosophical and sociological study of technology, and as one with a solid understanding of environmental policy issues.

The Role of Technology in Environmental Ethics

Technology, Environment, and Human Values was quite different from most works in Christian environmental ethics. The usual approach in these has been one of Christian apologetics. The key problems typically addressed are establishing the relevance and importance of the natural world for the Christian tradition and developing an ethic for the human relationship to nature.[7] The theological side of this project, which has involved searching scripture and tradition for resources and reinterpreting the tradition in a more nature-friendly way, has usually been more fully developed than has the ethical side. As valuable as this work has been, the connection between it and the immediate sources of environmental degradation has often been tenuous.[8] Likewise, although ecotheologians strongly affirm the importance of justice issues (hence the term 'ecojustice'), the practical relationship of environmental ethics and social ethics is not always as clear as one might hope.

Barbour's work has been distinctively different. First, he has approached ethical issues concerning the environment, not from the direction of theology, but from his study of technology. Barbour defines technology as 'the application of organized knowledge to practical tasks by ordered systems of people and machines.'[9] He prefers this broad definition for 'it allows us to include technologies based on practical experience and invention as well as those based on scientific theories' and because 'it directs attention to social institutions as well as to the hardware of technology.'[10] This starting point is critically important. For the most part our damage to the environment comes not from trampling the earth with our feet or plucking its fruits with our fingers. It comes instead through technologies and the social structures in which they are embedded. Likewise, our care for the earth, especially in those places where we must live and meet our needs, utilizes technologies. Ideas shape our behavior and provide motivation, but it is when they are translated into technologies that they most directly impact the earth.

This attention to technology and the environment distinguishes Barbour not only from other environmental ethicists, but also from others who have examined the ethics of technology from a Christian point of view. Most discussion of the ethics of technology has focused on human reproductive technologies, genetic engineering, cloning and, earlier, on nuclear war and nuclear power. Only indirectly, through concern for issues such as population, hunger, and energy did ethical discussions of technology involve the natural environment.[11] For Barbour, on the other hand, the environment has been a primary concern.

Since technology is the main way through which we relate to and impact the natural world, the ethics of technology and environmental ethics are inseparably related. Only if we understand how technology functions in human society, the relationship between technology and science, and the basic assumptions and attitudes that shape technology can we really understand our relationship with nature. Thus Barbour's discussion of views of technology in the first chapter of *Ethics in an Age of Technology* is of exceptional importance. He does not view technology as an autonomous force or as inherently neutral ethically; technology is never simply *technique*. Rather, he demonstrates that technologies are social constructions that are shaped by their cultural and social contexts and reflect particular purposes and interests. Thus technologies are inherently value-laden and ethics cannot be limited to the ways in which technologies are used. Ethical evaluation must extend to the social context and examine the purposes for which technologies are developed. Thus he rejects both technological optimism and technological pessimism, opting for a contextualist approach instead.

Values and Ethics

In *Ethics in an Age of Technology*, Barbour outlines the three major approaches to Christian ethics: the ethics of the good; the ethics of duty; and the ethics of response or context. Barbour finds that the ethics of the good 'is most helpful in the public discussion of policy issues because it involves the defense of values concerning which people holding diverse religious and philosophical positions can find common ground.'[12] He does not limit the ethics of the good to utilitarianism, however, which he finds lacking in a basis for rights. Rather, the ethics of the good, as he presents it, results in an ethical framework consisting of a series of values: individual values of food and health, meaningful work, and personal fulfillment; and social values of social justice, participatory freedom, and economic development.

Just as the ethics of the good provides the basis for his discussion of human values, so does it provide the basis for environmental values. He gives extensive attention to instrumental values of the natural environment, which he organizes into two sets of values: human benefits from the environment and duties to future generations. The former includes the need to protect human life-support systems as well as preserving wilderness for its recreational, character-building, and spiritual value. Duties to future generations involve using renewable resources sustainably, developing technologies to replace depleted resources, and limiting the risks passed on to future generations.[13]

Barbour also presents a third set of environmental values, respect for all forms of life. These values are based on the intrinsic value of nonhuman life. His primary rationale for the intrinsic value of living beings comes from process philosophy.

According to process thought, experience, which pervades all things, is the only intrinsic good. The capacity to experience, however, varies greatly and many beings have only insignificant intrinsic value. Thus respect for other beings is qualified by the *principle of discrimination*, in which different degrees of intrinsic value allow for assigning priorities where conflicts of interest occur.[14] Process thought also bases the intrinsic value of other beings on their value to God and their contribution to the richness of divine experience.[15] Despite the affirmation in process thought that relationality and interdependence are a fundamental part of being, its theory of value is focused on individuals, as is Barbour's respect for all forms of life. For Barbour, 'the integrity of the ecosystem is important because it makes possible *the welfare of interdependent individuals*, human and nonhuman.'[16] As Clare Palmer states in her detailed study of process thought and environmental ethics, process environmental ethics has more in common with individualistic environmental ethics, such as animal rights, than with communitarian ethics, such as that of Aldo Leopold.[17]

To a remarkable extent, Barbour's environmental values are human values, in contrast to most ecotheology, which focuses on intrinsic values in nature. In part, this reflects his interest in the public policy dimension of environmental problems. Public policy discourse takes place almost entirely in the language of human benefit. His emphasis on human values is also a result of Barbour's use of technology as a starting point. Technology is purposive and embodies human goals and values. Much of the critique of modern technology is in terms of its impact on persons, relationships, and culture. It is also critiqued, of course, on environmental grounds. But much of this critique, too, is human-centered as it is concerned with the degradation of the human environment and the depletion of natural resources. Where ethical regard for nonhumans does appear in his discussion of particular issues, it is in terms of respect for animals and their right to humane treatment. Thus Barbour's beginning point of technology leads to a largely human-centered environmental ethics. The challenge for further work in technology and the environment is to find a way to include a broader range of values that are not human-centered.

Ethics, Theology, and the Science of Ecology

Ecology and Ethics

Another reason Barbour's environmental ethics gives relatively little weight to intrinsic values in nature lies in the way he uses the science of ecology. For Barbour, the science of ecology is not a source of values; his use of ecology is prudential rather than normative. That ecosystems are complex systems of interaction and interdependence means that natural systems are fragile and that changes can have far-reaching and long-term consequences. The reality of finite limits indicates that there are limits to the growth of human populations and resource use. The dynamic stability and adaptability of ecosystems require biological diversity.[18] These characteristics of the natural world provide a set of parameters within which the realization of human and environmental values must take place rather than ethical norms.

Barbour is critical of basing ethics on science. In *Issues in Science and Religion*, he critiques evolutionary ethics at some length. The conclusions drawn from evolution, he asserts, 'seem to depend largely on the prior ethical commitments that lead an author to select particular aspects of evolution as definitive.'[19] In *Ethics in an Age of Technology*, Barbour rejects attempts to base ethics on ecology, on the grounds that it 'neglects the distinctive features of human nature and culture.'[20] He also asserts that Leopold's land ethic is not simply drawn from his work as a scientist, but from personal experience and is based on values that lie outside science.[21]

It seems here as if Barbour is drawing too sharp a line between facts and values, the *is* and the *ought*. Leopold's ideas on how land ought to be managed changed with the development of the science of ecology and his increasingly ecological understanding of the land. Whereas early in his career he saw game as a resource to be managed by eliminating predators, as he came to understand the role of predation in the health of the land he came to value all parts of the biotic community, apart from their usefulness to humans or their economic value.[22] It was from this realization that his land ethic had its origin. Furthermore, it is one thing to draw normative inferences from natural sciences about how human society should be structured, as in evolutionary ethics, and another to draw normative inferences about how we ought to relate to the natural world.

Holmes Rolston, who has examined the problem of values in nature in great depth, raises questions about the adequacy of dividing values into intrinsic and instrumental. Rolston finds that, at the level of the ecosystem, 'value-in-itself is smeared out to become value-in-togetherness. Value seeps out into the system, and we lose our capacity to identify the individual as the sole locus of value.'[23] He posits a third kind of value, systemic value, as an alternative to intrinsic and instrumental values. For Leopold, too, the unity of the land means that parts cannot be evaluated in terms of their utility, for the biota is 'so complex, so conditioned by interwoven cooperations and competitions, that no man can say where utility begins or ends.'[24] For both Leopold and Rolston, value is not limited to individuals, but is to be found in the community and in the relationships and processes by which that community functions.[25]

This discussion raises several important questions. First, are intrinsic and instrumental values adequate ways of thinking about value, especially in an ecosystemic context? Second, is creating priorities in order to resolve conflicts of interest what ethics – especially environmental ethics – is about, or is there a different way to think about ethics that focuses on *relationships* within the human community, within the biotic community, and between them? A ranking of values assumes that the role of ethics is the resolution of conflicts. However, it is the development of harmonious, mutually supportive relationships between humans and the natural world that Leopold sees as the goal of the land ethic. Furthermore, it is difficult to see how any hierarchy of intrinsic values, including one based on the capacity to experience, is compatible with our understanding of the natural world through the science of ecology.

Ecology and Worldviews

Where Barbour does affirm a role for ecology in ethics is its influence on our worldviews – the basic assumptions and ways of interpreting the world that impact our understanding of our place and role in the world. Science in general shapes our worldview and Barbour points to this as one of the important functions of science in ethics. In *Religion and Science: Historical and Contemporary Issues* (1997), he compares three views of nature: medieval, Newtonian, and twentieth-century. Of particular importance are the differences between the Newtonian view of nature and the twentieth-century view. In place of the Newtonian view of nature as atomistic and change as rearrangement of parts, the contemporary view sees nature as dynamic, historical, relational, and interdependent. Newtonian thought sees reality as reductionistic; the whole can be known by studying the most basic parts. The contemporary view, on the other hand, sees nature as layered; in each successive level new systems and characteristics emerge. The key image of nature in the Newtonian view is that of nature as a machine; in the contemporary view it is of nature 'as a community – a historical community of interdependent beings.'[26]

Barbour draws parallels between views of nature and views of technology, parallels that are clearer in *Technology, Environment, and Human Values* than in *Ethics in an Age of Technology*. He shows how the mechanistic view of nature is one of the roots of Western attitudes of domination and exploitation of nature.[27] Particularly in the American experience, such attitudes have also had their origins in belief in the inevitability of progress and a technological optimism that assumes that all problems have technological solutions.[28] Shifts in worldview are thus likely to significantly affect evaluations of particular technologies and different types of technologies emerge from different worldviews. As such, it would have been useful if Barbour had integrated the contemporary view of nature more fully into his discussion of technology and ethics in *Ethics in an Age of Technology*. In particular, it would be valuable to integrate his discussion of holistic environmental ethics with his discussion of the hierarchy of levels and the relationship of parts and wholes in *Religion in an Age of Science*.[29]

Ecology and Theology

Beyond its influence on worldviews, the science of ecology is a necessary dialogue partner in the discussion between science and theology. Physics, astronomy, and evolutionary biology have formed the science side of the science–religion dialogue, with neurology recently entering the conversation. In part, these sciences have been drawn on because they have been directly involved in challenges to the doctrine of creation, theological anthropology, and theism itself. The field of science and religion has arisen in large part as a response to these challenges. If the field of science and religion is to realize its promise for environmental theology and ethics, it must broaden the conversation to include the science of ecology.

The view of nature as historical and emergent coming from the sciences with which theology has been in dialogue, especially physics and evolutionary biology, has provided the basis for reinterpreting creation as continuous creation, rather than as a completed process. Divine purpose is worked out in this historical process, which leads to increasing complexity and self-consciousness. The science of ecology, however, tends to be\ more place-oriented. The word *ecology* is derived from the word *oikos*, meaning 'house' or 'place to live;' its very name implies place. Vine DeLoria, Jr, in *God is Red*, points out that, when primacy is given to time, it is very difficult to get to place. When priority is given to place, however, it is easy to get to time. Places exist in time; they have a history. Knowledge of the history of a place is an important part of knowing a place.[30] When we begin with place, there is a critical shift in the questions being asked. Rather than attending to the sweep of cosmic history and the human place in it, we are directed to the more immediate questions of what is going on in the natural world and what should we do here, in this place.

It is also important to attend to the science of ecology because ecosystems do not fit neatly into an organizational hierarchy of the sciences based on the relationship of parts and wholes, such as that described by Arthur Peacocke.[31] In this organizational scheme, ecology is located at the upper end of the living-organisms hierarchy that runs from cell components to organisms, populations, and ecosystems. R.V. O'Neill et al., in *A Hierarchical Concept of Ecosystems*[32] discuss the inadequacy of viewing ecosystems as an order of organization consisting of species populations. Ecosystems involve processes such as energy and nutrient cycling that do not fit into this part–whole hierarchy and include inanimate as well as animate components. The abiotic components of the ecosystem are as important as the biotic. 'In fact,' state O'Neill et al., 'the existence of abiotic functional components is a fundamental problem with breaking ecosystem structure into subsystems exclusively composed of populations.'[33] Thus, placing ecosystems at the end of the living organisms part–whole continuum is not really adequate.

More difficulties arise when we take into account the level of human culture and the sciences that describe it. Are ecosystems the part of economic systems that provides resources, as resource economics asserts? Or are economic systems parts of the ecosystems on which they rely?[34] As the science of ecosystems, ecology is a wild card that seems to have no fixed place in the hierarchy of sciences and can fit into all levels from the physical world to human culture. Perhaps this unruly quality of ecology is revelatory of something about the nature of nature and our place in it.

Including ecology in the science–religion dialogue has some important theological implications. Ecology would require asking how divine action might be present in the web of ecological relationships that sustain life. It would encourage greater emphasis on God as sustainer, for it is through the functioning of ecosystems that all life, including our own, is sustained. Creation and redemption, too, take on new meaning in the context of the ecosystem, for it is there that God continually creates and re-creates the world. It is through the processes of decay and decomposition that God's redemptive action continually brings life from death. Understanding God's action in this way makes serious ethical demands on us, for by fitting our actions to the land we inhabit and working cooperatively and creatively within ecological processes we are, in effect, responding to divine action.

Crossing Boundaries: Science and Ethics

What we have been looking at are what James M. Gustafson calls 'intersections' between disciplines – in this case theology, ethics, science, and the study of technology. Gustafson provides a useful way of thinking about these intersections by identifying a number of themes in the relationship between theological ethics and other disciplines, themes that also typify the traffic between philosophical ethics and other disciplines.[35] Five of these themes seem particularly relevant to environmental ethics. First, ethics can be independent of other disciplines, which do not affect the content of theological or philosophical ethics. Second, other disciplines can provide resources for the revision of ethics. This theme is best represented in the secular sphere; Leopold's land ethic is significantly shaped by ecology, as is Rolston's pluralistic environmental ethics. A third theme is that theological ethics can provide a larger religious narrative within which descriptions and explanations from other disciplines are 'redescribed, reexplained, and reinterpreted in religious and moral terms, and even in quite direct theological terms.'[36] Setting both evolution and ecology into a larger framework of meaning as the venue of God's action would fall within this theme. Fourth, Christian ethical principles are applied to situations described by other disciplines. The application of human and environmental values drawn from the Christian tradition to situations described by the natural and social sciences, as frequently occurs in Barbour's work, is an example. Fifth, theological ethics can challenge the descriptions and explanations of other disciplines. As Gustafson points out, examples of this can be found in work on ethics and economics, in which economic assumptions are questioned.

There are some interesting parallels between these themes and Barbour's four-part typology for the relationship of science and religion. What would different understandings of the relationship of science and ethics look like if we were to view them in terms of integration, dialogue, independence, and conflict? One caveat needs to be made. The relationship of science and ethics when considering environmental problems and policies is more complex than that of science and theology, for environmental issues almost always involve disputes between scientists themselves. Certainty about the facts is rare; thus the question of whether to err on the side of precaution or on the side of innovation is always present and is never soluble in purely scientific terms. The dialogue between science and theology, on the other hand, has tended to focus on well-established scientific theories – although it, too, cannot avoid involvement in scientific conflicts.

Conflict

Conflict between ethics and science, like conflict between religion and science, can take two forms. First, scientific materialism and reductionism allow little, if any, role for ethics. Issues concerning the environment and the development and use of new technologies such as genetic engineering are considered scientific questions. Science is objective and establishes the facts of the matter, while ethics is subjective and capable of multiple interpretations and conclusions. Religion and ethics should not be allowed to interfere with the development of science and technology, for the way to increase human well-being is through unfettered scientific and technological progress. If ethics has a role to play, it comes at the end of the process and applies only to the *uses* of science and technology, not to their development.[37]

Conflict between ethics and science can also have a religious or philosophical basis. There are those who have rejected genetic engineering on the grounds that it is 'playing God.' Thomas Berry rejects genetic engineering on the grounds that 'to enter into the genetic structure of any being is to enter into its most sacred and most intimate reality.'[38]

Independence: Differing Languages and Functions

The most common approach in environmental ethics involves extending established systems of human ethics to the natural world as described by science. This is effectively a 'differing language and functions' approach. Science may help us to understand environmental problems and their possible consequences for humanity and nonhuman nature; its role is descriptive or diagnostic. But the ethic that is applied is one that has been developed entirely in the context of human society. Thus science and ethics play different roles. Science provides the description; ethics provides the norms. This category is similar to the first and fourth of Gustafson's themes (see above). Much of Barbour's discussion of ethics is within this category.

Respect for sentient animals is another two-language approach. In Peter Singer's ethic of animal liberation, hedonistic utilitarian ethics is extended to other species that have the capacity to suffer.[39] Tom Regan's animal rights ethic is based on the assertion that animals, like humans, can be the subjects of a life and thus have rights.[40] Science does not shape the resulting ethic, although biology may help to determine what organisms meet the requirement for being of moral concern.

Dialogue

In environmental ethics, dialogue often takes the form of conceptual parallels. Ecological worldviews emphasize interconnection and interrelation in both human and biotic communities. Diversity is of value in both the natural world and the human social world. Deep Ecology is a notable example of a school of thought that draws on such parallels.

Another form of dialogue occurs when a philosophical or theological commitment is combined with concepts from science. J. Baird Callicott provides an example when he combines viewing the ecosystem as the center of value in terms of which the value of species and organisms is assessed with a set of philosophical commitments to ethical monism and the subjectivity of values.[41] These philosophical commitments are not revised in light of science, but are combined with values shaped by science to form a distinctively new ethic.

Integration

For Leopold and Rolston, environmental values arise with ecological knowledge; science informs and shapes the resulting ethic. It is not simply a human ethic extended to nature, contrary to what Leopold claims.[42] Nor, on the other hand, is it a monolithic ethic that subsumes human values into natural values. Leopold recognizes the legitimacy of human-made changes, as long as they maintain the health of the land. Relationships between people and the land must be ones of 'mutual and interdependent cooperation.'[43] The goal is a cooperative community of plants, animals, soil, and humans.[44]

Theological ethicists have tended to be much more reluctant to move beyond traditional sources of ethics. This is reflected in Barbour's discussion of human and environmental values in which he minimizes the role of science in ethics. Theology has been more willing to revise doctrines in light of science, resulting in a reinterpretation of creation as continuing creation and theological anthropology to include the concept of humans as co-creators. What theological ethicists must do is explore the ethical implications of these new theological insights, especially for environmental ethics.

Science and Ethics in Process Thought

Where in this typology does process thought fall? In the science and theology typology, process theology falls in the integration category. It does not seem to do so in the science and ethics typology. When process ethics structures its ethics on the intrinsic value of the experience, it moves away from its ecological view of beings as internally related to others and of reality as profoundly relational. Barbour cites John Cobb's affirmation that 'every integrated being ... is a center of experience, which is the only *intrinsic good*.'[45] This view of intrinsic value leads process ethics toward an individualistic ethic in which the intrinsic value of individuals is based on the capacity to experience, resulting in a hierarchy of intrinsic values. It is difficult to see what role relationships play in this ethic. Relationships, including that system of interrelationships we call the ecosystem, are of instrumental value as they support the lives of intrinsically valuable individuals. As such, process environmental ethics seems to have more in common with the two-language approach in the independence type than with either dialogue or integration.

Agriculture

In *Ethics in an Age of Technology*, Barbour provides an excellent overview of agriculture in both the West and in the Third World. His primary ethical concern is for hunger, a concern he justifies on three grounds: the basis of the right of persons to the basic necessities of life, the Rawlsian principle of justice in which inequalities are justifiable only if they benefit the least well-off, and the teachings in Judaism and Christianity that mandate feeding the hungry and eliminating the causes of hunger.[46] In the United States and Western Europe, he finds that social justice 'requires that economic efficiency and agricultural productivity be taken seriously for the sake of low food prices for consumers, especially the urban poor.'[47] In the Third World, social inequality, substitution of export crops in place of crops for local consumption, and displacement of food crops by feed crops for animals are major causes of rural poverty and hunger. In this setting Barbour favors more small farms.

In both the West and the Third World, he insists, agriculture must be sustainable. Environmental degradation caused by agriculture is a constraint on production. He provides an overview of alternative techniques that reduce or eliminate environmental damage, such as crop rotation, integrated pest management, and alternative tilling procedures. The ethical grounds for sustainable agriculture include duties to future generations, good stewardship, and animal welfare.

However, the question of what sustainability in agriculture means is a complex one that has received voluminous attention. Is sustainable agriculture simply a set of techniques for conserving natural resources, or does it involve a fundamental change in the meanings of agriculture? Can sustainability simply be an add-on to research programs aimed at increased agricultural productivity, or does it involve a fundamentally different view of nature and the human place in it? Can problems be solved separately through the development of technological solutions, or must they be solved systematically? Under these questions lurk fundamental attitudes toward technology. As Barbour points out, technological optimists tend to view problems in isolation from each other while pessimists see them as interrelated.

Many proponents of sustainable agriculture and many of its practitioners view the solution to agricultural problems as requiring systematic changes at all levels of the food system.[48] Furthermore, their goal is not simply to ameliorate the adverse environmental impacts of industrial agriculture, but to enter into a symbiotic relationship with the land, in which production is only one goal. Models for this relationship come from the land itself; as Wendell Berry states, it is necessary 'to consult the genius of the place.' For Berry, the relationship is like a conversation in which we must attend to the responses the land makes to our actions.[49] Of necessity this type of agriculture is place-oriented; techniques that work in one place may not work in another. The relationship of science and ethics in this view of sustainable agriculture is one of integration. Sciences, including ecology, conservation biology, and agroecology, provide an understanding of the land and what is required by it, an understanding that has an ethical dimension. Responsibility is not simply for the land, but to the land. It is significant that Leopold wrote 'The Land Ethic' for farmers, owners of wood lots, and game managers, not for protectors of wilderness.[50]

The view of nature in this understanding of sustainable agriculture is remarkably similar to Barbour's view of nature as a community of interdependent parts. What is frustrating is that Barbour does not explore the ethical implications of this for issues in agriculture. While Barbour's discussion of agriculture is clear, accurate, and insightful, one wishes for a more developed and audacious ethic that includes a broader range of values in nature as well as human values. Instead, Barbour's discussion seems limited to the independence of science and ethics category. The sciences, natural and social, provide an analysis of the problem, but the ethical principles called upon are separate from and unaffected by the sciences. Replying to a critique by Robert Stivers, Barbour states that process thought takes a middle ground between the holism of ecosystem ethics and the individualism of animal rights. 'Process thought portrays the interrelatedness of all entities (each constituted by its relationships), but it is pluralistic in distinguishing a variety of centers of experience, each valuable to itself, to other entities, and to God.'[51] Yet, it is difficult to see how ecological interrelatedness plays a role in his ethical analysis of contemporary agriculture.

Conclusion

In the end, I think my main critique is that *Ethics in an Age of Technology* leaves a lot of loose ends, and my essay has attempted to tease out a number of these. But this, for me, is actually part of Barbour's genius. I find myself working to knit the loose ends together into new patterns. I can do this because of the careful and orderly way Barbour has organized a vast body of scholarly material. I have been given a rich resource to inform and stimulate my own thinking, without which I would be overwhelmed by the vastness of the task. He has ordered the tangled skeins. To a great extent, the loose ends are the result of Barbour's meticulously honest and accurate treatment of the ideas of others; he never overgeneralizes or sets up straw men. He prefers to live with tension and ambiguity when values cannot be reconciled rather than creating a solution by discounting one side or the other. He imposes no easy order. Rather, his work empowers us to enter into these tensions and ambiguities to seek new and better answers.

Notes

1. I.G. Barbour, *Religion and Science: Historical and Contemporary Issues* (San Francisco: HarperSanFrancisco, 1997), 101.
2. Idem, *Technology, Environment, and Human Values* (Westport CT: Praeger, 1980).
3. Idem, *Science and Secularity: The Ethics of Technology* (New York: Harper & Row, 1970).
4. I.G. Barbour (ed.), *Earth Might Be Fair: Reflections on Ethics, Religion and Ecology* (Englewood Cliffs, NJ: Prentice Hall, 1972); I.G. Barbour (ed.), *Western Man and Environmental Ethics* (Reading, MA: Addison-Wesley, 1973).
5. I.G. Barbour (ed.), *Finite Resources and the Human Future* (Minneapolis: Augsburg Press, 1976).
6. I.G. Barbour et al., *Energy and American Values* (New York: Praeger, 1982).
7. Barbour describes this apologetic approach in his discussion of nature in historical Christianity and contemporary theology, *Ethics in an Age of Technology* (San Francisco: Harper Collins, 1993), 74–8 (*Ethics* hereafter).
8. A notable exception is work relating environmental theology and ethics to economics, such as that of John B. Cobb, Jr. See, for example, John B. Cobb, Jr, *Sustaining the Common Good: A Christian Perspective on the Global Economy* (Cleveland: Pilgrim Press, 1994) and Herman Daly and John B. Cobb, Jr, *For the Common Good* (Boston: Beacon Press, 1989).
9. Barbour, *Ethics*, 3.
10. Ibid., 4.
11. See, for example, Roger L. Shinn, *Forced Options* (Cleveland: Pilgrim Press, 1991).
12. Barbour, *Ethics*, 44.
13. Ibid., 64–9.
14. Ibid., 70–71.

15. Ibid., 72.
16. Ibid., 63 (emphasis original).
17. Clare Palmer, *Environmental Ethics and Process Thinking* (Oxford: Clarendon Press, 1998), 155–63.
18. Barbour, *Ethics*, 60.
19. I.G. Barbour, *Issues in Science and Religion*, edn (New York: Harper Torchbooks, 1971), 413.
20. Barbour, *Ethics*, 63.
21. Ibid., 61–2.
22. See, for example, Leopold's classic essay 'Thinking Like a Mountain' in *A Sand County Almanac* (New York: Oxford University Press, 1949), 129–33.
23. Holmes Rolston III, *Environmental Ethics: Duties to and Values in the Natural World* (Philadelphia: Temple University, 1988), 216.
24. Aldo Leopold, 'A Biotic View of Land', in Susan Flader and J. Baird Callicott (eds), *River of Mother of God* (Madison: University of Wisconsin, 1991), 267.
25. There is a similarity between Rolston's systemic value and H. Richard Niebuhr's concept of relational value. See Judith N. Scoville, 'Value Theory and Ecology in Environmental Ethics: A Comparison of Rolston and Niebuhr', *Environmental Ethics*, 17:2 (Summer 1995), 115–33; and Judith N. Scoville, 'Fitting Ethics to the Land: H. Richard Niebuhr's Ethic of Responsibility and Ecotheology', *Journal of Religious Ethics*, 30:2 (Summer 2002), 207–29.
26. I.G. Barbour, *Religion and Science: Historical and Contemporary Issues* (San Francisco: HarperSanFrancisco, 1997), 281–4.
27. Barbour, *Technology, Environment, and Human Values*, 15–16.
28. Ibid., 16–17.
29. Barbour, *Religion in an Age of Science*, 230–37.
30. Vine DeLoria, Jr, *God is Red* (Golden, CO: North American Press, 1992), ch. 4, esp. 71.
31. Arthur Peacocke, *Theology for a Scientific Age: Being and Becoming – Natural, Divine, Human* (Minneapolis: Fortress Press, 1993), 217.
32. R.V. O'Neill et al., *A Hierarchical Concept of Ecosystems* (Princeton: Princeton University, 1986).
33. Ibid., 63.
34. For an insightful discussion of the relation of human economies and the economy of nature, see Wendell Berry, 'Two Economies', in *Home Economics* (San Francisco: North Point Press, 1987), 54–75.
35. James M Gustafson, *Intersections: Science, Theology, and Ethics* (Cleveland: Pilgrim, 1996). My numbering in the following discussion is somewhat different from Gustafson's.
36. Ibid., 139.
37. For a discussion of science and ethics that expresses this view, see Klaus Leisinger, 'The Ethical Challenges of Green Biotechnology for Developing Countries', International Conference of Biotechnology, CGIAR-National Academy of Sciences, The World Bank, Washington, DC, October 21–22, 1999. Accessed at http://www.foundation.novartis.com/green-biotechnology.htm on April 27, 2001.
38. Quoted in Richard M. Clugston, 'The Ethics of Genetic Engineering', *Earth Ethics*, 6:1 (Fall 1994), 3.
39. Peter Singer, *Animal Liberation* (New York: Avon Books, 1977).
40. Tom Regan, *The Case for Animal Rights* (Berkeley: University of California Press, 1983).
41. J. Baird Callicott, *In Defense of the Land Ethic: Essays in Environmental Philosophy* (Albany: State University of New York Press, 1989).
42. Leopold, *Sand County Almanac*, 202–3.
43. A. Leopold, 'The Farmer as a Conservationist', in Flader and Callicott, *River of Mother of God*, 183.
44. Ibid., 188.
45. Barbour, *Ethics*, 71 (emphasis original).
46. Ibid., 110–12.

47. Ibid., 96.
48. Holistic management is an example of this systemic approach. See Allan Savory, *Holistic Management* (Washington, DC: Island Press, 1999).
49. Wendell Berry, 'Nature as Measure', in his *What are People For?* (San Francisco: North Point Press, 1990), 208–9.
50. Aldo Leopold, 'The Land Ethic', *Sand County Almanac*, 201–26.
51. I.G. Barbour, 'Response to Critiques of *Ethics in an Age of Technology*', *Zygon*, 31:1 (March 1996), 106–7.

Chapter 14

Environmental Ethics and the Science–Religion Debate: A British Perspective on Barbour

Christopher Southgate

Lord's Cricket Ground, St John's Wood, London N.W.6 may seem an odd place to start a tribute to a scholar based at Carleton College, Minnesota. But it was an involved and intense conversation while watching Oxford play Cambridge at Lord's in 1991 – with my then colleague the New Testament scholar Richard Burridge – which led to the idea that I use my background in experimental science to offer a university course on the science–religion debate.

The first book on my hastily assembled reading list was T.S. Kuhn's *The Structure of Scientific Revolutions*,[1] which like so many before me I found a compelling but contentious read. Kuhn described a grand narrative of scientific change very different from the experience of most scientists. He made ingenious use of certain striking examples, but I soon became aware that a different choice of examples would have led to a different and much more complex conclusion.

The second book on my list was Ian Barbour's *Religion in an Age of Science*,[2] the recently published first volume of his Gifford Lectures. Here I found a sensitive and judicious account of Kuhn's vaunted paradigms, as applied both in science and religion. More – and I could hardly believe my luck – here was also, in effect, a complete plan for a course of the sort I was about to offer, beautifully structured and laid out, and comprehensively referenced. (The relative lack of historical treatment in this book Barbour remedied later by revising elements of *Issues in Science and Religion* and fusing them with an update of the Giffords, the fusion being published as *Religion and Science*.[3] Like *Religion in an Age of Science*, this has been an excellent resource for students, a place where they could always find their bearings when the complexities of interdisciplinary study got the better of them.)

I shall return later to those texts, and Barbour's relation to the two British scientist-theologians with whom his name is most often linked, Arthur Peacocke and John Polkinghorne. But I begin by considering the line of investigation pursued by the second volume of the Giffords, published in 1992 as *Ethics in an Age of Technology*.[4] Like Barbour's work on the science–religion relationship this represented a strand of thinking stemming back over twenty years.[5] In 1970 Barbour had published *Science and Secularity: The Ethics of Technology*.[6] There his thinking about models in science and religion is directly applied to his understanding of the application of technology in the natural world. The book has a fine period ring to it now – Barbour quotes for example an advertisement in the *New York Times Magazine* for March 1, 1970, as follows:

And so it came to pass that nature made cotton. And it was good. But then it came to pass that man improved nature's cotton. And it was better.

It had more luster, more strength, and more richness of color. And it was called *Durene* mercerized cotton. And so, at last, man rested.

Helen Davis of *Carillon Fashions*, however, decided that instead of resting she'd make this elegant dress with double-breasted jacket ...

And it was very good.

It is the blithe optimism, as well as the naive drafting, of such an advertisement that strikes the twenty-first century reader so forcibly. That was still an era in which appeal can confidently be made to the improvement of nature. A strange paradox of our present situation is that our power to alter nature, especially through the use of the new genetic technologies, is now vastly greater than in 1970,[7] yet the rhetoric we tend to use is very different.[8] Not even at Monsanto.com do I find a claim that biotechnology is an improvement of nature.[9]

This was also the era of first publication of Lynn White Jr's seminal (though since much criticized) article on the 'ecologic crisis', in which White called Christianity 'the most anthropocentric religion the world has seen'[10] and alleged that it is the combination of Western Christianity with technology that has proved so devastating in its environmental effects. Indeed Barbour was content at that stage to endorse White's point, and to say that exploitative attitudes that lead to environmental deterioration are 'in part a by-product of the Christian tradition'.[11]

In 1972 Barbour edited *Earth Might Be Fair: Reflections on Ethics, Religion and Ecology*.[12] In his own chapter in this volume he comes, in effect, to the same conclusion as had the Norwegian philosopher Arne Naess in a much-cited essay of that same year. Barbour writes that:

> ecological concern will be short-lived and ineffectual unless it deals with the values and social institutions that have led to this ravaging of the environment. The basic disease is man's exploitative attitude towards both nature and his fellow man. If we treat a succession of symptoms – seeking technical remedies for one form of pollution after another – the task will be endless.[13]

Conservationists, Barbour notes, 'have usually assumed no fundamental changes are needed in society ... they have seldom been involved in the struggle for social justice.'[14] It was this 'shallow-ecological' thinking that Naess also condemned, but Barbour's analysis is less radical and more workable than the Norwegian's. Barbour's process ethic allows him to value different species differently, and protects him both from the extremism of Naess's 'deep-ecological' proposal, with its insistence on a 'biospherical egalitarianism' that holds all species equal – and from over-commitment to systemic values that denigrate the status of the individual.[15]

There is a passionate quality, a strength of exhortation, in these environmental writings of Barbour's, rather different from the tone of his other work. He sees clearly that the dispossessed have often benefited least from the effects of new technology, and that American society in particular, dominated as it has been by the 'masculine' aspirations of achievement, mastery, efficiency, progress, and success, needs to hear God's call to 'a more authentic human existence, not to affluence'.[16]

Barbour ends his 1972 essay by writing of the explosion in world population. He warns – and one senses the reluctance – that in the face of this crisis 'a society may well have to qualify individual freedom'.[17] We know now that the population in 2020 will probably be substantially less than was feared in 1972 (not least because the Government of China has so effectively 'qualified' individual freedom), but the threats posed by shortage of basic resources such as topsoil and fresh water are if anything even greater.[18] Barbour's fervent but compassionate tone of warning speaks to us from a time when there was greater hope that these issues would really be addressed. It was the time before what I believe will be seen in the future as the last great smash-and-grab raid on the Earth – the era inaugurated by the election of Ronald Reagan in the United States and Margaret Thatcher in the UK, an era in which environmental protection has tended to be sidelined in the zeal for economic growth. Any commentator writing at the end of the 1970s, and reviewing the rising trajectory of environmental concern and protection in the USA, would be astonished, I believe, to see where that graph has arrived at in 2002.[19]

In 1973 we find Barbour editing a further collection of essays on environmental issues, *Western Man and Environmental Ethics: Attitudes towards Nature and Technology*.[20] Here we find him proposing two principles that must underpin an environmental ethic – ecological wisdom, a concept now being recycled and developed by the British scholar Celia Deane-Drummond – and social justice.[21] Barbour's linking of these two concepts, and his recognition of the tension between them, foreshadows much later debate.

Importantly too, this collection offers Lynn White a chance to respond to his critics. And there is a fascinating clash evident here. Barbour makes much use in this period of the image of 'spaceship Earth.' This of course draws on the photographs taken by the Apollo missions, and on the personal testimony of those astronauts, on the strength of their reaction to seeing our planetary home from space. Barbour writes, 'The image of the earth as a spaceship symbolizes both our finite resources and our global interdependence. On this frail planet we travel together to a common destiny.'[22] From the vantage point of 2002 it is possible to see just what a modernist image 'spaceship Earth' is, with its connotations of a designed machine, human-piloted, making progress towards some destination. Even in 1973 White could write of this metaphor as 'ecologically terrifying – the final sophistication of this disastrous man-centred view of the nature of things and the things of nature … it has the present allurement of seeming to offer ecologic solutions without sacrifice of the old presuppositions.'[23] Typically Barbour takes the point, without giving up his own – in 1980 he writes of spaceship Earth:

> This is a striking image that forcefully represents the importance of life support and co-operation for human survival. But we must extend the spaceship image if it is not to mislead us. A spaceship is a mechanical man-made environment, devoid of life except for human beings. *Planet earth*, however, is enveloped in a marvellous web of life, a natural environment of which humanity is a part and on which it is dependent … Let us keep before us the image of the spinning globe, but let us imagine its natural environments and its social order. It is still possible to achieve a more just, participatory, and sustainable society on planet earth.[24]

It is intriguing to note the way the spaceship image has since been largely superseded by Gaia-language, by the notion of the Earth as a living organism.[25] This has caught at something deep in the contemporary imagination, to the extent that in 1989 'Gaia' was nominated by *People* magazine as one of the 25 most intriguing characters of the year.[26] And James Lovelock, progenitor of the Gaia Hypothesis, writes:

> Gaia, as I see her, is no doting mother tolerant of misdemeanors, nor is she some fragile and delicate damsel in danger from brutal mankind. She is stern and tough, always keeping the world warm and comfortable for those who obey the rules, but ruthless in her destruction of those who transgress.[27]

A very different trope to that of the spaceship, if no less terrifying.

In 1980 Barbour published *Technology, Environment, and Human Values*.[28] Here he joins the endless debate about stewardship, and shores up the concept with a process-based system of valuing the natural world. As noted above, this scheme enables him to justify valuing more complex organisms and systems more highly than simpler forms of life. To a British ecological theologian there is a poignancy to reading this 1980 book in particular. Barbour writes of the success of the environmental movement in the early 1970s, for example, in securing the banning of DDT in the USA, and in reversing the Nixon administration's decision to approve the manufacture of the 'Supersonic Transport,' the American rival to Concorde. He notes the way that eloquent ecological writing (such as that of Rachel Carson), broader scientific debate (not confined to federally-funded panels meeting in secret), and widespread public concern combined to overcome vested interests (despite those interests' powerful representation at congressional level). He notes too that these protests were also fuelled by an atmosphere of 'domestic discord' and suspicion of the activities of big government consequent on the Vietnam War.

As I write this President George W. Bush has just published his own somewhat derisory proposals on climate change, following the emphatic US rejection of the Accords reached at Kyoto. I would be the last to wish domestic discord on the USA, a country where I have lived happily in the past, and where I have many friends. But I cannot help reflecting that one consequence of the terrible tragedy that was the terrorist attack on New York and Washington of September 11, 2001 is that criticism of this US administration became (very understandably) profoundly muted, and the popular will to challenge its thinking on matters such as global warming seems weak. From a British, indeed from a European, perspective, this can only be an alarming development within an increasingly alarming world.[29]

I revert now to more formally academic considerations. It is both interesting and important that Barbour's thinking has continued to involve these parallel strands, environmentalism and the science–religion relationship. As I have remarked elsewhere,[30] there is all too often a needless and unhelpful polarization between, on the one hand, the way theology is done in dialogue with the physical sciences, and, on the other, what might be termed ecological theology. The former has largely, over the last 40 years, been constructed by certain key thinkers – Barbour much to the fore – whose background has been in the physical sciences, and who have placed a strong emphasis on a critical-realist approach to epistemology – relating the enterprise of theology both in content and in method as closely as possible to a realist view of the practice of science. There has been in this movement a profound skepticism of postmodernity as antithetical to the way scientists themselves perceive science as operating.

In contrast, the debate within ecological theology has been shaped largely by thinkers trained originally in the humanities, theologians often with an agenda skeptical of the power-structures underpinning 'big science'.[31] It is a debate characterized by a great plurality of approaches – from the discarding of the Christian tradition as being incapable of offering a basis for positive ecological proposals, all the way to fairly conservative restatements of the potential of that tradition.

Differences in approach between 'green' theology and theology which principally aims at conversation with physical science partly reflect the nature of different disciplines. The dismissal of grand narratives comes much more easily to some branches of theology than to others. The science–religion debate has constantly to engage with the sheer brute fact of the success of the sciences – in progressively describing in greater and greater depth the apparent character of the world, and in enabling technologists to design more and more intricate devices with which to interact with it. Reflection on ecosystems and modern human impact upon them has rather to reckon with a *failure* – human culture has seemed to develop in ways which are profoundly unsustainable and deeply damaging. The grand narratives of the West seem to have failed to give rise to understandings of nature that lead to sound ethical practice. So it is not surprising that much writing in ecological theology attempts a radical reframing of our understanding of the relationship between the divine and the nonhuman world, and does so accepting that a plurality of such reframings will emerge.[32]

Looking back to the 1970s shows me that the divergence of the two theological movements has not always been so marked – there is, for instance, evident ecological concern, sensitively and thoughtfully marshaled, in Peacocke's 1978 Bampton Lectures,[33] but Peacocke has developed this line of thinking little since then. It is a sad reflection of the way the modern academic process too often operates that such breadth of interest tends to be milled out by the specialization of conferences and journals, and by the volume of the literature in any one area, so that even scholars working across subject areas tend through sheer necessity to be confined to one field, one conversation. Even groups working in related areas of theology (which should be the most integrated and integrating of all disciplines) do not communicate as they should.

Barbour has been criticized for not making clearer links between his two areas of concern (for instance, between the two volumes of his Giffords[34]), and there is some justice to this criticism. However, his resolute insistence (and that of the other major figure to have retained a concern for both areas, Holmes Rolston III) as to the importance of science as a basis for environmental understanding is in refreshing contrast to some ecotheologizing.[35] It is vital that the science of ecosystems is taken seriously, both as outlining the parameters of our current crisis,[36] and in offering us opportunities to use our God-given ingenuity to alter the impact of our technology. (Not that Barbour is unrealistic about the complexities of the role played by technical experts – as witness a revealing section in *Technology, Environment, and Human Values* indicating the way the impact of 'insider' scientists has often been muted when their advice ran contrary to administration policy.[37])

I return now to Barbour's other main concern, the relationship between science and religion as it has been characterized through reflection on the physical sciences and on the *loci classici* of the Galileo Affair and the Darwinian controversies. Rereading *Myths, Models, and Paradigms,*[38] which Barbour researched in Cambridge on Fulbright and Guggenheim Fellowships, I am much struck by his evident zest for such thorny areas as the nature of metaphor. He embraces such debates with a breadth of enthusiasm which marks him out as the most philosophical of the trio in which he is often placed – the one that groups him with Arthur Peacocke and John Polkinghorne. The work of these two scientist-priests has surely been the major British contribution to the science–religion debate in recent years. And Ian Barbour's influence looks to have been very important to them. It encouraged them to look to the hope of a consonance of methodologies between science and religion, based on critical realism. Philosophically problematic though this may be, it has been profoundly catalytic of conversations between theologians and scientists ever since *Issues in Science and Religion* first appeared in 1966.

Peacocke's work is marked by the care with which he has formulated his theology, especially in the area of the debate on divine action, where Polkinghorne's more ambitious proposals, more generative of debate, have endured less well. Polkinghorne is of course the most distinguished of the three scientifically, and by his own confession his instincts are resolutely those of a 'bottom-up thinker'.[39] He is a critical realist to the core, a man endlessly challenged and fascinated by science's encounter with the diamond-hard edge of reality, and like Peacocke he wants to press the question that Barbour first brought to prominence: does not theology interrogate reality in a related way? Can critical realism not be seen to underpin method in both subjects? Peacocke's own review of *Myths, Models, and Paradigms* notes 'just how revolutionary the steady application of such a method might be'.[40] Peacocke saw clearly that a sense that theological and scientific communities might share an underlying epistemology would be very generative of conversation between theologians and working scientists, in particular because the latter tend to be realists at heart. He elaborates this in the Bampton Lectures to which I have already referred, and it is interesting to see how well his early writing, like Barbour's, still reads today.

Critical realism has had a long ride, and has had to be more and more carefully nuanced in the face of its critics. Its strength has also been its weakness; it has been a tempting basis for interdisciplinary conversation, but at the expense of philosophical precision. Roger Trigg has attacked critical realism as 'a vague umbrella concept that can encompass Polkinghorne's belief that our experience in both scientific and religious contexts is broadly reliable, and Barbour's more sceptical position that we are actually in the business of constructing models'.[41] Trigg makes an important point as to the spectrum that critical realism represents. Too many participants in the debate have been unwilling to recognize what Ian Barbour saw long ago – that the cautious end of the spectrum is not as distinct from competing epistemologies as is often claimed, that 'a reformulated instrumentalism which acknowledges an enduring and significant role for models, and which remains open and non-committal concerning their ontological status, is very close to critical realism'.[42] Equally, I would want to say, a reformulated critical realism, which acknowledges an enduring and significant role for coherence-testing, rather than holding out any hope of testing the correspondence to truth of any one statement, and which cannot be committed in any strong way to the ontological status of models, is very close to instrumentalism, indeed to pragmatism. (A more developed analysis of this issue is found in Niels Gregersen's chapter in this volume.)

I have not adverted so far to Barbour's famous typology of the relations between science and religion. This is the one aspect of his writings that I have found progressively less useful as time has gone on. I indicated some of the problems in the introduction to the textbook I edited in this area, a book which in many other ways draws great inspiration from Barbour.[43] Tempting as it is to define the science–religion relationship through a neat classification, such a scheme is a philosopher's stone fated always to elude us. That has been well demonstrated through the other great contribution made by British scholars to the recent science–religion debate – that of historians of science. John Brooke and Geoffrey Cantor come especially to mind. As Brooke has emphasized, the relations between the different sciences and different theological systems are disparate, and vary through time.[44] Even words like 'conflict' acquire different connotations as they are applied in different contexts.[45] Barbour determinedly retains his typological framework, but this retention tends to disguise the complexity of the matrix of relationships involved.[46] He has recently mounted a stout defence of his approach,[47] and I have to agree with him that a good typology offers a very useful introductory guide, a starting point for exploration. It thus has considerable pedagogic value. The problem as I perceive it has been that the sheer extent of the influence of Barbour's work has given the impression that his schemes are more than this – that they constitute the real map of the subject, rather than being mere introductions. For helpful further analysis, and an insight into why these typologies might have been so attractive to Barbour, see Christian Berg's essay in this volume (Chapter 3).

Barbour's emphasis on the potential of process theology to deliver an appropriate relation to the sciences and to generate a fruitful environmental ethic is one that appears strange to most British readers (though every time I teach on this area I 'make' a few converts to process thought). Again, it is to Barbour's credit that one can learn so much from him without having to espouse a process scheme. One or two distinguished British thinkers do work in process theology – I think particularly of David Pailin and his important book *God and the Processes of Reality*,[48] but there is no evidence of any great mutual influence between Pailin and Barbour. Nor would one expect Barbour's thought to have touched the work of T.F. Torrance, coming as that does very much out of a Barthian perspective.

Nancey Murphy has written of Barbour's style of scholarship as 'irenic' and 'encyclopedic',[49] and hence of the difficulty in finding points at which to take issue with him. Polkinghorne too has written: 'It is characteristic of Barbour's method that he prefaces each discussion with a careful and fair-minded survey of the views of others.'[50] It is this generosity of mind of Barbour's, always mapping out the territory with conspicuous fairness, that continues to be a great gift to the explorer. So his is the ideal introductory essay to the book on creation and kenosis recently edited by Polkinghorne.[51] Barbour does not believe in kenosis, in the usual sense of a voluntary self-limitation by the divine, but he maps out the ground. He once published a paper entitled 'Five Ways of Reading Teilhard'.[52] In the proceedings of the CTNS/Vatican Observatory Conference of 1996 we find him again offering five ways, this time to consider the relation of God to evolution.[53] He lays out possibilities, and invites his hearers and his readers to share his thinking; he empowers them to evaluate it.

For that gift of mapping the terrain, for his philosophical skill which did so much both to ground the science–religion conversation and to give it a wider audience, and for his breadth of interest, which has kept ecological concern alongside debates with metaphysics and with quantum theory, for all this we owe Ian Barbour a great debt, which it is a privilege to be able to acknowledge here.

Notes

1. Thomas S. Kuhn, *The Structure of Scientific Revolutions*. 2nd enlarged edn (Chicago: University of Chicago Press, 1970; first published 1962).
2. Ian G. Barbour, *Religion in an Age of Science: The Gifford Lectures 1989–1991, Vol. 1* (London: SCM Press, 1990).
3. I.G. Barbour, *Religion and Science: Historical and Contemporary Issues* (San Francisco: HarperSanFrancisco, 1997).
4. I.G. Barbour, *Ethics in an Age of Technology: The Gifford Lectures 1989–1991, Vol. 2* (London: SCM Press, 1993).
5. Indeed, as Roger Shinn notes, it may be that a sensitivity to the impermanence and vulnerability of Western society goes back to Barbour's early upbringing in China. Roger Shinn, 'Exploratory Ethics', *Zygon*, 31:1 (1996), 67–74, see p. 74.
6. I. G. Barbour, *Science and Secularity: The Ethics of Technology* (New York, Evanston and London: Harper & Row, 1970).
7. It is interesting to note the extent to which Barbour anticipates these in his 1970 book. See, for example, Barbour, *Science and Secularity*, 84–5.
8. There is a telling question mark in the title of Michael J. Reiss and Roger Straughan's *Improving Nature?: The Science and Ethics of Genetic Engineering* (Cambridge: Cambridge University Press, 2001; first published 1996). Perhaps the only modern author to insist on humans' improving, indeed redeeming, nature has been Ronald Cole-Turner in *The New Genesis: Theology and the Genetic Revolution* (Louisville, KY: Westminster/John Knox Press, 1993), esp. ch. 5.
9. Though I do find a very 'bullish' affirmation of the new biotechnologies which has attracted a lot of suspicion in Europe. Indeed an important element in 'the British perspective' in environmental matters is the contrast between attitudes to GM crops here and in the USA. See the papers by Celia Deane-Drummond et al. and myself in *ReOrdering Nature: Theology Society and the New Genetics*, ed. by Celia Deane-Drummond and Bronislaw Szerszynski with Robin Grove-White (Edinburgh: T.&T. Clark, 2003), also George Gaskell, Martin W. Bauer, John Durant, and Nicholas C. Allum, 'Worlds Apart? The Reception of Genetically Modified Foods in Europe and the U.S.', *Science*, 285:5426 (1999), 384–7.
10. Lynn White, Jr, 'The Historic Roots of our Ecologic Crisis', *Science*, 155 (1967), 1203–7, quotation on p. 1205.
11. Barbour, *Science and Secularity*, 66. Later, however, Barbour deployed some of the many critical responses White's writing has evoked. See, for example, *Ethics in an Age of Technology*, 75–6.

12. I.G. Barbour (ed.), *Earth Might Be Fair: Reflections on Ethics, Religion and Ecology* (Englewood Cliffs, NJ: Prentice Hall, 1972).

13. I.G. Barbour, 'Attitudes Towards Nature and Technology', in Barbour (ed.), *Earth Might Be Fair*, 146. See also Arne Naess, 'The Shallow and the Deep, Long-Range Ecology Movement. A Summary', *Inquiry*, vol. 16 (1972), 95–100.

14. Barbour, 'Attitudes', 159–60.

15. As Don Marietta has noted, consideration of the value of systems as a whole should supplement, rather than supplant, concern for the system's components. Don E. Marietta, Jr, *For People and the Planet: Holism and Humanism in Environmental Ethics* (Philadelphia, PA: Temple University Press, 1994).

16. Barbour, 'Attitudes', 161.

17. Ibid., 165.

18. See, for example, Reg Morrison, *The Spirit in the Gene: Humanity's Proud Illusion and the Laws of Nature* (Ithaca, NY: Cornell University Press, 1999), 14–53.

19. Though Barbour already sees the clouds gathering when he writes in 1980: 'The later 1970s have seen a resurgence of neoconservatism and isolationism in the United States, with groups campaigning to get us out of the UN, and to spend more on weapons' (I.G. Barbour, *Technology, Environment, and Human Values* [New York: Praeger, 1980], 314). And later he, all too rightly as it has proved, has no illusions that the election as Vice-President of Senator Al Gore, the author of *Earth in the Balance: Forging a New Common Purpose* (London: Earthscan, 1992), will shift the momentum of US policy far in a 'green' direction. See I.G. Barbour, 'Response to Critiques of *Ethics in an Age of Technology*', *Zygon*, 31:1 (1996), 101–10, esp. p. 110.

20. I.G. Barbour (ed.) *Western Man and Environmental Ethics: Attitudes towards Nature and Technology* (Reading, MA: Addison-Wesley, 1973).

21. I.G. Barbour, 'Introduction' in *Western Man*, 1–16, esp. p. 11. See also Celia Deane-Drummond, *Creation through Wisdom: Theology and the New Biology* (Edinburgh: T.&T. Clark, 2000).

22. Barbour, 'Introduction', 16; see also 'Attitudes', 168.

23. Lynn White, Jr (1973) 'Continuing the Conversation', in Barbour (ed.) *Western Man*, 63–4.

24. Barbour, *Technology, Environment, and Human Values*, 316.

25. This concept can be found in a lecture given by René Dubos in 1969, even before James Lovelock's formulation of the Gaia Hypothesis gave it a (albeit questionable) scientific status (see René Dubos, 'A Theology of the Earth', in Barbour (ed.) *Western Man*, 43–54, esp. 43–4).

26. See Lawrence Osborn, 'Archetypes, Angels and Gaia', *Ecotheology*, 10 (2001), 9–22, for an original and thought-provoking theological 'spin' on Gaia.

27. James Lovelock, *The Ages of Gaia* (Oxford: Oxford University Press, 1988), 212.

28. I.G. Barbour, *Technology, Environment, and Human Values* (New York: Praeger, 1980).

29. The strength of feeling in this area in the UK may surprise some in the USA. The tone of the following, from the front page of a major British newspaper on the opening day of the 'Earth Summit' in Johannesburg in August 2002, is indicative: 'The slowest ship in the world's convoy of environmental awareness is American public opinion. The bloated, resource-hungry American voter is the greatest obstacle to global sustainability. It is the US that blocks Kyoto, which will not even consider taxing international aviation fuel, which refuses to pick up the tab for preserving habitats outside its borders' (*The Independent*, 26 August 2002, p. 1).

30. What follows is drawn largely from my editorial in *Ecotheology*, 10 (2001).

31. Michael McGonigle touches on very much the same perception. He lists ecological thought as one of the diversity of counter-movements against structures of alienation of oppression (to which modernity has given rise). He seeks a 'new naturalism … not administered by the prince or the physicist'. See Michael McGonigle, 'A New Naturalism: Is There a (Radical) Truth beyond the (Postmodern) Abyss?' *Ecotheology*, 8 (2000), 8–39. My contention is rather that the natural scientist should be recognized as an invaluable consultant in the search for a wisdom held by 'beings-in-community-in-nature.'

32. A good example is a book such as Sallie McFague's, *The Body of God* (London: SCM Press, 1993).

33. Arthur Peacocke, *Creation and the World of Science: The Bampton Lectures, 1978* (Oxford: The Clarendon Press, 1979), 294–318.

34. See, for example, Mary Gerhart, 'Thinking Toward a Future', *Zygon*, 31:1, (1996), 87–92. Barbour seemed to respond to this in *Religion and Science*, by inserting some material on nature-centred spirituality into his basic schema (Barbour, *Religion and Science*, 95–8), but the material still does not seem entirely successfully integrated.

35. For consideration of the range of paradigms in ecological writing, see Carolyn Merchant's *Radical Ecology: The Search for a Livable World* (London and New York: Routledge, 1992).

36. As Barbour has recently written: 'Only science can supply the data for evaluating threats to our environment arising from our technologies and our life-styles' (I.G. Barbour, *When Science Meets Religion* [San Francisco: HarperSanFrancisco, 2000], 29).

37. Barbour, *Technology, Environment, and Human Values*, 125f.

38. I. G. Barbour, *Myths, Models, and Paradigms: A Comparative Study in Science and Religion* (San Francisco: Harper & Row, 1974).

39. See John Polkinghorne, *Science and Christian Belief: Reflections of a Bottom-up Thinker* (London: SPCK, 1994).

40. Arthur Peacocke, 'Review of *Myths, Models, and Paradigms* by Ian G. Barbour', *Journal of Theological Studies*, 27:1 (1976), 264–6.

41. Roger Trigg, *Rationality and Religion* (Oxford: Basil Blackwell, 1998), 86.

42. Barbour, *Myths, Models, and Paradigms*, 41.

43. Christopher Southgate (ed.), *God, Humanity and the Cosmos: A Textbook in Science and Religion* (Edinburgh: T.&T. Clark and Harrisburg, PA: Trinity Press International, 1999). See ch.1 for a comment on typologies.

44. John H. Brooke, *Science and Religion: Some Historical Perspectives* (Cambridge: Cambridge University Press, 1991), 2. See also John H. Brooke and Geoffrey Cantor, *Reconstructing Nature: The Engagement of Science with Religion* (Edinburgh: T.&T. Clark, 1998).

45. Geoffrey Cantor and Chris Kenny, 'Barbour's Fourfold Way: Problems with his Taxonomy of Science–Religion Relationships', in *Zygon*, 36:4, (2001), 765–81. Also the comments of Ted Peters in his 'Science and Theology: Towards Consonance', in Ted Peters (ed.), *Science and Theology: The New Consonance* (Oxford and Boulder, CO: Westview Press, 1998), 11–39, esp. 35, n. 5.

46. See Willem B. Drees, *Religion, Science and Naturalism* (Cambridge: Cambridge University Press, 1996), 43n, 44–5.

47. See I.G. Barbour, 'On Typologies for Relating Science and Religion', *Zygon*, 37:2 (2002), 345–59.

48. David Pailin, *God and the Processes of Reality* (London: Routledge, 1989).

49. Nancey Murphy, 'Ian Barbour on Religion and the Methods of Science: An Assessment', *Zygon*, 31:1 (1996), 11–19, esp. 12–13.

50. John Polkinghorne, *Scientists as Theologians* (London: SPCK, 1996), 8.

51. I.G. Barbour, 'God's Power: A Process View', in *The Work of Love: Creation as Kenosis*, ed. by John Polkinghorne (Cambridge, UK, and Grand Rapids, MI: Eerdmans, and London: SPCK, 2001): 1–20.

52. I.G. Barbour, 'Five Ways of Reading Teilhard', *Soundings*, 51 (1968), 115–45.

53. I.G. Barbour, 'Five Models of God and Evolution', in *Evolutionary and Molecular Biology: Scientific Perspectives on Divine Action* ed. by R.J. Russell, William R. Stoeger SJ, and Francisco J. Ayala (Vatican City: Vatican Observatory and Berkeley, CA: Center for Theology and the Natural Sciences, 1998), 419–42.

IV

THEOLOGICAL PERSPECTIVES ON BARBOUR'S WORK

A

Process Theology

Chapter 15

God and Physics in the Thought of Ian Barbour

John B. Cobb, Jr

The Process Project: Overcoming Fragmentation

This paper will not expound Barbour's thought. His own presentation is so clear that there is little need for commentary. My task, instead, will be to describe how his accomplishments fit into the larger project of process theology: what he has achieved for that project and what more is needed. My focus will be on the difference between the larger project and the one on which he has worked, not on any limitations of the way he has fulfilled his own. In this regard I can testify to its great value for me. I judge his work to be a brilliant success.

I should acknowledge that when I speak of the larger project that is different from the one Barbour has accomplished, I am speaking very much of my own project as a process theologian. It is not shared by all process theologians, certainly not in the specific form I propose. Nevertheless, within this community, in contrast to the larger scientific and theological communities, it is not unusual or strange. It is quite similar to Whitehead's own project.

The project of which I speak is, admittedly, grandiose. It is nothing short of reversing the dominant intellectual trends of the twentieth century. These trends were toward greater and greater modesty about the capacity of human thought to make sense of its world in any inclusive way. They accepted and even encouraged the fragmentation of thought in two ways. One is into 'disciplines,' each with its own separate subject matter and methodologies. The other is into perspectives reflecting the diverse life experiences of the thinkers.

Obviously there have been important reasons for affirming these fragmentations. With regard to the first, the ability of individual disciplines to explore much data with great rigor can be attributed partly to their freedom from concern with any larger picture of the world. With regard to the second, it is true that no two people have the same starting point for reflection, and, more significantly, diverse cultural and historical experiences lead to different perceptions of reality. These facts must not be denied or belittled in the effort to reverse the trend toward fragmentation.

My Assumptions and Convictions

Nevertheless, I find that I have certain assumptions that I am incapable of doubting. Here, I identify three. My inability to doubt them does not make them true, but it does mean that I cannot but regard them as true. First, I cannot avoid assuming that I am part of the real world, a world whose reality does not depend on me. Second, I cannot avoid assuming that this world is one rather than many. And, third, I cannot avoid assuming that all parts and aspects of this world are related to each other.

When I call these 'assumptions,' I mean that I have great difficulty imagining what kind of argument or evidence could dissuade me. It seems to me that the very act of arguing and providing evidence in some way presupposes a shared world in which things are related to one another. For example, to argue that the world of mind and the world of matter are separate and unrelated seems to presuppose a larger context in which they both fit. To argue that diverse cultures live in different worlds seems to presuppose that those who are to be persuaded of this idea live in the same world as those who seek to persuade them and those of whom they speak.

I find it difficult to believe that other people, at some level, lack these assumptions. But I know that here I may be quite wrong, and I am open to being persuaded. Certainly, I am already persuaded that people experience the world in very different ways and that communication among us is often difficult. Certainly, I am already persuaded that a very important problem in human history has been – and still is – our tendency to regard our own perceptions as normative for all. But in my view, that would not be a problem if, in fact, we did not all live in one world in which we are all interrelated, a world in which the imposition of the ideas of the powerful on the weak has been dreadfully destructive.

When I ask myself why these assumptions are so indubitable to me, I am unsure of the answer. I recognize that they are rooted in my Christian faith. On the other hand, I find them much more widely shared. I suspect that they are grounded in universal aspects of experience. In Whitehead's terms, deeper than our sense experience is perception in the mode of causal efficacy. We all experience ourselves as being brought into being by forces beyond ourselves and our control. Since we cannot find these forces through sense experience, we can deny them intellectually, but I doubt that we can really cease to believe that they occur.

Given these assumptions, I have developed some strong convictions. These are, I hope, unlike my assumptions, subject to correction. But however fallible, they direct my efforts and energies:

1   It is my conviction that human beings benefit from having as accurate a view of the real world as can be attained. This is not simply a matter of satisfying curiosity or gaining the ability to predict and control. It is also a matter of guiding action morally. The importance of how we understand the world can be shown in relation to the topics just discussed.

On the one hand, if we believe that there is one set of values and beliefs that correspond quite simply and unambiguously to the reality of the world, we are likely to undertake to impose them on others. Conversely, if we believe that whatever unity the world has is inaccessible or unimportant, we will adjust to the fragmentation of our time, regarding those who seek to understand the world's unity as threats to the freedom of others.

On the other hand, if we believe, as I do, that without some sense of commonality and a shared world, we are in danger of destroying the Earth and one another, we will seek to find and celebrate our interconnectedness and participation in a common world. And if we believe that the world is vastly more complex than any one approach can grasp, so that many different perspectives yield diverse elements of truth, we will approach others in expectation that they may have wisdom that we lack.

2   It is my conviction that the hold of substance thinking on the Western mind is a chief cause of the fragmentation that I find so dangerous. By substance thinking I mean any thinking that presumes that the objects of visual and tactile experience provide for us the best models for understanding what it is to exist or be. Most of the Greek philosophers operated in this way, and so did most medieval and early modern ones. Since substances cannot be internally related to one another, substance thinking inherently works toward separation and division. Hume and Kant exposed the philosophical problems in the idea of substance and pointed philosophy in phenomenalist and idealist directions. The result was to render the reality of a world apart from human experience conceptually doubtful or unknowable rather than to provide an alternative view of the nature of that world. Instead of countering the fragmenting tendencies of substance thought, these moves accelerated those tendencies.

3   It is my conviction that taking events, processes, or experiences as the primary clue to what is has dramatically different consequences. Entities conceived in this way are largely constituted by their relations to others. The apparent separability of the objects of visual and tactile experience from one another gives us an illusory view of what the world is really like. A full understanding of anything in fact requires understanding its relations to other things. Thinking in terms of the primacy of events and processes contributes to putting Humpty-Dumpty back together again.

Physics and Theology

In this paper I am focusing on one element in the fragmentation that has occurred, the split between theology and science, with special attention to physics. As a dominant factor in society, this split is rather recent. For Aristotle, metaphysics or theology went beyond physics but did so in a way that was continuous with it and built upon it. It deepened the understanding of the phenomena studied by physics. This general pattern of thought continued through the Middle Ages. Early modern philosophers and physicists continued to formulate coherent views of how God and the world studied by physics are related. This program did not collapse until the time of Hume and Kant. Since then, leading thinkers have taught that any attempt to think physics and theology together is a mistake. In my opinion both theology and physics have suffered from this fragmentation.

It is very doubtful that the physics and the theology that have developed in this period of radical separation can be brought back into a coherent relationship. Indeed, the separation itself, together with the general acceptance of fragmentation, has allowed each to accept internal incoherencies. One can hardly bring about a coherent connection between two internally incoherent bodies of thought.

Nevertheless, there were changes in both theology and physics during the twentieth century that a process theologian can regard as promising.

On the theological side, there has been a shift from metaphysical theology to historical thinking. Process theologians view this ambivalently. On the one hand, we believe metaphysical questions to be very important and the effort to avoid them as obscuring the metaphysical assumptions that continue to operate. On the other hand, the dominant metaphysics that has been rejected was substance metaphysics, and this metaphysics blocks theology from contributing to a coherent view of the world. When theology turns to narrative forms and is closer to lived experience, substance categories fade, and events assume a larger role.

On the philosophical side, the blatantly substantialist, materialist, mechanistic physics inherited from Descartes and Newton has been shown to have explanatory limits. It continues to have great usefulness, but as an account of reality, its limitations are shown by both relativity theory and quantum theory. Despite its continuing usefulness in a large domain, it can no longer be regarded as defining the limits of physical reality. There is an openness for new models of the world; although the major effect on the intellectual public may have been to further the assumption that thought does not lead us toward a world independent of that thinking.

Process theology sees this situation as an opening to a renewal of reflection about how physics and theology can relate coherently. It sees Whitehead as having developed the most promising proposals available to the twenty-first century. It recognizes that these proposals were made while quantum theory was still unfinished and fluid. It knows that there have been many important developments in physics since Whitehead wrote, especially in cosmology. For these reasons and others, it knows that the task he pioneered is one that must always be in process. At the same time, few process theologians are in a position to contribute significantly to this task. Barbour is one of the few exceptions.

The Contribution of Ian Barbour

In my own case, one main reason for the attraction of Whitehead was that I believed his way of thinking about God and human beings was coherent with our current empirical knowledge of the world. But even when I first studied him, the creative period of his own thinking was some decades past. Now another fifty years have passed. Again and again I have had to ask, does Whitehead still provide a way of relating theology to our knowledge of the physical world?

I have written before of my personal gratitude to Barbour for the reassurance I received from his book *Issues in Science and Religion*.[1] If his exposition was correct, then new developments in physics did not raise any serious challenge to the basic proposals of Whitehead. So far as I could judge from the response of physicists, Barbour's expositions were responsible. This liberated me to pursue my projects.

Religion in an Age of Science[2] carried further the demonstration of the compatibility of science as a whole, and physics in particular, with process thought in general, and the doctrine of God in particular. In many respects it implements the project of overcoming fragmentation between Christian theology and the natural sciences. From my point of view, that is an enormous achievement, even though most people in the field still prefer to keep the two disciplines somewhat further apart. To show that maintaining fragmentation is unnecessary is not sufficient to disrupt the habit of thinking in fragmented contexts. That fact has historical, sociological, and psychological explanations. I will return to the importance of these considerations in considering more specific developments in the field of physics.

Barbour's book not only relates Christian theology to the sciences, it also provides an excellent introduction to process thought. It offers an illuminating way of understanding alternative views of God and expounds and defends the process view with accuracy and insight. I commend it to all who are interested in understanding process philosophy and theology.

With regard to theology, and especially the doctrine of God, Barbour engages in the revisions called for by the shift from substance to process metaphysics. He shows that these revisions do not separate us from our biblical heritage. Indeed, in my opinion, the focus of Hebrew thought on narrative and human experience renders it far more congenial to process than to substance metaphysics.

In *Religion in an Age of Science*, Barbour does not discuss process thought until he has completed his presentation of the sciences. In that presentation, he summarizes dominant current theories, pointing out the philosophical issues that they raise. He shows how far these theories have already moved beyond the block universe criticized by William James, how far substance thought has eroded. He argues in ways convincing to me that process theology provides the best way of relating God's action to the world described by the sciences.

This structure of the material allows the reader to judge his account of science and of theology separately in addition to judging the congeniality of process theology to the current state of science. Even in other books, where the discussion of process thought is more intermixed with the account of science, the distinction and separation in principle are maintained. He is not giving us an account of where science *should go* from the point of view of process theology. He is showing us that process theology is compatible with where science is already heading.

I certainly do not criticize Barbour for this. To introduce the issue of how physics is handicapped by its substantialist assumptions and how it could be reshaped and redirected if it systematically adopted a process metaphysics would have vastly complicated his work and potentially alienated many potential readers. The approach he has taken is just what was needed.

Nevertheless, a fuller realization of the process project, as I understand it, requires as thoroughgoing a revision on the side of the sciences as on the side of theology. This task is enormous, and there are few people who are able to contribute to it, especially in physics. Because of the special difficulties of doing this in physics, I will first indicate how process thinking can contribute to the further development of the sciences in fields that I can discuss with less discomfort. The two disciplines into which I have personally made forays are economics and biology. I am confident that even in these fields a thoroughgoing shift from substance to process categories would have far more extensive consequences than I have yet been able to conceive. I hope, nevertheless, that the simple examples I offer will suffice to indicate the seriousness, and potential importance, of the project in these fields.

A Process Critique of Economic Theory

The most obvious influence of substance thinking on liberal and neo-liberal economic theory is with regard to the understanding of human beings. *Homo economicus* is a self-contained individual having all the characteristics of a substance. Relationships to other human beings and to everything else are external. He – and I use the masculine pronoun advisedly – is not affected by relations to others. For that reason there is no concept of community, or solidarity, or cooperation in economic theory. Each individual acts for his own gain. *Homo economicus* has no interest in the common good.

Let me make clear that I do not in the least deny that much economic behavior has always approximated this model. Let me make clear also that the early economists never affirmed that a human being is nothing other than *Homo economicus*. They intended to provide a model that illuminated one aspect of human behavior among others. As an academic discipline, economics took this aspect as its sole topic and isolated it from all other aspects of human behavior. Substantialist thinking encouraged this isolation. Let me make clear, finally, that this program has been brilliantly successful.

Nevertheless, from the point of view of a process thinker, the fundamental substantialist model is seriously deficient. People are in fact very deeply affected by their relationships with others. Viewing economic behavior broadly throughout history, one must say that it has been greatly affected by the communal character of human existence. In traditional societies, purely self-regarding individualistic behavior was not encouraged and did not dominate actual behavior. Those interested in economic development of the Third World in the decades after World War II complained about the 'irrational' behavior of those who preferred to continue their communal existence rather than advance themselves by leaving their villages to work for greater income in urban factories.

Describing individualistic, self-regarding, behavior as rational has given it normative weight in our society. The destruction of traditional societies, inherent in the industrializing process, has led to the 'modern' individualism the model prescribes. Now economic thinking extends into more and more fields, further discouraging the dimensions of mutual support and responsibility characteristic of community. The model becomes more and more 'true' because of its prestige. This illustrates the power of beliefs to shape life and society. In this case, at least from the process point of view, whatever gains this model once made possible, its effects today are pernicious.

We badly need a more accurate model whose implications are quite different. Process theology supports the model of person-in-community. This recognizes the importance of individuality, but by identifying persons rather than individuals as the agents, it recognizes dimensions of life and value other than 'rationality.' It also points to how persons have their being in and through their relations with others. It suggests that often the well-being of a person, even in strictly economic terms, may be better advanced by improvements in the community as a whole than by gaining competitive advantage within the community. It also indicates that economic values are not always the most important. They are often sacrificed, quite rationally, for the sake of human relations.

Shifting from strict individualism to person-in-community could also overcome the gap between economics and the other social sciences. Many of them understand how important culture and shared history are to people as well as human relationships. Anthropologists do not view the people they study with individualistic models. Neither do social psychologists. An economic theory that took community seriously could be integrated with other social sciences in a way that would provide far wiser guidance to human action.

Substance thinking led in the modern world to a sharp dualism between human beings and everything else. Economics took this dualism and its accompanying anthropocentrism from its context and built its theories accordingly. As a result the natural world has value only in terms of the price people will pay for any part of it. Other creatures have no value in themselves. This discourages attention to the natural world. Those shaped by the now dominant economic thinking, and they are many, employ models that assure them that market forces will generate the technology needed to respond to any shortages. As long as we give freedom to the market, they suppose, there is no need to examine the resources physically in order to determine that we should have no concerns about them.

If we adopt, instead, a different model, such as the one affirmed by process theology, we will understand human beings as integrally related to the rest of the natural world. Harming the natural world harms us quite directly. The simplification of the landscape damages the quality of human experience. In the long run it may also reduce the supply of food, but that is by no means the only reason to be concerned for the natural world and for the well-being of other species. The deterioration of the natural world impoverishes the life of God. God suffers in the suffering of all sentient creatures, not only human ones.

There is nothing in this that separates me from Barbour. The policies that Barbour advocates generally correspond with the judgments that follow from reordering economic theory around a person-in-community model. Our views of what is practically needed are quite similar. The only difference is that Barbour does not formulate his position in terms of a need to change economic theory.

A Process Critique of Biology

I turn now to the example of biology. The same substantialist model has affected its development as well. This shows up in the widespread reductionism of biological research. There is a strong tendency to think that detailed study of the parts will exhaustively explain the whole without attention to the relationship among the parts. In other words, the part is viewed as an entity, that is, what it is independently of its relations with other parts and with the whole.

As in the case of economics, this approach has been brilliantly successful. Much has been learned by this method that could never have been learned by observing the behavior of living animals in the wild. But it is equally true that one cannot predict the behavior of living animals in the wild from the detailed study of their organs or even their genes. Animals are far more than an assemblage of physical parts, and the neglect of this fact has limited biology.

We can take this one step further and say that the behavior of individual animals cannot be understood apart from their interrelationships. Just as human beings are not self-enclosed individuals, the same is true for all animals. They are what they are in particular environments, environments usually including other animals of the same species as well as other species. Examining the behavior of caged animals tells us little about the nature of those animals in a healthy wilderness setting.

Since biology is the science in which teleology once played its most dominant role, those who struggled to free it from this domination are particularly sensitive to the need to keep purpose out. There is no doubt that, by overcoming the temptation to explain biological phenomena by appeal to purpose, biologists have made great advances. This was a necessary step in the development of biology. It was embodied in the shift from organismic models to the mechanical ones suggested by substantialist thought.

Even so, process thinkers, along with other critics, emphasize the view that organisms are, in fact, not machines, but have intelligent purposes. Animals engage in exploratory behavior, and when such behavior has results they prize, they purposefully repeat it. Granted, even among humans, purposes are only rarely consciously formulated. But animal behavior is purposive nevertheless. Process thinkers hold that to suppose that this purposiveness has nothing to do with biological explanation is both arbitrary and dubious.

This issue is particularly important with respect to evolutionary theory. Standard neo-Darwinian theory has been formulated on mechanistic principles. It excludes from any role in explanation not only an overall purpose for the evolutionary process but also the purposes of individual animals. Without appeal to purpose, it certainly explains much. Nevertheless, if the entities that evolve are living animals, and if animals have intelligent purposes, it would be quite remarkable if it were true that their purposive behavior had no influence on the evolutionary process.

The evidence is, in any case, otherwise. When an animal finds a way of obtaining a new supply of food, pursues that way, and is imitated by others who seek the same result, intelligent purpose is involved. The result of beneficial changes in behavior is typically an evolutionary advantage for those members of the species that happen to be best adapted to it. The course of evolution is affected.

At one level, many biologists would agree. But it is remarkable how dogmatic the community as a whole remains in its exclusion of purpose from the theory. Chance and necessity alone are allowed.

One reason for resistance may be the fear that, if they speak of animal purposes, this could allow a role for divine purpose influencing creaturely purpose. The exclusion of divine influence is regarded as essential to scientific theory. From my point of view, they are correct in suspecting that this move may occur! But I do not see that denying God's role in the world should be an a priori condition of good science. From the point of view of process thought, this is just as inappropriately dogmatic as presupposing that such a role must be affirmed. A theory that includes a role for God should be considered on its merits.

What Barbour has written on biology is fully congenial with most of what I have said. His critique of reductionism is far more detailed and convincing than mine. The difference that is relevant in this essay is that he does not formulate what he says as a reconstruction of the basic models and theories of biology. In particular, he does not allow his own view of God to play any role in scientific theory. For him, as for almost all scientists, theology should not claim to contribute to science. Its task is distinct from that of science, although in Barbour's case, it should be congruent. For me the ultimate goal is a fuller integration.

A Process Critique of Quantum Theory

Now let us turn to physics. My interest here is to propose that a model of interrelated events, such as that supported by process thinking, can generate better theory than is possible where the conceptuality derived from substance thought is employed. This is not Barbour's project. He shows instead how the philosophical implications of quantum theory, as it is now formulated, are congenial with process philosophy. The present state of quantum theory points toward the importance of temporality and historicity, chance and law, and wholeness and emergence.[3] Thus physics supports central doctrines of process theology. There is no need to change quantum theory.

On topics of this sort, my ability to speak responsibly is very limited. My study of mathematics did not even take me as far as calculus; so I cannot read much of the discussion. Nevertheless, I have not allowed ignorance and incompetence to prevent me from forming judgments!

My judgment is that, despite the breakdown of classical substance models in physics, the major thinkers have still worked with substantialist models. The result is that formulations in quantum theory and in relativity are in some respects incoherent. My opinion is that physics could advance better if it approached its task employing process models. I will illustrate this in the present section with quantum theory and, in the next section, with relativity.

What has struck me is that when the evidence contradicted the idea of the atom as an indivisible substance, physicists described the entities into which it was analyzed as particles. 'Particle' is just as substantialist a notion as 'atom.' When it turned out that many of the observed phenomena did not fit the particle model, physicists appealed to the alternative model of a 'wave.' This is also a substantialist model. But to fit the substantialist way of thinking, waves require a substantial medium. The ether was posited. When it turned out that there was no ether, physics nevertheless retained the model of the wave. In other words, most physicists were not willing or able to develop a nonsubstantialist model even when the substantialist models led to incoherence.

What a process model would be is not all that obscure. It suggests that we think of the world as a field of events. These events are radically relational. This means that each event is almost exhaustively described as what the field is at that point-like locus. A fair amount of what I read seems to fit this model and even to use process language although not consistently. A consistent process model can gain plausibility only if mathematically-expressed theories, based on this way of thinking, explain in detail the phenomena that have been observed. I cannot make the slightest contribution to the development of such theories.

The quantum theorist who has most thoughtfully shared my conviction that a process model is needed is David Bohm. His most extensive philosophical discussion is in *Wholeness and the Implicate Order*.[4] There he even tries to develop a language that does not lead its users to think in substantialist terms. He also develops a holographic model that fits well with Whitehead's understanding of an event and makes sense of the comments I have made about a field of events.

Together with Basil Hiley, Bohm has more recently published *The Undivided Universe*.[5] I rejoice that this was virtually complete before Bohm's death. The more radical philosophical ideas are more clearly expressed in the concluding chapter than directly in connection with the mathematically formulated theories in the rest of the book. But at least they are coherent with the theory to which they led the authors.

It is my understanding that the quantum theory developed by Bohm and Hiley is able to explain all the phenomena covered by Bohr's dominant theory. It is, therefore, adequate to the data. It is conceptually coherent and realistic. Yet the great majority of quantum theorists apparently do not regard this as an advantage. They have been socialized to think in non-coherent terms and do not want to be disturbed.

Barbour writes that 'most physicists acknowledge that Bohm's view is consistent with … experiments, but they are reluctant to abandon Bohr's view until there is experimental evidence against it.'[6] Bohm does not expect that there will ever be experimental evidence against Bohr's theory. Bohm's motivation has been the achievement of coherence of thought, and this is not enough to interest most physicists. Bohm and Hiley do make the more limited claim that their theory may be able to make some predictions with regard to phenomena about which Bohr's is silent. Should that prove the case, such successful prediction may influence some of these reluctant physicists to consider it more seriously.

There is a second reason for failing to accept Bohm's theory. It embodies nonlocal relations. A straightforward interpretation of Bell's theorem seems to support the reality of such relations, but Einstein led the resistance. This was partly because he also operated with substantialist assumptions, which make nonlocal relations metaphysically impossible. It was also partly because nonlocal relations would appear to counter his relativity theory.

Bohm explains that when both relativity theory and nonlocal relations are carefully formulated, there is no contradiction. Nonlocal relations give direction to events but they do not transmit energy. Indeed, they cannot transmit signals. The parallel with Whitehead's speculations is striking. For Whitehead, causal feelings are simple physical feelings that transmit energy from contiguous events. But there are also hybrid physical feelings, which are feelings of the conceptual pole of other events. These do not require contiguity but can influence the form taken by an occasion of experience.

Not all of Bohm's earlier formulations were congenial to process thought. In particular, he seemed to be deterministic, using the language of determination in describing his vision. Years ago, in discussing with him, I came to the conclusion that his real interest was in insisting on determinateness over against the implication of such language as 'probability waves.' If the entities making up the quantum field are real, then they are what they are whether they are being measured or not. Of course, interaction with measuring devices changes them. But the determinateness of events does not imply that what they are is wholly determined by their past. Bohm tended to agree; in *The Undivided Universe* he makes clear that his theory does not depend on or imply ontological determinism.

Bohm found his chief philosophical influence in Spinoza. His own thinking moved a long way from Spinoza, at least as I understand Spinoza. But the Spinozistic influence continued to inform Bohm's language and imagery to some extent to the end. As a result, a process theologian cannot simply adopt it all. On the other hand, as far as I can tell, his theory as such is fully congenial to the process vision as informed by Whitehead. Needless to say, I am excited by this indication that Whiteheadian metaphysics can fit with all the empirical evidence derived from quantum theory.

I wish, of course, that physicists shared with me the preference for realism and coherence that make Bohm's theory preferable to Bohr's. Given the longer history of physics, their indifference seems odd. In this regard, James T. Cushing's book, *Quantum Mechanics: Historical Contingency and the Copenhagen Hegemony*,[7] provides a fascinating historical account, showing why Bohm's theory is so little considered. He makes clear how profound are the nonscientific elements in the determination of what theories are accepted. It is my assumption that new contingencies can lead to changes in the scientific climate. That is also my hope.

A Process Critique of Relativity Theory

When we turn to relativity theory, we can consider Whitehead's own response to Einstein regarding both special and general relativity. It is not clear that in all respects Whitehead's own work on these topics is consistent with his later philosophical system as embodied in *Process and Reality*.[8] Robert Russell, for example, has pointed out that the summation of multiple forces in the first of Whitehead's four proposed formulas for gravity (see below) does not reflect the complex pattern of interrelationships he affirmed in his later works.[9] Accordingly, I will ignore Whitehead's criticisms of Einstein in his book on relativity and keep in mind only the criticism he formulated in *Adventures of Ideas*[10] as I compare the approaches taken by Whitehead and Einstein in developing a relativistic theory of gravity.

Although, as I just noted, Whitehead agreed with Einstein formally regarding the special theory of relativity, when he came to a relativistic theory of gravity, Whitehead was troubled by Einstein's discussion of the curvature of space-time as a feature of the real world. For space-time as such to be curved, it would have to have a substantial character. For Whitehead, it could not. He argued that from the point of view of mathematics, any space that could be treated by Euclidean geometry could also be treated by elliptic and hyperbolic geometry. One may use one geometry or another for convenience, but one should not project a particular character on the space in question.

The question is, then, whether empirical facts support Einstein's substantialist metaphysics against that of Whitehead. In 1922, Whitehead developed an alternative relativistic theory based exclusively on multiple time systems.[11] When applied to the solar system, its predictions, such as the precession of Mercury, were identical to Einstein's. Eventually, however, evidence of the influence of the Milky Way galaxy on Earth's tides convinced the physics community that Whitehead's theory had been disproven.

Whitehead himself emphasized that, if the first formula that he unpacked in his book should be shown to be wrong by further empirical evidence, there were three other formulas that would be consonant with his metaphysical principles. The first of these three he called 'Einstein's Law' because he believed that its predictions were identical to those of Einstein. But he did not elaborate on the details of any of these additional formulas, and for many years no one else published anything regarding them. Since Whitehead himself indicated that the mathematical results of 'Einstein's Law' would be identical with Einstein's own theory, and since those who used Einstein's theory had been brilliantly successful and made vast progress, there would be no scientific gain in replacing Einstein's formulation of the theory with that of Whitehead. Only someone interested in philosophy as well as physics would have reason to study Whitehead's formula.

The situation was disheartening for one such as me committed to Whitehead's metaphysics. It seemed that physics could succeed only on the basis of the more substantialist metaphysics assumed by Einstein. It was hard to argue that the evidence could be interpreted equally well on the basis of Whitehead's metaphysics when this claim had to be taken on faith.

Fortunately the situation has changed. In 1974, Dean Fowler showed that Whitehead's first equation could be reinterpreted as consistent with the tidal data, although it had other technical problems.[12] In the mid-1980s, Robert Russell and Christoph Wassermann undertook an analysis of all four of Whitehead's equations.[13] They began by supporting Fowler's arguments regarding the first equation. Then through extensive mathematical arguments they showed explicitly that the second of the four equations is indeed equivalent to the free-space version of Einstein's field equations (as Whitehead had stated). Russell then went on to discover that Whitehead's third equation is yet another free-space field equation equivalent, physically, to Einstein's free-space field equations, and that his fourth equation appears to include non-gravitational sources. To date, two key questions remain unsettled: Is Whitehead's third equation identical in every respect to Einstein's free-space equations? How does Whitehead's fourth equation compare in detail with Einstein's field equations for non-gravitational sources? It should be emphasized, though, that Russell and Wassermann considered it remarkable that Whitehead achieved these results without appealing to the curvature of space.

Obviously, this does not prove that the whole range of phenomena predicted and explained by standard, Einsteinian, relativity theory can be accounted for without the curvature of space. This is particularly true when it comes to the problem of a Whiteheadian equivalent to the Big Bang cosmology. Still, the work of Russell and Wasserman does suggest that this may be the case. Whitehead's rejection of substance thinking in the context of relativity may not be in tension with the evidence.

The Prospects

Obviously, few physicists are interested in exploring this possibility. They are quite satisfied with the theories they have. Indeed, it is hard to think what might evoke attention from those who do not have strong philosophical interests. The one possibility I can imagine is that it might turn out that Bohmian quantum theory and Whiteheadian relativity theory could be shown to cohere better than Bohrian quantum theory and Einsteinian relativity theory. I certainly do not know this to be the case, and, indeed, I have little understanding of present problems in relating the two fields. But my hunch is that freeing both from substance thinking would help.

Now it is quite obvious that the disciplines of economics, biology, and physics have not changed direction as a result of the considerations I have rehearsed. Few of their practitioners are even interested in alternative assumptions and approaches. The abstract possibility that each could gain more internal coherence and adequacy by shifting to process categories has no effect on the general culture. The goal of achieving more coherence with other fields and disciplines is even less motivating. Hence the moves I am proposing have thus far not helped in the practical issue of bringing more wisdom to bear on our shared crises. Perhaps they never will.

Nevertheless, for that small group who find the fragmentation of thought harmful both to science and to society, the developments I have cited are encouraging. Of course, most of the work of displaying the fruitfulness of process thinking remains to be done. In the effort to do it, we may find that its potentialities are just as limited as those of substance thinking. But thus far, I think, the evidence is otherwise. The problem is that so few are prepared to work on the hundreds of tasks that need to be accomplished, not that anyone has shown that the project is hopeless or misdirected.

Is there any possibility that the new century will see a shift to process thinking on a large scale? Despite the absence of much interest now, I do see such a possibility. Although present orthodoxies in the sciences are well established, few are able to defend them thoughtfully. They have the strength of habit rather than of thought. Habit is very powerful, but when dogma is exposed as merely habit, its hold is weakened.

Furthermore, very few today intentionally affirm commitment to substance metaphysics. Most deny that they have any metaphysics at all. As I have noted, this makes it more difficult to get attention to the problems in all the disciplines caused by the substantialist conceptualities that still prevail. But when attention can be called to these assumptions, their defense is remarkably weak. It consists chiefly of saying that the present orthodoxy works well for the purposes of most practitioners. Few claim that it is true in any other sense.

This situation in the sciences is somewhat like that of traditional Christianity in Christendom. People have been Christian from long habit. They have accepted doctrines that they did not understand on the grounds that they were Christian. Christian society seemed to work fairly well. Christian belief seemed to ground the morality that society needed. For these reasons, even when Christian beliefs became increasingly doubtful, most continued to be Christians. But alternative ways of thinking gained greater and greater plausibility, and fewer and fewer open-minded persons found traditional Christian formulations fully convincing. Within Christianity new theologies emerged. The lack of real belief in the substance categories that continue to shape scientific inquiry can lead in a similar way to openness to quite new formulations.

Implications for Theology

One may ask what all this talk of changes in the sciences has to do with religion. If we take the root meaning of 'religion' to be binding together, then the answer is quite obvious. The interest of process theologians in changing the sciences is for the sake of binding them together with each other and with the rest of human experience and thought. For me, Christian faith is religious in this sense. Hence my own religious interest stems from my Christian faith.

Ian Barbour has led, among all process theologians, in reflection about the relation of process theology to the implications of the sciences. Of special interest and importance among these implications today is the Big Bang cosmology. This provides a picture of the past quite different from the one process theologians have derived from Whitehead. Whereas Whitehead envisioned one cosmic epoch evolving gradually out of another, we are now told that this cosmic epoch had a dramatic beginning, quite discontinuous from what preceded it. There are features of this beginning, and especially of the contingent order that so quickly emerged, that suggest a form of deism. Theologians who have separated theology from science are not affected by such changes, but we process theologians should be. Our slowness to engage in this discussion and our defensive arguments for the forms of thought that we had developed in relation to ideas of evolutionary change show how habit controls us as well as others. Whitehead's conceptuality has worked so well in so many ways, we would prefer to ignore the new challenges. But we must not do so.

Barbour has not been afflicted by these hesitations. He thinks that, whereas the theological doctrine of creation is fundamentally independent of scientific views, it should be congruent with them. He has shown that, in terms of basic principles, Big Bang cosmology supports and reinforces some of the themes of process theology. This is reassuring.

The problem for me, however, is one step more difficult than for Barbour. Throughout this essay I have emphasized that I look for something more than congruence. I seek the integration of science and theology. For me this involves reformulations in both science and theology. The Big Bang cosmology, therefore, requires of me more serious reflection about my theology than Barbour finds necessary.

The difference that I have stressed thus far is that I am more interested than Barbour in proposing changes in the sciences to bring them into accord with theology. That has led me to be slow to accept the Big Bang theory. As long as it was controversial within science, I could sympathize with alternative views that are more congenial to the thought of Whitehead and Hartshorne. I remain open to the possibility that Big Bang cosmology may not be the last word. Alternative interpretations of Big Bang cosmology, as well as alternatives to it, are still being proposed, and these would seem to have different implications for theology.

But as new knowledge is gained from the natural sciences, one who seeks integration must be concerned to change theology also. If the evidence for Big Bang cosmology is decisive, then it is time to make the theological adjustments that will integrate theology with that theory, even while recognizing that some day there may be the need of new changes to adapt to a different theory. For the present this integration amounts to something more than pointing out compatibilities. But one would need to understand Big Bang theory far better than I to carry out this project.

I have some ideas but little confidence in my own proposals. I am reassured by Barbour's treatment that there is nothing in Big Bang cosmology that cuts against the fundamental preference for process over substance. I do not think Whitehead's view of the organismic and relational character of actual entities is affected. The question is more the relation of divine persuasion to imposed law. Whitehead's thought includes both, but we process theologians have minimized the latter. Instead, we now need to reflect upon it in relation to the origins of our cosmic epoch. If we continue to emphasize persuasion as the way God works in the world now, we must explain why we do so. I believe we can do this, but if we neglect the challenge, our claim to a way of thinking about our faith that is integrated with what is known of the world will lose conviction. We will be defending one orthodoxy against others.

No doubt new challenges will arise from the sciences. Whitehead's advice is to take each challenge as an opportunity to purify, clarify, and advance understanding of our faith. We, like many others, prefer to cling to past understandings in order to articulate our faith. But faith itself calls for readiness to change.

Notes

1. Ian G. Barbour, *Issues in Science and Religion* (New York: Harper & Row, 1971; originally published in 1966 by Prentice Hall), 470.
2. I.G. Barbour, *Religion in an Age of Science: The Gifford Lectures 1989–1991 Volume I* (San Francisco: Harper & Row, 1990), 297.
3. Barbour, *Religion in an Age of Science*, 123–4.
4. David Bohm, *Wholeness and the Implicate Order* (London: Routledge & Kegan Paul, 1980).
5. D. Bohm and B.J. Hiley, *The Undivided Universe: An Ontological Interpretation of Quantum Theory* (London: Routledge, 1993).
6. Barbour, *Religion in an Age of Science*, 108.
7. James T. Cushing, *Quantum Mechanics: Historical Contingency and the Copenhagen Hegemony* (Chicago: University of Chicago Press, 1994).
8. Alfred North Whitehead, *Process and Reality*, corrected edn, ed. by David Ray Griffin and Donald W. Sherburne (New York: The Free Press, 1978).

9. Robert John Russell, 'Whitehead, Einstein and the Newtonian Legacy', in *Newton and the New Direction in Science*, ed. by G.V. Coyne, SJ. and M. Heller (Citta del Vaticano: Specola Vaticana, 1988), 183.

10. Alfred North Whitehead, *Adventures of Ideas* (New York: Mentor Book, The New American Library, 1933).

11. Alfred North Whitehead, *The Principle of Relativity with Applications to Physical Science* (Cambridge: Cambridge University Press, 1922).

12. Dean R. Fowler, 'Disconfirmation of Whitehead's Relativity Theory – A Critical Reply,' *Process Studies*, 4:4 (Winter 1974), 288–90.

13. Russell, 'Whitehead, Einstein and the Newtonian Legacy', including references to previous works.

Chapter 16

Barbour in Process: Contributions to Process Theology

Ernest Simmons

> When we consider what religion is for mankind and what science is, it is no
> exaggeration to say that the future course of history depends upon the decision
> of this generation as to the relations between them.
> Alfred North Whitehead, *Science and the Modern World* (1925)[1]

On April 30, 1968, I purchased my copy of Ian Barbour's *Issues in Science and
Religion*.[2] (I know because I still have the cash register receipt from the university
bookstore.) That text did nothing less than save my intellectual understanding of the
relationship of God and the world. As a recent physics-cum-philosophy major and
struggling with the deconstructions of analytic philosophy, it was restorative to read
someone who believed both in physics and God and kept the two together. In the
tumultuous spring of 1968, through the assassinations of Martin Luther King, Jr
and Robert Kennedy, this text also helped assure a college sophomore that reality
could still be understood coherently and intelligently, that the world was not really
coming apart at the seams. Indeed that momentous year ended with one of the most
remarkable feats of contemporary physics, namely the orbiting of the moon on
Christmas Eve. This text not only made sense to me from my study of physics but
also placed it in the context of the history of the philosophy of nature and introduced
me to the thought of Alfred North Whitehead for the first time. It is to this text that
I trace the beginning of my interest in process thought. It is rare that one book can
have such an impact on the intellectual career of a person but this was such a book
for me and, as this volume attests, also for many others. To Ian Barbour I owe a debt
of gratitude far beyond the ability of this modest essay to express.

As John Cobb indicates in his essay (Chapter 15), the greatest contribution
Barbour has made to process thought is to show its coherence with contemporary
physics, that Whitehead's thought, in particular, is not in fundamental contradiction
with contemporary physical theory. I will leave to others in this volume the task of
placing Barbour's work in the context of science and the science–religion dialogue.
My focus will be on Barbour's contributions to process theology. I would like to
address this in two ways, first of all through a careful summary of Barbour's
appropriation and critique of process theology in three of his major works
developed over his professional career: *Issues in Science and Religion, Religion in
an Age of Science, and Nature, Human Nature and God*,[3] including his reliance upon
the thought of Charles Hartshorne. Second, and much more briefly, I will assess his
contributions to process theology. My conclusion is that Barbour has primarily
focused on the relationship of God and the world in his treatment of process

theology, particularly in the area of creation and the theology of nature. While this has been essential, it is now critical to move more fully into the realms of redemption and eschatology if the science and religion dialogue is to indeed elicit hope as well as understanding. Although Barbour gives glimmers in this direction, he does not fully develop them. I believe that such development is possible but one will have to augment the Hartshornian expression of process theology that Barbour relies so heavily upon. Let us turn then to address Barbour's exposition of process theology.

Issues in Science and Religion (1966)

In *Issues in Science and Religion* (hereafter *Issues*) Barbour clearly summarizes, in the section entitled 'God and Nature,' the major themes of process thought particularly expressed by Whitehead. Barbour closes his introduction to this book with the Whitehead quote cited at the head of this essay and shows that his work will be a continuation of the important task of relating science and religion. Indeed it is this relationship that is definitive in Barbour's use of process theology throughout his major works and his contribution to a 'Theology of Nature.' While sympathetic to process thought, Barbour has not engaged in an uncritical adoption but rather has attempted to critique and enlarge process thought by relating it more fully to Christian religious experience and historical revelation through the understanding of continuing creation. It is in this context that we shall explore Barbour's place in process theology.

Whitehead's Metaphysics

In *Issues*, the central question, which continues throughout Barbour's work, is 'How can God act if the world is law-abiding?'[4] In response to the clearly failed 'God of the Gaps' approach where God is inserted as an explanatory hypothesis in the absence of human knowledge, and to advance beyond the separate realms approach where science and religion do not interact at all, Barbour employs process thought to forge a dynamic interaction in a theology of nature. The key to his approach is a recovery of the doctrine of *creatio continua*, of continuous creation, to supplement the understanding of an originating creation. It is through the understanding of continuing creation that God can be understood as active in the world. Employing Whitehead's metaphysics to demonstrate that divine action can be understood in a way that is coherent with contemporary science to forge a meaningful theology of nature is one of Barbour's greatest contributions to process theology. Let us briefly summarize Barbour's use of Whitehead and Hartshorne before turning to his critique, which would complement process metaphysics with religious experience and historical revelation to produce a doctrine of continuing creation that combines creation and providence.[5]

Barbour concisely summarizes Whitehead's metaphysics in terms of divine action through four major emphases. God is: (1) the Primordial Ground of Order; (2) the ground of novelty; (3) influenced by events in the world; and (4) acting by being experienced by the world.[6] This position allows for both divine immanence and transcendence in a relationship where, 'God's activity is more akin to *persuasion* than to compulsion.'[7] Barbour acknowledges that Whitehead's view of God is quite different than that of the traditional creator and while not having temporal priority does have priority of status over all else.[8] He then draws upon the thought of Charles Hartshorne to further develop Whitehead's concept of God, particularly in relationship to change and permanence. He observes, 'We may summarize Hartshorne's view by saying that God is *changing* in the content of his experience but *eternal* in his character and purpose.'[9] Hartshorne elaborates Whitehead's dipolar understanding of God to show the priority of becoming over being in relation to Divine experience but not in such a way as to lose continuity of Divine purpose. Hartshorne dynamizes the concept of perfection in order to relate an immanent, historical understanding of Deity in contrast to a transcendent more static understanding that flows from classical Greek thought.[10] Barbour finds this development by Hartshorne helpful because it moves the metaphysical understanding of God closer to the biblical one. This then leads to a constructive understanding of providence which does not result in divine determinism on the one hand or deny historical, physical change on the other. In Barbour's view Hartshorne qualifies God's sovereignty in the world by giving creatures their own degree of 'self-creation.' God's participation in this process achieves all that God intends while still allowing for us in our freedom to be part of that achievement.[11]

Here we see the change that process metaphysics can make to relate theology to contemporary science and historical analysis, the relating of the concept of God to the issues of freedom and determinism, of chance and necessity. This is essential for Barbour's theology of nature but, as he knows, it comes at a price, particularly in relation to divine power and the problem of evil. He develops this cost and possible solutions in his evaluation of process views at the end of *Issues*.

In his critique of Whitehead Barbour observes, 'Compared with the biblical God, it is clear that the God of system is limited in power whereas the God of the Bible is Whitehead's omnipotent.[12] This limitation protects God from being held responsible for the evils of this world, but the protection is costly, for God cannot unilaterally overcome these evils either. Such a God is lacking in both the degree of sovereignty and morality we see in the Biblical God.[13] Barbour goes on to point out things that God can do in Whitehead, such as, 'being omniscient, infinitely sensitive to events, responding to them with perfect adequacy,' and observing, 'This is a God of wisdom and compassion who shares in the world's suffering and is a transforming influence in it, even if he is not omnipotent.'[14] Barbour, pointing to a problem that process thinkers have struggled with from the beginning, asks whether, given these limitations on sovereignty and morality, Whitehead's God still evokes our worship. He suggests that it would if Whitehead's discussion of God were to include such characteristics as inevitable judgment along with persuasion, and if in the presence of Whitehead's God we would feel a profound sense of awe.[15] Here in his earlier reflections on Whitehead we see Barbour pointing to areas of response that he will develop in later writings. Before turning to these, however, we need to look at his initial development of a theology of nature.

Theology of Nature

Barbour is clear that his project is one of a theology of nature and different from that of John Cobb's in *A Christian Natural Theology*.[16] Indeed, he even sees his project in this regard as more amenable to the thought of Joseph Sittler and his elaboration of the relation of nature and grace. In a footnote Barbour observes that while Cobb would like to distinguish natural theology from its Christian roots so that it can stand more independently indeed as philosophy, Barbour insists that what he is calling a 'theology of nature' is an 'integral part of *theology*' (Barbour's italics). Like the writings of Joseph Sittler which called for 'A Theology for Earth,' Barbour wants to start with basic Christian beliefs, although, unlike Sittler's primary concern for the stewardship of nature, he is focused on the metaphysical issues regarding divine action in nature.[17] While this may be overstating Cobb's desire to separate natural theology from the Christian tradition, it is clear that Barbour's project is a theology of nature and not a natural theology. He is not interested in showing the cogency of belief in God so much as how God can act in a world understood by natural science. As such he sees his task involving both philosophy of religion and philosophy of science while clearly connecting to theology.

In *Issues* Barbour summarizes a theology of nature around five major themes. These themes will recur in his later thought so a brief summation of them is in order here. First of all, the goal of a theology of nature is to place nature in the context of theological discussion. Barbour is clear that the context of theological discourse is always the worshipping community, and, while employing religious experience and historical revelation, theology must include a theology of nature that does not disparage or neglect the natural order.[18] Nearly forty years later this observation seems rather obvious but in the 1960s society was only beginning to awaken to the environmental crisis and the importance of connecting theology to nature through the physical and life sciences. Barbour's insistence on a non-disparaging treatment of nature, by relating God to it in a way that bestows intrinsic and not just instrumental value, helped to create the emerging field of ecological or environmental theology.[19] In making his case for the importance of nature in theology, Barbour contrasts his 'critical realism' with neo-orthodoxy by rejecting its two-language treatment of nature as a mere stage for human salvation. He also contrasts it with the impersonal/personal alternatives of an existentialist treatment of nature/humanity, and with the attempt by linguistic analysts to separate discourse about nature from discourse about God. The role of nature is particularly important, for Barbour, in the doctrines of creation and providence even if it continues to play a secondary place even there.[20] He goes on to conclude secondly, that nature is seen as a dynamic process, which involves differing levels of activity and analysis, that are not mutually exclusive. This allows Barbour to then turn to the key issue of divine sovereignty.

Divine Sovereignty and Human Freedom

After pointing out that foreordination is not compatible with open alternatives and that time is not the unrolling of a previously written scroll but is a passage into the novel and indeterminate, Barbour asserts human freedom, indicating that humans can reject God's purposes and that such freedom is essential to voluntary love and uncoerced response. He concludes, 'But these conditions are God's self-limitation, not the imposition of restrictions by something external to God.'[21] We will pick up on this move later in the discussion of kenosis with John Polkinghorne but it is important to note here that for Barbour the idea of divine self-limitation is essential for human freedom although he will come to see it as a metaphysical condition not a divine choice as Polkinghorne does. The key, however, they would both agree upon and that is that theology must recover the concept of God's sovereignty through love and not coercive power. Here Barbour attempts to bring process thought and Christian theology closer together. He asserts:

> We need to recover the biblical motif that God's sovereignty is *the power of love* – coupled always with the righteousness, holiness, and judgment without which love becomes sentimentality. If Christ is our model of God, we must think of power in terms of the power of the Word, of the Cross, and the Spirit, rather than omnipotence imagined as coercive force.[22]

Here Barbour is in complete agreement with Whitehead, Hartshorne, Cobb, Griffin, and Suchocki in regard to divine power, but he, himself, does not develop these themes in his later writings. Instead he relies on the process theologians to attempt such reconciliation with the Christian tradition. But he does hold out a critique. Based on his concern, already mentioned above, that process theology places too severe a limitation on God's sovereignty, Barbour proposes that process theology would in fact not be 'incompatible' with a stronger sense of divine power and moral judgment. This, in turn, would be more in keeping with both religious experience and historical revelation. In addition, the sense of dependence on God which *creatio ex nihilo* carries could be maintained in the framework of continuing creation, with its integration of earlier notions of creation and providence, although the insistence on an absolute beginning of the world might be rejected. In such a theological revision, God retains 'priority in status' even if 'priority in time' is rescinded.[23] He concludes by restating his basic claim, namely that if process philosophy is 'adapted' in several ways it can indeed be used to convey and express the kerygma of the Bible to our contemporary culture. The metaphysical categories of process philosophy are crucial if we are to bring nature into the theological agenda, but the cost is their restriction to impersonal language. On the other hand, traditional theology's focus on salvation entails language about persons and history, but these are relatively inapplicable to the discussion of nature. Thus Barbour proposes a combined approach in which metaphysics would be placed within the articulation of the Christian message, resulting in the kind of 'integral world-view' that contemporary culture requires.[24]

We see then that for Barbour process metaphysics contributes to an integral worldview that will allow religion to be more adequately integrated with natural science. Process thought allows for this but not without further development that will allow the process God to be worthy of worship. Here one must leave the realm of metaphysics and allow for religious experience and historical revelation. Clearly Barbour sees this as most relevant for the community of faith but this tension is one that remains unresolved. Is the 'integral world-view' for everyone in society or primarily for the community of faith? In moving back and forth between philosophy of religion and theology Barbour is trying to please two masters at once and that is not easy. He clearly wants theology to be more respectful of nature but he also wants science to see that its analysis does not preclude divine action. This dual focus remains throughout *Issues* and is part of its value but reconciliations must be made and the elaborations more fully developed if they are to be enduring. How does Barbour develop these ideas in his later writings? For that we will turn primarily to Volume I of his Gifford Lectures, *Religion in an Age of Science*, and conclude with his most recent and personal work, *Nature, Human Nature, and God*.

Religion in an Age of Science (1990)

Twenty-four years after writing *Issues*, in *Religion in an Age of Science* (hereafter *Religion*) Barbour comes out more directly supportive of process theology than he had earlier. While restating the major themes of process thought and Whitehead's understanding of God that he had summarized in *Issues*, Barbour makes several significant additions to his treatment. Process thought is now referred to as an 'ecological metaphysics'[25] which reflects his deepening connection to environmental thought over the previous 25 years and there are major new sections on 'Christian Process Theology' and 'Process Theism' in which he develops the understanding of God as a 'Creative Participant' involving the biblical understanding of the Spirit. Finally, Barbour formulates four criteria for theological reformulation of classical theism (agreement with data, coherence, scope, and fertility) and concludes by stating: 'I believe that by these four criteria the reformulations of classical tradition proposed in process theology are indeed justified.'[26]

The Spirit

As we saw in *Issues*, Barbour wants to use the doctrine of continuing creation to connect creation and providence as a way of articulating divine action in the world coherent with the physical and life sciences. Process thought makes that connection possible but needs further elaboration. In *Religion* Barbour modifies Whitehead with some ideas of Hartshorne (drawing upon Cobb and Griffin) to propose a model of 'God as Creative Participant.'[27] The major addition in this volume is the proposal that the biblical understanding of Spirit is a way to connect in process theology the creative (*logos*) character of God with the loving participant (Christ). Barbour states that the Biblical view of Spirit is closely parallel to the proces idea of God's presence in the world. This view sees God's Spirit as involved with the initial and continuing creation of the world. Now we can understand grace as working in and through natural processes as well as religious experience without replacing or superseding them.[28]

This is a significant contribution to process thought, not because the insight was unique to Barbour but because he places it in the context of his very careful analysis of the physical and life sciences. By so doing he bridges science and process theology in a way which respects the integrity of each. He does not suggest that 'Spirit' is a scientific category but rather that its utilization in process theology will allow a coherent articulation of divine action in nature that affirms both creation and providence in a continuing creation, his goal from *Issues*. Unfortunately, Barbour does not develop this suggestion at any length, here, as in his later writings, deferring to process theologians like Cobb, Griffin, and Suchocki for further development. He subsequently concludes that process theism constructively addresses all six of the problems he raised with classical theism (human freedom, evil and suffering, 'masculine' and 'feminine' attributes, interreligious dialogue, evolutionary and ecological world, and chance and law).[29]

Theology and Metaphysics

In *Religion* Barbour does raise 'Problems in Process Theology' very briefly and they are the familiar ones from *Issues*, namely the relationship of Christianity and metaphysics and God's transcendence and power. Barbour acknowledges that all theology involves metaphysical thought but he states here a position which distinguishes him from other more 'scholastic' process thinkers. Insights from process philosophy can help the theologian modify inherited religious models to more accurately address both the ongoing experiences of the Christian community and the theories of contemporary science. The key here is to select certain philosophical insights without feeling one must take on board the entire Whiteheadian scheme: as Barbour writes, 'the theologian must adapt, not adopt, a metaphysics.'[30]

Here I think one sees as clearly as anywhere Barbour's working understanding of the relationship of theology, science, and process thought. Barbour does not engage in an uncritical adoption of process thought. He is not trying to reconcile theology and science with process thought but using process thought to reconcile theology and science. Theologically, speaking from the Christian Tradition, Barbour sees the Christian community and its religious experience as definitive for theological understanding. The issue is, of course, how to modify the classical understanding so that it is coherent with contemporary science thus enabling an integrated life of faith. Process thought helps Barbour to do that but he does not accept Whitehead or any other process thinker whole hog. It is important to point out that Barbour in his later writings, as in *Issues*, calls for Christian religious experience and tradition to augment process thought where it is inadequate for worship and theological completeness. A metaphysics is not a theology and as such must be 'adapted' not 'adopted.' The greatest adaptation comes in the understanding of divine power in relation to the world and the existence of evil and suffering within it. We shall consider the treatment of this understanding in *Religion* before turning to Barbour's most recent work.

God and Evil

By far, one of the greatest contributions that process theology has made to theological discourse is its reflection on the relationship of God and evil. Many other theologies – including the kenotic one to be discussed next – have borrowed from process thought in addressing this issue. In the postholocaust world of the 1950s and 1960s there was existential acknowledgement that the understanding of divine omnipotence had to be revised if theism was to remain viable. (For many, such as Richard Rubenstein it could not. See his *After Auschwitz* for a post-theistic Jewish consciousness.[31]) But could one modify divine power and still retain anything worthy of worship? That was the question in *Issues* that Barbour, among others, raised. In *Religion* Barbour returns to briefly address this issue. Does the process God because of metaphysical limitation, evoke more pity than devotion?[32] Barbour says no. He observes:

> The process God does have power, but it is the *evocative power* of love and inspiration, not controlling, unilateral power. It is the power that is also creative empowerment, not the abrogation of creaturely powers. The power of love and goodness is indeed worthy of worship, commitment, and also gratitude for what God has done, whereas sheer power would only be cause for awe and fear. God's love is not irresistible in the short run, but it is inexhaustible in the long run.[33]

Here you see Barbour's thought deepened particularly by the work of John Cobb and Daniel Day Williams but it also reflects a deepening religious conviction that power without love is only ruthlessness and manipulation. By tying this analysis of divine power and suffering to the wider context of biological evolution, Barbour provides additional support for such a process theological understanding. It is not only humanity that suffers but the whole evolutionary process, indeed with most species ending in extinction, even those as magnificent as the dinosaurs. This vision of God in relation to a 'trial and error' evolution makes more sense than one of divine determination that dictates such suffering and death. Barbour develops these themes in relation to nature most fully in his latest work.

Nature, Human Nature, and God (2002)

In his most recent work, *Nature, Human Nature and God* (hereafter *Nature*), Barbour gives his strongest endorsement of process theology ever. This is the book many of us have been waiting for where Barbour focuses primarily on his own positions. As he indicates in the Introduction, in his earlier works he has summarized many positions with which he does not agree and has worked mainly with the first three of his four types of relating science and religion. Here, all that changes. Barbour now focuses on his own thought and the use of process theology to achieve integration. He observes, 'In the present volume I restrict myself to the last of the four types, *Integration*, which I consider the most promising option. This allows me to spend more time developing my own views and less time trying to survey the field or offer criticisms of views with which I disagree.'[34] He goes on to reaffirm that he is doing a theology of nature and not natural theology so that he is not starting from science and trying to go to theology but, rather, starts from a religious tradition based upon religious experience and historical community and strives for theological doctrines that are consistent with the scientific evidence even if they are not derivable from current scientific theories.[35] (This is the same position as in *Issues* and differs in method from John Polkinghorne who does support a revised natural theology.) In developing his position Barbour advocates for holism over reductionism and the value of emergence in the evolutionary process. It is for these reasons that Barbour then finds process thought helpful. In one of the most straightforward and yet also critical endorsements of process thought to ever appear in his writings Barbour states,

> I have found the process philosophy of Alfred North Whitehead and his followers helpful in my attempt to integrate scientific and religious concepts. I have been indebted to the process theologians, especially John Cobb and David Griffin, who use Whitehead's philosophical ideas to interpret Christian faith without the technical terminology employed by Whitehead himself. While I accept the process critiques of divine omnipotence and of the body/soul dualism of classical Christianity, I defend a stronger assertion of God's power and a more integral view of selfhood than is found in Whitehead's writings.[36]

This is the clearest statement yet of where Barbour affirms and yet also wants to critique and revise Whitehead. We will turn to these two revisions by way of final summary.

Integrated Self

Barbour treats first the need for a more integrated sense of self than Whitehead has provided. While acknowledging the processual character of the self and disavowing any substantialist or dualist conceptions, Barbour nevertheless believes that Whitehead has given too much attention to the atomistic or quantum character of the process and not enough to the emergent capacities of higher, more complex levels. In his appeal to make everything exemplify the metaphysical system, Whitehead stresses the occasional character of the higher functions too much and loses the very 'becoming of continuity' which does result in a sense of self-identity in the higher organized societies. Here Barbour sides with Hartshorne's development of Whitehead, particularly in his societal understanding of both God and the world, as well as the further theological elaborations of Cobb and Griffin.[37] Barbour states:

> The unity of self is a unity of functioning, not the unity of a Cartesian thinker. We have seen that this view – that selfhood is constructed – is consistent with neuroscience. Yet I believe that Whitehead himself overemphasized the momentary and episodic character of the self. I have suggested that without accepting substantive categories we can modify Whitehead's ideas to allow for more continuity in the inheritance of the constructed self, which would provide stability of character and persistence of personal identity. Joseph Bracken agrees with my criticism of Whitehead and believes it can be remedied by emphasizing Whitehead's thesis that a temporal society maintains continuity among its momentary constituents ('actual occasions') ... Bracken proposes that a society that endures over time can be understood as a 'structured field of

activity' for successive generations of events … Such revisionist or neo-Whiteheadian proposals can remedy some of the problems in Whitehead's writings while supporting his fundamental vision of reality.[38]

The proposal is that a social order can emerge from the becoming of continuity, where the relation between the actual occasions constitutes the order and as such can begin to function as a field. Joseph Bracken develops this idea at some length in his article but, unfortunately, does not distinguish between classical field and quantum field theory. I believe that classical field theory cannot do what he wants because all points in classical field theory are local but in quantum field theory nonlocal relations are possible as well as superposition that would provide a more helpful revision of Whitehead allowing for a societal model.[39] Bracken is also interested in developing the societal model to facilitate a process understanding of the Trinity which Barbour is not particularly interested in doing.[40] Much earlier, John Cobb also developed the notion of a 'personally ordered society' in his *A Christian Natural Theology*.[41] Either vision of a social self provides a sense of greater identity and raises the possibility of subjective as well as objective immortality. We will return to that issue later but let us turn now to Barbour's second critique of Whitehead, that of divine power, and a way of understanding divine action which while not arguing for omnipotence does nevertheless present a vision of divine power worthy of worship.

Divine Power

Barbour begins this discussion by clarifying what he thinks in regard to divine self-limitation. In a section entitled 'Voluntary Self-Limitation or Metaphysical Necessity'[42] he clearly sides with process theology in stating a preference for the latter. Drawing upon the thought of Charles Hartshorne, Barbour states:

> Charles Hartshorne elaborates a metaphysics in which all beings, including God, are inherently social and interactive. Every being has passive and receptive capabilities as well as active and causally effective ones. No being can have a monopoly of power or effect unilateral control. It is not as if the presence of the world limits God's otherwise unlimited power, since any valid concept of God must include sociality and relationality.[43]

He goes on to point out that Hartshorne's 'dipolar' concept of God has attributes of relatedness to the world and also attributes more akin to the classical ones. For example, God alone is everlasting, omnipresent, and omniscient (in knowing all that can be known). Thus for Barbour the idea of metaphysical limitation is more attractive than saying that God 'self-limits'. After all, divine self-limitation implies that if God wanted to, God could exercise full omnipotence and then we would be back in the problem of theodicy. He observes:

> To say that the limitation of God's power is a metaphysical necessity rather than a voluntary self-limitation is not to say that it is imposed by something outside God. This is not a Gnostic or Manichean dualism in which recalcitrant matter restricts God's effort to embody pure eternal forms in the world. If God's nature

is to be loving and creative, it would be inconsistent to say that God might have chosen not to be loving and creative. We cannot say that God was once omnipotent and chose to set aside such powers temporarily. If behind God's kenotic actions there was an omnipotent God who refrained from rescuing the victims of pain and suffering. The problem of theodicy would still be acute, ... Within a social view of reality, persuasion has a higher moral status than coercion, even if it entails greater risk of evil and suffering.[44]

This is Barbour's alternative to Polkinghorne's kenotic self-limitation approach. Polkinghorne argues that while God is omnipotent divine power must be constrained by divine love. He states:

Love without power would correspond to a God who was a compassionate but impotent spectator of the history of the world. Power without love would correspond to a God who was the Cosmic Tyrant, holding the whole of history in an unrelenting grasp. Neither would be the God and Father of Our Lord Jesus Christ, for the Christian God can neither be the Creator of a divine puppet theater nor a deistic Bystander, watching the play of history unfold without any influence upon its course. Divine power and divine love must both be given their due importance.[45]

It is clear that both 'scientists as theologians' want to connect divine love and divine power, rejecting both theological determinism and deism, but Barbour sees it as less theologically objectionable to understand divine power as metaphysically limited than self-limited. To suppose that God could have omnipotence and choose not to use it is to obviate suffering. Polkinghorne's alternative opens up the shadow of theodicy while Barbour's (and process thought in general) opens up the question of the viability of hope of divine salvation and worship. Is such a metaphysically limited God so worthy?

God and Worship

Drawing upon the thought of Daniel Day Williams, Barbour says yes. Going beyond Hartshorne, Williams defends divine initiative in history including in the person of Christ seeing God's love as absolute and thus as invulnerable. Rejecting both the divine monarch and the divine aesthete, Williams portrays God as a divine companion whose influence is transformative and redemptive.[46] This God of absolute love is worthy of worship and as social may also provide a basis for subjective as well as objective immortality.[47]

In the final analysis Barbour seeks to understand divine power as empowerment rather than overpowering control. Understanding theology as originating in a religious community and out of their religious experience Barbour concludes his most recent assessment of process theology in this way:

Can process thought account for Easter? To be sure, scholars have questioned the historical accuracy of the resurrection stories. There are discrepancies among them, and Paul's letters, written earlier than the Gospels, never mention the empty tomb. But clearly the lives of the disciples were transformed in a dramatic way that changed the course of history ... Marjorie Suchocki speaks of both a confirmation and transformation: 'The resurrection is the confirmation of that which Jesus revealed in his life and death, and it is the catalyst that transforms the disciples, releasing the power that led to the foundation of the church.' In process thought, God provides initial aims relevant to particular occasions, so very specific divine initiatives are possible, though always in cooperation with finite beings in the world. The events of Easter can be understood as such a new initiative.[48]

Barbour raised two major concerns with process thought in this latest book, the need for a more integrated sense of selfhood and a stronger assertion of God's power making God worthy of worship. Drawing upon the thought of Charles Hartshorne and his social conception of God, Barbour argued that one could achieve greater integration of the self, approaching what human beings experience as self-identity. Drawing upon the further elaboration of Hartshorne in the thought of Williams and Suchocki, Barbour concludes that one can think of God's power in more absolute terms as empowerment that does not violate metaphysical principles but is nevertheless worthy of worship. God in Christ is more powerful than that envisioned by Whitehead but divine omnipotence is still qualified by love, persuasion still wins out over coercion. By way of concluding this chapter let us turn to a brief assessment of this affirmation of process theology in Barbour's work and where we need to go from here.

Assessment

Throughout his career Ian Barbour has affirmed the ability of process thought to effect a theology of nature and contribute to the relating of science and religion. As we have seen, however, he has not been an uncritical adopter of process thought but rather recommends that it be 'adapted' to theology. From the beginning he expressed concerns about some elements of Whitehead's thought while affirming the overall system. I have tried to summarize those critiques as well as his affirmations in this chapter. Whitehead's metaphysics contributed a way to affirm divine action in a world described by scientific law and made possible a connecting of creation and providence while retrieving the understanding of a continuous creation. This allowed Barbour to develop an ecological understanding and make a major contribution to environmental theology and ethics.

While accepting Whitehead's critique of divine omnipotence and the body/soul dualism, Barbour has been aware of the too atomistic charter of the actual occasion process and has sought to augment it with a more Hartshornian social understanding. This was made clear in his more recent work. Barbour has always sought for theology to complement process metaphysics with religious experience and historical revelation in order to make it useful to the Christian community. For those reasons he sought a more integral view of selfhood and a stronger understanding of God's power.[49] He believes that the further developments of process thought by Cobb, Griffin and Suchocki provide such renderings. He himself does not do so even though he may be considered a 'scientist theologian.'

While Barbour is certainly one of the 'Scientists as Theologians' that John Polkinghorne talks about in his book of the same title (along with himself and Arthur Peacocke), he has been far more the scientist than theologian. Sir John Polkinghorne concurs with this assessment. While Barbour argues for four ways of relating science and religion Polkinghorne argues for only two, establishing a continuum between consonance and assimilation. He observes, 'At issue is the degree to which scientific concepts should be allowed to mould and influence the conceptual apparatus of theological thought, and the degree to which theology must retain (as science does unquestioned) its own portfolio of irreducibly necessary ideas.'[50] In this context assimilation seeks to 'blend' scientific and theological categories without succumbing to absorption, while consonance – as Polkinghorne uses the term – affirms some constraint on theology in regard to theology's understanding of the natural world while asserting more autonomy for theological discourse than assimilation does.[51]

Clearly Polkinghorne sets up this continuum with his own position in mind. After acknowledging that none of the three scientists he discusses is a pure case of either of these extremes, in his closing evaluation Polkinghorne places himself closer to the position of seeking consonance and Barbour closer to the position of assimilation. He observes:

> It seems to me that Barbour is located towards the assimilation end of the spectrum. While there is an unmistakable Christian tone to his writing, he does not often engage with the detailed substance of traditional Christian theology. It may seem a trifle ironic that his preferred metaphysical framework for discussion is that provided by process philosophy, since I feel that Whitehead's thought is inadequately anchored in our knowledge of physical process.[52]

Polkinghorne thinks that Whitehead left England a year too soon (1924) – 'just before the "*anni mirabiles*" of 1925–26 in which modern quantum theory came to birth.'[53] He concludes that Whitehead's metaphysics is too 'episodic' in character as 'It jerks along rather than flows,'[54] and attributes a 'panpsychistic property' to matter rather than the 'dual-aspect monism' that Polkinghorne himself affirms.

While space does not permit a full exploration of this analysis of process thought, it is important to affirm that Barbour, as we have seen, expresses similar concerns though not in such a categorical fashion. He too wants more flow of continuity in the process and appeals to Hartshorne's societal view to provide it, especially for human self-identity. He also argues for use of the term 'panexperientialism' as over against 'panpsychism' stating that we are not talking about consciousness at the inorganic level. It is telling that, in his critique of Barbour's thought, Polkinghorne does not refer to the further developments of Whiteheadian thought that influence Barbour's own position. While there is a tremendous amount of respect between these great thinkers and Polkinghorne does seek to be fair in his assessments, he appears to be overhasty to lump Barbour's position with the early Whitehead and hence to see it as having limited metaphysical and therefore theological viability. I think this is an unfortunate oversight that leads to a portrayal of Barbour's thought that does not do justice either to his critical and qualified appropriation of process philosophy or to his suggestions for further development referred to above.

While affirming process theology in its various developments and offering suggestions for its expansion, Barbour has focused primarily on providing ways to relate science and religion rather than on doing constructive theology. Clearly, as mentioned earlier, his major contribution to process theology is showing its scientific cogency and usefulness for the dialogue across many different disciplines. Barbour's encyclopedic command of information and his excruciatingly detailed, fair and objective summaries, even of positions he disagrees with, have formed the academic field of science and religion. I think it is telling that in all of his books Barbour, unlike Polkinghorne or Peacocke for example, refers primarily to science and religion and not to science and theology. For example, his methodological text *Myths, Models, and Paradigms*[55] is primarily a discussion of the relationship of philosophy of science and philosophy of religion rather than theology. I believe it is fair to say that Barbour would not consider himself a theologian in the more technical and professional sense of that word (in contrast to Polkinghorne who would see himself as such, being an ordained Anglican priest) but rather a philosopher of religion and science with a commitment to the Christian community of faith. It is for this reason then, that Barbour supports but does not make major contributions to specific areas of theological reflection.

Barbour has encouraged the use of Spirit in process thought, affirms the Hartshornian social models, the further development of divine persuasive love and a viable affirmation of redemption and eschatology but has not himself made major theological contributions in these areas. Barbour prefers to report the work of process theologians and apply it to the relevant areas of science and religion rather than do the direct constructive theological work himself. While this may sound harsh it is not intended to be so because Barbour's great contribution is his ability to synthesize and clearly summarize the vast amount of literature in the field and to raise its ethical implications in relation to technological utilization. It is for this reason that I think Ian Barbour can fairly be considered the father of the field of science and religion in the United States. Without the widespread availability of the understanding that he has made possible the field would not be where it is today. He has contributed to process theology by employing it as a metaphysical platform from which to build the emerging dialogue. Along the way he has reminded theologians of the need to take adequate account of research in the physical and life sciences in order to include an adequate understanding of nature in their theological reflection. Barbour has had a singular purpose in mind throughout his career and it was stated in *Issues* at the very beginning: 'How can God act if the world is law-abiding?'[56] Everything that he has written and said can be seen as an attempt to answer that most important of questions.

Notes

1. Alfred North Whitehead, *Science and the Modern World* (New York: Macmillan, 1925), 180.
2. I.G. Barbour, *Issues in Science and Religion* (Englewood Cliffs, NJ: Prentice Hall, 1966).
3. I.G. Barbour, *Issues*; *Religion in an Age of Science* (San Francisco: HarperSanFrancisco, 1990); *Nature, Human Nature, and God* (Minneapolis: Fortress Press, 2002).
4. Barbour, *Issues*, 1.

5. Ibid., 458.
6. Ibid., 440–42.
7. Ibid., 442 (Barbour's italics).
8. Ibid.
9. Ibid., 445 (Barbour's italics).
10. See Hartshorne's *The Logic of Perfection and Other Essays in Neoclassical Metaphysic* (La Salle, IL: Open Court, 1962) and *The Divine Relativity: A Social Conception of God* (New Haven, CT: Yale University Press, 1983).
11. Barbour, *Issues*, 446.
12. Ibid., 447.
13. Ibid., 448.
14. Ibid.
15. Ibid.
16. John B. Cobb, Jr, *A Christian Natural Theology* (Philadelphia: Westminster Press, 1965).
17. Ibid., 453-4.
18. Ibid.,. 453.
19. See I.G. Barbour (ed.), *Earth Might Be Fair; Reflections on Ethics, Religion and Ecology* (Englewood Cliffs, NJ: Prentice Hall, 1972).
20. Barbour, *Issues*, 454.
21. Ibid., 457.
22. Ibid., (Barbour's italics).
23. Ibid., 457–8 (Barbour's italics).
24. Ibid., 460–61.
25. I.G. Barbour, *Religion*, 221.
26. Ibid., 267.
27. Ibid., 260.
28. Ibid., 236.
29. Ibid., 261–2.
30. Ibid., 263.
31. Richard Rubenstein, *After Auschwitz: History, Theology, and Contemporary Judaism*, 2nd edn (Baltimore: John Hopkins University Press, 1992; originally published 1966).
32. See Colin Gunton, *Becoming and Being: The Doctrine of God in Charles Hartshorne and Karl Barth* (Oxford: Oxford University Press, 1978). Reference cited in Barbour, *Religion*, 264.
33. Barbour, *Religion*, 264 (Barbour's italics).
34. Barbour, *Nature*, 2 (Barbour's italics).
35. Ibid., 3.
36. Ibid., 6–7, see also p. 37.
37. See Hartshorne's 'The Compound Individual' in *Philosophic Essays for Alfred North Whitehead*, ed. by F.S.C. Northrup (New York: Russell and Russell, 1967), also John B. Cobb, Jr and David Griffin's *Process Theology: An Introduction* (Philadelphia: Westminster Press, 1976).
38. Barbour, *Nature*, 98. See also Joseph A. Bracken, SJ, 'Revising Process Metaphysics in Response to Ian Barbour's Critique', *Zygon*, 33 (1998), 407–8.
39. See Ernest Simmons, 'Quantum Field Theory and the Theology of the Cross: Towards a Kenotic Pneumatology', *CTNS Bulletin*, 1998.
40. See Joseph A. Bracken, SJ, 'Panentheism from a Process Perspective', in *Trinity in Process: A Relational Theology of God*, ed. by Joseph A. Bracken and Marjorie Hewitt Suchocki (New York: Continuum, 1992).
41. See n. 16 above.
42. An earlier version of this chapter was published as 'God's Power: A Process View', in *The Work of Love: Creation as Kenosis*, ed. by John Polkinghorne (Grand Rapids: Eerdmans, 2001).
43. Barbour, *Nature*, 112.

44. Ibid., 112–13. See also Charles Hartshorne's *Reality as Social Process* (Glencoe, IL: Free Press, 1953).

45. John Polkinghorne, 'Kenotic Creation and Divine Action', in *The Work of Love*, 91. See also his *The Faith of a Physicist* (Minneapolis: Fortress Press, 1996).

46. Ibid., 113. See Daniel Day Williams, *The Spirit and the Forms of Love* (New York: Harper & Row, 1968).

47. Ibid., 117.

48. Ibid., 118. See Marjorie Hewett Suchocki, *God, Christ, Church: A Practical Guide to Process Theology* (New York: Crossroad, 1982).

49. Barbour, *Nature*, 3.

50. John Polkinghorne, *Scientists as Theologians* (London: SPCK, 1996), 82.

51. Ibid., 82–3. For a different understanding of consonance in science and religion dialogue see Ted Peters, *Cosmos as Creation: Theology and Science in Consonance* (Nashville: Abingdon, 1989).

52. Ibid., 83.

53. Polkinghorne, *The Faith of a Physicist*, 23.

54. Ibid., 22.

55. I.G. Barbour, *Myths, Models, and Paradigms: A Comparative Study in Science and Religion* (San Francisco: Harper Collins, 1976).

56. Barbour, *Issues*, 1.

B

Roman Catholic Theology

Chapter 17

Catholicism and Ian Barbour on Theology and Science

Anne M. Clifford

If scientific endeavor, philosophical inquiry and theological reflection are to bring genuine benefit to the human family, they must always be grounded in truth, the truth that shines forth in the works of the creator ...

Pope John Paul II[1]

'Catholic' Universal and Confessional

Derived from the Greek *kath'holou*, meaning 'on the whole,' the reality but not the actual term 'catholic' is found in the New Testament, especially in Ephesians 4, when it speaks of the global dimensions of the church as the body of Christ, stressing in that context the importance of speaking 'the truth, each one to his or her neighbor, for we are members one of another' (Eph. 4:25). The explicit application of 'catholic' to Christianity was first made by Ignatius of Antioch (died *c.* 107–10) who, in reference to the nascent Christian *ecclesia*, argued that wherever Jesus Christ is, the catholic church is (*Letter to Smyrnians*, 8.2). Catholicity, however, is more than a matter of geographical extension. Cyril of Jerusalem (died 386) makes this clear when among the reasons he gives for the church being called 'catholic' is that it teaches 'universally and without omission all the doctrines that ought to come to human knowledge, concerning things both visible and invisible' (*Catechetical Lectures*, 18.23). Concerned not only with heavenly and spiritual matters, but also with the earthly and material ones, the church 'catholic' seeks truth both in the self-communication of God revealed in human history, and also in the divine self-manifestation through nature (cf. Paul's sermon at Lystra in Acts 14:15–17). Since the Nicene-Constantinopolitan Creed (381), widely accepted by Christians, 'catholic' has been regarded as one of the essential attributes of the Christian church. When the word 'catholic' is read in the creed it refers to these multiple understandings, including pursuing 'the truth that shines forth in the works of the creator.'

I begin with this brief early history of the term 'catholic,' not only to underscore its vast scope, but also its applicability to the life-project of Ian Barbour who, as a Christian and scientist, has traveled around the globe, diligently exploring with scientists and theologians the respective truths of both communities with the goal of enabling their doctrines to become meaningful parts of human knowledge for the benefit of people and the good of the planet.

Since the Reformation, however, 'catholic' has also acquired a confessional meaning, associated with the churches who accept the authority of the Petrine office in contrast and often in opposition to the churches that do not. At the Second Vatican Council of 1962–65, the oppositional stance of Counter-Reformation Catholicism was replaced with emphasis on a fundamental unity in Christ that encompasses diversity among Christians. All Roman Catholics were exhorted 'to recognize the signs of the times and to take an active and intelligent part in the work of ecumenism' (*Unitatis redintegratio*, 'Decree on Ecumenism,' #4). Since then dialogue and cooperation have become guiding principles for conversations, both formal and informal, as Roman Catholics and Protestants together seek deeper understanding, rooted in the fundamental unity we recognize in our common faith in Jesus Christ. By confession and church membership Ian Barbour is not a Roman Catholic, however, even a cursory perusal of Barbour's extensive involvement in science and religion dialogues, find him often seated at a common table with Roman Catholics and Protestants representing a wide variety of confessional perspectives. This reveals Barbour's commitment to the catholicity that can be achieved only through a dedicated ecumenism, an ecumenism that acknowledges that although there are some real and substantive differences among Christians about specific religious beliefs, communion with the 'religious other,' centered in love for the God revealed in Jesus Christ, is worth seeking in the context of conversation about science. It is in the spirit of ecumenism, that I, a Roman Catholic by confession and commitment, dialogue with elements of Ian Barbour's theology.

Roman Catholic theology today manifests its catholicity in ways that exhibit anything but a bland uniformity of thought. There are both unity and considerable diversity about how to interpret Roman Catholic doctrines, including those, such as creation, that are particularly germane to science and religion. However, since the Petrine office does symbolize the Roman Catholic Church's visible unity to the world, the teachings related to the relations of science and Catholic belief of our current Pope, John Paul II, will feature strongly in my treatment of Catholicism and the theological contributions of Ian Barbour.

Roman Catholicism's Neglect of Science

Virtually until the papacy of Pope John Paul II (1978–) the Roman Catholic hierarchy had not shown any great concern with the natural sciences except when scientific claims seemed to raise major problems with a particular doctrine or moral issue. In part this was due to the tendency in western Christianity – both Roman Catholic and Protestant – to subordinate earthly existence to the 'after life.' Beyond this reason, there are additional factors specific to Roman Catholicism that provide reasons for neglecting the natural sciences when doing theology. The first reason is that institutional Catholicism, prior to the Second Vatican Council, interpreted the Bible and Christian doctrine in the framework of medieval metaphysics. This pattern, which the hierarchy encouraged as central to Catholic identity, continued even when the medieval metaphysics and the worldview wed to it were no longer tenable to educated laity and many of the clergy. The second reason is related to the first but is more specific. It is the conviction that faith and reason do not conflict, but rather exist in harmony. This position, traceable to Thomas Aquinas and developed at the First Vatican Council of 1869–70,[2] held that there ought not to be major conflicts between Roman Catholic theology and any discipline because all truth has God as its ultimate ground. In principle, therefore, divine revelation, which for Catholics encompasses both the Bible and Tradition (faith), and accurate knowledge of the natural realm provided by the sciences (reason) should not contradict. Faith, in order to be understandable, requires the full development of reason; reason requires faith to strengthen, guide, and supplement its inherent limitations. Ian Barbour's conviction that a partnership between natural science and Christian theology is both possible and desirable resonates with the Roman Catholic conviction that faith and reason 'walk hand in hand.'

Barbour has analyzed the historical manifestations of the presence and absence of partnership between Christian theology and the natural sciences in terms of four 'typologies' – conflict, independence, dialogue and integration. These typologies, on the whole, are not directly tied to the confessional identities of Christian churches, but rather depend on other exigencies. Since his four typologies are widely regarded as a helpful pedagogical tool, they will be given attention in the pages that follow.

The Galileo Affair Revisited

The Galileo affair will be given attention for two reasons, first, Ian Barbour has commented on it at some length in several of his writings.[3] Second, Pope John Paul II has addressed it on several occasions to not only formally accept what the Roman Catholic Church had long tacitly accepted: the validity of Galileo's Copernicanism, but also to create 'teaching moments' to clarify the perspective of the Roman Catholic Church on its relationship to the scientific community.

Barbour, in company with many commentators, speaks of the Galileo affair as an example of conflict, although he does so with carefully worded disclaimers that draw attention to its overall complexity. There are elements of the Galileo affair that lend it to being included in the conflict topology, especially the famous trial of 1633, in which Galileo's acceptance of Nicholas Copernicus's *De revolutionibus orbum coelestium* was condemned. Yet, there are also factors, some of which Barbour neglects, that make the Galileo story difficult to categorize.

Prior to the 1633 trial, Copernicanism – specifically the propositions made in print by two of Galileo's contemporaries, Fr Paulo Antonio Foscarini and Fr Diego de Zuñiga – was judged to be heretical in a decree of the Congregation of the Index of Forbidden Books (*Librorum Prohibitorum*), made on March 5, 1616, on the grounds that it disagreed with biblical revelation.[4] Galileo's name appears nowhere in the decree, although he had publically supported Copernican astronomy in his *Sunspot Letters* (1613), arguing that the sun was motionless in the center of the solar system, and that the earth moves in orbit around the sun-center, while rotating on its axis. The reason is that after considerable private interchange he acquiesced to a request made by Cardinal Robert Bellarmine, to treat Copernican's heliocentricism as a hypothesis.

Cardinal Robert Bellarmine (1542–1621), a Jesuit who, as consultor to the Holy Office, had considerable experience in defending Roman Catholicism against the challenges of Protestantism,[5] found Galileo's position on the mutability of the heavens being compatible with truths of Sacred Scripture heretical and held that 'the motion of the earth is without any doubt against Scripture.'[6] Even before Galileo's ideas had been brought to the cardinal's attention, Bellarmine had projected a literal interpretation of the Bible onto questions of astronomy in a way that supported a static, geocentric world. However, beyond the actual content of Galileo's Copernicanism, Galileo held a position on the interpretation of the Bible that was also problematic for Bellarmine: he believed that the Bible, concerned with salvation, can never speak untruth, but its interpreters can. Science has nothing to say about salvation, but when biblical texts become the focus of disputes about the natural world, then the expositors of the Bible (the Catholic Church hierarchy) should commit themselves to finding interpretations that agreed with the well-established conclusions of natural philosophy (in other words, the new Copernican science).[7] This position, put forward by a scientist and not a theologian, was highly problematic for Bellarmine who, following the teachings of the Council of Trent, held that sacred scripture without the authorities of the Church to interpret it rightly could never resolve any question.[8] According to the Council of Trent, the authorities of the Catholic Church were bound to interpret the Bible in ways that did not conflict with the opinion of the early Fathers, all of whom in Bellarmine's opinion, interpreted the critical biblical passages literally, concluding that the sun revolves around the earth, which is at rest.[9] Bellarmine's ecclesiastical biblicism led him to conclude that the theories of astronomy could only be treated as hypothetical. He, therefore, admonished Galileo to treat the Copernican theory as a hypothesis; something to which Galileo agreed.

No doubt, Bellarmine expected Galileo to acquiesce because during this era, Roman Catholic Church authorities, many of whom like Bellarmine were well schooled in medieval scholastic theology and philosophy, believed that the findings of natural philosophy (the 'new science') were necessarily subordinate to the ultimate end of humankind, salvation of one's soul and eternal beatitude with God in heaven, and therefore must be carried out within the boundaries of revealed truth as God inspired the church authorities to define it.

Another issue worth noting is the impact of Copernicanism on the doctrines of Roman Catholicism. Barbour does not ignore this issue, giving some attention to 'humanity in the new cosmology' and the challenge to 'God's particular concern for human life.'[10] My purpose is to add nuance to Barbour's treatment. The cosmology of Ptolemy, which the Church on biblical and theological grounds accepted, presumed a hierarchy of being, something Barbour notes. Why is this significant? If the earth is the center of the whole universe with the sun revolving around it, there is a certain logic to concluding that human beings are the center of the earth, and by divine design God's primary concern. It makes sense to say that, of all the creatures, only humans image God. In the Copernican system, the sun displaces the earth as center, and so humans are pushed toward the margin of cosmic order, losing their special status. The new cosmology of the heliocentric system was a dangerous idea because it had the potential of drawing into question all that the Bible was believed to have revealed, including especially the divine Son becoming incarnate as a human for the sake of our salvation and human beings' special status as *imago Dei*.

From the standpoint of seventeenth-century history, the interaction between Galileo and Bellarmine was likely not so much a conflict between science and Roman Catholic theology as two worldviews bypassing each other without substantive contact: a nascent scientific worldview with a yet-to-be-proved hypotheses, which accepted the Bible as a source of truth but demanded it be reinterpreted, and an older Ptolemaic worldview that judged the Copernican to be merely hypothetical and in conflict with the truth God had entrusted to the guardianship of Catholic Church authorities. Galileo believed that the 'new science' would enable human knowledge of nature to increase over time. Bellarmine believed that the truth, representative of a union between faith and reason, was already known. Expanding the truth was unnecessary, defending it against erosion was a necessity.

My reason for going into some detail here is not to be dismissive of Barbour's strategy of analyzing the history of the relations of natural science and Christian theology in terms of typologies; indeed, they are helpful in negotiating the unfolding history of the interaction of Christian theology and science. Rather, I wish to emphasize the importance of a point that Barbour himself makes and to which he consistently attempts to be faithful: 'historical studies are of great value in any attempt to understand the interaction of science and religion today.'[11] Galileo possibly did not believe that his *Dialogue Concerning the Two Chief World Systems, Ptolemaic and Copernican* (1632)[12] constituted a disregard for the agreement made earlier with Bellarmine to treat Copernicanism as a hypothesis. Galileo's *Dialogue* was condemned in 1633, but no direct assessment of science versus religion played a role. The reason was his failure to honor the agreement associated with the decree of 1616. Galileo recanted and was placed under house arrest. Nevertheless, he chose to remain a Roman Catholic and continued his scientific work to the degree that his failing health and eyesight allowed. To the end Galileo seemed no more capable of comprehending the position of Bellarmine and those who after his death espoused his line of thinking, than they were his.[13]

The Roman Catholic Church's condemnation of Galileo may have more importance as a post-Darwin symbol of conflict between religion and science – a way to underscore how long the supposed 'warfare' has been going on – than was actually the case in the years following Galileo's trial. Within the Roman Catholic Church, there is evidence that Galileo underwent gradual rehabilitation after his death. For one thing, church authorities granted permission in 1734 to move Galileo's remains from a simple grave to a mausoleum suitable for an important personage in the Church of Santa Croce in Florence. Galileo's *Dialogue Concerning the Two Chief World Systems, Ptolemaic and Copernican* was removed from the Index of Forbidden Books in 1835, after which time scholars were granted access to the documents surrounding his Copernicanism. In 1893 Pope Leo XIII penned the often quoted words 'truth cannot contradict truth,'[14] reminiscent of Galileo's 'the two truths of faith and science can never contradict each other.'[15] Leo XIII, comes to his conclusion, however, in a manner more realistic about the state of science in the nineteenth century than Galileo had been capable of in the seventeenth:

> The Catholic interpreter [of Sacred Scripture] although he should know that
> these facts of natural science which investigators affirm to be now quite certain
> are not contrary to the Scripture *rightly explained*, must, nevertheless, always
> bear in mind, that much which has been held and proved as certain has
> afterwards been called in question and rejected.[16]

Likely to make the tacit rehabilitation of Galileo explicit and to correct the
perception that Roman Catholic belief about creation conflicts with science, John
Paul II sent a message in which he addressed the Galileo affair to the Pontifical
Academy of Science in 1979. Seeking to overcome the obstacles to fruitful concord
between science and the Catholic faith, John Paul II called theologians, scholars,
and historians to sincere collaboration, in an examination of the Galileo case. To that
end, he established a special commission.[17] In 1983, to honor the 350th anniversary
of Galileo's *Two Dialogues*, he remarked that the Galileo case has led to the
church's adoption of a more accurate grasp of its own proper authority.[18] In 1989,
while addressing the faculty of the University of Pisa, where Galileo once taught,
he again drew attention to Galileo and spoke of the 'people of science'
metaphorically as practicing 'a special priesthood' in and for the world.[19] In 1992,
Pope John Paul II officially closed the work of the commission and made a
statement before the Pontifical Academy of Science that is widely interpreted as an
official rehabilitation of Galileo. He called the Galileo case a 'myth' in which 'the
image fabricated from the events was quite removed from [the historical] reality.'[20]
Nevertheless, he argues:

> From the Galileo case we can draw a lesson which is applicable today in
> analogous cases which arise in our times and which may arise in the future ...
> It often happens that, beyond two partial points of view which are in contrast,
> there exists a wider view of things which embraces both and integrates them.[21]

Pope John Paul II's Call for Conversation

The attention given to Galileo by John Paul II manifests the recognition that modern
science has shaped the intellectual landscape within which Christianity, Roman
Catholic and Protestant, must engage in doing theology. This recognition did not
begin with John Paul II. It is found in the Second Vatican Council's *Gaudium et
spes*, 'The Pastoral Constitution on the Modern World' (1965). Focusing on the
influence of science on culture, *Gaudium et spes* made it clear that Roman
Catholicism did not have an oppositional relationship with the natural sciences. The
writers of this document acknowledge 'the lawful freedom and affirm the legitimate
autonomy of the sciences' (#59). *Gaudium et spes* also drew attention to the positive
values of the study of the sciences, including fidelity to truth in scientific
investigation (#57).

In the midst of the multiple addresses in which John Paul II gave attention to
Galileo, he sent an official message to George V. Coyne, the head of the Vatican
Observatory, in support of an open assessment of the relations between theology and
science.[22] If analyzed in terms of Barbour's helpful typologies, it is immediately

clear that John Paul II does not subscribe to 'conflict' between Christian theology and the natural sciences. Yet, like Barbour, John Paul II is aware that the conflict between the two is often the clash of scientism, which reduces truth to only one kind of knowing, thereby becoming an unconscious pseudo-theology,[23] with religionism, which opposes science in the name of faith, degenerating into a pseudo-science (M14). While emphasizing that the integrity and autonomy of science and theology must be respected, his position also goes beyond the independence typology. John Paul II believes that it is shortsighted for theologians to ignore the scientific character of modern society. He, therefore, advocates honest and in-depth conversation: 'Knowledge of each other leads us to be more authentically ourselves' (M14). Clearly, his preference is for conversation and dialogue. To that end, he calls for theologians and scientists to search together for a more thorough understanding of one another's disciplines. There are positive outcomes to this common search: 'a rational unity between science and religion,' can be achieved, which would result not in identity or assimilation but in dynamic interchange, with each 'radically open to the discoveries and insights of the other' (M9). Further, '[s]cience can purify religion from error and superstition; religion can purify science from idolatry and false absolutisms. Each can draw the other into a wider world, a world in which both can flourish' (M13).

John Paul II attaches a sense of urgency to theology's ability to incorporate the discoveries of scientists. He writes:

> Contemporary developments in science challenge theology far more deeply than did the introduction of Aristotle into Western Europe in the thirteenth century. Yet these developments also offer to theology a potentially important resource. Just as Aristotelian philosophy, through the ministry of such great scholars as St. Thomas Aquinas, ultimately came to shape some of the most profound expressions of theological doctrine, so can we not hope that the sciences today, along with all forms of human knowing, may invigorate and inform those parts of the theological enterprise that bear on the relation of nature, humanity and God? (M12)

Here John Paul II cites the philosophy of Aristotle and the highly philosophical theology of Thomas Aquinas. Elsewhere in *Fides et ratio* (1998), he makes it clear that the Catholic Church today has no preference for any one philosopher and will not 'canonize any one particular philosophy in preference to others.' The reason given is that, 'even when it engages theology, philosophy must remain faithful to its own principles and methods' (#49). The autonomy that exists where theology and science are concerned is extended to philosophy (#49). Yet, philosophy can provide an important and necessary bridge between the two, providing the critical thinking required for a fruitful exchange (#69).

While it is impossible to conceive of Pope John Paul II, a person well versed in classical, personalist, and phenomenological philosophies, using process philosophy to create a bridge between theology and the natural sciences, Ian Barbour has. In the interest of systematic integration and the articulation of a coherent worldview, Barbour proposes process philosophy as a promising candidate for a mediating role today because it was itself formulated under the influence of both scientific and religious ideas. Of particular importance is the primacy given to event, as the basic constituent category of reality, and of God, as the source of novelty and order. The dipolar God of process thought, both transcends the world and is immanent in it. In Barbour's assessment, the dipolar God of Process theism is more in tune with the biblical God, who is intimately involved with creation and with history than the classical immutable God found in the thought of Aristotle and Thomas Aquinas.[24] Among North American Roman Catholic theologians, some agree with this assessment, especially John F. Haught.[25]

In the 1988 *Message* and in other statements made by John Paul II, his concern about constructive relations of science and theology and their benefit for the two communities and for the human community and culture, as a whole, is clearly evident. There is sufficient evidence in Barbour's writings to conclude that he is in agreement with the Pope's concerns and goals, but would extend them – to the whole of reality, the cosmos. For Barbour, one of the hoped-for outcomes of fruitful dialogue between theology and science is to develop the foundation for an environmental ethics relevant to today's world.[26] The environment is not a topic neglected by John Paul II,[27] but it is not given specific attention in this particular message. Interaction of theology and science will certainly result in a moral commitment to a sustainable *oikos* commensurate with the natural order discernable by science and attributed to God by religion.

Biological Evolution and the Human Species

In his 1988 *Message* to Coyne, Pope John Paul II devotes one small paragraph to the 'life sciences,' noting that molecular biologists have discovered the same underlying constituents in the make-up of all living organisms on earth (M7). Some years later, in 1996, Pope John Paul II addressed biological evolution at a meeting of the Pontifical Academy of Sciences in which he argued that 'at first sight, there are apparent contradictions' between biological evolution and the message of Revelation (#2).[28] Going beyond the position of Pope Pius XII (1950) that there is no necessary opposition between evolution as a scientific hypothesis and the doctrine of the faith,[29] John Paul II stated even more strongly the Roman Catholic Church's recognition of the reasonableness of evolution on the basis of the scientific evidence and wide acceptance in the scientific community. 'Truth cannot contradict truth.'[30]

Pope John Paul II is not willing, however, to give all theories of biological evolution *carte blanche* acceptance. Of particular concern are the reductionist and materialist philosophies taken by some scientists. By taking this position, John Paul II invites scientists to be attuned to how ideology can affect their positions. He rejects any philosophical ideology that denies that humans are ontologically different – different in the very nature of their being – from all animals. If a scientist denies this fundamental truth, then she has overstepped the boundaries of science. For John Paul II, what makes humans ontologically different from animals is their 'spiritual soul.' This leads him to repeat Pope Pius XII's position that the human body evolved, taking its 'origin from pre-existing living matter, [but] the spiritual soul is immediately created by God.'[31] This is the Roman Catholic form of 'creationism.'[32] John Paul II associates the human soul especially with the possession of a 'speculative intellect,' a notion which he takes from Thomas Aquinas.[33] Apparently closely connecting (if not equating) the spiritual soul with the human mind, John Paul II stresses that those theories of evolution that treat 'the mind as emerging from the forces of matter, or as the epiphenomenon of this matter' are incompatible with the truth about humanity.[34] What is this truth? It is a special dignity God has granted to humans alone, for 'man is the only creature on earth that God wanted for its own sake.'[35]

In a historical context very different from that of the seventeenth century, Pope John Paul II's creationist position on the spiritual soul exhibits a similar purpose to the Church rejecting Copernicanism: to safeguard belief that to God humans are special and are made in God's image and likeness. To a scientist this position may indicate that John Paul II himself is not free from 'ideology.' Although, as already noted in *Fides et ratio* (written two years after his message on evolution), Pope John Paul II believes that no particular philosophy is to be given preference when doing theology, in the position that the human body is the product of biological evolution, but the spiritual soul of the human is created directly by God, there is evidence for a preference for classical Greek metaphysics, which is far removed from contemporary philosophies that take into account the science of evolution. John Paul II's creationism treats the human soul, and one might also presume the human mind, as a great exception to evolution, a 'special creation,' made directly by God. This results in a philosophical dualism with a line of demarcation between the spiritual soul, with its rational mind and spiritual capacities, and the human body, the material product of natural evolutionary processes. Part of what is at stake in John Paul II's insistence on this position, is to support not only the dignity of humankind but also a belief in the immortality of the soul. Although this concept is not given explicit attention in his message on evolution, one may draw this conclusion from the subject matter of the final section of Pope John Paul II's message, which focuses on the call to human beings to eternal life (#7).[36]

Ian Barbour has briefly treated Pope John Paul II's position in *When Science Meets Religion*, locating it in the typology of 'independence.'[37] On theological grounds, Barbour is unwilling to embrace soul/body dualism of any kind because he believes such dualism is inconsistent with biblical anthropology. He points out that biblical anthropology, especially that of the Jews who first composed the initial chapters of Genesis, conceives the human to be an undivided self (*nephesh* in Hebrew). A human self, he writes, 'is a unified activity of thinking, feeling, willing and acting.'[38] Further, most scientists do not accept soul/body dualism.[39] They speak of the mind and brain as two aspects of one unified process. Therefore, Barbour writes: 'I do not myself accept ... the classical body/soul dualism ...' Instead, he defends 'an integral view of the person as a psychosomatic unity,' which he believes is 'closer to both the biblical view and the evidence from contemporary science.'[40]

Barbour, seeks to integrate biblical anthropology with what biology reveals about the evolution of the human species by incorporating elements of process philosophy. He judges classical metaphysics and its reliance on substance categories (such as mind and matter; soul and body) for reality, to be inadequate because it infers a static sameness to entities no matter what their context. In contrast, process philosophy conceives of reality as 'one kind of event with two aspects or phases.' According to Whitehead, events are constituted by their relationships and their contexts in space and time. This is true for diverse types of systems, to which subjective experience can be attributed in progressively more attenuated forms to persons, animals, lower organisms and cells. Consciousness (associated with classical understandings of 'soul life' or mind) is found only at the higher levels, which makes humans the newest emergents in cosmic history. The unified self (cf. the biblical *nephesh*) is not an enduring entity but a stream of experience that is momentarily constructed through a unity of functioning, that always includes God. This is so because the dipolar God of process theism is present in all time and space, while also transcending time and space. In Barbour's proposal the immortality of the human person is not abandoned but, rather than it being an unchanging property of individual souls, it is conceived in terms of a relationship of persons to God and other beings.

Barbour's process conception of the self, which he believes is compatible with biblical anthropology and current neuroscience raises the question: What is the most adequate and appropriate way for conceiving of the human? Is it John Paul II's acceptance of evolution in a framework that retains the classical anthropology, founded on soul/body dualism? Or is it Barbour's process conception of the self as the unified activity of thinking, feeling, and acting? The reader is left with a clear choice: which approach honors the emerging consensus of scientists about human evolution and also safeguards the spiritual capacity of humans for self-integration through self-transcendence toward God? How one responds, no doubt, will reveal the extent to which one locates oneself in the typologies of conflict, independence, dialogue, and integration.

Conclusion

In this essay I have drawn attention to the catholicity of Ian Barbour's work in terms of the global and ecumenical dimensions of his commitment to partnership between scientists and theologians. I have set up a 'conversation' about some of his positions as they relate directly to Roman Catholicism, with emphasis on the writings of his contemporary, Pope John Paul II. In Barbour's thought we find a consistent example of John Paul II's 'two wings' of faith and reason rising 'to the contemplation of truth'[41] which has its ultimate source in God. In this regard he is indeed very catholic.

In her 1996 Catholic Theological Society of America 'Presidential Address,' Elizabeth A. Johnson expressed concern about the neglect among North American Catholic theologians of attending to 'the whole world as God's good creation.'[42] This neglect, she argues, 'enfeebles theology in its basic task of interpreting the *whole* of reality in the light of faith, thereby compromising the intellectual integrity of theology.'[43] The situation as described by Johnson has only slightly improved in the past six years. Catholic theologians can learn a great deal about interpreting the whole of reality with intellectual integrity from Ian Barbour. One may not agree with all of Barbour's analyses of the history of the relationship of science and theology (for example, the Galileo affair) or may prefer something other than his choice of process philosophy for bridging science and religion. However, any person who seeks to discover 'the truth that shines forth in the works of the creator'[44] and develop a theology of nature suitable for our time, can benefit greatly from a careful study of Barbour's in-depth and careful scholarship.

Notes

1. Pope John Paul II, 'Message to the Vatican Observatory Conference on Evolution and Molecular Biology' (June 28, 1996), in *Evolution and Molecular Biology, Scientific Perspectives on Divine Action*, ed. by Robert John Russell et al. (Vatican City State: Vatican Observatory and Berkeley, CA: Center for Theology and the Natural Sciences, 1998), 1.
2. *Dei Filius* (Dogmatic Constitution on Faith), esp. ch. 4.
3. I.G. Barbour, *Religion and Science, Historical and Contemporary Issues* (San Francisco: HarperSanFrancisco, 1997), 9–17, 77; *When Science Meets Religion* (San Francisco: HarperSanFrancisco, 2000), 7–8.
4. Found in Annibale Fantoli, *Galileo for Copernicus and for the Church*, trans. George V. Coyne, SJ (Vatican City State: Vatican Observatory Publications, 1994), 206. Since the decree came from the Congregation of the Index and not the Holy Office (or Inquisition), it did not carry the weight of an official pronouncement central to the faith.
5. By 1616 Bellarmine had distinguished himself as a professor of theology at the Catholic University at Louvain and at the Collegio Romano, where his speciality was 'Controversial Theology.' (At a special convocation held at the Collegio Romano in 1611 Galileo was honored for his contributions to mathematics and astronomy.)
6. Bellarmine's letter to Prince Federico Cesi (January 12, 1615), cited in Ernan McMullan, 'Galileo on Science and Scripture', in *The Cambridge Companion to Galileo*, ed. by Peter Machamer (Cambridge: Cambridge University Press, 1998), 278.
7. 'Galileo to Castelli' (December 21, 1613), in *The Galileo Affair, A Documentary History*, ed. and trans. by Maurice A. Finochiaro (Berkeley: University of California Press, 1989), 49–54. For commentary on the letter, see Richard J. Blackwell, *Galileo, Bellarmine and the Bible* (Notre Dame: University of Notre Dame Press, 1991), 67.
8. 'Letter to Foscarini' (April 12, 1615) in Blackwell, *Galileo, Bellarmine and the Bible*, 265–7; in the letter Bellarmine refers to the decrees of the Council of Trent (Session IV, April 8, 1546).
9. Bellarmine's letter to Foscarini was forwarded to Galileo through an emissary, Msgr Dini on April 18, 1615; see James Broderick, *Robert Bellarmine, Saint and Scholar* (Westminster: Newman Press, 1961), 362–3.
10. Barbour, *Religion and Science*, 16–17.
11. I.G. Barbour, 'Responses on Typologies for relating Science and Religion', *Zygon*, 37 (2002), 346.
12. *The Dialogue* is a witty conversation between Salviati (representing Galileo), Sagredo (the intelligent layman), and Simplicio (the dyed-in-the-wool Aristotelian). In support of the Copernican heliocentric theory, Galileo gathered together all the arguments (mostly based on his own telescopic discoveries) and used them against the traditional geocentric cosmology of Ptolemy [*c*.100–170]. As opposed to Aristotle's static cosmology, Galileo's approach to cosmology is fundamentally spatial and geometric. In giving Simplicio the final word, that God could have made the universe any way he wanted to and still made it appear to us the way it does, he put Pope Urban VIII's favorite argument in the mouth of the person who had been ridiculed throughout the dialogue. The reaction against the book was swift. The pope convened a special commission to examine the book and make recommendations; the commission found that Galileo had broken the 1616 agreement that he treat

the Copernican theory hypothetically and recommended that a case be brought against him by the Holy Office (Inquisition).

13. Church authorities at the 1633 trial of Galileo failed to appreciate the underlying history of their own position. In the thirteenth century, Aristotle's 'science' had presented the Catholic Church with a similar challenge. Although at first resistant to it and to Thomas Aquinas's theology because of its use of Aristotle's metaphysics, the Catholic Church authorities learned to state its fundamental doctrines in Aristotle's idiom and made the resulting scholastic theology the official theology of Catholicism. Unfortunately, the scholasticism wed to Aristotlean thought, to which they were committed, prevented them from benefiting from a potential lesson of history.

14. Pope Leo XIII, *Providentissimus Deus, On the Study of Holy Scripture* (Washington, DC: National Catholic Welfare Office, 1893), 27.

15. 'Galileo to Castelli' (December 21, 1613), in *The Galileo Affair, A Documentary History*, 51.

16. *Providentissimus Deus, On the Study of Holy Scripture*, #2, 23. (emphasis is mine).

17. Pope John Paul II, 'Faith, Science and the Search for Truth,' *Origins*, 9 (1979), 389.

18. Pope John Paul II, 'Papal Address on the Church and the Sciences', *Origins*, 13 (1983), 52.

19. Pope John Paul II, 'The Links between Faith and Science', *Origins*, 19 (1989), 373.

20. Ibid.

21. Pope John Paul II, 'Lessons of the Galileo Case', *Origins*, 22 (1992), 374.

22. 'Message of His Holiness Pope John Paul II to the Reverend George V. Coyne, SJ, Director of the Vatican Observatory', in *John Paul II on Science and Religion, Reflections on the New View from Rome*, ed. by Robert John Russell et al. (Vatican City State: Vatican Observatory and Notre Dame: University of Notre Dame Press, 1990). The occasion was a response to a conference in honor of the 300th anniversary of the publication of Isaac Newton's *Philosophiae Naturalis Principia Mathematica* (*Mathematical Principles of Natural Philosophy*). 'M' before a number corresponds to the pagination of the original message.

23. In '*Fides et ratio*', *Origins*, 28 (1998), 318–46. In this encyclical Pope John Paul II defines scientism as 'the philosophical notion which refuses to admit the validity of forms of knowledge other than those of the positive sciences; and it relegates religious, theological, ethical and aesthetic knowledge to the realm of mere fantasy' (339).

24. Barbour, *When Science Meets Religion*, 34–6.

25. See especially Haught's *Science and Religion from Conflict to Conversation* (New York: Paulist Press, 1995).

26. Ibid., 33.

27. Pope John Paul II, 'The Ecological Crisis: A Common Responsibility, Message of His Holiness Pope John Paul II for the celebration of the World Day of Peace' (January 1, 1990), in '*And God Saw That It Was Good*', ed. by Drew Christiansen, SJ, and Walter Grazer (Washington, DC: United States Catholic Conference, 1996), 215–22. In this message, the pope draws attention to the negative long-term effects resulting from 'the indiscriminate application of advances in science' (#6) and stresses that remedying the crisis is the 'responsibility of everyone' (#15). Throughout, his focus is anthropological.

28. Pope John Paul II, 'Message to Pontifical Academy of Sciences on Evolution', *Origins*, 26 (1996), 351. This message was given five months after the Vatican Observatory and Center for Theology and the Natural Sciences sponsored a conference on evolutionary and molecular biology, held at the papal summer residence in Castel Gandolfo. The papers discussed at this conference in which Ian Barbour participated are found in *Evolutionary and Molecular Biology, Scientific Perspectives on Divine Action*; Barbour's paper is entitled 'Five Models of God and Evolution', 419–42.

29. Pius XII, *Humani generis* ('Concerning Certain False Opinions'), in *Acta Apostolicae Sedis* 42 (1950), 575–6. This encyclical was written to address the issue of biological evolution and its relation to the biblical accounts of creation and the scholastic version of creation theology being debated in the 1940s. Although during Darwin's lifetime the Vatican authorities did not place any of his books on the Index of Forbidden Books, nor did Pius IX mention Darwinian evolution in the

Syllabus of Errors (1864), some Catholic theologians believed that evolution as described by scientists was unreasonable on philosophical grounds. Others, however, were beginning to explore the implications of the theory for theology. Although Pius XII did not condemn the speculations, he did express caution about the origin of the soul and about polygenetic theories of the origin of the human species. His reasons were theological and had to do with the uniqueness of humans as the only creatures that image God, the universality of original sin, and the universal need for salvation through Christ.

30. Pope John Paul II, 'Message to Pontifical Academy of Sciences on Evolution', 351. (The quote, as already noted, is Leo XIII's *Providentissimus Deus*, #5).

31. Ibid.

32. The Roman Catholic form of creationism assumes that God creates every individual soul directly out of nothing (see Heinrich Denzinger, *Enchiridion Symbolorum, Definitionum et Declarationum de rebus fidei et morum*, ed. by Karl Rahner, 31st edn (Freiburg im Briesgan: Herder, 1950), 738 (p. 272), 1100 (p. 363), 2327 (p. 713)). This position first emerged early in Christianity. Hilary of Poitiers (*c*. 315–67) argued that, although flesh is always born of flesh, 'the soul of the body [can] be from nowhere else than from God' (Hilary of Poitiers, *On the Trinity*, book 10, trans. by Stephen McKenna [New York: Fathers of the Church, Inc., 1954], Book 10, 22, p. 413). In the Middle Ages, Thomas Aquinas also made a creationist claim when he argued that the rational soul of humans could be made only by [direct] creation, even though other life forms [species] could come into existence by generation and presumably, therefore, by evolution (although evolution would have been very foreign to Aquinas's mind set); see the *Summa Theologiae*, I, q. 90, a. 2. (See also Aquinas, *Summa Contra Gentiles*, Book 2, q. 87 where he takes a creationist position to argue against the soul's source being semen of the father.)

33. 'Message to Pontifical Academy of Sciences on Evolution', 352. Here Pope John Paul II cites the *Summa Theologica*, I–II, q. 3, a.5, ad 1. In addition to the speculative intellect, humans also have a practical intellect and the capacity for knowing through the application of the senses.

34. 'Message to Pontifical Academy of Sciences on Evolution', 352. John Paul II upholds a tradition of rejecting 'generationism' that held that the souls of human offspring are derived from living matter in the act of procreation. This position, argued by Jakob Froschammer (1812–93) a priest, philosopher and Darwinian scholar, in *Uber den Ursprung der menschlichen: Rechtfertigung des Generationismus* (1855; 'On the Origin of Human Souls: Justification for Generationism') and *Menschseele und Physiologie* (1855; 'Human Souls and Physiology') was condemned and his books placed on the Index of Forbidden Books in 1857. In 1910 the church's magisterium condemned the opinion that the human soul was in any way generated by parents (D 170, 533, in Denzinger, *Enchiridion Symbolorum*).

35. 'Message to Pontifical Academy of Sciences on Evolution', 352. The quote is from *Gaudium et spes* (#24).

36. John Paul II, 'Message to Pontifical Academy of Sciences on Evolution', 353. It is important to bear in mind, however, that Christian eschatology is not dependent on Plato's conception of the soul as by nature immortal, although this belief is one of the contributing factors to Platonism's adoption by many early Christian theologians. Christian eschatology is rooted in belief, not in the natural immortality of the soul, but in bodily resurrection, revealed in Jesus Christ.

37. Barbour, *When Science Meets Religion*, 131. George Coyne, SJ, of the Vatican Observatory holds a different opinion, seeing the papal message on evolution to be an expression of 'openness in dialogue;' see his 'Evolution and the Human Person: The Pope in Dialogue', in *Science and Theology, the New Consonance*, ed. by Ted Peters (Boulder: Westview Press, 1998), 158. In this case, I share the judgment of Barbour; see my 'Biological Evolution and the Human Soul: A Theological Proposal for Generationism', in *Science and Theology, the New Consonance*, 162–73.

38. Ibid., 129.

39. Ibid., 132.

40. Ibid., 134–5.

41. *Fides et ratio*, Preface, 318.
42. Elizabeth A. Johnson, 'Presidential Address, Turn to the Heavens and Earth: Retrieval of the Cosmos in Theology', *Proceedings of the Catholic Theological Society of America*, 51 (1996), 1.
43. Ibid.
44. Pope John Paul II, 'Message to the Vatican Observatory Conference on Evolution and Molecular Biology', #2, 1.

Chapter 18

'Seeing' the Universe: Ian Barbour and Teilhard de Chardin

John F. Haught

As I reflect on the earliest stages of the trail that led to my concentrating on science and religion, I can see now that two markers stand out above all others. The first was my encountering the ideas of Teilhard de Chardin in my early twenties, during the period of the Second Vatican Council. The second was Ian Barbour's book *Issues in Science and Religion* (1966), a work that not only helped me organize my earliest courses on science and religion, but one that also convinced me of the abiding relevance of Alfred North Whitehead's thought to theology's encounter with the natural sciences.[1]

Barbour, in his first major book on science and religion, I was gratified to observe, expressed considerable appreciation of Teilhard.[2] And today when I reflect on Barbour's work I cannot help noting how well it complements and clarifies Teilhard's way of 'seeing' the universe. Barbour has long been an admirer of Teilhard, though not an uncritical one.[3] His esteem is perhaps as much for the person of Teilhard as for the latter's bold attempts to connect evolution and religious thought. Barbour's own father George was a scientific associate and close personal friend of Teilhard, especially in their days together in China. And one needs only to read a little of their mutual correspondence to appreciate the religious as well as scientific interests that bound the two scientists together. George Barbour has even written a moving book about their work and life together.[4]

In his later synthesis *Religion and Science* (1997), Barbour has devoted less attention to Teilhard's ideas than in his earlier book.[5] Perhaps this reflects a general waning of interest in Teilhard over the last 30 years. The renowned Jesuit geologist and paleontologist is no longer the towering pillar of inspiration he was during the 1960s and 1970s. Clear evidence of this decline can be gathered from the fact that some English translations of Teilhard's books have now gone out of print. This erosion of interest is especially surprising in light of the recent revelation that out of all the many books on religious thought published during the twentieth century by Harper & Row (and HarperCollins), Teilhard's *Phenomenon of Man* was the number one best-seller. In spite of the fall-off of interest in Teilhard, however, I believe that he still has much to contribute to our understanding of the role of religion in an age of science. I shall make this point by comparing his emphasis on 'seeing' the universe with Barbour's Whiteheadian interpretation of nature.

Teilhard: A Brief Introduction

Pierre Teilhard de Chardin (1881–1955) was a French Jesuit whose expertise in geology and paleontology led him to a life of reflection on the religious and specifically Christian meaning of evolution. For Teilhard, evolution is not an obstacle to Christian faith, but the most appropriate framework in which to articulate the meaning of that faith. Ordained a priest in 1911, Teilhard became a stretcher bearer during World War I where his courage in battle led to a military medal and the Legion of Honour. His most important work is *Le Phénomène humain* (1955; translated as *The Human Phenomenon*, 1999).[6] He began work on the book in China during the 1920s and 1930s, but his religious superiors forbade its publication throughout his lifetime, causing its author enormous anguish. Because his ideas on faith and evolution were considered too adventurous, Teilhard was almost literally 'exiled' to China where he became involved in significant geological expeditions and earned a sterling scientific reputation. Meanwhile, though, his growing understanding of earth history reinforced his urgent sense of the need for a radical reinterpretation of Christianity in the context of evolution. He composed numerous essays on religious faith and science, but this material saw the light of day only after he died. Returning to France from China in 1946, Teilhard hoped to gain an academic position at the Collège de Frances, but again his superiors, still afraid of his new religious vision, refused him permission. Following this disappointment, Teilhard came to the United States, where he worked at the Wenner-Gren Foundation for Anthropological Research. He participated in two more paleontological and archeological expeditions and died virtually alone and unknown in New York City on Easter Sunday, 1955.

Passed over during his lifetime, the modest and brilliant Jesuit scientist has turned out to be one of the most important Christian thinkers of the past century.[7] And to those who believe that religion – for the sake of its intellectual credibility – must eventually come to grips with evolution, Teilhard will continue to be an encouraging, even heroic, model. Speaking for myself, a great deal of my appreciation of Ian Barbour stems from the fact that the latter's work, though in many ways distinct from Teilhard's, carries forward and clarifies philosophically and theologically the sort of synthesis that Teilhard began.[8] The occasion of this *Festschrift*, therefore, provides an opportunity to revisit briefly Teilhard's revolutionary ideas on religious faith and natural science. Can they still contribute to the kind of philosophically sophisticated and theologically informed discussions that Barbour's work exemplifies?

Why the Neglect of Teilhard?

During his lifetime Teilhard was held in the highest esteem as a scientist, commonly acknowledged by his peers to be one of the top geologists of the Asian continent. But since his death and the publication of *The Phenomenon*, he has not fared well in the scientific community, particularly among evolutionary biologists. This disparagement is due in great measure to the predominantly materialist disposition of molecular and evolutionary biology. Because of Teilhard's insistence that the data of evolution do not require a materialist setting, evolutionists have often mistaken him for a vitalist, not realizing that he was carving out an alternative to both materialism and vitalism. Others have interpreted his vision of cosmic directionality as an illegitimate importing of teleological intuitions into science. The French Nobel laureate and biochemist Jacques Monod accused him of systematically 'truckling' to millenarian dreams.[9] Stephen Jay Gould, annoyed by Teilhard's conviction that evolution is patently directional, arbitrarily exiled him to the province of scientific cheaters.[10] Daniel Dennett recently referred to him as a 'loser,' ultimately because of Teilhard's firm rejection of materialist metaphysics and his allowance that evolution does not entail atheism.[11] Early on, many respected scientists in France embraced Teilhard, but today his critics often explain this affection as due to the residual Lamarckian bias of much French biology. In the English-speaking world the biologists Julian Huxley and Theodosius Dobzhansky energetically defended him, but even his close friend G.G. Simpson found it impossible to reconcile Teilhard's ideas with his own conviction – shared by many biologists to this day – that evolution rules out divine providence and cosmic purpose.

A notable exception to the current scientific dismissal of Teilhard is the commendatory appraisal by the widely respected biologist Harold Morowitz.[12] In fact, Morowitz expresses enormous regard for Teilhard's scientific ingenuity. He correctly observes, for example, that many years prior to Stephen Jay Gould's and Niles Eldredge's theory of 'punctuated equilibrium,' Teilhard had already provided a substantively identical explanation of the 'gaps' in the fossil record.[13] Morowitz might also have noted that Teilhard's work, even more pointedly than that of contemporary evolutionary biologists, anticipated and dismantled anti-Darwinian creationist efforts to interpret the gaps as making room for the notion of divine 'special creation,' an idea that, according to Teilhard, actually diminishes rather than honors the creative power of God.

Morowitz does not follow Teilhard's religious vision, but he is at least fair enough to distinguish clearly between Teilhard as a scientist and Teilhard as a religious thinker. Teilhard did not always make this distinction easy. He expressed the hope early in his major work *The Human Phenomenon*, for example, that his broad and novel vision of humanity would be taken simply as 'science,' even though the book includes obviously metaphysical assertions. Probably nothing has injured Teilhard's reputation among scientists more than a remark he makes at the beginning of the *Phenomenon* advising readers to take the book not 'as a metaphysical work, still less as some kind of theological essay, but solely and exclusively as a scientific study.'[14]

It is important, however, to understand just what Teilhard meant by 'scientific.' Above all, he intended that science should take into account the full range of 'phenomena.' Science, he thought, must not arbitrarily leave anything out that impresses itself upon our 'vision.' This means that science must also take into account the fact of our own 'consciousness,' since its emergence surely tells us something about the character of the universe that is its home. In other words, consciousness is not alien to nature, but nature's inner side, and as such inseparable from any adequate definition of nature. And yet, science thus far has done its best to close its eyes to the dimension of interiority, 'consciousness' or 'thought' that is clearly part of the universe. Why so? Teilhard's answer is clear:

> The apparent restriction of the phenomenon of consciousness to higher forms of life has long served science as a pretext for eliminating it from its construction of the universe. To dismiss it thought has been classed as a bizarre exception, an aberrant function, an epiphenomenon ... 'Full evidence of consciousness appears only in the human,' we had been tempted to say, 'therefore it is an isolated case and of no interest to science.'

But, Teilhard goes on, we must now enlarge our vision:

> Evidence of consciousness appears in the human, 'we must begin again, correcting ourselves,' therefore half-seen in this single flash of light, it has cosmic extension and as such takes on an aura of indefinite spatial and temporal prolongations.
>   Indisputably, deep within ourselves, through a rent or a tear, an 'interior' appears at the heart of beings. This is enough to establish the existence of this interior in some degree or other everywhere forever in nature. Since the stuff of the universe has an internal face at one point in itself, its structure is necessarily *bifacial*; that is, in every region of time and space, as well, for example, as being granular, *coextensive with its outside, everything has an inside.*[15]

Teilhard assumed that those who embrace the scientific spirit should, of all people, be willing to open their eyes. Doesn't science, after all, boast an allegiance to the empirical imperative? Then should it not take into account *all* of the data available to our experience, including the experience of ourselves as subjects, as conscious beings? Why, if we intend to be truly scientific, do we post a 'no entry' sign at the point where the cosmos exposes an 'interior' dimension. Surely subjectivity is an *objective* aspect of the universe, and not something floating in from outside? As Teilhard sees it:

> The time has come for us to realize that to be satisfactory, any interpretation of the universe, even a positivistic one, must cover the inside as well as the outside of things – spirit as well as matter. True physics is that which will someday succeed in integrating the totality of the human being into a coherent representation of the world.[16]

Interestingly, Teilhard's materialist critics, though pretending to be metaphysical monists ('only matter is real') remain implicitly dualists in their clean separation of their own mental life from the rest of the universe.[17] On this point I believe that Barbour's work has done much to clarify, with the help of process philosophy, Teilhard's entirely appropriate intuition that a thoroughgoing empiricism should not exclude consciousness or 'thought' from the field of its inquiry into the cosmos. Teilhard's is a universe, after all, that includes the human, a universe that cannot be understood objectively without taking the fact of human awareness into account as a terrestrial and, by extension, a *cosmic* phenomenon.[18]

Like William James and Alfred North Whitehead, Teilhard thought that the true spirit of science should lead us to practice a *radical* form of empiricism. Science should take into account *all* the data of experience. And this means that science should extend its sweep to include the datum experienced most immediately by each of us, namely, our own consciousness. An adequate science should attend to the 'inside' of things and not restrict its gaze to the outside.[19]

Although Barbour may not be willing, for methodological reasons, to extend the work of science itself to include the formal investigation of the 'withinness' in nature, it seems clear to me that he does agree with Teilhard that these are data deserving of *empirical* study. The question remains, however, whether we should expand our understanding of science itself to include the study of subjective consciousness, as Teilhard proposed that we do. Or should we instead make these the object of metaphysical inquiry only? I believe that Barbour agrees with Teilhard that consciousness is a *phenomenon*, a reality that we can 'see,' to use Teilhard's term, but that the 'seeing' is more appropriate to an experientially grounded metaphysics, such as that of Alfred North Whitehead, than to the conventional method of the natural sciences.

To Teilhard, in any case, it is irritating that the natural sciences almost completely suppress any sincere inquiry into the recently emergent human phenomenon, even though the intense fire of our species' consciousness is blazing right there in front of our eyes. Scientists, like everyone else, can be blind to certain realities in the universe until they have had their eyes opened. It is for this reason that Teilhard places a special emphasis on 'seeing.' At the beginning of *The Human Phenomenon* he writes: 'These pages represent an effort *to see* and *to show* what the human being becomes, what the human being requires, if placed wholly and completely in the context of appearance.' Then he adds:

> *Seeing*. One could say that the whole of life lies in seeing – if not ultimately, at least essentially. To be more is to be more united – and this sums up and is the very conclusion of the work to follow. But unity grows, and we will affirm this again, only if it is supported by an increase of consciousness, of vision. That is why the history of the living world can be reduced to the elaboration of ever more perfect eyes at the heart of a cosmos where it is always possible to discern more ... To try to see more and to see better is not, therefore, just a fantasy, curiosity, or a luxury. See or perish. This is the situation imposed on every element of the universe by the mysterious gift of existence.[20]

Ironically, however, natural science itself has not yet really *seen* that the human phenomenon is part of nature, and that because of this fact nature itself can no longer mean exactly what it has meant in modern times as the result of science's virtual expulsion of human subjectivity, or what Teilhard calls 'thought,' from nature. Moreover, even when scientists bother gingerly to investigate the human phenomenon, they almost invariably resort to reductive explanatory categories that are unable to illuminate what is distinctively human about the phenomenon. Evolutionists, for example, typically bracket out what each of us already knows intimately to be our most distinctive trait – our subjectivity, our capacity for thought. And in doing so they inevitably end up understanding not only the human phenomenon but also the universe in terms too small for either. The fact of consciousness actually provides a clue to what the *universe* essentially is, but science's myopic habit of methodologically abstracting from the inside of things, ends up blurring rather than clarifying our understanding of both humans and the cosmic totality.

While Barbour is appreciative of Teilhard's plea for a wider empiricism, however, he does not wish to burden the natural sciences themselves with the task of opening our eyes so widely to the fact of subjectivity as Teilhard did. Physics, for example, does not need to do the work of metaphysics as long as we do not forget that physics abstracts from much of the real world. For Barbour it seems that we can put up with the fact that science filters things out, methodologically excluding certain aspects of nature, provided that we allow for finer nets to retrieve what gets left behind. Barbour can live with the broad meshes of natural science's net only because he is fortunate enough to have found, as a complement, an empirically based *metaphysics* (that of Whitehead) that keeps bringing back before our senses what scientific method typically leaves out.

In process philosophy Barbour has found an empirically based complement to the abstractions of physics and other natural sciences. With Whitehead he understands metaphysics as providing an interpretive set of general categories which can apply to all types of experience and represent their fundamental characteristics.[21] An inclusive metaphysics can acknowledge more explicitly than natural science that subjectivity is pervasive in nature. Parallel to Teilhard's expansive understanding of 'science,' Barbour's metaphysics takes into account the 'inside' aspect in all of nature, though his Whiteheadian way of doing so is not exactly the same as Teilhard's. It is not essential to set forth the subtle differences here in order for us to register how close Barbour's empirically oriented metaphysics is in spirit to Teilhard's extending the boundaries of empirical inquiry to include the fact of consciousness. Process thinkers, Barbour notes, believe that the characteristics of lower levels are more developed at later, higher levels, thus providing both continuity and novelty at all levels of reality. All events are characterized by two aspects, mental and material, which see from within and from without. This view sharply distinguishes process thought from an ontological dualism of matter and mind and from a materialistic reductionism which excludes mind. Instead, process thought holds that all events at all levels are characterized by a single set of metaphysical categories. Thus human experience provides a clue to the kinds of experience at all levels, even while including what is truly unique, reflective self-consciousness.[22]

Teilhard did not have available such an empirically capacious metaphysics as Barbour has found in Whiteheadian process thought. For this reason I believe we should treat somewhat amiably Teilhard's audacious efforts to expand the understanding of *science* in the direction of the more radical empiricism that for Whitehead and his followers is more characteristic of a suitable metaphysics. For Whitehead, metaphysics is a kind of 'descriptive generalization' that must take into account not only scientific experience but all other kinds of experience as well.[23] For Teilhard, since neither the science of his day nor the Thomistic metaphysics he had absorbed during his theological training was adequate to capture the emergent 'withinness' of nature, he opted to stretch the boundaries of science so that the search for truth would not pass over in silence what is clearly an aspect of nature. Teilhard shared with Whitehead, for example, the conviction that every mental event is an aspect *of* nature, and not something that occurs outside the cosmos. They both agreed that we need to keep our search for truth open to whatever is phenomenally available, and this includes the experience of our own subjectivity. If science fails to 'see' the fact of interiority in nature, Teilhard is asking in effect, then what other mode of inquiry will do so?

Barbour, for his part, is apparently willing to allow science to abstract from the obvious fact of subjectivity provided that we make it integral to our metaphysical worldview. 'Metaphysics,' he rightly insists, 'is the province of the philosopher,'[24] and not of the scientist, a precept that Teilhard, for reasons that we have seen, could not follow scrupulously. Nevertheless, even though Teilhard used the word 'science' too loosely for the tastes of most scientists today, there can be no doubt that he was simply trying to get truth-seekers to accept as an empirical datum the human phenomenon as it has emerged in the context of an evolving universe. It is not so much that he was unscientific, but that he thought science should become *more integrally empirical* than it usually is. He wanted to stretch science's vision to embrace natural data that science generally ignores. Because he lacked an empirically grounded metaphysics such as Whitehead's, Teilhard could only fall back on *science* to do the job of *seeing* the universe.

This is not as grievous a sin, then, as it is often made out to be. We may object to Teilhard's widening the notion of science, but we have no cause for accusing him of being unempirical. Barbour, on the other hand, is blessed with a Whiteheadian metaphysics that gets its data from experiences of all kinds and is therefore able to apprehend empirically what science leaves out, including the fact of inwardness or subjectivity.

The phenomena that Teilhard wants us to view are available to everyone's immediate experience, and that is why he thought science, which claims to be rooted in experience, should look at them. There can be no reasonable objection on the part of scientists, he thought, to having their eyes opened to entirely new phenomena and to new ways of seeing. It is evident in the history of science, after all, that scientists of one age may fail to regard what scientists of another age can visualize quite readily. For example, until quite recently scientists, conditioned by atomism, Newtonian physics, and mechanistic models of representation, failed to notice the phenomena of chaos and complexity.[25] Today it is not unheard of that scientists of the old school still refuse to allow that chaos and complexity are really scientific ideas, and that they then relegate discussion of them to the arena of metaphysics. In a sense, they cannot yet *see* them as aspects of the natural world.

What Teilhard was trying to do was to turn scientific attention toward an aspect of nature that modern science had not looked at before in a penetrating fashion, but which the tools of geology and paleontology now render transparent, namely, the human phenomenon as a new *layer* in evolution. Since it is only artificially, and through almost violent abstraction, that science tears off the 'inside' from the outside of this phenomenon, it seems to me that it is not an absence, but perhaps an excess, of empirical concern that led Teilhard to envisage the phenomenon of consciousness as essential to a true scientific grasp of nature. I believe that

Barbour's work expresses a similarly broad empirical concern, but that he is more willing than Teilhard to divide between science and metaphysics the work of *seeing* things in their entirety.

Teilhard's Universe: What Did He 'See'?

Teilhard was also one of the first scientists in the twentieth century to have both noted and seriously reflected on the fact that the entire universe, and not just the stages of life and human existence, has a fundamentally historical character. The cosmos, he often repeated, is a genesis. On earth evolution has brought about the spheres of matter (the geosphere) and of life (the biosphere). But terrestrial evolution is now seamlessly weaving a new 'geological' stratum onto our planet. The sphere of mind, the noosphere, is the latest obvious dimension of cosmogenesis.[26]

So it is clearly within the legitimate compass of natural science, Teilhard insisted, to explore this new layer now emerging over our heads and beneath our feet. But, curiously and most disappointingly, scientists for the most part ignore it. The human phenomenon is clearly visible, and if we but opened our eyes we could *see* it. Yet this reality, containing in itself perhaps the deepest clues to the very nature of the *universe*, has not yet become a serious datum for scientists.[27] The eye of the geologist or paleontologist is ideally trained to look for emerging *levels* in the record of planetary evolution, and so it should not have missed the recent eruption onto the planetary surface of a whole new such level, the noosphere. Yet the scientific attention even of the vast majority of earth scientists has not yet truly begun to focus on the human phenomenon as a natural, terrestrial and cosmic, development. Behind this reserve there lies a suspicion that we humans – beings endowed with mind or consciousness – do not really belong to the cosmos. Subjectivity, to this day a scientific taboo, is seldom formally considered to be a real part of the natural world.[28]

Ian Barbour, very early on, recognized in Teilhard as well as in Alfred North Whitehead, a new breadth of empirical interest, one that situates the fact of mind or consciousness directly in nature itself.[29] As far as the relationship of religion to science is concerned, the advantages that come from placing mind on a continuum with nature cannot be overstated. Once mind is returned to its proper matrix in nature, two of the major difficulties that religion faces in an age of science begin to dissolve. The first of these is the challenge to religion posed by mechanism–materialism, a vision of things that Teilhard, Whitehead, and Barbour all expose as at best a useful abstraction. The second is the question of how to think of divine action in the world of nature.[30] By recognizing the continuity of emergent human subjectivity (the 'inside') with the entire history of the universe, Teilhard realized that there is no clearly defined threshold in evolution where we can trace a crisp line separating 'matter' sharply from the realm of mind or spirit. Consequently the interactivity of God (whom religions identify as the epitome of 'spirit') with the physical world should no longer pose an insurmountable problem in principle – since the 'stuff' of the universe has *never* been separable from consciousness and spirit.

Once dualism is destroyed, there can be no such thing as an essentially mindless kingdom of matter inherently closed to the realm of spirit or to the influence of God. What we casually refer to as 'matter' has never in fact been separable from spirit. The whole idea of 'matter' is for both Teilhard and Whitehead – and later for Barbour – a scientifically helpful abstraction that has illegitimately and illogically assumed the status of being the metaphysical foundation of modern science's understanding of nature.[31] Mindless 'matter' still constitutes ultimate reality in the assumptions of many contemporary evolutionists.

It is our modern fictitious substantializing of a realm of spiritless matter that makes it seem impossible that God could influence nature. For Teilhard, however, matter and spirit are terms that properly refer not to distinct substances, but to *tendencies* in the evolution of the universe. 'Matter' designates the inclination of entities to slide back entropically toward the condition of multiplicity and dispersal that constitute the primordial stages of evolution, whereas 'spirit' stands for the propensity of beings to converge toward complex, differentiated unity around a center or goal. What we need today, Teilhard argues, is a 'generalized physics, where the internal face of things as well as the external face of the world will be taken into account. Otherwise ... it would be impossible to cover the totality of the cosmic phenomenon with a coherent explanation, as science must aim to do.'[32]

Spirit, henceforth, cannot logically be taken as epiphenomenal, but as a 'fundamental' aspect of evolution, spanning the entirety of the process, though becoming manifest in different degrees of transparency along the way. The cosmic *tendency* toward unity, a nisus that has never deserted the universe, renders incoherent any attempt by science to comprehend evolution's impetus toward life, consciousness and spirit in terms of totally materialized atomic units. Since the most serious challenges by modern thought to religion have come from materialist metaphysics, we cannot exaggerate the significance of Teilhard's critique of the 'analytical illusion' that supposes we can get to the bottom of the phenomena of life and mind by mentally decomposing them into lifeless droplets of 'matter.'[33]

The simple fact is that there is no such *thing* as matter. Thus the ongoing project by modern eliminative materialism to account for life and mind in terms of frozen abstract entities that are falsely assumed to be concretely real is logically doomed from the outset. It is to Barbour's considerable credit that he has persistently recognized along with Whitehead and Teilhard that the whole modern project of scientific materialism is rooted in simultaneous failures both of logic and of vision. In ways that he has not always clarified explicitly himself, I believe that Barbour's way of 'seeing' the world, and teaching others to see it, has deep affinities not only with Whitehead but also with Teilhard. One of Barbour's most important contributions to contemporary thought is that – in association with other scientifically informed thinkers like Teilhard and Whitehead[34] – he has persistently declined to edit out the fact of subjectivity from what he knows to be objectively part of the *natural* world. Along with Teilhard and Whitehead, he has been concerned to understand the non-human evolutionary world in terms that will allow a real place for subjectivity in the unfolding of the universe.

Modern thought, on the other hand, has not prepared us well for such an inclusion. The typical scientific picture of the natural world out of which humans evolved has been one in which there is no logical space for subjects of any sort.[35] Thus, when evolutionary biology perforce located the roots of our own existence deep down in the subsoil of the *objective* universe, the only way modern thought could consistently conceive of an inclusive continuum of humans and nature was to rule out our own subjectivity as at best epiphenomenal. To fit humans into a mindless universe it had to divest us of mind. It still tries to do so.

Barbour, on the other hand, while allowing that there is an inclusive continuum of human subjects and the natural world, wants to make sure that our understanding of this continuum is categorically copious enough to fit the totality – rather than just an abstracted portion – of our being into the whole scheme of things. If science itself cannot do this work, then an empirically based process metaphysics must take up the task. Carrying on the spirit, if not the letter, of Teilhard's way of 'seeing,' Barbour has kept our eyes open to aspects of the universe and its evolution that we would otherwise have failed to notice. In doing so, it seems to me, he has contributed to a vision of nature that Teilhard would have been honored to endorse.

Notes

1. I.G. Barbour, *Issues in Science and Religion* (New York: Harper Torchbooks, 1966).
2. Ibid., 400–408.
3. See, for example, I.G. Barbour, 'Five Ways of Reading Teilhard', *The Teilhard Review*, 3 (1968), 3–20.
4. George Brown Barbour, *In the Field with Teilhard de Chardin* (New York: Herder & Herder, 1965).
5. I.G. Barbour, *Religion and Science: Historical and Contemporary Issues* (San Francisco: HarperSanFrancisco, 1997).
6. Pierre Teilhard de Chardin, *The Human Phenomenon*, trans. by Sarah Appleton-Weber (Portland, OR: Sussex Academic Press, 1999).
7. See, for example, Christopher F. Mooney, *Teilhard de Chardin and the Mystery of Christ* (Garden City, NY: Doubleday, 1968).
8. To those interested in pursuing Teilhard's ideas, my own recommendation is to begin with collections of his essays, especially *The Future of Man*, trans. by Norman Denny (New York: Harper & Row, 1964) and *Human Energy*, trans. by J.M. Cohen (New York: Harcourt Brace Jovanovich, 1971), rather than plunging immediately into *The Human Phenomenon*. Next to the latter, Teilhard's best known work is *The Divine Milieu* (New York: Harper & Row, 1968), a fertile and provocative interpretation of spirituality framed by an evolutionary sense of the world. For a lucid and blunt presentation of Teilhard's critique of classical theology, see his book *Christianity and Evolution*, trans. by René Hague (New York: Harcourt Brace Jovanovich, 1971). There are also many works available by critics of Teilhard, and certainly Teilhard would have welcomed such evaluations – if only he had been given the opportunity while still living. As it is, it is left for others to refine, develop and apply his ideas to our contemporary situation.
9. Jacques Monod, *Chance and Necessity: An Essay on the Natural Philosophy of Modern Biology*, trans. by Austryn Wainhouse (New York: Knopf, 1971), 32.
10. See Stephen Jay Gould's essays in *Natural History*, March, 1979; August, 1980; June, 1981. For a discussion of Gould's charges against Teilhard and a decisive refutation of them see Thomas King, SJ, 'Teilhard and Piltdow,' in *Teilhard and the Unity of Knowledge*, ed. by Thomas King, SJ, and James Salmon, SJ (New York: Paulist Press, 1983), 159–69.

11. Daniel C. Dennett, *Darwin's Dangerous Idea: Evolution and the Meaning of Life* (New York: Simon & Schuster, 1995), 320.
12. Harold J. Morowitz, *The Kindly Dr. Guillotin and Other Essays on Science and Life* (Washington, DC: Counterpoint, 1997), 21–7.
13. See especially Teilhard's unfortunately neglected work *The Vision of the Past*, trans. by J.M. Cohen (New York, Harper & Row, 1966). Reading this important book might remove many of the caricatures of Teilhard as unscientific. The book also includes brilliant defenses of evolution against the attacks of creationists and other critics of Darwinian biology.
14. Teilhard de Chardin, *The Human Phenomenon*, 1.
15. Ibid., 24 (emphasis original).
16. Ibid., 6.
17. Perhaps the best example is Jacques Monod's book, *Chance and Necessity* which combines Cartesian dualism with existentialism and mechanism as the only 'objective' context for understanding evolution.
18. Teilhard de Chardin, *The Human Phenomenon*, 109–63.
19. Ibid., 22–32.
20. Ibid., 3. If it appears to the reader that I will be employing the verb 'to see' to excess in the following, it is only because Teilhard has given to 'seeing' a richer meaning than it ordinarily has. To substitute other terms might cause us to overlook the technical meaning that Teilhard gives to the verb.
21. Barbour, *Religion and Science*, 103.
22. Ibid., 104.
23. Alfred North Whitehead, *Process and Reality*, corrected edition, ed. by David Ray Griffin and Donald W. Sherburne (New York: The Free Press, 1978).
24. Barbour, *Religion and Science*, 103.
25. See Stephen H. Kellert, *In the Wake of Chaos: Unpredictable Order in Dynamical Systems* (Chicago: University of Chicago Press, 1993).
26. Teilhard de Chardin, *The Human Phenomenon*, 122–5.
27. Ibid., xxvi–xxviii, 3–7.
28. See also B. Alan Wallace, *The Taboo of Subjectivity: Toward a New Science of Consciousness* (New York: Oxford University Press, 2000).
29. For Barbour as for Whitehead not only science but also metaphysics must be grounded empirically: 'Metaphysics is not, as its critics hold, sheer speculation unrelated to experience' (*Issues in Science and Religion*, 461). The function of metaphysics is not to move the mind away from the empirical, but to root it more completely in a wide range of experience. Hence, as Whitehead insisted, the philosopher's job is to criticize scientific abstractions for leaving out too much of the real world. Ironically science gives us representations of the universe that abstract from most of its real depth. Physics, for example, gives us not fundamental reality, as many physicists claim, but an abstract set of ideas and models that have already left out most of what we actually experience. Metaphysics is essential, therefore, as Barbour put it, to give us an 'integral world view' (ibid., 461).
30. It is not possible for me in this essay to argue this point in detail, but I would turn the reader's attention to Ian Barbour's whole synthesis of science and religion, which among other things does provide just this sort of argumentation.
31. See also E.A. Burtt, *The Metaphysical Foundations of Modern Physical Science* (Garden City, NY: Doubleday, 1954).
32. Teilhard de Chardin, *The Human Phenomenon*, 22.
33. Pierre Teilhard de Chardin, *Activation of Energy*, trans, by René Hague (New York: Harcourt Brace Jovonovich, Inc., 1970), 139.
34. In addition to Whitehead's, Michael Polanyi's thought is also relevant as an attempt to bring back the reality of subjectivity as part of the real world. See his book *Personal Knowledge* (New York: Harper Torchbooks, 1964).
35. See Wallace, *The Taboo of Subjectivity*.

C

Buddhist Theology

Chapter 19

A Reflection on Buddhist–Christian Dialogue with the Natural Sciences

Paul O. Ingram

Throughout his distinguished career Ian Barbour has argued that the two most important topics for Christian theological reflection are (1) dialogue with the natural sciences and (2) how the practice of interreligious dialogue for Christians should be contextualized by what the natural sciences are discovering about the physical processes structuring the universe. In *Religion and Science*, he discusses four criteria that define successful scientific models and theories: agreement with data, coherence, scope, and fertility.[1] While these criteria can be employed in analyzing religious models and claims, no religious tradition can claim to be scientific, 'even though they exemplify the same spirit of inquiry found in the standards of science.'[2] Theology is critical reflection on the life and thought of various religious communities. Yet while it is always revisable, there exist neither controlled experiments nor proofs in theology. Still there is a process of testing in the life and experience of a religious community and theologians can build cumulative cases from lines of argument. Furthermore, persons of faith should demand that concepts and theological models be closely related to the widest body of human experience.

Barbour's discussion of the world's religions in the context of his own Christian dialogue with the natural sciences demonstrates his breadth of thought. Yet, knowledgeable about the world's religions as Barbour is, the generalist character of his understanding of non-Christian religious traditions has limited the data, coherence, scope, and fertility of his theological vision. Even so, the fact that Barbour has acknowledged the need to encounter the natural sciences within the wider contexts of religious pluralism furthers the evolution of current religion–science dialogue. Inspired by Barbour's thought, this essay seeks to contribute to the evolution of both the religion–science dialogue and contemporary Buddhist–Christian dialogue by focusing on how Christian theology and Buddhist philosophy have interacted with certain aspects of the contemporary scientific origin narrative known as the 'Big Bang'. My thesis is that, while Buddhist and Christians do not interact with Big Bang cosmology in identical ways, including current scientific accounts of the evolution of the universe as a third partner in Buddhist–Christian encounter will engender new opportunities for mutual creative transformation. But first, some preliminary observations.

Preliminary Observations

Barbour identifies five features of contemporary scientific thought that constitute a challenge not only to Christian tradition, but to all religious traditions: the success of the methods of scientific investigation; the differences between scientific cosmologies and traditional religious cosmologies; the new contexts that science provides for theological reflection on religious understandings of human nature, particularly the doctrine of creation in the monotheistic religions; the fact of religious pluralism, which calls into question exclusive claims for any one religious tradition; and global threats to the environment and the subsequent necessity for religious people to turn toward science to understand the ecological interdependence of all life forms.[3] Given these challenges, this essay is based on four assumptions.

First, it seems clear that what the natural sciences are revealing about the universe have become epistemological models for other disciplines of inquiry. The sciences appear to give us real knowledge of the physical structure of the universe because scientific theories and laws bear some resemblance to the actuality of the universe they describe That is, they have ontological reference to physical reality.[4] But, as John Cobb warns, human beings cannot live by scientific abstractions alone because patterns of scientific abstractions cannot tell us how to constitute ourselves in community with each other and with other sentient life forms with whom we share this planet.[5] Such issues are the proper focus of theological reflection in dialogue with the natural sciences.

Second, it is also clear that scientific theories cannot be taken as literal descriptions of the physical universe, as classical realism assumed. Nor are scientific theories merely calculating devices whose only function is to allow the correlation and prediction of experimental observations, as instrumentalism holds. As Barbour notes, most working scientists hold a middle position between classical realism and instrumentalism he calls 'critical realism:' scientific theories and models are 'abstract symbol systems, which inadequately and selectively represent particular physical aspects of the world for specific purposes.'[6] Critical realism thereby points to a working scientist's real intention while recognizing that scientific theories and models are imaginative human constructs that are always intended to bear ontological correspondence to reality; they are neither literal pictures nor useful fictions, but limited – and revisable – ways of imagining what the physical structures of the universe are. This essay appropriates Barbour's understanding of critical realism as its primary epistemological assumption.

Third, both scientific and theological insights demand response and carry ethical implications for human action. Because both science and theology are concerned with the question of truth and how persons should live in accord with truth, neither science nor theology can be ethically neutral. Nor will either discipline ever attain a total grasp of reality – the way things really are as opposed to the way we wish them to be. Yet for both disciplines there is reasonable hope for developing approximate understandings of reality.

Finally, while there are many problems in the overall perspectives that the various natural sciences – and the diverse theories within each particular science – give us of the history of the universe, there exists a surprisingly unified origin narrative starting from Plank time to the present. In broad strokes, this narrative claims that some twelve to fourteen billion years ago the universe began as an explosion of matter from a singularity that was infinitely small, infinitely hot, and infinitely concentrated outward to create some hundred billion galaxies, including our galaxy, the Milky Way, which in itself contains billions of stars and our sun and its planets. All things that have existed, now exist, and will ever exist are the evolutionary effects of this primal 'Big Bang' and its evolutionary history.

A metaphysical conclusion this essay draws from this narrative is that the universe is dynamic and open ended – creative of ever new novelty, things and events never before imagined, yet always coming to be in interdependence with what went on before – ideas that should bring a smile of recognition to Buddhists and Christian process theologians. If this conclusion is valid, it is reasonable to conclude that current scientific cosmology provides us with a 'metadiscourse' of the universe by which it is possible to link individual discourses such as theology, ethics, or politics, or the teachings and practices of different religious traditions. That is against the postmodern insistence – itself a universal truth claim that is, when pushed to its logical conclusion, incoherent with its own assumptions – that every theological and religious claim based on universal criteria is nothing but a social construction of the politically powerful, valid only for its own back yard, we can hold up a common origin narrative of the universe that tells us that all things and events are interrelated and interdependent.

The Origin of the Universe: Buddhist and Christian perspectives

But there is a hiccup. As a Lutheran Christian historian of religion, I am more sure of the theological challenges and contributions of dialogue with the natural science for Christian faith and practice than I am of the contributions dialogue with the sciences might make for Buddhist faith and practice. It's not just that Buddhists need to decide this for themselves. Buddhists who write about the natural sciences seem agreed that Buddhist doctrine is supported rather than challenged by the natural sciences. Accordingly, Buddhism may be evidence against my thesis that current scientific cosmology provides a common origin narrative that can be appropriated by most of the world's religious traditions.

Since Christian monotheism and Buddhist non-theism seem so incommensurable, reflection on the current scientific origin narrative that both Christians and Buddhists now share will serve as an illustration of my dilemma. According to this narrative, a plausible reconstruction of cosmic history has emerged. Some fourteen billion years ago the contents of the universe were together in an initial singularity, meaning a region of infinite curvature and energy density at which the known laws of physics break down ($t = 0$).[7] There was a Big Bang. The history of the cosmos began three minutes after this event, when protons and neutrons were combining to form nuclei. Five hundred thousand years later, atoms were coming into existence. One billion years from $t = 0$, galaxies and stars were being formed, followed by planets at ten billion years. After another two billion years, microscopic forms of life were beginning to appear on our planet.

The farther back we go beyond three minutes, the more tentative cosmological theory becomes because it deals with states of matter and energy increasingly farther from anything physicists can experimentally duplicate in the laboratory.[8]

Protons and neutrons form from their constituent quarks at 10^{-4} seconds (a ten-thousandth of a second from t = 0), when temperature had cooled to 10^{12} (1,000 billion degrees). This sea of hot quarks would have formed at about 10^{-10} seconds from an even smaller and hotter fireball. According to the inflationary theories proposed by Alan Guth, the universe underwent a very rapid expansion at about 10^{-35} seconds due to the tremendous energy released in the breaking of symmetry when the strong force separated from the other forces.[9] Before 10^{-35} temperatures would have been so hot that all the forces except gravity were of comparable strength. Physicists have almost no idea about events before t = 10^{-43} (Plank time), when the temperature was about 10^{32} degrees, and the universe was about the size of an atom with an incredible density of 10^{96} times that of water.

If this origin narrative is accurate, it seems reasonable to ask what caused the Big Bang. The Christian answer is that God created the universe. But there is a problem with the Christian doctrine of creation that seems, at first glance, to point in the direction of Buddhist non-theism. The problem is that cosmologists claim that the Big Bang marked not only beginning of the universe, but also the start of time. There was not time before the Big Bang, so there could have been no cause of the Big Bang. 'What place then for a creator?' asks Stephen Hawking in *A Brief History of Time*,[10] to which one might add, 'or divine agency in the continuing processes of nature?'.

The Buddhist answer to Hawking's question is that there is no place for a creator or for divine agency. Non-theism has always been the center of the Buddhist worldview so that Buddhists like Geoffrey Redmond argue that contemporary cosmology readily harmonizes with Buddhism since Buddhism's cosmology can be construed as a metaphor without 'weakening the Buddhist edifice.' Furthermore, Redmond argues, cosmology never had the centrality that creation has in Christian and Jewish tradition. 'Buddhism never committed itself to a particular ontology,' he writes, 'which could be contradicted by modern psychological or anthropological conceptions of such beliefs as metaphorical or archetypal.'[11] Therefore, 'Buddhism is closer to science than is revealed religion in the way it seeks truth.'[12]

Of course, the challenge of Big Bang cosmology to the Christian doctrine of creation is crystal clear. One way theologians have responded is by reflecting on the relation between space and time in the scientific origin narrative. As I understand this narrative, the Big Bang was an unusual explosion because it did not take place at a particular location in space. This means there existed no space outside the Big Bang. A common analogy to visualize this conclusion is a rubber balloon onto which are glued a number of coins. The coins represent galaxies. As air is pumped into the balloon, it expands. Suppose a fly were to land on one of the coins, what would it see? All the other coins moving away from it, which is, of course, the observed motion of the galaxies relative to scientists studying them from the Earth.

Astronomers now interpret the motion of the galaxies as being due to the space between galaxies expanding, rather than the galaxies moving through space. In other words, the galaxies are being carried outward from the singularity of the Big Bang on a tide of expanding space, just as coins glued to a balloon are carried apart by its rubber as the balloon expands. Furthermore, just as there is no empty stretch of rubber surface 'outside' the region where the coins are glued, so there is no empty three-dimensional space outside where galaxies are to be found. It is this interpretation of the recession of the galaxies that leads cosmologists to conclude that all space that now exists was squashed to an infinitesimal singularity at the Big Bang. In other words, space began as nothing and has continued to expand ever since.

There is also an even more extraordinary element of this cosmology. According to Einstein's theory of general relativity, space and time are welded together as a four-dimensional continuum called 'space-time.' One cannot have space without time or time without space. In Buddhist language, they are 'co-originated,' meaning 'interdependent.' This being so, the Big Bang marked not only the coming into existence of space, but also the existence of time. This means that as there is no space before the Big Bang, there is also no time before the Big Bang.

It is this aspect of contemporary scientific cosmology that many Buddhists believe gets rid of the sort of creator God that most people have in mind when they think of the Genesis creation story: a God who first exists alone and then at some point in time decides to create the universe. God says some words, there is a Big Bang, and WHAM, creation begins. Indeed if the word 'God' refers to this sort of entity, Buddhist non-theism seems more closely allied with current scientific cosmology than Christian monotheism.

However, much depends on the meaning of the word 'God.' Consider the following quotation from St Augustine:

> It is idle to look for time before creation, as if time can be found before time. If there were no motion of either a spiritual or corporal creature by which the future, moving through the present, would succeed the past, there would be no time at all. We should therefore say that time began with creation, rather than creation began with time.[13]

In other words, for God, there is neither before nor after; God simply *is* in a motionless eternity. Time and space are part of creation. Before creation, there is neither time nor space, and therefore, literally 'nothing.'[14] Deeply influenced by Platonic ideas, Augustine could write as early as his *Confessions*: 'It is not in time that you [God] precede all times; all your "years" subsist in simultaneity, because they do not change; your "years" are "one day" and your today is eternity.'[15]

So, Augustine argued, we know time exists because things change – in Buddhist language, all things change because all things are impermanent. If nothing changed, if nothing 'moved' in Augustine's language, we could not distinguish one point in time from another and there would be no way of determining to what the word 'time' referred. Accordingly, Augustine argued, if there were no objects that change, that is, 'move,' there would be no objects at all. 'Time' would be a meaningless category. Furthermore, if there is no time, there is no space ('either') through which objects move or occupy. In other words, no moving objects, no time; no time, no space.[16] In this way, Augustine's theology of creation distinguished between ontological and historical origination, and he concluded that time and space are as much a property of the universe as anything else and it makes no sense to think of God pre-dating the creation of the universe. Yet none of this had an adverse affect on Augustine's theology because he noted that there is an important distinction between the words 'creation' and 'origins.' While in everyday conversations, we might use these words interchangeably, in Christian theological discourse since Augustine, each word has its own distinctive meanings. For example, if one has in mind a question like 'How did the universe begin?' one is asking a question about historical 'origins.' Questions or origins are empirical matters for scientists to decide, their current research pointing to the Big Bang cosmology.

The question of 'creation' poses ontological issues that are different from the question of the universe's historical 'origins.' In Christian teaching, 'creation' has as much to do with the present instant of time as any other instant of time. Why is there something and not nothing? Why are we here? To whom or what do we owe our existence? What keeps us in existence? Thus Christian theological reflection on creation concerns the underlying 'ground' of all things and events in space-time, past, present, and future. On the other hand, the question of the universe's origins has to do with what started the processes that ended up as the universe.

Barbour continues Augustine's line of argument in his interpretation of the doctrine of *creation ex nihilo* in light of Big Bang cosmology. In *Science and Religion*, he makes as sharp a distinction between ontological/historical categories as Langdon Gilkey makes in *Maker of Heaven and Earth*[17] (which is a contemporary neo-orthodox restatement of Augustine's distinctions). According to Barbour, creation is an ontological issue and is the central meaning of *ex nihilo*, while t = 0 in Big Bang theory is an empirical issue and plays no role in the doctrine of creation *ex nihilo*.[18] Accordingly, Barbour thinks it wise that theologians do not employ Big Bang cosmology as a means of demonstrating the reasonableness of theism. However, in his criticism of Barbour's position, Robert John Russell reports that should an initial singularity (t = 0) be supported scientifically, Barbour believes this *would* provide an 'impressive example of dependence on God.'[19] Russell also notes that the inclusion of a marginal significance of t = 0 in Barbour's theology represents something of a shift in his thought. Nevertheless, Barbour continues to sharply distinguish between ontological and historical origins and places most of the theological weight of his theology on the ontological interpretation of the universe's creation, with 'only nodding attention to the possibility of the historical interpretation being relevant.'[20]

The point of the foregoing discussion is to show that questions about the universe's ontological or historical origins are seen by Buddhists as posing no significant challenges to Buddhist thought and practice. In fact, contemporary Buddhist writers tend to dismiss such questions as meaningless. In Buddhist cosmology, the universe is portrayed as an eternally changing system of interdependent interrelationships without beginning or end. Contemporary Western Buddhists especially think we should simply accept the universe as a brute fact and ask what, if anything, is gained by affirming that God created it. For Buddhists, the Christian doctrine of creation not only raises the question of who created God; it also implies that any notion of divine creation encourages clinging (*tanha*) to an imagined permanent sacred reality. The karmic result of such clinging to imagined permanent realities can only be suffering (*duhkha*).[21]

From a Christian perspective, however, Buddhist criticism of Christian notions of creation often misinterprets how Christian theology uses the word 'God.' For example, Paul Tillich appropriated Augustine's notions of time when he wrote that God is not an existent object or 'being.'[22] In other words, one cannot say that God 'exists' in the same way that one can say 'apples exist,' or, for that matter, 'the universe exists.' The point of the Christian doctrine of creation is that God is the source of all existence; 'God' is the name Christians (and Jews and Muslims) give to whatever is responsible for the existence of all space-time things and events, including human beings. However, most Buddhist interpretations of the Christian doctrine of creation mistakenly assume that Christians affirm God as an object confined within the limits of space and time or that God can only exist 'in time.' Certainly, one hears such theological talk among some evangelical and fundamentalist Christians. But the mainline teaching is that, while we experience God in time and space, God is not confined by time and space.

If none of the challenges posed to the themes of traditional Christian theism – God as creator, both 'in the beginning' and continually in the present – seemingly pose any challenge to Buddhism's non-theistic worldview, how can Buddhist faith and practice be creatively transformed through conceptual dialogue with Christian theology mediated by the sciences as a 'third party'? Reflection on this question will require a brief description of the sorts of conversations with the sciences Buddhists are now undertaking.

Contemporary Buddhist Writings and the Natural Sciences

For the most part, Buddhists have to this date stressed environmental ethics and psychology in their conversations with the natural sciences.[23] This assertion does not imply that Buddhists have paid no attention to physics and biology. Rather, as in Christian theology, the focus of Buddhist interest in the natural sciences has stressed those areas where traditional Buddhist teachings might be supported by current scientific views of physical reality. In general, Buddhists interpret the natural sciences as a support for its doctrine of interdependence (*pratītya-samuptpāda*), which teaches that every thing and event at every moment of space-time is co-created and constituted by the interdependently interpenetrating nexus of relationships it undergoes from moment to moment of its existence. Thus Buddhist interest in ecology is closely linked to the Buddhist doctrine of dependent co-origination, as are Buddhist teachings about non-self (*anatta, anatman*). Furthermore, the practice of meditation has led Buddhists to contemporary psychology and a means of translating its traditional doctrines of suffering and its causes (*duḥkha* and *taṇha*), the meaning of 'liberation' (*nirvana*), and the practice of meditation into a more contemporary context.

B. Alan Wallace, who writes about the relation between scientific theory and reality through the lenses of a practicing Tibetan Buddhist, will serve to illustrate both a Buddhist critique of physics and biology and Buddhist interest in psychology. In contrast to Barbour, Wallace is highly critical of the principle of 'critical realism' in that he thinks that scientific theories do not have ontological correspondence to physical realities.[24] Barbour's 'independence model'[25] best describes Wallace's thesis about the relation between science and Buddhism, since according to Wallace, 'while the sciences give us objective knowledge about physical processes, the sciences do not give us knowledge of an objective world.'[26] This means that the function of scientific theories is to make natural events intelligible for the purpose of developing technology that improves the quality of life for 'all sentient beings.' In other words, Wallace takes an instrumentalist approach to scientific inquiry that views scientific truth as pragmatic, meaning leading to practical technological applications that improve the quality of life for all sentient beings.

Wallace's interpretation of the natural sciences is based on his appropriation of the 'two-truth' epistemology that originated with the second-century Indian Buddhist logician, Nāgārjuna.[27] As pragmatic truths about the physical world, scientific truths are 'secondary truths' that in themselves shed little light on the nature of reality. Absolute truth, however, is metaphysical and is named by Wallace in particular, and Nāgārjuna in general, 'Emptying' (*śūnyatā*); 'Emptying' is the Absolute Truth to which Buddhas awaken through the practice of meditation. Therefore, Wallace concludes, 'we err if we expect the natural sciences to solve issues of a metaphysical or religious nature, for it was never designed to probe such questions.'[28] Furthermore, as 'secondary truths,' the primary weakness of physics and the biological sciences is that 'neither discipline the mind and mental experience.'[29]

Redmond notes that Buddhism first encountered Western science as part of its experiences of sixteenth-century colonialism in South and East Asia. In this encounter, Buddhists do not appear to have felt the need to oppose Western science. Nor did the sciences challenge the fundamentals of Buddhism's worldview and doctrines in the way it challenged Christian theology. According to Redmond, this is because Buddhism is not committed to the prescientific ideas associated with it since Buddhism's traditional cosmology was never its essential core. Therefore, Buddhism was, and still is, less threatened by science than other world religions.[30] Like Wallace, Redmond thinks Buddhism and the sciences are independent enterprises.

Victor Mansfield takes Redmond's conclusions farther. He argues that similarities between Madhyamika philosophy and modern physics in their understanding of time is evidence that Buddhism is particularly compatible with the natural sciences, especially in the area of psychology.[31] But compatibility with the natural sciences does not imply that Buddhism is 'scientific.' Both Redmond and Mansfield, as well as most Buddhists, think that asserting that Buddhism is 'scientific' is a distortion of Buddhism. So while science is no threat to Buddhist teachings and practice (because they are independent enterprises), Buddhism has resources that can fill in the 'gaps' of Western science relative to analyzing subjective mental and emotional experiences that can help the psychological sciences overcome its Cartesian emphasis on objectivity and thereby develop coherent theories of cognition. In other words, through dialogue with Buddhism science is more apt to be creatively transformed than is Buddhism because of Buddhism's 'strong empirical foundations' and the 'deconstructive traditions of Nāgārjuna's Madhyamika ("middle Way") dialectics,' which Mansfield believes overcome the 'objectivist weakness' he perceives in Western physics and biology.[32]

Finally, writing from a Theravada Buddhist perspective, Shoyo Taniguchi asserts that Buddhism is scientific in a way other religions are not. She scrutinizes the Pali suttas and early Buddhist philosophy and pushes the interdependence model as far as it can probably go. She concludes that early Theravada Buddhism employs empirical and experimental methods equivalent to those of modern science and is therefore a 'scientific' religion, meaning that Buddhist doctrines harmonize with current scientific models of physical reality in a way other religions do not.[33] Her tacit conclusion is that Buddhism is thereby superior to other religions, particularly Judaism, Christianity, and Islam. In her view, physics and evolutionary biology leave no room for a Creator.

It is clear that neither Redmond, Mansfield, nor Taniguchi experience or interpret the natural sciences – particularly Big Bang cosmology – as a challenge to Buddhist doctrine and practice. The distinct impression that contemporary Buddhist writing on the natural sciences seems to give is that the structure of Buddhist tradition remains untouched by the sciences, either positively or negatively.

Current Buddhist–Christian Dialogue and the Natural Sciences

It's now time to bring this essay to a conclusion and ask, 'So what?' What, if anything, would Buddhist–Christian dialogue with the natural sciences add to current Buddhist–Christian encounter, here illustrated by aspects of Big Bang cosmology? While my conclusions are very much in process, I want to be crystal clear about what I am not arguing: (1) that Buddhism is deficient because the natural sciences have not challenged Buddhist doctrines in the same way that the natural sciences have challenged Christian doctrines; (2) that Christian tradition is 'truer' than or 'superior' to Buddhist tradition because the current scientific origin narrative can be read as a confirmation of certain Christian doctrines; or (3) that Buddhist dialogue with natural sciences should be modeled after Christian encounter with the natural sciences. Consequently, what follows should be understood as descriptive and a bit tentative.

First, it is clear that Buddhists tend to read Big Bang cosmology as supportive of the Buddhist worldview.[34] Buddhists seem not to have experienced the natural sciences as a conceptual challenge in the same degree as Christians. Some Buddhist writers point to parallels between Buddhism's 'non-theistic' worldview and current scientific cosmology as evidence that Buddhism is more in harmony with the sciences than is Christian theism (Wallace, Redmond and Mansfield). A few Buddhist writers take a stronger stance and affirm scientific accounts of reality are proof of the superiority of Buddhism to all theistic religions (Taniguchi). Such arguments have a familiar ring. Nineteenth- and early twentieth-century Western scholarly interpretations of Buddhism tended to see Buddhism as 'rational,' 'experimental,' 'empirical,' and critical of authority beyond an individual's own experience – all treasured ideals of the Western Enlightenment. And indeed, Buddhists have generally not thought it necessary to rethink or reformulate the fundamental doctrines that shape Buddhist thought and practice because of challenges posed by its encounter with the natural sciences. Those Buddhists writing from Mahayana Buddhist perspectives often apply Nāgārjuna's two-truths epistemology in their encounter with the sciences: scientific conclusions, models, paradigms, theories, and laws are identified as 'secondary truths.' The measure of the truth of scientific conclusions is 'relative' and 'pragmatic,' meaning they 'work,' especially in the realm of technology. But the absolute truth – that is, 'Emptying' or *sūnyatā* – is absolutely beyond the 'discriminating mind' based on cause–effect relations, which themselves are 'empty' of 'self-nature' (*svabhava*).[35] Such notions seem contrary to Barbour's notion of the 'critical realism,' as well as the self-understanding of most working scientists, for whom scientific theories and paradigms are not 'secondary truths.'

Second, Buddhism's conceptual encounter with the natural sciences parallels its conceptual dialogue with Christian theology. In conceptual dialogue with Christian theology, Buddhists have not experienced the same degree of creative transformation as have Christians in their dialogue with Buddhist philosophy – perhaps because Buddhism is more worldview specific than Christian tradition. Delete or redefine any of the doctrines implicit in Buddhism's worldview – non-self, impermanence, interdependence, nontheism – Buddhism ceases to be Buddhism. So while a Christian theologian in dialogue with Buddhism, such as John Cobb, can affirm in print that 'A Christian can be a Buddhist, too'[36] – provided that one is careful to explain what this means – no Buddhist writer in dialogue with Christian theology has yet written that 'A Buddhist can be a Christian, too.' It seems that Buddhists have concluded that conceptual dialogue with the natural sciences as a 'third party' would contribute as little to Buddhism's creative transformation as has its conceptual dialogue with Christian theology.

Nevertheless, Buddhists are as interested in the natural sciences as Christians, particularly in the practice of 'socially engaged dialogue' with Christian traditions of social activism. Buddhists have learned much from Christian tradition about confronting issues of oppression and injustice that are not religion-specific: consumerism, gender issues, social justice issues, environmental issues, racism, war. Christians have learned much from Buddhist traditions of social engagement as well. The biological sciences have been particularly helpful to Buddhists and Christians in their socially engaged dialogue on environmental issues because these problems cannot be addressed apart from what evolutionary theory tells us about the structure of biological processes. Accordingly, a point of entry for Buddhist–Christian dialogue with the natural sciences might well be socially engaged dialogue.[37] Including the sciences as a partner in socially engaged dialogue – especially the biological sciences and economics – would greatly empower current Buddhist and Christian cooperation on confronting justice and environmental issues.

Third, the neurobiological sciences might also make important contributions to the practice of Buddhist–Christian interior dialogue. The psychological dynamics and neurophysiological processes underlying disciplines like meditation and contemplative prayer, liturgical practices, and forms of spirituality and community might shed light on Buddhist and Christian traditions of 'practice,' in terms of both similarities and differences between the experiences such practices engender. In this way, new information might be added to what is already known about Buddhist and Christian practice traditions.

My final conclusion in process begins with a question. Is it really true that encounter with the natural sciences poses no important conceptual challenges to Buddhism's worldview or to Buddhist doctrines? Consider the following.

It is a fact that in the late twentieth century and now the twenty-first century, the displacement of God in scientific writing is almost complete.[38] In my opinion, this is a good thing and no scientist should place God in scientific equations. The result is pseudoscience and incoherent theology. But watch what happens when some scientists step outside of their work as scientists and draw metaphysical conclusions relative to religious claims on the basis of their understanding and practice of science. In 1978, Edmond O. Wilson won the Pulitzer Prize for his book *On Human Nature*. Wilson's work on the social behavior of insects is widely admired as pioneering and led directly to his founding contributions of a new field which he called 'social biology,' defined as the study of the biological foundations of social behavior. In the beginning of his book, Wilson clearly stated what he believed was the final displacement of God by Darwinian evolution: 'If humankind evolved by Darwinian natural selection, genetic chance and environmental necessity, not God, made the species.'[39] So much for the Christian doctrine of creation, scientists like Wilson declare. 'No problem,' Buddhists like Redmond believe, since Buddhist non-theism does not posit a doctrine of creation.

But watch what happens when scientific theory filtered through the lenses of scientific materialism is pushed to its logical conclusions. Richard Dawkins agrees with Wilson and asserts that the Darwinian universe not only displaces God, it leaves no real place for values of genuine good or evil. 'This is one of the hardest lessons for humans to learn,' he writes. 'We cannot admit that things might be neither good nor evil, cruel nor kind, but simply callous – indifferent to all suffering, lacking all purpose.[40] Physicist Steven Weinberg draws the same conclusion from his work in reconstructing Big Bang cosmology: 'The universe is pointless.'[41] First, Copernicus displaces humanity as the center of the universe. Then materialist interpretations of Big Bang cosmology and evolutionary biology set aside God as the creator of the universe. And finally, according to this interpretation of the history of science, biochemistry and molecular biology remove all doubt that the properties of all living things can be explained in terms of the physics and chemistry of ordinary matter. Everything is molecules.

For me, scientific materialist assertions of the illusory character of religious teachings, Christian or Buddhist, are summarized by the following description of the mating system of a species of monkeys, the Hanuman Langurs of Northern India, by George C. Williams, a scientist who has made important contributions to understanding the complexities of natural selection.

> Their mating system is what biologists call harem polygony: dominant males have exclusive sexual access to a group of adult females, as long as they can keep other males away. Sooner or later, a stronger male usurps the harem and the defeated one must join the ranks of celibate outcastes. The new male shows his love for his new wives by trying to kill their unweaned infants. For each successful killing, a mother stops lactating and goes into estrous ... Deprived of her nursing baby, a female soon starts ovulating. She accepts the advances of her baby's murderer, and he becomes the father of her next child. *Do you still think that God is good?*[42]

So there it is. If the universe is pointless and meaningless, then what is the meaning of any religious tradition? Certainly, such conclusions are radically opposed to Christian notions of God and the whole edifice of Christian doctrine and practice. But these same views also contradict the whole edifice of Buddhism as well – if the scientific materialism of persons like Wilson, Weinberg, Dawkins, and Williams are accurate descriptions of the way things really are in this universe.

Of course, the issue for Buddhism is not the 'displacement of God.' Nevertheless, the notion that all living things have evolved through accidental forces of random mutation and natural selection in the struggle for existence seems to raise as many questions regarding fundamental Buddhist doctrines as it does for Christian theology. Is the teaching that, since all sentient beings are interdependent, we should experience the suffering of others as our suffering and act to relieve suffering by non-violent expedient means based on an illusion? In a universe where the Second Law of Thermodynamics seems to demand suffering and death as the price for life itself, does it make any sense to say we cause our own suffering by clinging to impermanence and that we can free ourselves of suffering by training ourselves not to cling to it? Does universal suffering have anything to do with 'clinging'? If the universe really is 'pointless' and 'without value,' can Awakening mean anything more than becoming experientially aware of universal pointlessness? If the universe is valueless, what's the value of Awakening? Are compassion and non-violence merely fantasies? In a pointless and valueless universe, in what and for what can one reasonably hope? What is the connection between Buddhism's defining teachings and what are the sciences discovering about the physical processes of nature?

Only Buddhists can answer these questions. They are there to be answered whether or not Buddhists chose to confront them. Doing so in the context of conceptual dialogue with Christian theology and the natural sciences would, I believe, engender new forms of creative transformation in both Buddhist and Christian tradition. Exactly how remains an open question, since the sciences have not as yet been included as dialogical partners in current Buddhist–Christian encounter. Perhaps it is time to start.

Notes

1. I.G. Barbour, *Religion and Science: Historical and Contemporary Issues* (San Francisco: HarperSanFrancisco, 1997), 113, 158–9.
2. Ibid., 159.
3. Ibid., xii–xv.
4. Ibid., 117–19.
5. John B. Cobb, Jr, 'Global Theology in a Pluralistic Age', in *Transforming Christianity and the World*, ed. by Paul F. Knitter (Maryknoll, NY: Orbis Books, 1999), 53.
6. Barbour, *Religion and Science*, 106–10.
7. See Jonathan J. Halliwell, 'Quantum Cosmology and the Creation of the Universe', in *Cosmology: Historical, Literary, Philosophical, Religious, and Scientific Perspectives*, ed. by Noriss S. Hetherington (New York: Garland Publishing, 1993) 477–97.
8. See Steven Weinberg, *The First Three Minutes* (New York: Basic Books, 1988).
9. Alan Guth and Paul Steinhard, 'The Inflationary Universe', *Scientific American*, 250 (May 1984), 116–28.

10. Stephen W. Hawking, *A Brief History of Time* (New York: Bantam Books, 1988), 141.
11. Geoffrey P. Redmond, 'Comparing Science and Buddhism', *Pacific World*, 11–12 (1995–96), 106.
12. Ibid., 111.
13. *De Civitate Dei (The City of God)*, XII. 15; cited by Russell Stannard, 'Where in the World is God?', *Research News and Opportunities in Science and Theology*, 1 (October 2000), 13.
14. See Etienne Gilson, *The Christian Philosophy of Saint Augustine* (New York: Random House, 1960), 190–91.
15. Augustine, *Confessiones*, Book 11; *Confessions* (Oxford: Oxford University Press, 1991), 230.
16. *De Civitate Dei (The City of God)*, XII. 15: 'For where there is no creature whose changing movements admits to succession, there cannot be time at all.' So also XI. 6: '... time does not exist without some movement and transition ...' Also see Robert Jordan, 'Time and Contingency in St. Augustine', in *Augustine: A Collection of Critical Essays*, ed. by R.A. Markus (New York: Anchor Books, 1972), 255–79 and Hugh Lacy, 'Empiricism and Augustine's Problem About Time', *Augustine: A Collection of Critical Essays*, 280–308.
17. Langdon Gilkey, *Maker of Heaven and Earth: The Christian Doctrine of Creation in Light of Modern Knowledge* (Garden City: Doubleday, 1959), 310–15.
18. Barbour, *Religion and Science*, 128–9.
19. Ibid., 129.
20. Robert John Russell, 'Finite Creation Without a Beginning', in *Quantum Cosmology and the Laws of Nature: Scientific Perspectives on Divine Action*, ed. by Robert John Russell, Nancey Murphy, and C.J. Isham (Vatican City and Berkeley, CA: Vatican Observatory and The Center for Theology and the Natural Sciences, 1996), 302.
21. See Shoyo Taniguchi, 'Modern Science and Early Buddhist Ethics: Methodology of Two Disciplines,' *Pacific World*, 45–53.
22. Paul Tillich, *Systematic Theology* I (Chicago: University of Chicago Press, 1951), 235–92.
23. See, for example, Mary Evelyn Tucker and Duncan Ryukan Williams (eds), *Buddhism and Ecology* (Cambridge, MA: Harvard University), 1997 and three essays in J. Baird Callicott and Roger T. Ames (eds), *Nature in Asian Traditions of Thought* (Albany, NY: State University of New York, 1989): 'The Jeweled Net of Indra' by Francis Cook (213–30); 'Environmental Problems' by Kenneth K. Inada (231–46); and 'Toward a Middle Path of Survival' by David J. Kaluphana (247–58).
24. B. Alan Wallace, *Choosing Reality: A Buddhist View of Physics and Mind* (Ithaca, NY: Snow Lion Press, 1996), ch. 11.
25. The independence model asserts that science and theology are independently autonomous enterprises. Each should keep off the other's turf; each should tend to its own specific affairs and not meddle in the concerns of the other. See Barbour, *Religion and Science*, 84–90.
26. Wallace, *Choosing Reality*, 14.
27. For an interpretation and translation of Nāgārjuna's writings, see Frederick J. Streng, *Emptiness: A Study in Religious Meaning* (Nashville: Abingdon Press, 1967).
28. Ibid., 9.
29. Ibid., 9–10.
30. Geoffrey Redmond, 'Introduction', *The Pacific World*, 11–12 (1995–96), 2–3. Also see 'Comparing Science and Buddhism', ibid., 101–14.
31. Victor Mansfield, 'Time in Madhyamika Buddhism and Modern Physics', ibid., 28–67.
32. Ibid., 65–7.
33. Shoyo Taniguchi, 'Modern Science and Early Buddhist Ethics', ibid., 28–67.
34. In the essays cited in this essay, the Buddhist authors also reflect on the usefulness of evolutionary and psychological theory as these relate to the doctrine of impermanence and the practice of meditation. They conclude that these sciences are particularly useful in understanding environmental issues as well as enhancing the practice of meditation through the development of a coherent theory of consciousness free from the 'objectivist bias of Western psychology.' Given the

limitations of space for this essay, I have focused mostly on Buddhist–Christian encounters with contemporary Big Bang cosmology.

35. Frederick J. Streng, *Emptiness*, chs. 2–3.
36. John B. Cobb, Jr, 'Can a Christian Be a Buddhist, Too?', *Japanese Religions*, 10 (December 1978), 1.–20.
37. Cf. Mary Evelyn Tucker and Duncan Ryukan Williams (eds), *Buddhism and Ecology* (Cambridge, MA: Harvard University for the Study of World Religions, 1997); Christopher S. Queen and Sallie B. King (eds), *Engaged Buddhism: Buddhist Liberation Movements in Asia* (New York: State University of New York, 1996); and Christopher S. Queen (ed.), *Engaged Buddhism in the West* (Boston: Wisdom Publications, 2000).
38. See Kenneth R. Miller, *Finding Darwin's God: A Scientist's Search for Common Ground between God and Evolution* (New York: Cliff Street Books, 1999), 15.
39. E.O. Wilson, *On Human Nature* (Cambridge, MA: Harvard University Press, 1978), 1.
40. Richard Dawkins, *River Out of Eden* (New York: Harper Collins, 1995), 95–6.
41. Steven Weinberg, *The First Three Minutes*, 150–55.
42. George C. Williams, *The Pony Fish's Glow* (New York: Harper Collins, 1997), 156–67; cited by Miller, *Finding Darwin's God*, 16.

Chapter 20

Barbour, Buddhism, Bohm, and Beyond

Jensine Andresen

Though we are at the end, perhaps we should begin at the beginning, and, in Barbour's case, the beginning began in Beijing. Having been born in China, Barbour developed a deep interest in Asian culture and thought that he continues to pursue today. My first memory of Ian takes me back to a Templeton Foundation event in Tallahassee, Florida in 1997, at which time, being aware of my background in Buddhist Studies, he made a point of introducing himself to me and subsequently engaging me in a conversation about Buddhist philosophy. Over the years, Ian continues to contribute to the intellectual expansion of religion and science conversations by encouraging the input of specialists in Asian thought, and his discussions with colleagues, such as Mark Unno (previously on the faculty at Carleton College and now at the University of Oregon), have deepened his own interest in points of overlap between Christian theology and Buddhist thought.

Despite the significant breadth of his writings on history, method, theorizing, values, language, and metaphysical holism in religion and science, Barbour does not discuss Asian perspectives on these topics in considerable depth. Nevertheless, he does mention Asian views in many of his central writings. For example, in *Religion and Science: Historical and Contemporary Issues,*[1] Barbour critiques certain scholars' descriptions of parallels between physics and eastern mysticism; in *Ethics in an Age of Technology: The Gifford Lectures 1989–1991, Volume 2,*[2] he discusses how Eastern religions, biblical traditions, and contemporary theology can work together to develop the underpinnings of an efficacious environmental ethics; in *Myths, Models, and Paradigms: The Nature of Scientific and Religious Language,*[3] he considers whether the transposition of the notion of 'complementary models' in physics to the realm of religion can illuminate our understanding of religious experience; and in his private ruminations, Barbour allows himself to speculate on interesting connections between process thought and Buddhist philosophy, particularly Buddhist views of consciousness.[4] While all of these treatments helpfully extend present religion and science conversation towards a meaningful dialogue with world religions, Barbour's dependency on secondary sources as opposed to primary ones curtails the depth of these important beginnings. In this paper, then, I will discuss various Buddhist views on consciousness and will also explicate elements of Madhyamika Buddhist philosophy as articulated by the seminal, second-century philosopher, Nāgārjuna, that shed light on the important theme of 'timelessness' upon which Barbour himself focuses in his own writing. At the same time, I will survey Barbour's own perspectives on Eastern religions to provide readers with an overview of his valuable contributions in this area.

Barbour describes writings from the 1970s and 1980s that purport to describe parallels between physics and eastern mysticism, such as Fritjof Capra's *The Tao of*

Physics, which argues for parallels along three dimensions, 'the limitations of human thought and language,' 'the wholeness of reality,' and the 'dynamic and ever-changing' nature of the world.[5] Barbour helpfully critiques Capra's comparisons, arguing that he has made them without attending to the differences in their contexts. On the topic of unity and wholeness, for example, Barbour claims that the meaning of these terms differs significantly in the contexts of Asian traditions versus Western physics. Whereas the former suggests a lack of differentiation, the latter suggests something highly structured by constraints, principles, and laws.[6]

Although Barbour's subtle distinction between different perspectives on unity in physics and mysticism adds clarity to discussions of wholeness, his subsequent comments regarding Hinduism and Buddhism generally cut too broad a swath. For example, in the context of his discussion of how the relation 'between *time* and *timelessness*' differs in physics versus mysticism, Barbour overgeneralizes when he states, 'In Buddhism, timelessness also refers to the realization of our unity with all things, which releases us from bondage to time and the threat of impermanence and suffering.'[7] Similar to Capra's overgeneralizations regarding mysticism, Barbour treats 'Buddhism' as a monolithic entity, thereby ignoring the diversity of viewpoints available within the Buddhist pantheon of philosophical positions and failing to specify arguments from a specific Buddhist tradition in support of his own important distinction between the relation of time and timelessness in physics versus mysticism.

How could Barbour better justify the claim that Buddhism holds a different view than physics concerning the relation of time and timelessness? In the case of physics, Barbour states:

> Physics deals with the realm of temporal change. I agree with Capra that in the atomic world there is impermanence and an ever-changing flux of events. But I do not agree that space-time is a static and timeless block. I have argued that relativity points to the temporalization of space rather than the spatialization of time.[8]

How can we compare this characterization of space-time to a perspective from Buddhist thought?

We can begin by specifying a particular aspect of Buddhist philosophy that addresses time – for example, Madhyamika Buddhist philosophy – and the work of a particular thinker – for example, the Madhyamika Buddhist philosopher, Nāgārjuna, author of the *Mūlamadhyamakakārikā*. To understand this specific Madhyamika position on time and timelessness, we can begin with Nāgārjuna's distinction between two levels of truth: 'The Buddha's teaching of the Dharma / Is based on two truths: / A truth of worldly convention / And an ultimate truth.'[9] The distinction between conventional and ultimate levels of truth enables Buddhists to recognize the apparently paradoxical coexistence of both time and timelessness – that is, 'time,' a facet of conventional reality, appears to beings with sense consciousness as a helpful way to mark and organize experience; while 'timelessness,' a subjective and qualitative description, describes both sentient beings' experience of ultimate reality and the ontological nature of reality itself. Because Madhyamika thinkers such as Nāgārjuna and those who adopt his viewpoint on time admit to the non-dual juxtaposition of two levels of reality, they inhabit a perceptual field in which both time and timelessness coexist completely. Indeed, according to Madhyamika Buddhists, the perceptual ability to experience such paradoxical awareness constitutes the experience of enlightened Buddhahood.

Now, let us return to Barbour's claim that physics and mysticism (in this case, a certain branch of Buddhist thought) conceive the relation between time and timelessness differently. Putting physics into the philosophical matrix of Nāgārjuna's Madhamika Buddhism, it appears that, in 'deal[ing] with the realm of temporal change,' physics situates itself in Nāgārjuna's conventional reality. One also could situate Barbour's portrayal of space-time as other than 'a static and timeless block' within the context of conventional reality. And, Barbour's idea that 'relativity points to the temporalization of space rather than the spatialization of time' also sits more comfortably within a conventional reality framework. In short, one could argue that, in comparison to Madhyamika Buddhism's differentiation of two levels of truth to accommodate apparently paradoxical realities of time and timelessness, physics, as Barbour describes it, stands firmly within the realm of conventional reality.

Barbour's discussion helpfully differentiates 'spatializing' time from 'temporalizing' space. Let me make a few preliminary comments before turning to Barbour's treatment of Bohm to help shed light on our options regarding the possible primacy of either space or time. First, the literature describing the experiential accounts of Buddhist practitioners, particularly in the 'Great Perfection' (Tib. *Rdzogs chen*) tradition of the Tibetan *Rnying ma* branch of Buddhism, one encounters myriad descriptions of deep layers of reality in which one experiences timelessness in conjunction with spaciousness – in other words, the experience of vastness and spaciousness also occurs as an experience of timelessness. So, if one experiences the outer reaches of spaciousness as timeless, it makes no sense from a phenomenological perspective to 'temporalize space' theoretically and/or ontologically. In other words, even though relativity theory in physics may point us towards temporalizing space, unless we want to think of the temporalizing of space as leading to an experience of timelessness – a somewhat absurd conclusion! – we might have to interpret this viewpoint merely as a provisional step towards a more complete understanding of both space and time.

Next, let us look at space and time from the opposite viewpoint, that is, with regard to the spatialization of time. At one level, I certainly agree with Barbour that we do not want to spatialize time such that we subject time to the rigid constraints of locality. However, Buddhist meditative experience introduces a phenomenological perspective here that may assist us in conceiving of a kind of spatializing of time that creates possibilities instead of closing them. Such a phenomenological and intuitive/experiential perspective helps orient our analytical and concept-based theorizing. Early Buddhist thought, for example, in the context of the *Abhidharmakośabhāṣyam*, refers to the importance of recognizing the present – the 'now,' to speak colloquially – while viewing concepts of 'past' and 'future' as mental imputations upon the present. In the *Abhidharmakośabhāṣyam*, Vasubandhu writes: 'Five causes grasp their results only when they are in the present; in the past, they have already grasped their results; in the future, they have no activity.'[10] Indeed, David Bohm and John Cobb also defend a version of this idea, as Barbour notes when he states: 'Cobb cites Bohm's assertion that "past, present and future are all together as one in the implicate order.""[11] In this sense, early Buddhist thought 'opens up' one's experience of time, specifically, of the present, making it more spacious. Again, drawing upon Bohm, Barbour states: 'Bohm's paper[12] maintains that as consciousness turns to deeper unconscious levels the moments become more similar; at a very deep level, "all 'nows' would not only be similar – they would all be one and essentially the same. So one could say that in its inward depths, now is eternity."'[13] That which one previously may have passed over unreflectively – the present – opens up in one's perceptual field as the experience of spacious, liberative potentiality.[14]

In essence, one can observe that various branches of Buddhism recognize both the temporalization of space and the spatialization of time. Bohm appears to recognize both 'conventional' and 'ultimate' aspects of time, stating:

> one no longer implies that the ordinary level of experience has no fundamental kind of significance, nor does one imply that the timeless or the eternal is the only basic reality. Rather, what is crucial is the *relationship* between the two ... In establishing such a relationship, it is clear that eternity or the timeless should not be considered as absolute. Rather, one may think in terms of what may be called 'relative eternity.' ... For example, it has been said that Mozart was able to perceive the whole of a composition in such a moment, which was then unfolded in time in all its detail. The proposal is that a similar relationship between time and timelessness may be universal and that we may see it in many areas of experience. Such a relationship may then be the very essence of what is to be meant by freedom and creativity.[15]

Bohm,[16] whom Barbour generally commends for being 'more cautious in delineating parallels between physics and mysticism,'[17] also raises the issue of an apparent paradox between the perceived necessity of local connection versus wholeness. Bohm writes, 'in a certain sub-order, within the whole set of implicate order, there is a totality of forms that have an approximate kind of recurrence, stability and separability. Evidently, these forms are capable of appearing as the relatively solid, tangible and stable elements that make up our "manifest world."'[18] Bohm asserts that this so-called explicate order, which manifests as a result of the pattern recurrence of the implicate order, presents itself to our senses, which, ironically, delimit it. Because what we perceive as solid forms appear stable and independent, and as a result of our embodiment, we relate to inputed objects in patterns of local connections. As Lakoff and Johnson point out,[19] the sensorimotor patterns of human embodiment play a crucial role in structuring the scaffolding of human cognition. Said differently, I would claim that the physical constraints imposed by human embodiment cause us to observe the apparent necessity of local connection in the sense that we move 'locally' from point A to point B, without non-local leaps through space-time. Our experience of movement, then, predisposes us to think 'locally' and to extrapolate, or project, from our experience of local movement onto our conceptualization regarding reality itself and regarding aspects of it, for example, the experience of time, which we tend to think of 'chronologically' in terms of linear progression. Additionally, however, many of us also enjoy the phenomenological experience of wholeness via intuition and contemplative endeavors. If the localness of the embodied, human experience of space causes us to assume the necessity of chronological, local connections in time, we obviously can unmask the notion of linear time as an assumption.

The aforementioned discussion of human embodiment points to the importance of different views of consciousness in any discussion of physics and mysticism. Although quantum physics certainly recognizes the role of human consciousness in contributing to the manifestation of observed realities, consciousness remains somewhat of a 'black box' for Western science despite recent scholarly attempts to understand it.[20] Let me spend a few paragraphs outlining Buddhist views on consciousness, then, to help supplement the discussion of physics and mysticism.

Buddhism presents diverse views of consciousness, mind, and personhood reflective of the different traditions of Buddhist thought and practice popular in different time periods, regions, and communities in India. Much scholarship in Buddhist Studies differentiates three Buddhist 'vehicles' – Nikāya (of which Theravāda constitutes one division); Mahāyāna; and Vajrayāna (also known as Tantric). Viewing consciousness and embodiment from the perspective of so-called classical Indian Buddhism, for example, shows that Nikāya Buddhist theories focus on 'mind' and its activities, whereas later Nikāya and Mahāyāna formulations differentiate 'mental events,' 'mind,' and 'consciousness.' Later Vajrayāna Buddhist theories emphasize the relationship between consciousness and embodiment. In general, then, Buddhism's historical development across the centuries, which occurred within the context of tremendously rich contemplative practice tradition and intellectual discussion in both India and Tibet, results in a careful typology of different aspects and manifestations of human consciousness.

During the classical period, spanning the period from the life of the historical Buddha (born approximately 560 BCE) until the fourth century of the common era and the writings of the Yogācāra philosopher Vasubandhu, early Buddhist psychology describes a mutually dependent 'body/mind,' that is, 'substance dualism.' According to the literature of this early period, the Buddha rejects the conception of an 'inherent self' (Skt. *ātman*), continues to describe human beings as 'mind/matter-form' (Pali *nāmarūpa*), and introduces the unique notion of human beings as 'aggregates of addiction' (Pali *upādānakkhandha*). 'Mind' and 'matter-form' couple ontologically because they both share the same underlying principle of 'contact' (Pali *samphassa*) – matter involves 'contact with resistance' (Pali *paṭigha-samphassa*), and mind involves 'contact with concepts' (Pali *adhivacana-samphassa*). Interacting with the world through the principle of 'contact,' humans create a 'dependently arisen' (Pali *paṭiccasamuppana*) and 'dispositionally conditioned' (Pali *sankhata*) world. In this framework, consciousness depends upon form at the same time that it molds and shapes form. According to the Nikāya tradition, the 'five aggregates' (Pali *pañcakkhandha*) comprise the mind/body. All five comprise 'aggregates of addiction' (Pali *upādānakkhandha*) in the sense that one experiences addiction to: (1) form/matter (Pali *rūpa*); (2) feeling/sensation (Pali *vedanā*); (3) ideation/perception (Pali *sañña*); (4) dispositions (Pali *sankhārā*); and (5) consciousness (Pali *viññāna*).

Departing somewhat from classical ideas regarding consciousness, Buddhist Tantra introduces a continuum of consciousness from 'coarse' to 'very subtle' measured according to relative materiality. In order to transform into an enlightened Buddha, tantric practitioners must transform both the coarse level of their psychophysical form and also its more subtle manifestations (described in the Indo-Tibetan theory of the 'subtle body': Skt. *sūkṣma-deha*; Tib. *sku phra mo*). Tantric texts, an Āyurvedic schema of the body, various ritual prescriptions, and embodied yogic practice. As in earlier Buddhism, Tantra describes consciousness experientially. And as in Mahāyāna, tantric practitioners seek to transform their ordinary 'consciousness' (Skt. *vijñāna*; Tib. *rnam par shes pa*) into a 'non-dual consciousness' (Tib. *gnyis med kyi shes pa*) mentioned earlier in connection with the juxtaposition of conventional and ultimate levels of reality. One experiences this 'non-dual consciousness' as the union of 'clear light' (Skt. *prabhāsvara*; Tib. '*od gsal*) and the realization of 'emptiness' (Skt. *śūnyatā*; Tib. *stong pa nyid*). Departing from earlier forms of Buddhism, which comparatively focus more on consciousness and philosophy, Tantra utilizes human embodiment to expedite the journey towards enlightened Buddhahood. A contemporary Tibetan scholar states: 'According to the tantras, there is no moment of consciousness or mind which is not associated with some sort of corporeal element that serves as its vehicle. Thus, the tantras will not admit to a realm of disembodied consciousness' such as that found in Nikāya formulations.[21]

Indeed, in Chapter 19 in this volume, Paul Ingram claims that science has not issued the same degree of challenge to Buddhism that it has to Christianity. While Ingram may accurately note that Buddhism appears somewhat nonplussed by transitions in cosmological understandings in the sciences (probably because Buddhist cosmology as articulated in the *Abhidharmakośabhāṣyam* admits for infinite cycles of expansion and contraction), I would argue that brain sciences, specifically neuroscience, pose a significant challenge to Buddhism because of their potential to upset Buddhist notions of enlightenment by explaining unusual experiential realities by means of exceptional occurrences in the brain.

As noted earlier in connection with the three primary Buddhist vehicles, Buddhist meditation styles evolved over time, reflecting engagement with different internal schemas relating to mind and body. While earlier meditative traditions focus on 'mind' (Skt. *citta*) in the context of 'stabilizing' (Skt. *śamatha*) and 'analytic' (Skt. *vipassana*) meditations, later tantric practice focuses on subtle transformations within the body in terms of 'generation stage' (Skt. *utpattikrama*; Tib. *bskyed rim*) and 'completion stage' (Skt. *niṣpannakrama*; Tib. *rdzogs rim*) practices. In this sense, Barbour makes an accurate observation when he observes that physics and mysticism hold very different goals.[22] He states: 'The goal of meditation is not primarily a new conceptual system but the transformation of personal existence, a new state of consciousness and being, an experience of enlightenment.'[23] Barbour correctly points to the deep integration of theory and practice in Buddhism, since Buddhists pursue philosophical analysis and rigorous practice explicitly for the sake of furthering their progress towards the soteriological outcome of enlightenment. Though he does not differentiate varieties of meditative experience, which do often exhibit vastly different practical methods and experiential outcomes, Barbour describes mystical experience and meditation graciously as 'participation in eternity':

> Persons in many religious traditions have indeed described mystical experience as timeless ... The intense experience of unity with all things seems to transcend all boundaries of space and time. Meditation may achieve a level of consciousness in which the normal flow of thought and the shifting patterns of attention cease, and one is not aware of the passage of time. There is also a liberation from bondage to time and the transitory world of impermanence and flux. Such an enduring, all-encompassing relationship beyond the vicissitudes of time can be described as participation in eternity.[24]

In addition to his survey of certain Asian traditions' views on time and timelessness, Barbour also discusses Asian traditions' value systems and proposes that Eastern religions, biblical traditions, and contemporary theology can all work together to develop a successful ethic regarding the environment.[25] Barbour comments upon the Taoist view of 'the world as an organic, interconnected system,' in which 'Humanity and nature are intimately linked, and there is an ontological equality among all the manifestations of the Tao.'[26] He also describes mutuality between humankind and nature in the context of Zen Buddhism, which holds that 'nature is to be contemplated and appreciated rather than mastered. Humankind should act on nature with restraint, bringing out the latent beauty and power of the natural world.'[27] He concludes:

> I believe we have much to learn from *Taoism* and *Zen*, especially about disciplines of meditation and respect for the natural world, both of which have been neglected in the West. But most Westerners are not familiar with these religions. Furthermore, Asian traditions have had less to say about social justice, which I take to be a crucial value today. It seems to me more promising to use the insights we can gain from the East to help us recover neglected strands of our own heritage.[28]

Since 1993 when Barbour wrote *Ethics in an Age of Technology*, however, many scholars have worked to convey to Western audiences important features of Asian thought that will support a more global and pluralistic ethic relating to the environment. For example, a recent series of books, 'Religions of the World and Ecology', published by the Center for the Study of World Religions of Harvard University, describes the relationship of Eastern traditions to ecology and the environment. In their introduction to *Confucianism and Ecology*, Berthrong and Tucker claim that Confucianism's holistic and dynamic worldview, its understanding of self in a triad with Heaven and Earth, and its respect and compassion for all aspects of life contribute to a broadened perspective on global ecological concerns.[29] With respect to Daoism, Girardot et al. argue that Daoism does not present any particular intellectual principle concerning ecology; instead, 'knowing in the Daoist sense is always alchemical and ecological in nature since it depends on the revelatory experience and practice that comes in and through the transformation of the human body in corporate relation with all other particular bodies.'[30] In this epistemology-cum-ecology, knowing itself involves an ethical rapport with the environment. According to Daoist cosmology, the universe expresses itself as 'a single, vital organism, not created according to some fixed principle, but spontaneously regenerating itself from the primal empty-potency lodged within all organic forms of life.'[31]

Moving on to Hinduism, Christopher Chapple cites the growing number of environmental activist organizations in India as evidence that ecological concerns fit within the wide variety of traditions we refer to as 'Hinduism.' He cautions, however, against any kind of monolithic assessment of Hinduism and ecology, saying that while 'several avenues can be pursued to lift up Hindu religious imagery in the name of environmental protection ... it is just as likely that the same religious symbols might be used to promote the latest consumer product.'[32] Finally, in *Buddhism and Ecology*, Duncan Williams calls attention to the central role Buddhism has played in the American environmentalist movements by means of Buddhist notions of Buddha-nature present within living beings, a non-anthropocentric worldview, and the importance of various forms of introspective, meditative practice. According to Williams, 'Environmental philosophers have turned to Buddhism as a conceptual resource for a new ecological ethics.'[33] Clearly, then, each of these Eastern traditions supports an engaged and multifaceted approach to environmental ethics.

In concert with Asian traditions' integrated ecological models, Barbour describes the usefulness of 'complementary models' in physics, 'in the domain of the unobservably small, whose characteristics seem to be radically unlike those of everyday objects; the electron cannot be adequately visualized or consistently described by familiar analogies.' Because we may find ourselves unable to grasp dimensions of religious realities by means of 'visualizable models and familiar analogies,' Barbour suggests that we consider 'whether personal and impersonal models of Ultimate Reality may be thought of as complementary representations.'[34] Referencing the work of Ninian Smart,[35] Barbour suggests that we begin from the experiential basis of religion to consider two fundamental types of cross-culturally valid experience – 'numinous encounter (associated with worship); and mystical union (associated with meditation).' While one interprets numinous experience by personal models of God, often one tends to interpret mystical union with impersonal models;[36] and, states Barbour, 'Ninian Smart has shown that although Western religious traditions have been predominantly numinous and Eastern traditions predominantly mystical, all the major world religions have in fact included *both types of experience*.'[37] Furthermore, citing the work of Rudolf Otto, evidently as described by Smart, Barbour also mentions Otto's discussion of the '*mysterium tremendum et fascinans*, the mystery which evokes fear and awe, and yet also attracts and fascinates.'[38] Barbour suggests that a 'universal typology might correlate the *tremendum* pole with the prophet's feeling of the unapproachability of God' and the '*fascinans* pole' with 'the mystic's feeling of the nearness of the divine.' In this sense, Barbour helpfully distills the polarity of withdrawal/approach, or distance/identity, that characterizes one element of our experience of the sacred. Overcoming such dichotomous modes of relationality may assist us in embodying a more integrated mutuality with nature.

Barbour's theological interest in complementary personal and impersonal models of the divine involves the significance of theism. He states: 'This relative priority of personal or impersonal models has far-reaching implications. Only with a personal God can there be divine initiative and freedom rather than cosmic necessity.'[39] For this reason, Barbour appears suspicious of, for example, Vedanta Hinduism, which, while 'allow[ing] a place for theism, ... tends to see it as a lower stage of spiritual development ... At the highest level of truth, the personal in both man and God is swallowed up in the impersonal Absolute.' For Barbour, then, one requires the personal, or local dimensions of the divine in order to privilege theism over pantheism. As he puts it, 'Divine initiative, together with the ontological and epistemological distance assumed between man and God, is a correlate of the ideas of historical revelation, grace and redemption; the gulf can only be bridged from the side of the divine.'[40] For Barbour, Hinduism and Christianity represent separate paradigms, with the term 'paradigm' referring to historical unfodings that shape life and thought in particular communities. Unlike wave-particle duality in quantum physics, they do not function as complementary models, which only occur within the same paradigm. Barbour does, however, recognize an analogy to complementarity in the relation between personal and impersonal models in Hinduism and also in Christianity.[41]

Regardless of whether one conceptualizes the divine relatively more personally or more impersonally, Barbour argues for the importance of experience to theology. For Barbour, grace and redemption function experientially, supporting the healing of rifts between human beings. In this context, Barbour describes God as the structuring element of reality that personally transforms human life by means of love and forgiveness and also ontologically transforms the human experience by means of reuniting that which has been separated.[42] In the context of both Buddhist and Christian understandings of personhood and conceptions of 'self,' I have often wondered what part of the 'self' or the 'I' experiences theological happenings, as opposed to merely conceptual ones. Presumably, 'grace,' for example, does not occur as a perception directly accessible to what Buddhism refers to as the 'five sense consciousnesses.' Experiences of grace, redemption, and reconciliation transcend more conventional experiences, just as the experience of love includes a transcendental quality that reorients levels of the self not moved by ordinary events.

Contributing to the broadening of discussion in religion and science circles, Barbour helpfully includes mention of Asian thought in many of his major works. Barbour's parallels between quantum physics and Asian thought serve as important points of departure for future research and speculation in this area. Unfortunately, however, the sheer magnitude of the area Barbour covers – and his own dependency on secondary as opposed to primary Asian sources – cause him to tend to reify Asian perspectives and to present such viewpoints too generally. As a result, one sometimes comes away from Barbour's comparative work wondering about Asian traditions' subtleties regarding ontological and metaphysical matters. Nevertheless, Barbour's conscientiousness in including Asian viewpoints in his major works certainly furthers the development of religion–science dialogue.

More recently, too, Barbour comments that he has 'been interested in some parallels between process thought and Buddhist thought traced by John Cobb and others, and in the Buddhist view of consciousness as explored by Alan Wallace.'[43] This research holds much promise, since a deep reconciliation between physics and mysticism will illuminate how consciousness and so-called external reality co-create one another. Unno also acknowledges the importance of including mind in our overall assessment of reality.[44] Citing Barbour's comments from *Religion and Science*,[45] Unno questions the accuracy of 'Barbour's characterization of Bohm's conception of an holistic underlying implicate order as an instance of classical realism', since, '[a]ccording to Barbour, classically realistic theories in science hold the view that "valid models and theories provide a representation of the world as it is in itself apart from the observer."' Unno continues:

> While this may be true at one level, the inclusion of mind or consciousness within the implicate order complicates the pictures. Once the mind is included as integral to the 'world as it is in itself,' the world can never really be separated from the observer because to do so would mean the separation of the observer from his own mind and nature.[46]

Francisco Varela's work at the intersection of Madhyamika Buddhism and Western science describes the more comprehensive and immediate role of consciousness in the creation of the realities we experience and observe, thereby problematizing rigid separation between the self and the world.[47] Although Barbour comments that he only has 'rough notes on these presentations,' we can expect from the careful and copious contributions Barbour has made already to religion–science discussion that he will continue to develop the depth of contribution. As regards the co-creation of mind and so-called external reality, however, I believe we still continue to underestimate our own enfoldedness in the realities we experience around us – that is, the way in which the depths of individual psyches interpenetrate one another and create particular realities; the way in which thoughts and events far removed from one another in space-time co-determine one another, and the extent to which all events and happenings integrate at the level of the whole. Many models in both science and technology still fail to capture the thick layers of interpenetration that characterize this deep structure of mutual, enfolded reality. In the end, we may need to resign ourselves to living out deep reality fully, modeling it only for the sake of pedagogy. Losing out on the living for the sake of the modeling would make for an incomplete response to the fullness of our situatedness.

Notes

1.   I.G. Barbour, *Religion and Science: Historical and Contemporary Issues* (New York: HarperSanFrancisco, 1997).
2.   I.G. Barbour, *Ethics in an Age of Technology: The Gifford Lectures 1989–1991, Vol. 2* (San Francisco CA: HarperSanFrancisco, 1993).
3.   I.G. Barbour, *Myths, Models, and Paradigms: The Nature of Scientific and Religious Language* (London: SCM Press, 1974).
4.   I.G. Barbour, e-mail correspondence with Jensine Andresen, 2001.

5. Barbour, *Religion and Science*, 188–9.

6. Ibid., 189.

7. I.G. Barbour, *Religion in an Age of Science: The Gifford Lectures 1989–1991, Vol. 1* (San Francisco, CA: Harper & Row, 1990), 119–20.

8. Barbour, *Religion and Science*, 189.

9. Jay Garfield (trans.), *The Fundamental Wisdom of the Middle Way: Nāgārjuna's Mūlamadhyamakakārikā* (New York and Oxford: Oxford University Press, 1995), 68.

10. Louis de La Vallée Poussin, *Abhidharmakośabhāṣyam of Vasubandhu*, vol. 1 (Berkeley: Asian Humanities, 1988), 292.

11. I.G. Barbour, 'Bohm and Process Philosophy: A Response to Griffin and Cobb', in *Physics and the Ultimate Significance of Time: Bohm, Prigogine, and Process Philosophy*, ed. by David Ray Griffin (Albany: State University of New York, 1986), 167.

12. David Bohm, 'Reply to Comments of John Cobb and David Griffin', in *Physics and the Ultimate Significance of Time*, ed. by Griffin, 199.

13. Barbour, 'Bohm and Process Philosophy', 167.

14. Jensine Andresen, 'Enchanted Presence', forthcoming in *The End of Materialism: the Primacy of Consciousness*, edited by Trish Pfeiffer and John E. Mack.

15. David Bohm, 'Time, the Implicate Order and Pre-Space', in *Physics and the Ultimate Significance of Time*, ed. by Griffin, 175.

16. Idem, *Wholeness and the Implicate Order* (London: Routledge, 1995).

17. Barbour, *Religion and Science*, 190.

18. Bohm, *Wholeness*, 186.

19. George Lakoff and Mark Johnson, *Philosophy in the Flesh: The Embodied Mind and Its Challenge to Western Thought* (New York: Basic, 1999).

20. Daniel C. Dennett, *Consciousness Explained* (Boston: Little, Brown, & Co., 1991); S. Hameroff, A. Kaszniak, and A. Scott (eds), *Toward a Science of Consciousness I – The First Tucson Discussions and Debates* (Cambridge, MA: MIT/Bradford, 1996), *Toward a Science of Consciousness II – The Second Tucson Discussions and Debates* (Cambridge, MA: MIT/Bradford, 1998), *Toward a Science of Consciousness III – The Third Tucson Discussions and Debates* (Cambridge, MA: MIT/Bradford, 1999).

21. G.L. Sopa, 'The Subtle Body in Tantric Buddhism', in *Wheel of Time: The Kalachakra in Context*, ed. by His Holiness the 14th Dalai Lama (Madison: Deer Park, 1985), 153 and fn. 18.

22. Barbour, *Religion and Science*, 189.

23. Ibid., 190.

24. Barbour, *Bohm and Process Philosophy*, 167.

25. Barbour, *Ethics*.

26. Ibid., 72.

27. Ibid., 73.

28. Ibid., 74.

29. John Berthrong and Mary Evelyn Tucker (eds), *Confucianism and Ecology: The Interrelation of Heaven, Earth, and Humans*, in Religions of the World and Ecology Series, ed. by John Grim and Mary Evelyn Tucker (Cambridge, MA: Harvard University Center for the Study of World Religions, 1998), xxxv–xxxviii.

30. Ibid., xlix.

31. N.J. Girardot, James Miller, and Liu Xiaogan (eds), *Daoism and Ecology: Ways Within a Cosmic Landscape*, in Religions of the World and Ecology Series, ed. by John Grim and Mary Evelyn Tucker (Cambridge, MA: Harvard University Center for the Study of World Religions, 2001), xlviii.

32. Christopher K. Chapple and Mary Evelyn Tucker (eds), *Hinduism and Ecology: The Intersection of Earth, Sky, and Water*, in Religions of the World and Ecology Series, ed. by John Grim and Mary Evelyn Tucker (Cambridge, MA: Harvard University Center for the Study of World Religions, 2000), xlv–xlvi.

33. Mary Evelyn Tucker and Duncan Ryukan Williams, *Buddhism and Ecology: The Interconnection of Dharma and Deeds*, in Religions of the World and Ecology Series, ed. by John Grim and Mary Evelyn Tucker (Cambridge, MA: Harvard University Center for the Study of World Religions, 1997), xxxv.

34. Barbour, *Myths, Models, and Paradigms*, 78.

35. Ninian Smart, *The Concept of Worship* (London: Macmillan, 1972); *Reasons and Faiths: An Investigation of Religious Discourse* (London: Routledge and Paul, 1958); 'Revelation, Reason and Religions', in *Prospect for Metaphysics: Essays of Metaphysical Exploration*, ed. by Ian Ramsey (London: Allen and Unwin, 1961); *World Religions: A Dialogue* (Harmondsworth: Penguin, 1969).

36. Barbour, *Myths, Models, and Paradigms*, 79–80.

37. Ibid., 80 (in reference to Smart, *Reasons and Faith*).

38. Ibid., 81.

39. Ibid., 83.

40. Ibid., 83–4.

41. Ibid., 84.

42. Ibid., 89.

43. I. G. Barbour, e-mail correspondence with Jensine Andresen, 2001.

44. Mark T. Unno, 'The Anthropic Principle: The Personal and the Impersonal, Mind and Matter, from a Mahayana Buddhist Perspective', address to the American Academy of Religion Annual Meeting (Orlando Florida, November, 1998), 11.

45. Barbour, *Religion and Science*, 176, 359.

46. Unno, 'The Anthropic Principle', 11.

47. Francisco Varela, *The Embodied Mind: Cognitive Science and Human Experience* (Cambridge, MA: MIT, 1991); Francisco Varela and Jonathan Shear (eds), *The View From Within: First-Person Approaches to the Study of Consciousness* (Imprint Academic, 1999); Francisco Varela, 'Why a Proper Science of Mind Implies a Transcendence of Nature', in *Religion in Mind: Cognitive Perspectives on Religious Belief, Ritual, and Experience*, ed. by Jensine Andresen (Cambridge, UK: Cambridge University Press, 2001).

Published Works of Ian Graeme Barbour

Christian Berg

Barbour, Ian Graeme, 'An Automatic Low Frequency Analyzer', *Review of Scientific Instruments*, 18:7 (1947), 516–22.
———— with Marcel Schein and Thomas D. Carr, 'Cosmic Ray Investigations on Mt. McKinley', *Physical Review*, 73 (1948), 1419–23.
———— 'On the Use of Nuclear Plates in a Magnetic Field', *Physical Review*, 74 (1948), 507.
———— 'Magnetic Deflection of Cosmic-Ray Mesons Using Nuclear Plates', *Physical Review*, 76 (1949), 320.
———— 'A Pantograph and Tilting Stage for Use with Nuclear Plates', *Review of Scientific Instruments*, 20 (1949), 530.
———— with L. Greene, 'Emulsion Studies of Cosmic-Ray Stars Produced in Metal Foils', *Physical Review*, 79 (1950), 406–7.
———— 'Magnetic Deflection of Cosmic-Ray Mesons Using Nuclear Plates', *Physical Review*, 78 (1950), 518–25.
———— 'Emulsion Studies of Cosmic-Ray Stars Produced in Metal Foils', *Physical Review*, 82 (1951), 280.
———— with R.O. Kerman, 'An "Original" Experiment in Heat for the First-Year Laboratory', *American Journal of Physics*, 20 (1952), 493–6.
———— 'Integration as an Objective in the Physical Sciences', *American Journal of Physics*, 20 (1952), 565–68.
———— 'The Faculty Christian Fellowship', *Christian Century*, 70 (March 25, 1953), 348–50.
———— 'Emulsion Studies of Cosmic-Ray Stars Produced in Metal Foils', *Physical Review*, 93 (1954), 535–43.
———— 'Indeterminacy and Freedom: A Reappraisal', *Philosophy of Science*, 20 (1955), 8–20.
———— 'Karl Heim on Christian Faith and Natural Science', *The Christian Scholar*, 39 (1956), 229–37.
———— 'Are There Religious Perspectives in the Physical Sciences?', *Religion in Life*, 26 (1957), 513–25.
———— 'On the Contribution of Physics to Theology', *Religious Education*, 52 (1957), 329–36.
———— *Christianity and the Scientist*, New York: Association Press (1960).
———— 'The Methods of Science and Religion', in Harlow Shapley (ed.), *Science Ponders Religion*, New York: Appleton-Century-Crofts (1960) 196–215.
———— 'Responses to Strom: An Analysis', *Christian Century*, 78 (March 29, 1961), 383–4.

————— 'Science, Ethics, and Education', in John Dunning (ed.), *The Nurture of Scientists in America*, New York: Columbia University Press (1961), 11–36.

————— 'The Natural Sciences', in Ralph Raughley (ed.), *New Frontiers of Christianity*, New York: Association Press (1962), 19–42.

————— 'Cosmic-Ray Neutron Monitor Data for Northfield, Minnesota', *Annals of the Internal Geophysical Year*, 36 (1964), 11–36.

————— 'Some Problems of Religious Language', in Robert Wicks (ed.), *The Edge of Wisdom*, New York: Charles Scribner's Sons (1964), 43–8.

————— *Issues in Science and Religion*, Englewood Cliffs, NJ: Prentice Hall (1966); reprinted, New York: Harper & Row (1971).

————— 'Resources from the Physical Sciences', *Zygon: Journal of Religion and Science*, 1 (1966), 27–30.

————— 'The Significance of Teilhard', *Christian Century*, 84 (August 30, 1967), 1098–1102.

————— 'The Significance of Teilhard', in Kyle Haselden and Philip Hefner (eds), *Changing Man: The Threat and the Promise*, Garden City, NY: Doubleday and Co. (1968), 130–41.

————— 'Five Ways of Reading Teilhard', *The Teilhard Review*, 3 (1968), 3–20.

————— 'Five Ways of Reading Teilhard', *Soundings*, 51 (1968), 115–45.

————— (ed.), *Science and Religion: New Perspectives on the Dialogue*, London, UK: SCM Press (1968).

————— 'Science and Religion Today', in Ian Barbour (ed.), *Science and Religion: New Perspectives on the Dialogue*, London, UK: SCM Press (1968), 3–29.

————— 'On to Mars?', *Christian Century*, 86 (November 16, 1969), 1487–90.

————— 'Teilhard's Process Metaphysics', *Journal of Religion*, 59 (1969), 136–59.

————— 'An Ecological Ethic', *Christian Century*, 87 (October 7, 1970), 1180–84.

————— *Science and Secularity: The Ethics of Technology*, New York: Harper & Row (1970).

————— *Issues in Science and Religion*, Spanish translation, Guevara, Spain: Sal Terrae (1971).

————— 'An Ecological Ethic', in S.T. Reid and D.L. Lyon (eds), *Population Crisis*, Glenview, IL: Scott, Foresman & Co. (1972).

————— (ed.), *Earth Might Be Fair: Reflections on Ethics, Religion and Ecology*, Englewood Cliffs, NJ: Prentice Hall (1972).

————— (ed.), *Western Man and Environmental Ethics: Attitudes towards Nature and Technology*, Reading, MA: Addison-Wesley (1973).

————— *Myths, Models, and Paradigms: A Comparative Study in Science and Religion*, London, UK: SCM Press (1974).

————— *Myths, Models, and Paradigms: A Comparative Study in Science and Religion*, New York: Harper & Row (1974); 2nd edn, New York: Harper (1976).

————— 'Science, Religion, and the Counterculture', *Zygon: Journal of Religion and Science*, 10 (1975), 380–97.

————— (ed.), *Finite Resources and the Human Future*, Minneapolis, MN: Augsburg Fortress (1976).

————— 'Introduction', in Ian Barbour (ed.), *Finite Resources and the Human Future*, Minneapolis, MN: Augsburg Fortress (1976), 7–31.

————— with Kenneth Boulding and Donella Meadows, 'Panel on Resources and Growth', in Ian Barbour (ed.), *Finite Resources and the Human Future*, Minneapolis, MN: Augsburg Press (1976), 129–37.

————— 'Comments on the Future of Science' (paper delivered at the 1975 Nobel conference organized by Gustavus Adolphus College, MN), in John White and Stanley Krippner (eds), *Future of Science*, Garden City, NY: Anchor Books (1977), 23–4.

————— 'Environment and Man: Western Thought', in Warren T. Reich (ed.), *Encyclopedia of Bioethics*, New York, NY: Macmillan (1977), 366–74.

————— 'Justice, Participation, and Sustainability at MIT', *Ecumenical Review*, 31 (1979), 380–87.

————— 'Justice, Freedom, and Sustainability', in Clair N. McRostie (ed.), *Global Resources: Perspectives and Alternatives*, Baltimore, MD: University Park Press (1980), 73–94.

————— 'Paradigms in Science and Religion', in Gary Gutting (ed.), *Paradigms and Revolutions: Appraisals and Applications of Thomas Kuhn's Philosophy of Science*, Notre Dame, IN: University of Notre Dame Press (1980), 223–45.

————— *Technology, Environment, and Human Values*, Westport, CT: Praeger (1980).

————— with Harvey Brooks, Sanford Lakoff, and John Opie, *Energy and American Values*, New York: Praeger (1982).

————— 'Stewardship, Justice and Judgment', *Rituals of the Earth*, 3 (1982), 18–19.

————— 'Democracy and Expertise in a Technological Society', *National Forum*, 63/1 (Winter 1983), 3–6.

————— *Mity, Modelt, Paradygmaty,* Polish translation of *Myths, Models and Paradigms*, Krakow, Poland: Solecyny Instytut Wydawniczy Znak (1984).

————— 'Towards a Theology of Technology', *CTNS Bulletin*, 4 (Winter 1984), 1–13.

————— Book Review: *Intimations of Reality: Critical Realism in Science and Religion* by Arthur Peacocke, *Religion and Intellectual Life*, 2:4 (1985), 111–14.

————— 'Religion, Values and Science Education', in David Gosling and Bert Musschenga (eds), *Science Education and Ethical Values*, Washington DC: Georgetown University Press (1985), 10–19.

————— with Robert John Russell, 'David Bohm's Implicate Order: Physics, Philosophy and Theology', *Zygon: Journal of Religion and Science*, 20 (1985), 107–10.

————— 'Intimations of Reality: Critical Realism in Science and Religion', *Religion and Intellectual Life*, 2 (Summer 1985), 11–114.

————— 'The Liberation of Life', *Zygon: Journal of Religion and Science*, 20 (September 1985), 360–63.

————— 'Bohm and Process Philosophy: A Response to Griffin and Cobb', in David R. Griffin (ed.), *Physics and the Ultimate Significance of Time: Bohm, Prigogine, and Process Philosophy*, Albany, NY: State University of New York Press (1986), 167–71.

————— 'The Coolidge Research Colloquium: An Evaluation', *Religion and Intellectual Life*, 3 (Fall 1986), 65–7.

———— 'Theology for a Nuclear Age', *Zygon: Journal of Religion and Science*, 21 (1986), 535–7.

———— 'The Relationship between Science and Religion', in David M. Byers (ed.), *Religion, Science, and the Search for Wisdom: Proceedings of a Conference on Religion and Science*, Washington, DC: United States Catholic Conference (1987), 166–91.

———— 'For Further Exploration', *Religion and Intellectual Life*, 5 (Spring 1988), 59–63.

———— 'On Two Issues in Science and Religion: A Response to David Griffin', *Zygon: Journal of Religion and Science*, 23 (1988), 83–8.

———— 'Ways of Relating Science and Theology', in Robert John Russell, William R. Stoeger, and George V. Coyne (eds), *Physics, Philosophy, and Theology: A Common Quest for Understanding*, Vatican City: Vatican Observatory (1988), 21–48.

———— 'Creation and Cosmology', in Ted Peters (ed.), *Cosmos as Creation: Theology and Science in Consonance*, Nashville, TN: Abington Press (1989), 115–51.

———— 'Consultation Summation', in James Miller (ed.), *The Church and Contemporary Cosmology*, Pittsburgh, PA: Carnegie Mellon University Press (1990), 297–312.

———— *Religion in an Age of Science: The Gifford Lectures 1989–1991 Volume 1*, San Francisco, CA: Harper & Row; London SCM Press (1990).

———— 'Time and Eternity', *CTNS Bulletin*, 10 (Spring 1990), 25–7.

———— 'Response to Panel on "The Church and the Environmental Crisis"', *CTNS Bulletin*, 10 (Autumn 1990), 26–8.

———— *Ethics in an Age of Technology: The Gifford Lectures 1989–1991 Volume 2*, San Francisco, CA: Harper Collins; London: SCM Press (1993).

———— 'Surveying the Possibilities: Ways of Relating Science and Religion', in James E. Huchingson (ed.), *Religion and the Natural Sciences*, Fort Worth, TX: Harcourt Brace Jovanovich College Publishers (1993), 6–34.

———— 'Experiencing and Interpreting Nature in Science and Religion', *Zygon: Journal of Religion and Science*, 29 (1994), 457–87.

———— 'Science, Technology, and the Church', lecture presented at the United Church of Christ, Cleveland, Ohio (1994).

———— 'Religious Responses to the Big Bang', in Clifford N. Matthews and Roy Abraham Varghese (eds), *Cosmic Beginnings and Human Ends: Where Science and Religion Meet*, Chicago, IL: Open Court Publishing Company (1995), 379–402.

———— 'Science, God, and Nature', The Idreos Lectures, Manchester College, Oxford (1995).

———— 'Three Paths from Nature to Religious Belief', The Idreos Lectures, Manchester College, Oxford (1995).

———— 'The Churches and the Global Environment: The Challenge of Al Gore', *Dialog*, 35 (Fall 1996), 278–86.

———— 'Responses to Critiques of *Religion in an Age of Science*', *Zygon: Journal of Religion and Science*, 31 (1996), 51–65.

———— 'Responses to Critiques of *Ethics in an Age of Technology*', *Zygon: Journal of Religion and Science*, 31 (1996), 101–10.

———— 'The Churches and the Global Environment', *CTNS Bulletin*, 16 (Summer 1996), 1–9.

———— *Religion and Science: Historical and Contemporary Issues*, a revised and expanded edition of *Religion in an Age of Science* (1990), San Francisco, CA: HarperSanFrancisco (1997).

———— 'Five Models of God and Evolution', in Robert John Russell, William R. Stoeger, SJ, and Francisco J. Ayala (eds), *Evolutionary and Molecular Biology: Scientific Perspectives on Divine Action*, Vatican City: Vatican Observatory and Berkeley, CA: Center for Theology and the Natural Sciences (1998), 419–42.

———— 'Neuroscience, Artificial Intelligence, and Human Nature', in Robert John Russell, Nancey Murphy, Theo C. Meyering, and Michael A. Arbib (eds), *Neuroscience and the Human Person: Scientific Perspectives on Divine Action*, Vatican City: Vatican Observatory and Berkeley, CA: Center for Theology and the Natural Sciences (1999), 249–80.

———— 'Neuroscience, Artificial Intelligence, and Human Nature: Theological and Philosophical Reflections', *Zygon: Journal of Religion and Science*, 34 (1999), 361–98.

———— 'Religion in an Environmental Age', in Donald B. Conroy and Rodney Laurence Peterson (eds), *Earth at Risk: An Environmental Dialogue Between Religion and Science*, Amherst, NY: Humanity Books (2000), 27–54.

———— *When Science Meets Religion: Enemies, Strangers, or Partners?*, San Francisco, CA: HarperSanFrancisco (2000).

———— 'Perspectives on Sustainability', in Audrey R. Chapman and Rodney Petersen (eds), *Consumption, Population, and Sustainability: Perspectives from Science and Religion*, Washington, DC: Island Press (2000), 23–35.

———— 'Scientific and Religious Perspectives on Sustainability', in Dieter T. Hessel and Rosemary Radford Ruether (eds), *Christianity and Ecology: Seeking the Well-Being of Earth and Humans*, Cambridge, MA: Harvard University Press (2000), 385–401.

———— 'The Church in an Environmental Age', in Donald Conroy and Rodney Petersen (eds), *Earth at Risk: An Environmental Dialogue Between Religion and Science*, Amherst, NY: Prometheus Books (2000), 27–54.

———— 'God's Power: A Process View', in John Polkinghorne (ed.), *The Work of Love: Creation as Kenosis*, Cambridge, UK and Grand Rapids, MI: Eerdmans, and London: SPCK (2001), 1–20.

———— 'Science and Scientism in Huston Smith's *Why Religion Matters*', *Zygon: Journal of Religion and Science*, 36 (June 2001), 207–14.

———— *Nature, Human Nature, and God*, Minneapolis, MN: Fortress Press (2002).

———— 'On Typologies for Relating Science and Religion', *Zygon: Journal of Religion and Science*, 37 (June 2002), 345–59.

Index of Authors

Index of Subjects